GRAIN EXPORT CARTELS

GRAIN EXPORT CARTELS

ANDREW SCHMITZ
University of California, Berkeley
ALEX F. McCALLA
University of California, Davis
DONALD O. MITCHELL
Michigan State University
COLIN CARTER
University of Manitoba, Canada

BALLINGER PUBLISHING COMPANY
Cambridge, Massachusetts
A Subsidiary of Harper & Row, Publishers, Inc.

International Standard Book Number: 0–88410–690–X

Library of Congress Catalog Card Number: 81–3448

Printed in the United States of America

Library of Congress Cataloging in Publication Data
Schmitz, Andrew.
Grain export cartels.

Includes bibliographical references and index.
1. Grain trade. 2. Grain trade—Political aspects. 3. Monopolies. 4. Monopolies—Political aspects. 5. Prices. I. Title.
HD9030.6.S35 382'.4131 81–3448
ISBN 0–88410–690–X AACR2

CONTENTS

LIST OF FIGURES

LIST OF TABLES

ACKNOWLEDGEMENTS

We would like to thank Ed Schuh, Edward Rossmiller, Lowell Hill, Ray Goldberg, Vern Sorenson, and Tim Josling for comments on various aspects of this topic; also, the support from the University of Manitoba, Michigan State University, and the University of California is appreciated. A special acknowledgement goes to Dale Hathaway and Kelly Harrison. In addition, while acknowledgement is made to the members of the Word Processing Unit who were involved in the final typing of the manuscript, we thank especially Frances A. Hammond and Ikuko Takeshita of the Giannini Foundation and the Department of Agricultural and Resource Economics, University of California, Berkeley.

INTRODUCTION

Many of us have heard statements such as the following: "Bread is the staff of life," "A bushel for a barrel," "We shall not feed the armies of aggressors," "A poor man's bread is his life," and "Regimes rise and fall on the price of a loaf of bread." These statements suggest that the way in which food is produced, consumed, and distributed among the nations of the world is of critical importance. This book deals with grain export cartels which is a lively and controversial subject for many reasons. (One example is that cartels are opposed by the private grain trade in the United States since they imply government pricing.) The cartel coverage in this book encompasses both wheat and feed grains—the two most important grains consumed and traded worldwide. The proposed formation of an exporter cartel in food and feed grains, where exporters cooperate in the pricing and exporting of grain abroad, has generally taken place in response to large increases in oil prices during the 1970s. In large part, oil prices are due to the formation of the oil export cartel which has given rise to the "A bushel for a barrel" phrase. In this book, we explore the economic significance of a grain export cartel which, if effective, would place the major grain exporters in a position to deal more effectively in international trade and in essence command real prices for grain in line with the prices for oil and the other key raw materials. However, since the oil-exporting countries import relatively small amounts of grain, the major source of increased revenues to the grain cartel has to come from nonoil-exporting nations.

Unlike nations such as Canada and Australia which export mainly wheat, the United States exports many agricultural products, among the most important being wheat, corn, soybeans, and rice. This book focuses largely on wheat and feed grains in analyzing the effects of a grain export cartel; in addition, it considers the effects of a cartel in wheat and feed grains on the livestock sector—a sector highly dependent on the prices and volume of feed grains available.

Chapter 1 focuses largely on the issues which have led to the many and varied proposals for a grain export cartel. The growing importance of state trading by importers, the decline in grain prices relative to other commodity prices and the prices of key imports, and the use of tariffs by importers which improve their economic welfare are among the factors discussed.

Chapter 2 highlights the market structure for grains along with pricing and institutions in the international grain trade. The role of the state and the private sector is discussed. In addition, the impact of tariff and other trade restrictive policies is analyzed with reference to the implementation of a cartel.

Chapter 3 presents an empirical review of the world grain trade. It presents production and trade trends, exporter market shares, and origin and destination trade flows, and discusses the relevance of these data for a grain cartel.

Chapter 4 presents the theory of cartels as it applies to the grain trade. A simple cartel model is first presented; it is then broadened to incorporate fringe suppliers, market intermediaries, stocks, and multiple pricing. In the analysis, a distinction is made between a government export cartel and a producer export cartel.

In Chapter 5, the operation of a grain cartel is discussed. Possible cartel instruments and institutions are presented and compared. The problems of supply management and quota allocations among countries are also spelled out. Lastly, the successes and failures of past cartels are highlighted.

Chapter 6 focuses on the critical issues involved in the successful operation of a cartel. These include the (1) demand characteristics for grain, (2) response of importers, and (3) interface with domestic markets (including futures markets and the role of the private firms). Single and multiple price cartels are discussed, and a summary of the models to be tested empirically is presented.

Chapters 7 and 8 present the empirical results of the effects of different forms of cartels. Aggregate gains and losses for both the grain and livestock sectors are presented along with disaggregate effects.

Chapter 9 discusses policy implications and the limitations of the empirical analysis presented on possible cartel outcomes. Such issues as acreage controls, production quotas, risk reduction, and stability in world grain markets are discussed. In addition, this chapter discusses grain cartels in the broader context of political economy and food policy.

1 PROBLEMS AND ISSUES IN INTERNATIONAL GRAIN MARKETS

The international market for grains is both complex and highly unstable. Millions of producers and consumers, along with hundreds of firms, participate in the transportation, handling, and consumption of grain. The grain trade is characterized by a greater number of importers than exporters. There are more than fifty countries that import grain, and no single importer buys more than 10 percent of shipments each year on the average. On the other hand, the United States alone makes up over 50 percent of yearly grain exports. Figure 1–1 shows the world's degree of dependence on U.S. grain exports.

The market is unstable largely because of weather and government policy. Weather variations affect production conditions and thus cause fluctuations in both export supply and import demand. Policy affects international supply via embargoes, acreage controls, and price supports. On the demand side, policies maintaining fixed internal prices (regardless of domestic supply and demand conditions), accompanied by trade restrictions, produce substantial fluctuations in import demand as importing countries export domestic production instability.

To illustrate the impact of such factors as weather and policy on commodities, it is useful to compare the prices of wheat and corn to that of petroleum. Figure 1–2 reveals that the degree of price instability for both corn and wheat is much greater than that of oil. In

Figure 1–1. Total world grain trade, including rice, 1971–72 to 1980–81

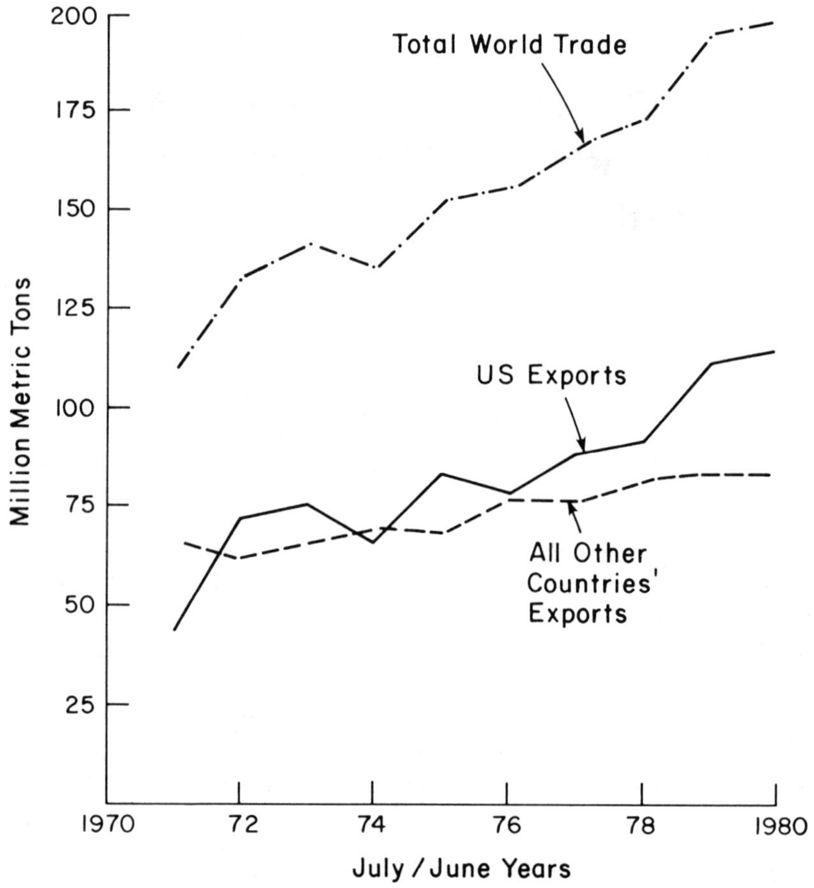

Source: U.S. Department of Agriculture, Foreign Agricultural Service, *Foreign Aricultural Circular,* July 15, 1980.

fact, there is little instability in oil prices. (Note that since 1970, they have not, on a yearly basis, declined).

The price relationships in Figure 1-2 between grains and oil may be explained largely by two important determinants: weather and market structure. Weather has little or no adverse effect on oil production and consumption. In terms of market structure, a major characteristic of the oil market is supply control by the major exporters: for example, the Organization of Petroleum Exporting

Figure 1–2. Degree of price stability in selected basic commodities

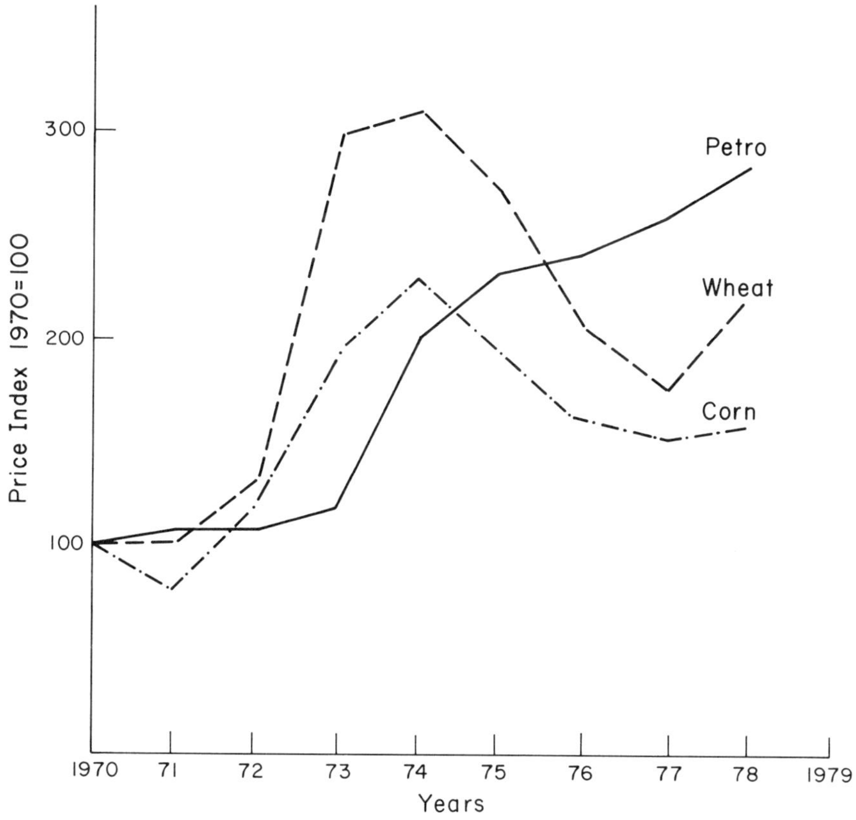

Petroleum: Average price of crude, at wells.
Wheat: Season average price received by farmers.
Corn: Season average price received by farmers.

Source: *Commodity Yearbook* (Various Issues) New York: Commodity Research Bureau.

Countries (OPEC). The formation of OPEC has stabilized the "real price" of oil at a level far higher than would otherwise have prevailed. As pointed out, it is partly in response to OPEC that proposals for a grain export cartel expressed in the phrase, "A bushel for a barrel," have been made.

There is also an important relationship between grain prices and livestock prices, as shown in Figure 1–3. In 1973–74, for example, when the prices of both wheat and feed grains increased, the prices

Figure 1–3. Relationship between corn and cattle prices, 1970–1980.

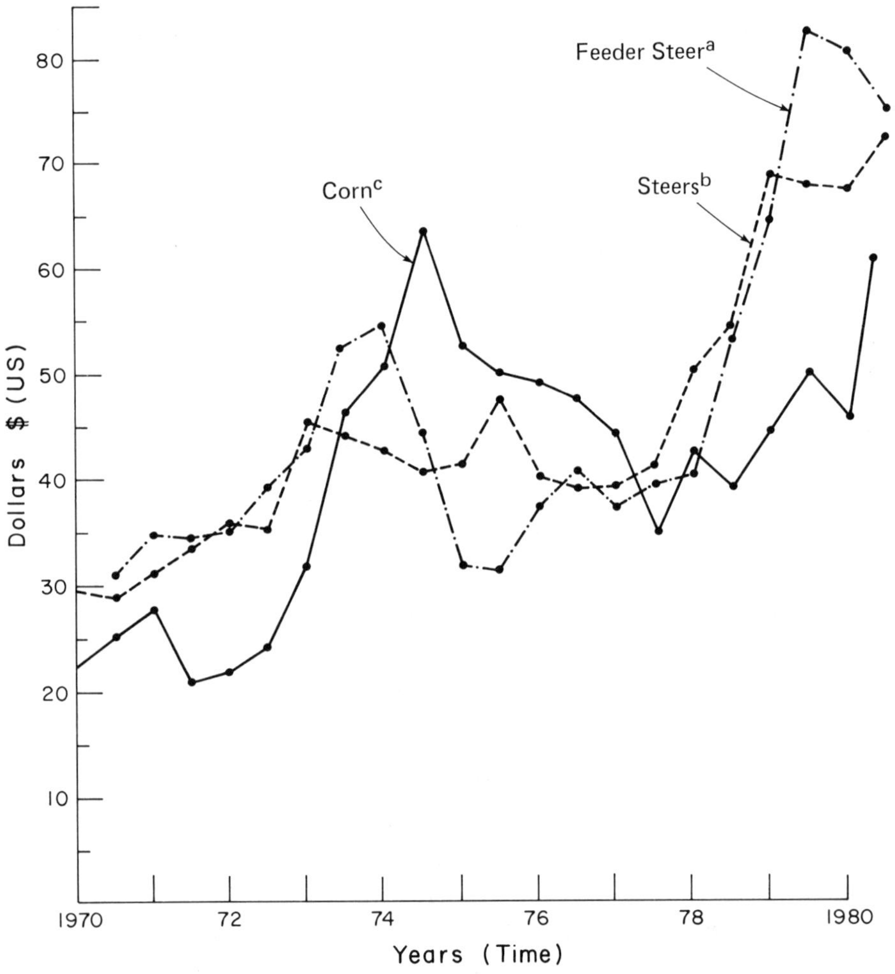

a. Semi-annual weighted average price ($/cwt) led by 6 months. Choice Feeder Steers, Kansas City, 600–700 lbs. (prior to 1972, 550–750 lbs.).

Source: *Livestock and Meat Situation* (various issues), Economics and Statistics Service (formerly ESCS), USDA.

b. Semi-annual weighted average price $/cwt. Choice Steers at Omaha, 900–1100 lbs.

Source: *Livestock and Meat Situation* (various issues), Economics and Statistics Service (formerly ESCS), USDA.

c. Semi-annual weighted average price (actual $/cwt multiplied by 10 to make figure consistent). #2 Yellow Chicago.

Source: *Feed Situation* (various issues), Economics and Statistics Service (formerly ESCS), USDA.

of feeder steers (those animals bought by feedlot operators from cow-calf ranches) decreased. This caused the returns to ranchers to diminish and triggered both a reduction in cattle numbers and the supply of beef available for domestic consumers. This resulted in higher retail prices in the late 1970s. Thus, the domestic demand for grains (for both wheat and feed grains) is an important component of this study. Domestic demand is influenced by foreign demand. For example, if short-run export demand increases, grain prices rise, resulting in an economic loss to the cow-calf ranching sector and the final consumers of beef. Because the livestock sector is such an important component of the agricultural sector in the grain-exporting countries, grain export policies cannot be adequately analyzed without taking into account the domestic livestock sector. Often, for example, there are gains from trade in grains but losses to the livestock industry which can greatly reduce or eliminate the gains from trade in grains.

PUBLIC CONCERN

A number of factors have contributed to heightened public concern about international grain markets and have stimulated the demand for alternative market arrangements including export cartels. First among them is the increased instability in grain markets and its effect on the livestock sector as suggested above. The events of 1972–1974—most importantly, massive Soviet grain purchases—led to the rapid depletion of exporter-held stocks and to a rapid rise in prices (Table 1–1).[a] Although international prices have subsequently fallen, they continue to exhibit much greater instability than was the case in the 1950s and 1960s.

Secondly, during the late 1970s, higher petroleum costs, coupled with higher debt service costs on land resulting from land price escalation, caused an increase in the costs of production. This increase aggravated the effect of falling and unstable prices, and grain producers were placed back in a cost-price squeeze.

A third factor is the rapid change in the structure of international

[a]Many other factors also contributed to this instability (for example, exchange rate effects and poor anchovy catches). A discussion of these is contained in Johnson (1979).

Table 1-1. World wheat and coarse grains supply and demand, 1960-61 through 1979-80 (million metric tons/hectares)

Total Wheat and Coarse Grains	*Area Harvested*	*Yield*	*Production*	*July-June Trade*[b]	*Total*[c] *Utilization*	*Ending Stocks*[a]	*Stocks As % of Util.*
1960-61	531	1.30	690.6	66	576.8	188.6	27.9
1961-62	524	1.26	660.3	77	687.0	161.9	23.6
1962-63	527	1.36	714.8	75	712.4	164.2	23.0
1963-64	532	1.33	705.3	90	706.5	162.8	23.0
1964-65	539	1.39	747.5	87	746.0	164.0	22.0
1965-66	535	1.40	749.3	103	783.5	130.0	16.6
1966-67	535	1.55	830.4	96	802.2	157.8	19.7
1967-68	546	1.55	848.0	90	830.7	175.1	21.1
1968-69	550	1.60	879.8	82	851.8	203.1	23.8
1969-70	547	1.62	885.8	89	901.6	186.8	20.7
1970-71	537	1.66	891.2	101	933.6	146.8	15.7
1971-72	545	1.79	977.6	101	956.0	167.2	17.5
1972-73	540	1.76	952.1	126	988.1	131.4	13.3
1973-74	560	1.86	1040.7	134	1037.0	134.2	12.9
1974-75	562	1.75	985.1	128	995.0	119.5	12.0
1975-76	574	1.73	995.1	143	995.8	119.9	12.0
1976-77	584	1.92	1118.7	146	1061.4	177.1	16.7
1977-78	575	1.89	1086.7	156	1094.7	169.1	15.4
1978-79[d]	574	2.09	1195.8	161	1164.0	200.9	17.3
1979-80[e]	571	2.01	1147.2	184	1171.5	176.7	15.1
1980-81[e]	580	2.01	1164.1	185	1175.9	164.9	14.0

Note: Stocks as % of utilization is the ratio of marketing year-ending stocks and total utilization.

[a]Stocks data are based on an aggregate of differing local marketing years and should not be construed as representing world stock levels at a fixed point in time. Stocks data are not available for all countries and exclude those such as the People's Republic of China and parts of Eastern Europe: the world stock levels have been adjusted for estimated year-to-year changes in USSR grain stocks, but do not purport to include the entire absolute level of USSR stocks.

[b]Trade data as expressed in this table excludes intra-EC-9 trade.

[c]For countries for which stocks data are not available (excluding the USSR), utilization estimates represent "apparent" utilization, that is, they are inclusive of annual stock level adjustments.

[d]Preliminary.

[e]Projection.

Source: U.S. Department of Agriculture, Foreign Agricultural Service, 1980. *Foreign Agricultural Circular,* August 13.

grain markets. Particularly in the wheat market, the rising importance of Third World and centrally planned economies as importers has made state trading in grain more common. Roughly 95 percent of the transactions in the world wheat market involve state traders on one or both sides of the transaction (McCalla and Schmitz 1979). At the same time, a small number of multinational private grain firms are involved in an increasing percentage of grain transactions, acting either as principals or as handlers of the logistical elements of state trading transactions. Both of these trends raise questions about who benefits from international trade and, in particular, about the impact of these changes on small producers and individual consumers.

Fourth, as a result of the dramatic distributional changes that have taken place in the world grain market (Table 1–2), most of the world has become heavily dependent on North American grain exports. Nevertheless, most nations involved in the grain trade continue to pursue inward-looking and often protectionist farm policies which seek to stabilize domestic markets and, therefore, tend to export instability to the open grain market of the United States. The European Economic Community (EEC), Japan, and the centrally planned economies are the most frequently discussed cases;

Table 1-2. The changing pattern of the world grain trade: exports and imports[a] of major cereals:[b] 1934-1977 (million metric tons)

	Year				
Region	*1934–1938*[c]	*1947*	*1957*	*1967*	*1977*
North America	+5	+23	+27	+51	+87
South America	+10	+3	+3	+3	+11
Oceania	+3	+1	+3	+8	+12
Western Europe	-24	-22	-28	-25	-27
Eastern Europe and USSR	+5	n/a	+7	+2	-16
Asia	+2	-5	-10	-31	-48
Africa	+1	+1	0	-10	-13

[a]Plus sign denotes net exports; minus sign denotes net imports.

[b]Includes wheat, rice, barley, maize, rye, and oats.

[c]An average for the period covering all the years, 1934 through 1938.

Source: *Food and Agricultural Organization of the United Nations Trade Yearbook* (various volumes).

some economists have suggested that importers, through protectionist policies and state trading, are exploiting grain exporting nations (Carter and Schmitz 1979).

The fifth disturbing observation is the fact that world stocks of grain relative to annual utilization have fallen to approximately one-half of what they were twenty years ago. Table 1–1 indicates that world grain reserves presently represent only 14 percent of annual utilization and thus points out the increased vulnerability of the world to major crop failures.

Sixth, at the Tokyo Round of the General Agreement on Tariffs and Trade (GATT) negotiations, major traders failed to reach an international grains agreement; the absence of such an agreement can make the market more unstable. In addition, many of the barriers to trade in wheat and feed grains were not lowered which has caused concern to exporters.

Seventh, government officials—partly through jealousy of OPEC's success in enhancing export earnings—are considering "food power" as a counter to rising petroleum prices. However, on this issue it is a mistake to argue that all the gains from a cartel would come from OPEC countries.

Finally, the U.S. grain embargo against the Soviet Union in 1980, in response to the latter's invasion of Afghanistan, clearly demonstrates how grain can be used in an attempt to exert political and economic power against trading partners. Communist countries such as the Soviet Union and China are important components in the international trade in grains, and the instability of grain markets in the past has been partly due to erratic purchases by the Soviet Union, caused mainly by fluctuations in crop conditions in the Communist bloc. As a result, the United States and the Soviet Union signed an agreement whereby the Soviet Union was to buy annually a minimum of 8 million metric tons of grain from the United States.

These points may explain why a grain export cartel has been proposed. It is difficult to understand, in the light of the growing dependency on North American grain exports (Table 1–2), why importers can create instability for North American exporters and at the same time exert buying power against them. A formal arrangement among exporters, by reducing price instability and increasing producer income in the exporting countries, might correct these apparent anomolies in the international market.

REAL PRICES OF BASIC COMMODITIES

To place the cartel issue in a broader context, Table 1–3 presents data on the prices of selected primary commodities and inputs in the United States for the period of 1965 through 1978. Corn and wheat prices at the farm level are presented along with prices for gold, silver, petroleum, and basic farm inputs. It is apparent that prices for the latter have gone up much faster than prices for wheat and corn—a reason often given in favor of grain exporters forming a cartel.

It is also interesting to compare corn and wheat prices directly with farm machinery and equipment and farm real estate which includes farmland. Land values, for example, have increased more than twice as fast as wheat and corn prices. Until the early 1970s, land values generally reflected the value of the products which they produce. Land values at the end of the 1970s reflect more the rate of inflation since it has been shown that assets such as land and gold act as stores of value during times of inflation. The data already reflect how individual producers (especially those who own their own farms) can be in a desirable wealth position due to real price increases in land values in the 1970s and still have a severe cash-flow problem because of low commodity prices (columns 1 and 2 of Table 1–3).

Also, it is interesting to note the increase in farm production since 1965 due to such factors as technological change and less severe acreage controls on production. This production increase in part explains why producer prices for basic commodities are relatively low and why the rise in the consumer price index (last column of Table 1–3) was not more severe.

The last point of interest concerns machinery and oil prices—two basic inputs to the food production system. Since 1965, crude petroleum prices have increased by 213 percent, while farm machinery has increased by 181 percent. Some of the supporters of a cartel view oil as the culprit because of OPEC's success. However, as stressed in this book, the economic gains from grain exporters retaliating against OPEC countries is relatively small due to their small imports of food and feed grains. In terms of the cost of machinery and equipment, there are also input markets about which the cartel could do very little. If the high price of machinery is partly due to the fact that four firms manufacture the bulk of the major cost

Table 1-3. Prices of selected commodities, U.S. 1965–1978

	Corn[a] (Average $ per Bu.)	Wheat[a] (Average Received by Farmers: $ per Bu.)	Gold[b] (Average $ per Fine Oz.)	Silver[b] (Average $ per Fine Oz.)	Crude[b] Petroleum (Average $ per Barrel Domestic U.S.)	Tractors[a] and Self-Propelled Machinery 1967 = 100	Farm[a] Production (All Commodities) 1967 = 100	Farm[a] Real Estate 1967 = 100	Consumer[a] Prices 1967 = 100
1965	$1.16	$1.35	$35.00	1.29	2.86	92	96	86	94.5
1966	1.24	1.63	35.00	1.29	2.88	96	100	93	97.2
1967	1.03	1.39	35.00	1.55	2.92	100	100	100	100
1968	1.08	1.24	39.30	2.14	2.94	104	100	107	104.2
1969	1.16	1.25	41.50	1.79	3.09	111	104	113	109.8
1970	1.33	1.33	36.70	1.77	3.18	116	108	117	116.3
1971	1.08	1.34	41.20	1.55	3.39	122	113	122	121.3
1972	1.57	1.76	58.60	1.69	3.39	128	121	132	125.3
1973	2.55	3.95	97.80	2.56	3.89	137	146	150	133.1
1974	3.02	4.09	159.70	4.71	6.74	161	166	187	147.7
1975	2.54	3.56	161.50	4.42	7.56	195	182	213	161.2
1976	2.15	2.73	125.30	4.35	8.14	217	193	242	170.5
1977	2.02	2.33	148.30	4.62	8.57	238	200	283	181.5
1978	2.11	2.94	193.60	5.40	8.96	259	216	308	195.4

Sources: for columns[a]: U.S. Department of Agriculture. *Agricultural Statistics,* (various issues); for columns[b]: U.S. Department of Commerce, Statistical Abstract of the U.S., (various issues).

items, then the policy instrument to make this industry more competitive is not an export cartel. It is interesting, however, that the degree of concentration of both buyers of farm commodities and suppliers of farm inputs is great. As pointed out, the buyers of grain—at least at one stage of the market transaction—are state traders and a few large private grain firms. In terms of inputs—oil and fuel, farm machinery and equipment, and fertilizers—supplies are controlled by relatively few companies or countries. Perhaps it is because of this overall structure that groups are proposing a grain export cartel which, depending on how it is organized, would give producers a greater share of real income.

ATTEMPTS TO ORGANIZE INTERNATIONAL MARKETS

The drastic price declines caused by the Great Depression created an increased interest both in governmental intervention in nations' markets and in intergovernmental market regulation. The Monetary and Economic Conference held in London in 1933 adopted a resolution favoring international commodity agreements. During the interwar period, stabilization schemes were designed for a number of commodities including wheat, sugar, tea, rubber, tin, copper, and potash.

Commodity agreements, however, have been difficult both to negotiate and to operate. As recently as 1977, only five commodity agreements remained: coffee, cocoa, sugar, wheat, and tin (see Table 1–4 for a brief summary of these five agreements). These were ineffective in regulating world markets and have been denounced as restricting supplies and thus interfering with economic efficiency.

Wheat pricing has generated a good deal of discussion. The issue of stabilizing wheat prices emerged in the 1930s, and there have been seven agreements since 1949. The International Wheat Agreement (IWA), negotiated during the GATT Kennedy Round of 1967, was a multilateral contract under which exporters and importers agreed to buy or sell wheat from each other at prices within an agreed-upon range. It attempted to raise wheat prices but broke down in 1968 under the pressure of surpluses, and in 1971 negotiators were unable to agree on a new price range. Since then, the IWA has contained no commercial trade provisions. Although it

Table 1–4. Principal features of formal international commodity agreements

Title	*Entry into Force*	*Partici-pating Countries*	*Price Targets*	*Formal Export or Production Quotas*	*Buffer Stocks*	*Other Policy Measures*	*Institutional Support*
International Wheat Agreement	1971. Preceding agreements 1949, 1953, 1956, 1959, 1962, 1965, 1966, 1967.	Major exporting and importing countries, with exceptions during certain periods.[a]	Not at present. Earlier agreements included a range between max. and min. prices.	No	No	From 1959 until 1971 importers undertook to buy a min. share of their imports from member countries and exporters to sell the equivalent of their average exports over the preceding 4 years to member countries at prices within the agreed range.[b]	Administered by the International Wheat Council.
International Sugar Agreement	1969. Preceding agreements	All major exporting and im-	Not at present. A range of trigger prices ap-	Not at present. Export quotas applied to free	Not at present. Min. and max. stocks to be	Not at present. Trigger mechanism linking	Administered by the International

	1954 and 1959.	porting countries trading on free world market.	plied from 1969 to 1973, when the economic provisions of the agreement lapsed.	market from 1961 to 1973.	held in producing countries were stipulated from 1969 to 1973.	quota adjustments and stock releases to movements in market prices operated from 1969 to 1973.	Sugar Organization.
International Tin Agreement	1976. Preceding agreements 1956, 1961, 1966, 1971, and 1976.	All major producing and importing countries.	Yes. Range between max. and min. prices.	Yes. Export quotas.	Yes. Producing and consuming countries contribute to the buffer stock.		Administered by the International Tin Council.
International Coffee Agreement	1976.[c] Preceding agreements 1962 and 1968.	All major exporting and importing countries.	Yes. Range between min. and max. prices to be established by the ICO.	Yes. Export quotas consisting of a fixed part and a variable part, linked to the price range established by the ICO, or in its absence to average indicator prices for "other milds" and Robusta coffees in 1975.	No.	No.	Administered by the International Coffee Organization

(continued)

Table 1–4. Principal features of formal international commodity agreements (continued)

Title	*Entry into Force*	*Partici-pating Countries*	*Price Targets*	*Formal Export or Production Quotas*	*Buffer Stocks*	*Other Policy Measures*	*Institutional Support*
International Cocoa Agreement	1976.[c] Preceding agreement 1973.	All major exporting and im-porting countries except USA	Yes. Range between min. and max. prices.	Yes. Export quotas. The agreement provides for dif-ferent combina-tions of export quotas and buffer stock operations at different price levels.	Yes.	No.	Administered by the International Cocoa Organization

[a]For example, U.K. in 1953 and 1956. Argentina in 1949 and 1953, and USSR in 1949, 1953, 1956, 1959, and 1967.

[b]The 1967 and 1971 agreements include a Food Aid Convention involving a commitment on the part of each member to supply a fixed quantity of cereals in the form of aid to the developing countries.

[c]Not yet operative.

Source: Hillman, J.S., Peck, A.E.; and Schmitz, A., 1978. "International Trade Arrangements." *Speaking of Trade: Its Effect on Agriculture.* University of Minnesota Agricultural Extension Service, Special Report No. 72, p. 68.

appeared in 1979 that a successful wheat agreement would be reached which would include storage and reserves as instruments, no agreement was achieved.

A GRAIN CARTEL

The previously identified public concerns and the failure of the Tokyo Round to develop a grains' agreement have led in the United States to the introduction of a number of legislative proposals along cartel lines. Discussions of grain export cartels have also taken place in two large wheat-exporting countries: Canada and Australia. In these countries there appears to be considerable support for a cartel. However, the discussion and proposals introduced there are not included here.

The following are among the proposals introduced in the United States.

1. H.R. 3042 was introduced by Congressman Weaver on March 15, 1979. This bill would amend the Commodity Credit Corporation (CCC) Charter Act to create within the CCC a National Grain Board to provide the highest possible prices in foreign markets for American agricultural producers and to provide price and supply stability in domestic markets. The CCC would become the marketing agent for all export sales of wheat, rice, corn, grain sorghum, barley, oats, rye, and soybeans. It would be authorized to negotiate sales for export of such commodities, barter such commodities for other goods, accept purchase bids from foreign purchasers, and offer selling bids in the world market. A private exporter could still export such commodities at prices, terms, and conditions approved by the Corporation.

2. On May 14, 1979, Congressman Mottl introduced H.R. 120 which urged the President to establish an international food cartel with Canada, Australia, Argentina, and other major food-exporting countries. It would negotiate with OPEC using food commodities as a bargaining tool.

3. Senator Bellman introduced S. 356 (the International Wheat Exporting Commission Act of 1979) on February 6, 1979. This bill requests that the President take action to create such a commission to establish a minimum world market price of wheat from member nations, prescribe the share of wheat each one may export, initiate

and carry out any actions needed to insure an adequate supply of wheat, protect purchasers of wheat against wide price fluctuations, and assist producers in recovering at least their costs of production.

4. The National Farmers Union requested the Congress and the President "to appoint a commission to reach an agreement with Canada, Australia, and Argentina on the world market share of wheat for each country and on a minimum price" (Terpstra 1979).

5. The American Agriculture Movement (AAM) passed a resolution stating that the President "must act to correct the balance of trade deficit and halt inflation by establishing a pricing policy for grain exports equivalent to a bushel of wheat for a barrel of oil" (Terpstra 1979). In addition, the AAM proposed that

> a National Board of Agricultural Producers be created to devise and approve agricultural production and marketing policy. The United States shall establish its parity level as the export price level in all trade transactions with other countries, and will not bring its price down below that level. The Board must approve the prices, conditions and terms of all import and export sales [Committee on Agriculture 1978]

6. On May 23, 1979, the Senate considered and approved by a vote of 80 to 15 a resolution offered by Senator Church that asked the President to

> actively work toward convening a negotiating conference of wheat exporting nations with the intent of reaching a cooperative arrangement to improve wheat trade policy and achieve equitable prices for producers while assuring adequate supplies for consumers.

There has, however, been strong opposition to the notion of a grain export cartel among certain sectors of the economy. During the hearings before the Senate Committee on Foreign Relations on May 8, 1979, the Western Wheat Associates, U.S.A., Inc., commented:

> We do not believe it is possible to manage an OPEC-type monopoly on world wheat production to raise prices regardless of supply and demand factors. Setting an artificially high price for wheat would stimulate production in many nations that would not be part of the agreement and, in effect, would defeat the purpose of the cartel. Wheat can be produced in more than 100 countries around the world [McCalla and Schmitz 1979].

The president of the National Association of Wheat Growers stated: "I want to make it clear that the National Association of Wheat

Growers does not advocate a wheat cartel, fixed exporting pricing, or market sharing" (Terpstra 1979). In *Agricultural World* (1979:1), Robbin S. Johnson, assistant vice president of Cargill, Inc., concluded:

> Those involved in producing or marketing wheat reject a cartel for three reasons: they know it will not work, they know that they will be hurt most by the attempt to make it work, and they know that their long-term interests are better served by treating customers fairly and supplying them dependably.

At the time of writing this book, none of the legislative proposals had been passed, but the question of a cartel continues. Thus, this book will explore those issues important in the future resolution of this issue; one of these issues is the objectives of a cartel.

OBJECTIVES OF A CARTEL

A quick review of public statements reveals that those who propose a grain cartel as an international policy alternative to deal with trade in grains do so with at least four possible objectives: (1) market stabilization to prevent wide swings in international prices; (2) agreements to establish international minimum trading prices in order to prevent price wars and allow major exporters to maintain market shares, particularly in a static or declining market; (3) use as a bargaining threat to induce major importers to reduce trade barriers to grain imports; and (4) increases in international grain prices so as to improve producers' incomes and extract part of the economic gains currently accruing to importers as a result of variable levies or quotas.

These objectives are not necessarily inconsistent within a cartel arrangement. However, the degree of international control necessary increases in moving from the first objective to the fourth objective.

In terms of the above, a cartel need not be established to achieve, for example, the first objective. An effective cartel, as we perceive it in this book, incorporates all of the above objectives. Its overall intention is to devise an organizational means whereby trade in grains will result in an increase in real income to exporters for producers, consumers, or both. The first two above, for example, are merely part of a cartel package.

WHAT IS A CARTEL?

In simplest terms, a cartel is an association of producers or governments who jointly determine levels of output, prices, and profits or returns. Its closest relative in terms of conventional economics is monopoly or collusive oligopoly (a market characterized by a small number of sellers). The conditions under which a monopoly can be successful in enhancing its position, relative to a free trade equilibrium, are as follows:

1. The monopolist (cartel) must have control over all supply or at least a sufficiently high percentage of it to dominate the market.
2. The demand for the product should be relatively steep, which means that a small reduction in quantity will result in a large increase in price. Steepness of demand or inelasticity results when a product has no close substitute, is a differentiated product, or is a necessary commodity. In technical terms, for an exporter cartel to achieve large gains, the prices which exist prior to the formation of a cartel should lie in the inelastic portion of the demand curve. If demands are linear, a producer cartel will raise prices to the elastic portion.
3. Entry of new producers into the market must be blocked, or at least limited, so that new producers cannot enter and undercut monopoly (cartel) prices.
4. The monopolist (cartel) must have a clearly defined objective function such as maximizing profit, gross returns, or the like.
5. Buyers of the product should be sufficiently small and dispersed so that they cannot exercise countervailing market power.

If these conditions are generally met, a government or producer cartel is able to set prices via the management of supply in such a way as to maximize its stated objectives. The outcomes of a producer cartel, unlike those of a government cartel, are higher prices both at home and abroad. Consumers lose relative to a competitive market situation (if a competitive market alternative exists), and the producer (monopolist) gains profits. Similar results could come from an international cartel if members agreed on objectives and submitted to centralized decision-making.

An international export cartel in grains could take one of several forms which are discussed in detail later. At one extreme, the major institutions in the grain trade (for example, the Canadian Wheat Board and Cargill, Inc.) would remain; but the United States, Canada, and Australia would agree on a minimum price to be used in export sales. This price would be set by government negotiations among exporters, and the trade would be subject to this price minimum. At the other extreme, a government export selling agency would be set up in the United States; and importers would have to buy directly from this and from other country government marketing boards now in existence at a common minimum price set by all of the export boards.

ANALYSIS OF CARTELS—WHAT IS NEEDED?

An analysis of grain export cartels must focus on at least three areas of inquiry: the nature of the grain trade, an understanding of cartel theory specific to renewable resources, and the structure of the international market. A series of examples will highlight the importance of each of these areas in determining the effectiveness of this policy alternative and in evaluating the various forms proposed.

Nature of the Grain Trade

Many grain cartel proposals are based on the notion of bartering U.S. wheat for oil produced by OPEC countries. Yet, an examination of the significance of wheat exports to OPEC nations reveals that the potential gains from such a cartel are limited. Table 1–5, which shows U.S. exports of wheat, corn, and soybeans to OPEC countries, illustrates that, except for wheat, the percentage of exports to OPEC is extremely low and that, even in wheat, less than 20 percent of U.S. exports go to OPEC nations.

Cartel Theory

A cartel could take several forms, depending on its objective. A government export cartel is very different from a producer export cartel. The former, which maximizes welfare for everyone in the exporting countries, could result in lower grain prices for domestic

Table 1-5. U.S. exports to OPEC: average price and percent of total wheat, corn, and soybean exports, 1973-1978

	Wheat		*Corn*		*Soybeans*	
Year	*Average Price per Bushel*	*Percent*	*Average Price per Bushel*	*Percent*	*Average Price per Bushel*	*Percent*
1973	3.10	6.3	2.99	1.0	5.29	0.3
1974	5.15	14.9	3.71	0.4	7.87	0.4
1975	5.05	10.4	3.25	0.4	5.85	0.4
1976	4.22	10.5	3.09	0.6	6.16	0.7
1977	3.06	17.0	2.95	1.0	7.16	1.0
1978	3.50	14.8	2.70	0.9	7.03	0.8

Source: Terpstra, A.E. 1979. "An Analysis of Possible Cartel and Barter Arrangements to Influence the Price and Availability of Wheat on the International Market." Unpublished paper, The Library of Congress, May 30, p. CRS-15.

consumers than would otherwise be the case, whereas a producer cartel which maximizes only producer welfare would result in higher consumer prices. An important point from this distinction, as will be shown later, is that domestic prices of food derived from grain products may rise or fall depending on the form of a grain export cartel. This distinction is not needed in dealing with nonrenewable resources, such as oil, largely because the domestic demand for oil by major exporters is relatively unimportant compared to worldwide demand—this is not the case for grains.

Structure of the International Market

The effects of an international grain cartel depend, in part, on the structure of the grain market at the time of the formation of the cartel. Is the market essentially characterized by free trade, or does it consist of price leaders or strong import buyers? The degree to which a cartel can achieve its objectives, as well as the form it should take, depends partly on this structure. For example, if major importers are exerting monopsony power in trade through their relative strength as buyers, then an effective cartel by exporters could at least force the importers to free trade and gain by so doing.

At the extreme, the exporters could go further and exert monopoly power in the selling of the product. That is, an effective cartel could shift the market from a "buyer's market" to a "seller's market."

REFERENCES

Agricultural World: Insight into the Forces Affecting Agriculture. 1969. 5 (July/August):1.

Carter, C., and A. Schmitz. 1979. "Import Tariffs and Price Formation in the World Wheat Market." *American Journal of Agricultural Economics* 61 (August):517–522.

Committee on Agriculture, U.S. House of Representatives. 1978. "Evaluations of Proposals Guaranteeing Full Parity for Farmers in the Market Place." Washington, D.C.: U.S. Government Printing Office.

Johnson, D.G. 1979. "Food Reserves and International Trade Policy." In *International Trade and Agriculture: Theory and Policy,* edited by J.S. Hillman and A. Schmitz. Boulder, Colo.: Westview Press.

McCalla, A.F., and A. Schmitz. 1979. "State Trading in Grain." Paper presented to the conference, State Trading in Industrialized and Developing Countries, Ecole des Hautes Études Commerciales, Montreal, Quebec, Canada, April 19.

Terpstra, E. 1979. "An Analysis of Possible Cartel and Barter Arrangements to Influence the Price and Availability of Wheat on the International Market." Washington, D.C.: Library of Congress.

2 THE NATURE OF GRAIN MARKETS AND TRADE

The international grain industry has been the subject of a great deal of controversy, such as the question of whether grain markets are competitive and function efficiently. During the Russian wheat deal of 1972–73, for example, many felt that a few large private traders manipulated market prices.[a] Morgan (1979), furthermore, implies that the private grain trade has a substantial amount of market power, while Food West Resource Consultants (1979) have suggested that the Canadian marketing system, with its focal point, the Canadian Wheat Board, is inefficient in comparison to that of the United States.

In order to discuss such issues, it is necessary to define the major components of the international grain market and to understand their roles and interaction. Governments, for example, influence the grain trade in many ways: they can use export subsidies to promote exports or tariffs and quotas to restrict trade; they can curtail production by the use of acreage controls or increase it by price supports; they can also influence price by direct involvement in the price negotiations between exporters and importers (that is, by state trading). This chapter discusses first the role of governments and marketing boards in negotiating world market prices for grain, and

[a]The history of this period is well documented and discussed by Biggs (1976).

then the impact of governments' agricultural policies on the grain trade. It focuses on the interactions among governments, marketing boards, and the private grain trade, and considers how the market might change in response to the formation of a grain export cartel. For example, if a grain cartel were created, would there be any need for the futures market which, unlike the situation in many countries of the world, has been an integral part of marketing U.S. grains? Given that the degree of state trading has increased through time and that the United States is the largest nonstate trader in grains, what would be the significance of the formation of an export cartel?

GOVERNMENTS, MARKETING BOARDS, AND THE PRIVATE TRADE PARTICIPANTS

Governments and Boards As Price Setters

To illustrate a contrast, the Canadian Wheat Board is a producer marketing board (PMB) and the sole seller of Canadian wheat for the export market; all buyers outside Canada have to deal with the board. Its sales to the Soviet Union are examples of state trading. In the United States, as has been well documented elsewhere, a few major private grain companies export a large proportion of U.S. grain, that is, they buy grain privately within the United States for sale in export markets. A sale by one of these private firms to the Soviet Union would be viewed as a private-to-state sale.

There have been some interesting changes in the degree to which governments and boards are involved in international pricing of grains. Major exporters, such as Canada and Australia, have been state traders since the interwar period; Argentina was a state trader until the mid-1970s but now relies on the private trade; and the United States of America, the ECC-9, and Thailand rely on private traders. Thus, on the export side, the growing dominance of the United States means that the volume of grain trade originating in state-trading nations has declined. On the import side, the opposite is occurring: traditional markets in Western Europe which relied on private traders have declined, while the importance of the centrally planned economies (CPs) and the developing countries has increased.

Table 2–1 presents a summary of state trading in wheat in the postwar period (McCalla and Schmitz 1979a). Several things stand

Table 2-1. State trading in wheat: percentage of volume of principal exporters accounted for by state traders

Years	*Private Exporters to Private Importers*	*Private Exporters to State Importers*	*State Exporters to Private Importers*	*State Exporters to State Importers*
	1[a]	2[a]	3[a]	4[a]
1953-1957	10.7	33.3	28.3	27.7
1963-1967	5.9	51.2	8.1	34.8
1973-1977	4.4	56.6	4.3	34.7
	Exports by Private Traders	*Exports by State Traders*	*Imports by Private Traders*	*Imports by State Traders*
	Cols. 1 + 2[a]	Cols. 3 + 4[a]	Cols. 1 + 3[a]	Cols. 2 + 4[a]
1953-1957	44.0	56.0	39.0	61.0
1963-1967	57.1	42.9	14.0	86.0
1973-1977	61.0	39.0	8.7	91.3
	Volume of Trade Included Above[b]		*Total World Exports*[b]	
1953-1957	23,475		25,596	
1963-1967	49,891		56,397	
1973-1977	60,386		63,506	

[a]Given in percentages.
[b]Given in million metric tons.
Sources: For 1953-1957: United Nations, Food and Agriculture Organization. *World Grain Trade Statistics* (various issues). For 1963-1967 and 1973-1977: International Wheat Council, *Review of the World Wheat Situation* (various issues).

out. First, the proportion of wheat trade which involves only private traders is small and declining, involving about 5 percent of the trade during 1973–77. The reciprocal, of course, is that 95 percent of the world trade in wheat involves a state trader on at least one side of the transaction. Second, state trader-to-state trader transactions account for about one-third of the trade and seem to be stable. Third, the importance of state trading on the export side of the market is declining, reflecting the rising importance of the United States as an exporter and the discontinuance of state trading by Argentina. And fourth, the rise in importance of state trading importers is substantial, reflecting the rising importance in the wheat market of CP and less developed country (LDC) importers, most of whom pursue state trading.

Comparable data for coarse grains cannot easily (if at all) be generated. It can be postulated, however, that the role of private traders is significantly greater in coarse grains than in wheat for the following reasons: (1) the United States is a more important element in the market; (2) Australia does not state trade in coarse grains; (3) Japan imports only barley as a state trader—other coarse grains are imported by trading companies; (4) the relative importance of LDCs is much smaller; and (5) many countries (particularly in Other Western Europe) which state trade in food grains do not do so for coarse grains.

Partially offsetting these factors is the rising volume of coarse grain exports to the USSR and Eastern Europe which do state trade. As the data in McCalla and Schmitz (1979a) indicate, in 1975–76 more than 85 percent of world coarse grain exports originated with private traders. Similarly, more than 60 percent of coarse grain imports were imported by private traders. More details on specific bilateral trading relationships are, unfortunately, not available; neither are trend data.

This review of wheat and feed grain markets shows clear differences in the importance of state trading in the two markets. State trading is becoming increasingly important in the wheat market principally because of the increasing importance of LDCs and CPs. It is relatively less important in coarse grain markets because coarse grains are primarily imported by high-income countries as livestock feed, and these countries are less inclined to state trade in feed inputs.

It is clear that most state trading occurs in importing nations largely because the major grain exporter, the United States, relies heavily on private trade to carry out market transactions.

Interactions Among Governments, Marketing Boards, and the Private Grain Trade

In spite of governments' and marketing boards' increased involvement in the pricing of grains, the private grain trade still plays a major role in the marketing of wheat and feed grains. The private grain firms, which are multinational in scope, carry out several functions crucial to the marketing of grain. Even in cases where wheat is sold by the Canadian and Australian Wheat Boards, for example, the private trade is involved since it carries out shipping and other activities related to getting the grain from Canada and Australia to importers. As McCalla and Schmitz (1979b) point out, the private grain traders act as "agents" to the wheat boards.

The grain trade is similar to any other form of international market as it involves the production and collection of a product in dispersed locations in an exporting country and its movement to dispersed consumption points in the importing country. At some point between production and consumption, a contractual transfer of ownership occurs. In the grain trade, the contractual arrangement involves many factors including price, quantity, quality, point of ownership transfer, terms of payment (when and in what currency), marine insurance, carrying charges, responsibiity for unforeseen events, time period of delivery, and means for settlement of disputes. The first three factors—price, quantity, and quality—we call basic terms and conditions; the latter set of factors, logistical factors. Given the variety of factors involved and the spatial distribution of trade, contractual arrangements in grain can have many forms. Table 2–2 outlines six basic contractual types which are common in the grain trade. The first three—free on board (F.O.B.), free alongside ship (F.A.S.), and free, stowed, and trimmed on boat (F.S.T.)—require the exporter to deliver only to the exporting port; all other functions are provided by the importer either directly or through the middlemen. The last three—cost and freight (C.&F.); cost, insurance, and freight (C.I.F.); and delivered to final destination (D.F.D.)—involve the exporter in movement of the grain to at least the importer port of entry. The most frequent forms of trade are F.O.B. and C.I.F.

The role of private trade, and its interaction with state traders, becomes further apparent when one considers the following facts about the way state traders operate. First, state-trading exporters almost never become directly involved in the logistical terms of grain handling. The Canadian Wheat Board, for example, sells principally on an F.O.B. basis, leaving the importer to deal with the risks involved in shipping, freight, and foreign exchange. Similarly, state-trading importers typically buy on a C.I.F. or D.F.D. basis. This means that, in contractual arrangements involving a state-trading

Table 2-2. The taxonomy of the grain trade exporter and importer responsibilities and point of contract (*)

Type of Contract	*Functions: (1) Production*	*(2) Transport to Export Point*	*(3) Loading*	*(4) Ocean Transport*	*(5) Insurance*	*(6) Foreign Exchange Arrangements*	*(7) Unloading*	*(8) Transport to Final Destination*	*(9) Consumption*
1. F.O.B. Free on Board—in spout to boat (bulk)	Farmers	EX *	IMP	IMP	IMP	IMP	IMP	IMP	Domestic users
2. F.A.S. Free Along Side—bags on wharf	Farmers	EX *	IMP	IMP	IMP	IMP	IMP	IMP	Domestic users
3. F.S.T.—F.O.B. Free plus stowed and trimmed on boat	Farmers	EX	EX *	IMP	IMP	IMP	IMP	IMP	Domestic users
4. C&F—Cost and freight to importer dock	Farmers	EX	EX	EX *	IMP	IMP	IMP	IMP	Domestic users
5. C.I.F.—Cost, insurance and freight	Farmers	EX	EX	EX	EX *	EX/IMP	IMP	IMP	Domestic users
6. D.F.D.—Delivered to final destination	Farmers	EX	EX	EX	EX	EX	EX	EX *	Domestic users

Note: An exporter or importer could contract with a third party (grain merchandiser) for any or all of functions 3, 4, 5, 6, 7, and 8. If these are fixed fee-for-service contracts, who does them will not alter the principal contractual factors of price, quantity, and quality.

exporter and a state-trading importer, a middleman (usually a multinational grain firm) is almost always involved at least in the logistics of the trade. Second, a private trader buying grain from a state-trading exporter F.O.B. without a prior sales contract has a large range of contractual variables on which to negotiate with importers—private or state. Thus, in these cases considerable scope for price variation exists. Also, in a trade with a significant number of state traders, the role of any origin sales by private traders gives these traders considerable scope for intermarket arbitrage and price discrimination which a state trader may not have. Third, the complexity of international grain markets, with the attendant risk, places a large premium on good information. Thus, a state-trading exporter which sells only F.O.B. or a state-trading importer which buys only C.I.F. may not have access to information regarding market variables that an active middleman may have.

In addition to the private sector carrying out F.O.B. activities for many of the state-trading agencies, it also buys grains directly from these agencies. For example, Cargill Grain, Inc., has at times purchased sizable quantities of wheat from the Canadian Wheat Board; therefore, in these transactions it does not act as an agent to the board (McCalla and Schmitz 1979a). The private sector is also heavily involved in carrying out the merchandising activity for U.S. government sales under Public Law 480 shipments; very few of these shipments, for example, are carried in U.S. government ships.

Because of the size of its exports, any successful grain exporter cartel will require cooperation from the United States. Also, because of the largely private nature of its export trade, a cartel would probably have a substantial impact on the marketing institutions in the United States. As a result, a more detailed discussion of the U.S. marketing system follows.

The Private Trade and Grain Coops in the United States

Although many grain merchandising and processing firms export U.S. grain, the export grain industry is dominated by a few firms that account for a large portion of U.S. grain exports. According to the United States Department of Agriculture (USDA) report of Thurston, Phillips, Haskell, and Volkin (1976), the remaining share of the market is divided among four regional grain cooperatives and other small private firms. Add this to the involvement of the private trade in state trading, and one can easily imagine the large volume of exports handled by the private trade.

Cargill Grain, Inc., and Continental Grain, Inc., may account for as much as one half of U.S. grain exports. These companies, which are privately held by a small number of individuals, are also diversified. For example, Cargill, the third largest rock salt producer, also produces molasses; owns and operates cattle-feeding operations in the United States and a fishing fleet in Peru; and has interests in real estate, paint and glass manufacturing, steel plants, and flour milling. Generally, the five major exporters have the following characteristics: they are diversified; are multinational in scope; cross-subsidize operations; have worldwide market intelligence systems; and are closely held private corporations. These characteristics have an important bearing on the functioning of the grain trade. For example, as discussed later, the major export cooperatives in the United States have limited scope largely because of the size and structure of the private trade.

The USDA report of Thurston, Phillips, Haskell, and Volkin (1976) categorizes the types of markets in which the export firms operate into the open market, the public tender market, and the private tender market. In the open market—for example, Rotterdam, Hamburg, and London—there is a continuous two-way flow of offers, bids, and market information; private traders and processors typically use this type of market. The public market is one in which the buyers issue tenders ahead of the requested offering date; among buyers who operate in this manner are recipients under Public Law 480 agreements and the Japanese Food Agency. In the private tender market, private mills or processors request selected exporters to submit offers.

Farm cooperatives also play a role in the U.S. grain trade. Cooperatives have relatively more control of grain used within the United States than that exported; flour mills and feed manufacturers buy substantial amounts of grain from farm cooperatives, while farmer cooperatives are themselves involved in processing grain for animal feed. Since the largest percentage of U.S. feed grains is used domestically, feed processing is a gigantic business and accounts for the largest single purchased input made by U.S. farmers in a single year.[b]

Table 2–3 illustrates that in the United States, the amount of corn (which is by far the most important feedgrain) consumed domestically is a large percentage of the amount produced. The numbers

Table 2-3. Corn: production, exports, and domestic use in the United States, 1960-1979

Year	*Production*	*Exports*	*Domestic Use*[a]	*Percent of Production in Domestic Use*
	Million Bushels			
1960	3,907	292	3,387	.87
1961	3,598	435	3,527	.98
1962	3,606	416	3,479	.96
1963	4,019	500	3,348	.83
1964	3,484	570	3,305	.95
1965	4,103	687	3,722	.91
1966	4,168	487	3,698	.89
1967	4,860	633	3,885	.80
1968	4,450	536	3,966	.89
1969	4,687	612	4,189	.89
1970	4,152	517	3,977	.96
1971	5,646	796	4,391	.77
1972	5,580	1,258	4,742	.85
1973	5,671	1,243	4,653	.82
1974	4,701	1,149	3,677	.78
1975	5,829	1,711	4,082	.70
1976	6,266	1,684	4,100	.65
1977	6,426	1,948	4,260	.66
1978	7,087	2,133	4,773	.67
1979	7,764	2,433	5,021	.65
		2 550	4850	

[a]Roughly 35 percent of domestic use is in hog production.

Sources: U.S. Department of Agriculture. 1969. *Agricultural Statistics,* p. 34. U.S. Department of Agriculture. 1979. *Agricultural Statistics,* p. 31. *Feed Situation.* 1980. (October): 8.

[b]Information on the growth of the U.S. feeding industry is contained in Pearce (1976).

clearly show the importance of domestic demand for feed grains relative to foreign demand and the reasons why pricing on the foreign market has a direct impact on domestic feed grain prices which in turn affect their usage by the meat sector of the U.S. economy. This is why later in the book a sharp distinction is drawn between a producer and government export cartel. Because of the large size of domestic demand for grains via the livestock sector, a producer cartel in grains could have serious detrimental effects on this industry.

Grain is stored in the United States on farms, in local elevators, and at ports (for example, Gulf ports). Inland cooperative elevators handle roughly 40 percent of the total U.S. grain; thus, they represent buyers when grain first leaves the farm level. In addition to coop elevators, there are many small private elevator companies, not connected with the large private export firms, who buy grain directly from the farmer. However, as grain moves into export position, it is increasingly controlled by the large private export firms, which have roughly 50 percent of the U.S. port capacity. (Cargill, Inc., alone has 25 percent.) Farm cooperatives, on the other hand, have less than 20 percent. Thus, cooperative control of grain is rapidly diminished as it moves through marketing channels. As the USDA study (Thurston et al. 1976) points out, in 1973 cooperative direct export sales accounted for only 7.5 percent of total U.S. grain exports, while indirect exports (that is, those made to major exporters who, in turn, make the sale) accounted for 18 percent. Thus, although cooperatives are a major factor through origination, they turn about 70 percent of their potential export volume over to the other grain companies. The USDA study gives the following reasons: (1) lack of access to cooperative export facilities; (2) less risk in indirect sales; (3) better price; (4) economies of size; (5) lack of expertise; (6) unwillingness to coordinate; and (7) fear of the unknown. The main differences between coops making direct export sales and the private trade are the former's lack of (1) a market intelligence system; (2) diversification; (3) multiple grain sources; (4) flexibility; (5) overseas facilities and sales offices; and (6) secrecy of operations. For example, lack of diversification for coops means that they cannot spread the risks inherent in the exporting business.

The U.S. marketing system contrasts sharply with that of Canada and Australia because of the different role played by the private sector. Private firms in Canada own very few country elevators; the majority of elevators are cooperatives. In addition, private firms do not export Canadian or Australian wheat or feed grains except to the extent already mentioned. The wheat boards are the sole sellers of Canadian and Australian wheat and feed grains for export markets. The structure of the Canadian Wheat Board has been described elsewhere by Schmitz and McCalla, (1979a) while the Canadian and U.S. grain marketing systems have been compared in studies by McCalla and Schmitz (1979a) and Stickland of Food West Resource Consultants (1979).

Establishing an export cartel implies government involvement, in some form or another, in the pricing and exportation of grain. One extreme would be the creation of a U.S. marketing board similar to that of Canada and Australia. As the above data suggest, however, this would be a major departure from the current structure. If major changes in market structure are needed to implement an export cartel, the efficiency of different market structures must be considered. For example, would an all-marketing-board arrangement for North America lead to the same grain marketing efficiency that now exists?

GOVERNMENT POLICY

Two kinds of actions by governments in international markets directly or indirectly influence grain flows and prices. The first consists of government policies which fundamentally alter trading relationships in the international market; an example is the establishment of the EEC and its Common Agricultural Policy (CAP). The second type, already discussed, could result from the exercise of power by governments through state trading.

Nearly every government pursues some form of domestic food and agriculture policy which influences internal prices or production. In almost all cases, a necessary element of these policies is the management of international trade so that changes in international prices do not offset or pervert domestic price objectives. The result is that participation in international markets is in residuals (either exports or imports) resulting from domestic policymaking (Josling 1977). These facts seem incontrovertible, and it does not seem productive to further belabor the point. The more important question is whether or not the pursuit of generally protectionist domestic policies simply alters net flows into or out of the market (the quantity impact) or whether actions by governments significantly influence price. Debate on this point continues.

It is obvious that U.S. domestic agricultural policies, such as acreage controls, have an effect on grain stocks and prices. Therefore, we focus on the less obvious aspects of government policy. Attempts to include traditional structural parameters, particularly government policy, as endogenous parts of price formation models are limited. The work of Josling (1979) begins by assuming domestic agricultural policy as given and attempts to analyze an international market of policy-induced residual supplies and demands. The problem arises when government, by pursuing price-insulating domestic policy, makes import demand or export supply perfectly inelastic with respect to world price. Summations of perfectly inelastic net supply and demand functions yield perfectly inelastic aggregate world supply and demand functions which, if by chance they coincide, yield an infinity of price solutions. Josling introduces a stock function which has a slope and allows a determinate price outcome. Earlier work by McCalla and Learn (1967) also deal with these issues. The work of Abbott (1979) attempts, in world econometric models, to introduce government policy endogenously; but the number of parameters it is possible to include is limited, and the ultimate pricing solution is a market-clearing competitive one. Heidhues (1979) and Warley (1976), among others,have delved quantitatively into the political economy of interactions of domestic agricultural policy and international markets.[c]

Exporters With Market Power

In addition to the above, several writers have attempted to look at the international wheat market in an oligopolistic framework made up of major exporters. McCalla (1966, 1967) postulates a cooperative duopoly with price leadership by one of the duopolists (Canada) and a fringe of competitive followers; Abel (1966) also considers a

[c]In part of the discussion that follows, a theoretical approach is used. We present an intuitive approach as well so as, hopefully, not to discourage the nontechnical readers.

price discrimination trade model. In a more recent work, Alaouze, Watson, and Sturgess (1978) postulate a tripoly model of the world wheat market with Canada as a revenue-maximizing price leader.[d] All of these models achieve deterministic price solutions on the basis of simplistic pricing rules, suggesting implicit, if not explicit, collusion. None of them recognizes the possible existence of private intermediaries. Recently, McCalla (1979) attempted to include both governmental entities (state traders) and private intermediaries, pursuing different objective functions, in a model of the international grain market; but the analysis fails to provide a rational price formation model.

Importers As Monopsony Buyers

A recent paper by Carter and Schmitz (1979) views the wheat market as a buyer's market and postulates that large importers exercise market power by the application of an optimum, or near optimum, tariff. This represents an alternative approach to price formation. They contend that buyers, such as Japan and the EEC, use tariffs to improve their economic situation at the expense of exporters.[e] There are generally three effects from a tariff: (1) an increase in price to producers which results in a producer economic gain; (2) an increase in the price to consumers—a loss to consumers; and (3) an increase in tariff revenue. In the optimal tariff argument, the producer gain plus the tariff revenue gain more than offsets the consumer loss.

Because the argument that grain importers impose welfare-improving tariffs (from their viewpoint) against exporters has important implications for the possible formation of a grain export cartel in that a cartel could at least take back the importer gains, the theory is discussed below.

The optimal import tariff solution is given in Figure 2–1. The supply schedule in the exporting country is given by S_f with MC_f

[d]For counterarguments, see Grennes and Johnson (1979).

[e]Carter and Schmitz (1979) admit that even in a seller's market, exporters may have power. The model of optimal tariffs has more recently been employed by Sampson and Snape (1980) to study specifically the EEC. The analysis also included feed grains. These results strongly support those by Carter and Schmitz (1979). In addition Sampson and Snape (1980) found that the feed grain market was also a buyer's market.

Figure 2–1. The optimum tariff solution

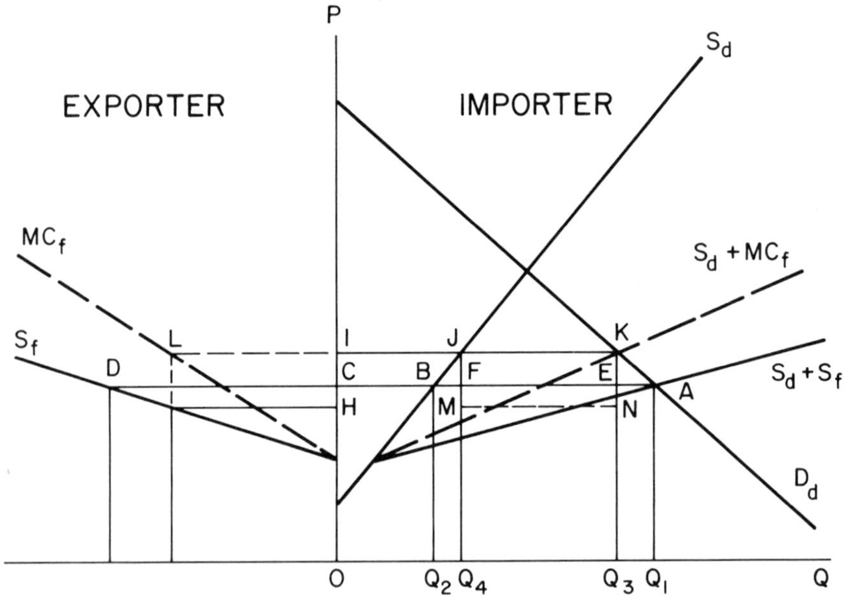

Source: Enke S. (1944)

being the marginal cost of importation when the importing country exerts monopsony power. In the importing country, S_d and D_d are the supply and demand schedules, respectively. Under free trade, imports are BA. However, the importing country can do better by imposing an optimum tariff. This solution is derived by summing $S_d + MC_f$. Imports are reduced to *JK*. In the importing country, producers gain *BCIJ*, consumers lose *IKAC*, and there is a gain in tariff revenue of *JKNM*. The gain in tariff revenue plus the producer gain more than offsets the consumer loss.

Note that with the optimal tariff solution benefits accrue to more than just producers in the importing country; if the tariff revenue is redistributed to consumers, the country as a whole gains from the tariff. Thus, while a government may use tariffs primarily for the purpose of protecting producers, the net result may be an overall improvement in society's welfare if the tariff imposed is close to being optimal.

The model in Figure 2–1 was used as a reference point to empirically test the hypothesis that importers exert monopsony power in the world wheat market.[f] The aggregate empirical model and the results are presented in the appendix to this chapter. Because the actual prices in some cases are reasonably similar to the empirical estimates (Figure 2A-1), there is reason to argue that the major importers of wheat could be acting in a fashion similar to tacit collusive behavior and that they are effectively imposing close to an optimal import tariff on wheat. Even though there seems to be no formal arrangement, it is conceivable that one of the major importers of wheat (for example, Japan or the EEC) acts as a price leader in setting an optimal or nearly optimal tariff; a mechanism used to achieve this might be the variable levy or the equivalent quota. Even though there is no evidence that overt collusion among importers exists, one could argue that collusion without formal agreement is both feasible and tempting.

It is unrealistic to argue that importers each day impose the exact optimal tariff solution, the assumption on which the welfare gains presented are based.[g] However, it is not necessary for the importers to impose the exact optimum tariff for them to become better off than under free trade. There is a wide range of tariffs which make importers better off than they would be in the absence of tariffs (Carter and Schmitz forthcoming).

How does one reconcile Carter and Schmitz's conclusions that Japan and the EEC-9 set prices with Josling's plausible assertion that importing nations which isolate domestic prices from external prices by absolute quantitative (or equivalent) barriers give up any inherent market power? Further, a policy of using optimum tariffs to set world prices would suggest that importers should constantly adjust internal prices to capture benefits from changing world market conditions, but the community's internal prices seem only to rise as a

[f]To test the model presented in Figure 2–1, estimates of national supply and demand equations for wheat were obtained from an econometric study of the world wheat economy by the U.S. Department of Agriculture's Economic Research Service (ERS) (1971). From the estimates, aggregate supply and demand functions were computed for the major wheat exporters and importers. The estimated slope coefficients and elasticities provided by the ERS are not too dissimilar from those reported by Schmitz and Bawden (1973).

[g]Empirical estimates of the welfare gain accruing to the importing group as a result of the optimal tariff are shown in Figure 2A–1. Consumers in the importing countries lose a surplus equivalent to the area CZAB. On the other hand, producers in these countries gain a surplus equal to the area CDEB. Government revenue from the import tariff is equal to DZGF. Therefore, the total net gain to the importing nations is equal to the area (HJGF)–[(DHE) + (ZAJ)] ´ 0. This estimated net welfare gain accumulated per annum by the wheat importers is shown later to be approximately $3.7 billion.

result of internal price-support considerations. Because of these complications, pricing models should include the potential for both exporters and importers to exercise market power.

MARKETING BOARDS, MULTINATIONAL GRAIN FIRMS, AND FUTURES MARKETS[h]

As already pointed out, central governments, producer marketing boards (PMBs), and private grain firms play a key role in the pricing of wheat and feed grains. In essence, the world grain markets involve different types of marketing agencies. If the theory, presented earlier, that buyers exert monopsony power in world grain markets is correct, then how did this happen? Clearly, collusion in the pricing of grains could not have existed among the major exporters, in part perhaps because the goals which the different marketing agencies pursue cannot lead to collusive marketing behavior among exporters. If this is true, a successful cartel organized among exporters would require some change in the way exporters currently price grain.

State and Private Trading

In a market in which different intermediaries are involved, the question arises as to the objectives pursued by each marketing firm and the effect of differing objectives in determining the level of prices. In the grain market, one can defend the hypothesis that the objective of the Canadian and Australian Wheat Boards is different from that of the private trade. Among the objectives of the boards is the maximization of producer returns, whereas one of the main objectives of the private trade is to maximize profits and returns to shareholders; and, as will be demonstrated in a noncompetitive environment, the outcome for one is quite different from that for the other.

Consider an international market where only a PMB exists as a marketing intermediary. In Figure 2–2, *D* is the foreign excess demand schedule, and *S* is the domestic excess supply curve. Assume

[h]For a theoretical treatise on this subject, see Just, Schmitz, and Zilberman (1979).

Figure 2–2. A producer marketing board versus a private firm as an international intermediary

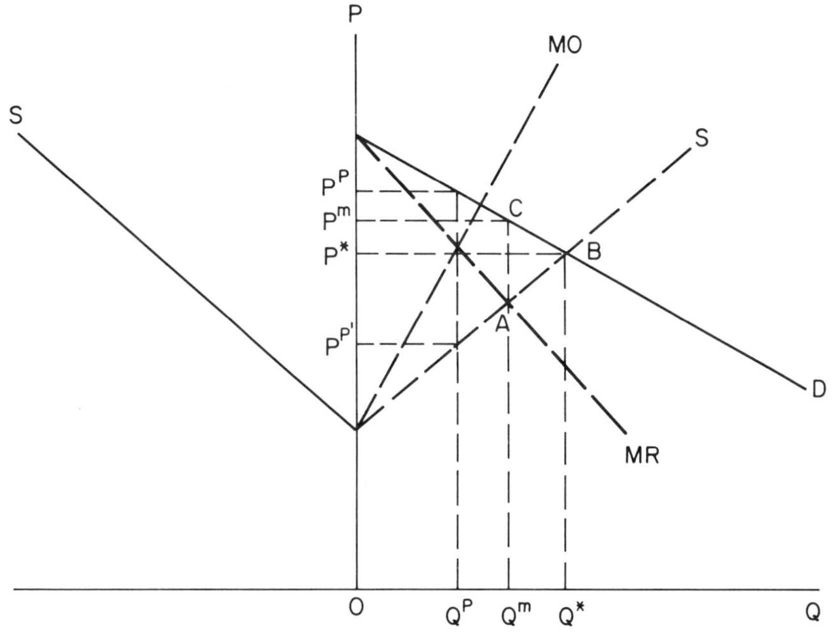

that "normal marketing costs" are already included in *S*—the simplest of all possible models. With competition, the free trade price is *P**, and *OQ** of the product is exported. At the extreme, the board can improve the welfare position of producers by behaving as a monopolist. The board will charge P^m to foreign consumers and restrict sales from *OQ** to OQ^m.

The very different solution for a private trader can also be represented in Figure 2–2. In the former case, the surplus was extracted from consumers; now it is extracted from both producers and consumers. The private sector will equate the marginal outlay curve to *S*(*MO*) with *MR* to arrive at the optimal pricing solution. Note that the price difference between the amount received by producers and that paid by consumers ($P^pP^{p'}$) goes to the private marketing firm, unlike the case with the board.

The above models have ignored stocks and have not incorporated price instability. As Bieri and Schmitz (1974) have shown, a PMB will use stocks so as to create price stability for producers, whereas the private firm will use stocks to "manufacture" price instability for producers. Stocks can be used advantageously by the private sector in order to create a situation of buying low and selling high.

Clearly, *both* the private traders and the PMBs operate in the same international market. Thus, it is interesting to hypothesize how prices are determined in a market consisting of different marketing institutions that are pursuing different objectives. One model is presented in Figure 2–3. Suppose that S^* represents the excess supply schedule for the exporting country whose marketing is carried out by a board arrangement. S is the excess supply in the country whose exports are sold by the private trade. The foreign excess demand is represented by D. With competition, the free trade price is P_f. Suppose now that the marketing board acts as a price leader by equating the sum of S^* and S with MR. Exports are reduced from OQ_f to OQ_m. Accordingly, production in each country is reduced.

Figure 2–3. Producer marketing board together with a private firm in international trade

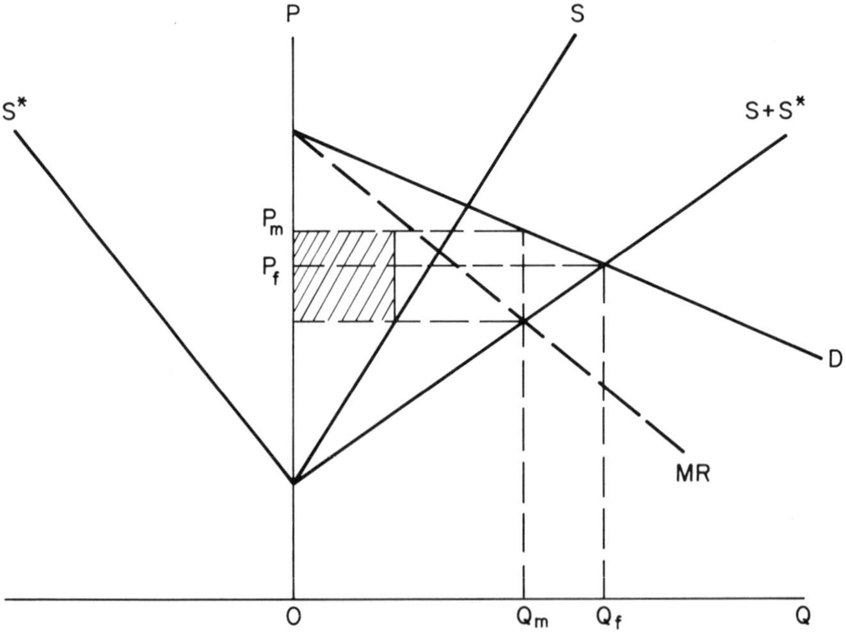

Note that in the country where the board exists, while production is reduced, prices for producers increase from P_f to P_m, resulting in a net welfare gain. If, as has to be the case in this model, the private sector also charges P_m, the real producer prices will depend on the degree of monopoly power exercised by the private sector. On one hand, the crosshatched area could be given to producers, with the result that only normal profits would be made by the private sector. On the other hand, the private trade could keep the same area in the form of excess profits. Thus, it is interesting that, even though the board and the private sector price the same on the demand side, a wide discrepancy can exist between producer prices in both countries.

The above model would also hold if the private sector acted as a price leader or if there were some form of price collusion in the marketplace. The important point is that one cannot argue that competition always prevails when marketing institutions from different countries set identical prices for buyers.

Multinational Firms

A striking difference between the operations of the PMBs and the private grain traders is that some of the latter companies are of a multinational nature. In order to meet export commitments,they buy grain not only from U.S. producers but also, for example, from the Canadian Wheat Board. The boards, however, do not buy from other countries in order to make export sales. To our knowledge, for instance, Canada has not bought grain from other nations to meet its export commitments; its export sales are confined to the magnitude of domestic production.

This raises the question of producer welfare at any point in time since, when the large companies shop around for the best deal for themselves, their actions do not necessarily always benefit the producers in the country in which the parent company is located (or in any particular country, for that matter).

Also, what are the implications for pricing? Consider Figure 2–4 where S* is the supply in the country where the board does the marketing. The competitive price is P^c. However, the multinational nature of the private sector enables it to use both S and S^* to meet the foreign demand, provided that the board will sell to it. This is

Figure 2–4. Operations of a multinational trading firm

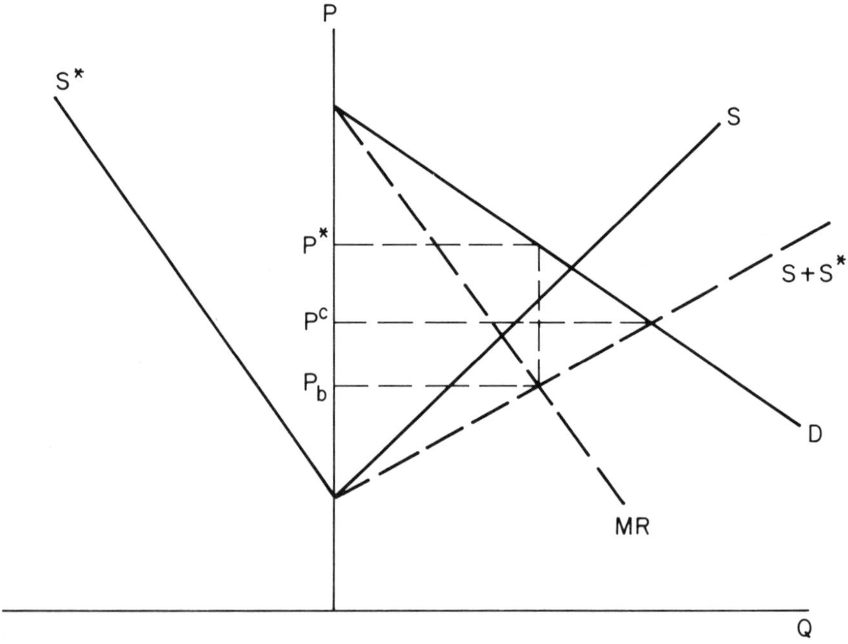

unrealistic since the board will market at least part of the crop produced directly to foreign buyers; thus, it is more realistic to think of S^* as an excess supply curve. If this is true, the private sector could price at P^* and reap excess profits on production from both countries. The extent to which this is possible depends on how knowledgeable the board is with respect to current and future marketing conditions. As the figure shows, the excess price of the multinational is $P^* - P_b$. This can be captured by the monopolist trader only if the board sells its remaining supplies at prices close to P_b; otherwise, the monopolist would capture a smaller portion of the profits. Clearly, the returns to the private sector from gathering information are very high since it can use the information not only to capture quasi rents on S but also rents on S^*.

The models have ignored storage facilities and transportation. Generally, the large multinational marketing firms have the means of shipping commodities more easily than marketing boards can. Thus, the board may be willing to sell an amount (excess supply being determined by shipping capacity) to the private sector just because it does not have the physical facilities to market the commodity. Hence, if the private sector has access to better physical facilities, it can easily capture excess profits on the part of the good it buys from the board countries. The board may know that this is the case but may still permit such sales in order to avoid a large buildup of stocks in that country.

The Futures Market

Futures markets, used extensively by the private grain companies and, to some extent, by importers as well, are an integral part of the grain trade. In a sense, these markets provide information to the entire grain trade. They are used by exporters in setting asking prices and by importers in negotiating buyer prices, and thus futures prices have an impact on both exporters and importers. In addition, even though there is no active wheat futures market in Canada due to the wheat board system, the Canadians still can use U.S. futures for more than just providing information. For example, when making outright sales to private firms in the United States, the board hedges in the sense that private firms can hedge the purchase in U.S. futures.

The role of futures markets is highly controversial, as is the need for these markets if a cartel were formed. Assuming futures markets are efficient, economists have supported these markets for the following reasons (Carter 1980):

1. A firm can cope with changes in price uncertainty by participating in the futures market.
2. A futures market will stabilize spot prices.
3. Futures prices dampen price fluctuations.
4. A futures market may be an effective and cheaper alternative to buffer stock stabilization.
5. Spot market prices provide more accurate signals for resource allocation when there is futures trading in a commodity.

There is some question, however, as to whether or not futures markets are efficient (Carter 1980).

The volume of futures trading has increased drastically in the past few years (Figure 2–5). As Figure 2–6 shows, an important factor for the increase in volume is that recent commodity prices have been highly unstable. Producers and consumers of commodities for which there are futures markets have begun participating in the markets with the expectation of being able to reduce their exposure to price instability. Surely, if a cartel were to reduce instability, the volume of futures trades would be unlikely to increase.

The involvement of different segments of the grain industry in the United States is substantial. However the use of futures markets among producers is small compared to that of millers, elevator companies, and the private grain trade. As well, importers such as Japan participate in the U.S. future markets directly, in addition to using the markets as a source of price information. The latter is also true for the Canadian and Australian Wheat Boards. Some have argued (for example, Pearce [1976] and Caves [1977–78]) that the futures market acts as a price discovery mechanism for the U.S. and world grain trade. Information is gathered from all sources and is

Figure 2–5. Futures trading on the U.S. exchanges fiscal years 1965—1979[a]

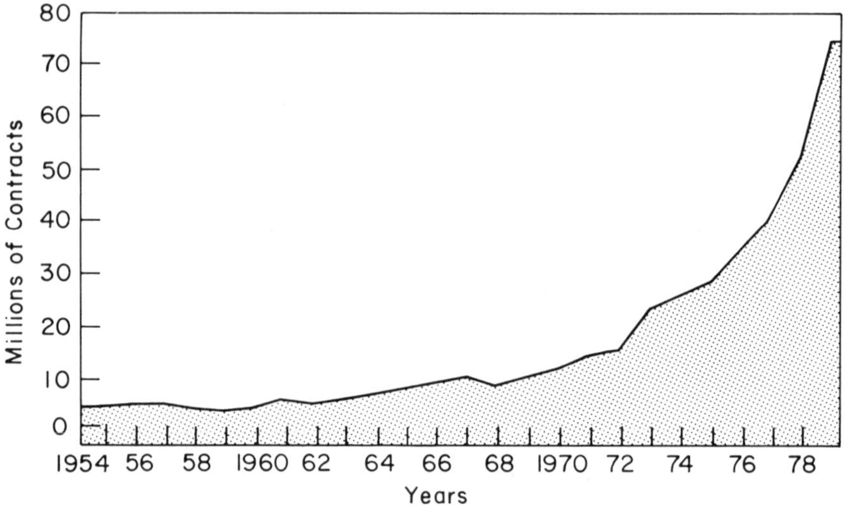

[a]Figures include volume of trading of nonregulated commodities for the years 1955 through 1974.

Source: Commodity Futures Trading Commission *Annual Report* 1979, Washington, D.C.

Figure 2–6. Commodity research bureau futures price index (1967 = 100)

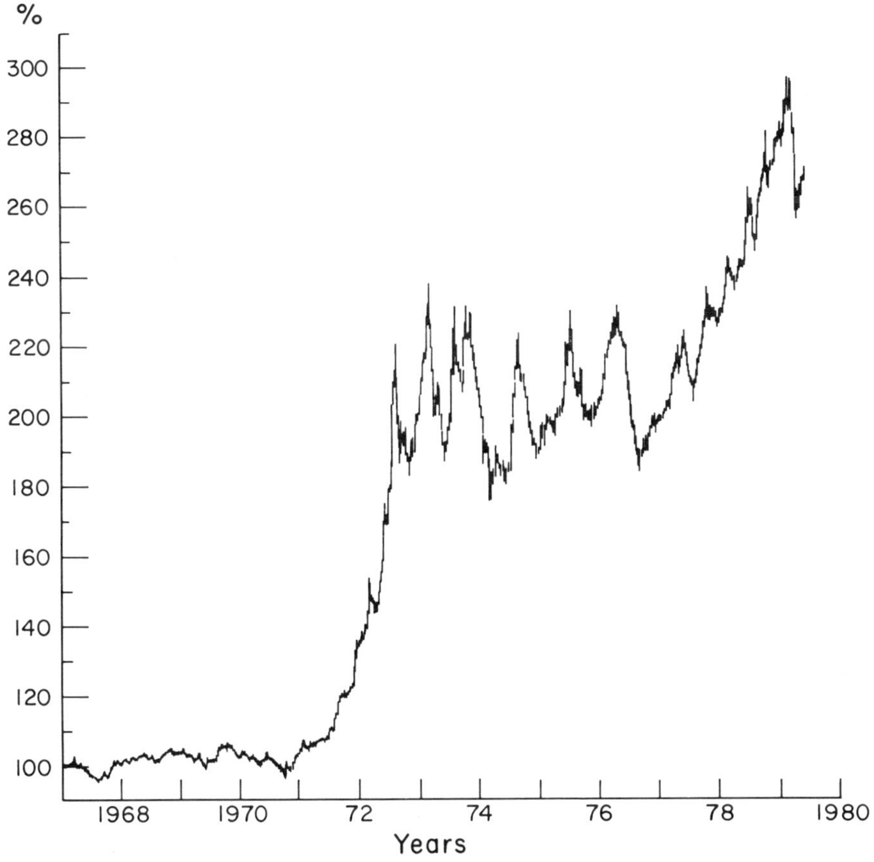

Source: *Commodity Yearbook 1980,* (New York Commodity Research Bureau) p. 6.

revealed in futures market prices which are available to exporters, importers, producers, and the like. In a sense, one could argue that the futures market is the central pricing point in the international grain market. In a recent paper, Caves (1977–78) argued that the existence of an active futures market assures that the private grain trade is highly competitive.

Whether or not this is the case is not debated here. What is more important is that futures markets have income distributional implications. They aid the large private firms and large producers because of the superior information these groups have. Thus, a cartel would probably change the role of futures; that is, the information would be distributed to all producers through the actual prices that both large and small producers would receive. The marketing advantage presently held by large private companies, including large producers, would be reduced.

Performance of the Grain Marketing System

A number of studies have been conducted in recent years which examine various aspects of the performance of the grain marketing system (Frevalds 1976; Goldberg and McGinity 1979; Grennes, Johnson, and Thursby 1978). A lively debate has focused on a comparison of the Canadian and U.S. systems, which are markedly different. These studies have often formed the basis for discussions of the Weaver Bill, which proposes both a grain marketing board for the United states similar to that of Canada and an implied cartel. Meanwhile, debate continues in Canada as to the appropriateness of their system of using the Canadian Wheat Board as the key element. This debate is important since it puts pressure on the grain trade to do a good job of marketing grain and adds to an understanding of the price determination process. The issues raised in comparisons of the two systems also have direct relevance for the cartel question addressed in this book. For example, if the U.S. system is performing poorly and, as a result, more goverment pricing is introduced, the possibility for a successful grain export cartel is increased since its coordination among countries is easier in a system where central selling agencies do the pricing rather than in a system which contains a mixture of public and private entities. However, as will be discussed in a later chapter, even if goverments were the major price-setting institutions, there is no guarantee that an export grain cartel could be effectively maintained.

The study by McCalla and Schmitz (1979a) uses several criteria to evaluate the peformance of the Canadian and U.S. systems—producer prices and equity, market shares, price stability, and technological change in grain handling. Their findings suggest that strengths exist in both systems and that it would be extremely difficult to conclude which had the "best" system. More recent studies by Peltier and Anderson (1979) and Food West Resouce

Consultants (1979) suggest that the American system has outperformed the Canadian one—at least on the basis of a returns-to-producers criterion.

Two other studies have focused on the efficiency of the U.S. grain marketing system (Caves [1977–78]) and Thompson and Dahl [1979]); they conclude that the system is efficient. The whole question of the competitiveness of international agricultural markets is questioned and extensively discussed in several chapters by McCalla and Josling (forthcoming). In addition, it is possible for a market to be efficient in terms of price differentials reflecting costs of transportation, transformation, and storage, even though it may be imperfect in a structural sense. It is entirely possible for a spatially and time-separated market to be efficient in this sense but still have levels of price influenced by monopolistic elements in market structure. Logistically, grain markets may be efficient even though price formation is imperfect.

CONCLUSIONS

This chapter has briefly discussed the key components in the world grain industry with a focus on the issue of the possible formation of grain export cartels. In a different context, this chapter itself could be easily expanded into a book. For example, one could write at length about the efficiency of the Canadian and U.S. grain marketing systems. One issue in this regard (not discussed in the literature) is the role played by multinational grain firms in technological change in grain marketing because they are not only multinational but also multiproduct. They spread their operations over more than just grains and, hence, may appear to be willing to take more risks than, say, the Canadian Wheat Board. Also, multinational firms are engaged in more facets of the trade than are marketing boards. For example, the profit function of a multinational grain trader includes elements such as several potential price-quantity trades (primary delivery point, inland terminal, export terminal, and import port); hedging and speculative transactions; inland transportation and ocean shipping; handling and storage; and insurance and foreign exchange. A major house presumably maximizes short-run profits from all of these elements in several commodities. It is conceivable—in fact, likely—that a house could lose money on a particular price-quantity element in a single commodity and still maximize its profit function. Clearly, if economists are mesmerized by the price-quantity dimension to the exclusion of others, they are likely to provide at best very partial explanations of international grain prices.

This chaper presents a key argument and suggests reasons why importers may well be exerting monopsony power in trade. The world grain market could well be a buyer's market largely because of the existence of competition among exporters. On the other hand, an export cartel, to be effective, requires that some form of collusion exist among exporters. In addition, if a cartel is to result in net gains to exporters,there has to be a source of these gains. As already shown, the OPEC countries are very small grain importers; hence, the gain from exporters acting as a cartel against them cannot be great. However, a major source of gain from an export cartel is introduced in this chaper; as shown later, if it could succeed in greatly reducing the buying power of such importers as the EEC and Japan, the gain to exporters could be substantial. The sources of gains to exporters from a cartel will be discussed in detail later.

APPENDIX A
THE OPTIMAL WHEAT TARIFF

In Figure 2A–1, D_E and S_E represent the empirical demand and supply functions of the major wheat exporters. The amount of excess supply of the major exporters is $ES_E(S_E–D_E)$. The function marginal to ES_E is labeled MO_E. On the other side of the market, D_I and S_I represent the demand and supply functions of the major importers.

To integrate transportation costs into the analysis, the horizontal axis of the major exporters is shifted upward. The prices in Figure 2A–1 are in 1964–1966 dollars.

From Figure 2A–1, free-trade imports of wheat would equal EA, and the free-trade price of wheat would be approximately *OB* per bushel. However, if, as hypothesized, the importers are exerting monopsony power in trade and, at the extreme, are imposing an optimum tariff, wheat imports would be restricted to *DZ*. Relative to the free-trade position, the price in the importing countries would be raised from *OB* to *OC*, and the price of wheat in the exporting countries would be reduced from *OB* to *OM*. The world price of

Figure 2A–1. Empirical estimate of the optimal import tariff solution (1964–1966 prices)

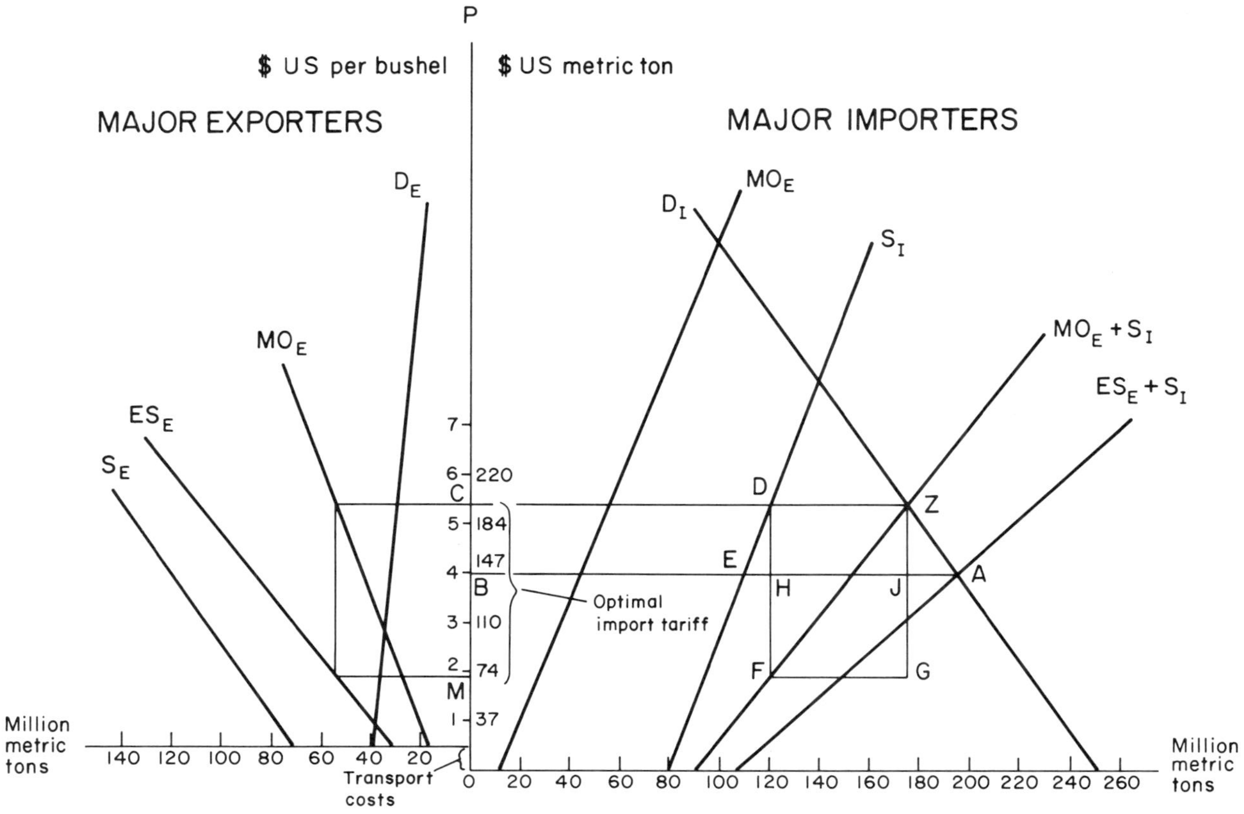

Source: Carter C. and A. Schmitz (1979).

wheat would be *OM*. The price is depressed due to the influence of the importers in the market.

To test informally the hypothesis that importers are exerting monopsony-like power in trade, one can compare actual prices (Table 2A–1) with the empirical estimates of the optimal tariff solution (Figure 2A–1). The export prices of Argentina, Australia, Canada, and the United States (Table 2A–1) should be compared for equivalence with the estimated price of *OM* (Figure 2A-1).

Table 2A-1. World wheat prices, 1966-67 to 1976-77

	Export Prices ($U.S. per Metric Ton)				*Basic Support Levels*[d]	
Crop Year	*Argentina Trigo Pan*	*Australia*[a]	*Canada*[b]	*United States*[c]	*Japan*	*EEC*
1966-67	59	63	72	67	140	[e]
1967-68	62	58	66	63	145	99
1968-69	58	58	68	63	152	99
1969-70	56	54	64	57	153	99
1970-71	57	58	67	63	164	99
1971-72	62	58	65	62	175	101
1972-73	86	91	92	92	217	114
1973-74	[f]	195	202	178	282	128
1974-75	163	167	198	170	334	148
1975-76	144	147	174	161	354	163
1976-77	104	113	130	118	401	183
Mean 1966-73 + 1976-77	68	69	78	73	193	113

[a]Australian Wheat Board selling price (f.o.b.); Australian Standard White.

[b]Canadian Wheat Board official "in store" price converted to f.o.b. at current fobbing rates (price basis: Thunder Bay); Canada Western Red Spring.

[c]F.o.b. Gulf; U.S. No. 2, Hard Winter.

[d]These prices are those used for government guaranteed prices.

[e]No data available.

[f]Due to the limited trading in this wheat in the 1973-74 crop year, no representative average export price is available.

Source: International Wheat Council (various issues).

Similarly, the support levels in Japan and in the EEC should be compared with the estimated *OC*. It is not argued that the buyer's market hypothesis in this study is completely robust over time since, during the 1973–74 to 1975–76 period, the "power" in the market temporarily reverted to the sellers as a consequence of the general commodity boom at the time.

The export prices, interestingly enough, for the 1966–1973 and 1976–77 periods are very similar in Table 2A–1 and Figure 2A–1. The actual average export price for this period is $72 per ton, while the estimated export (world) price is $70 per ton (*OM*). The estimated and actual prices in the importing nations do not compare quite so favorably. The estimated price in the importing nations is approximately $198 per ton. The average support price in Japan, $193, is very near the optimal $198 figure, but the support price in the EEC is less and is approximately equal to $113. The results suggest that perhaps, relative to Japan, the EEC is not taking full advantage of its position as a major wheat importer.

The EEC, China, the USSR, and Japan account for between 30 and 40 percent of the world wheat imports, and they directly influence the world price of wheat. The results in the Appendix suggest that the major importers are regulating consumption, production, and imports so that the least possible marginal cost to the group of obtaining wheat (shown by $MO_E + S_I$) is equal to its marginal value in consumption (shown by D_I) at point *Z*. As shown in Figure 2A–1, consumption of wheat in the importing countries under the optimal tariff is reduced to approximately 174 million metric tons per annum (*CZ*) with production of 119 million metric tons (*CD*). Imports of wheat to the group are approximately 55 million metric tons annually (*DZ*). The importers would set the optimum tariff at close to $3.50 per bushel, and the exporting countries would receive approximately $1.90 per bushel net of transport costs. Under this solution, producers in the importing countries receive slightly over $5.00 per bushel.

The results pertaining to volumes of wheat traded are very close to actual world wheat statistics. The International Wheat Council (n.d.) reports that for the periods 1966–1973 and 1976–77, the major wheat importers restricted their purchases to an average of 55.1 million metric tons per year. The model in this study predicted that, with an optimal tariff solution, imports of wheat to the group would

Table 2A-2. Welfare gains to wheat-importing nations with the imposition of the optimal import tariff

Welfare Effect	*Net Gain Million Dollars (U.S.)*
1. Loss in consumers' surplus	-9,439
2. Gain in producers' surplus	5,971
3. Import tariff revenue	7,202
4. Net gain (3 + 2 - 1)	3,734

be approximately 55 million metric tons annually, as shown in Table 2A–2.

REFERENCES

Abel, M.E. 1966. "Price Discrimination in the World Trade of Agricultural Commodities."*Journal of Farm Economics* 48 (May): 194–208.

Abbott, P.C. 1979. "Modeling International Grain Trade with Government Controlled Markets." *American Journal of Agricultural Economics* 61 (February): 22–31.

Alaouze, C. M.; A.S. Watson; and N.H. Sturgess. 1978. "Oligopoly Pricing in the World Wheat Market." *American Journal of Agricultural Economics* 60 (May): 173–185.

Bieri, J., and A. Schmitz. 1974. "Market Intermediaries and Price Instability: Some Welfare Implications." *American Journal of Agricultural Economics* 56 (May): 280–285.

Biggs, T.S. 1976. "Political Economy of East-West Trade: The Case of the 1972–1973 U.S.-Russian Wheat Deal." Ph.D. dissertation, University of California, Berkeley.

Carter, C., and A. Schmitz. 1979. "Import Tariffs and Price Formation in the World Wheat Market." *American Journal of Agricultural Economics* 61 (August): 517–522.

———. Forthcoming. "World Wheat Tariffs As Optimum Levies: Reply." *American Journal of Agricultural Economics.*

Carter, H.O. 1976. "World and U.S. Food Trends: A Current Perspective for Policy." In *Contemporary Economic Problems,* edited by W. Fellner, pp. 293-322. Washington, D.C.: American Enterprise Institute.

Caves, R.E. 1977–78. "Organization, Scale and Performance of the Grain Trade." *Food Research Institute Studies* 16: 107–123.

Food West Resource Consultants. 1979. *U.S. Grain Handling and Transportation With Selected Comparisons to the Canadian System.* Edmonton, Alberta, Canada.

Enke, S. 1944. "The Monopsony Case for Tariffs." *Quarterly Journal of Economics* 58 (February): 229–45.

Frevalds, J. 1976. *Grain Trade: The Key to World Power and Human Survival.* New York: Stein and Day.

Goldberg, R.A., and R.C. McGinity. 1979. *Agribusiness Management for Developing Countries.* Cambridge, Mass.: Ballinger Publishing Co.

Grennes, T. and P.R. Johnson. 1979. "Oligopoly Pricing in the World Wheat Market: Comment." *American Journal of Agricultural Economics* 61 (August): 574–577.

Grennes, T.; P.R. Johnson; and M. Thursby. 1978. *The Economics of World Grain Trade.* New York: Praeger Publishers.

Heidhues, T. 1979. "The Gains from Trade: An Applied Political Analysis." In *International Trade and Agriculture: Theory and Policy,* edited by J. Hillman and A. Schmitz, pp. 117–145. Boulder, Colo.: Westview Press.

International Wheat Council. *World Wheat Statistics.*

Josling, T. 1977. "Government Price Policies and the Structure of International Trade." *Journal of Agricultural Economics* 28 (September): 261–276.

Just, R.E.; A. Schmitz; and D. Zilberman. 1979. "Price Controls and Optimal Export Policies Under Alternative Market Structures." *American Economic Review* 69 (September): 706–714.

McCalla, A.F. 1966. "A Duopoly Model of World Wheat Pricing." *Journal of Farm Economics* 48 (August): 711–727.

———. 1967. "Pricing in the World Feed Grain Market." *Agricultural Economics Research* 19 (October): 93–102.

———. 1979. "Strategies in International Agricultural Marketing: Public vs. Private Sector." In *International Trade and Agriculture: Theory and Policy,* edited by J. Hillman and A. Schmitz, pp.209–238. Boulder, Colo.: Westview Press.

McCalla, A.F., and E.W. Learn. 1967. "Nonequilibrium Fixed-Price Schemes in Agricultural Trade." *Agricultural Economics Research* 19 (October): 111-116.

McCalla, A.F., and A. Schmitz, 1979a. "Grain Marketing Systems: The Case of the United States versus Canada." *American Journal of Agricultural Economics* 61 (May): 200-212.

———. 1979b. "State Trading in Grain." Paper presented to the Conference on State Trading in Industrialized and Developing Countries, Montreal, Quebec, Canada, April 19 and 20.

McCalla, A.F., and T. Josling. editors, 1981. *Imperfect Markets in Agricultural Trade.* Montclair, N.J.: Allanheld Osmun and Co.

Morgan, D. 1979. *Merchants of Grain.* New York: Viking Press.

Pearce, B. 1976. *The U.S. Grain Industry.* Minneapolis: Cargill, Inc.

Peltier, K., and D.E. Anderson. 1978. "The Canadian Grain Marketing System." No. 130, Department of Agricultural Economics, North Dakota State University, Fargo.

Sampson, G.P. and R. H. Snape, 1980. "Effects of EEC's Variable Import Levies." *Journal of Political Economy* 88 (October): 1026–1040.

Schmitz, A., and D.L. Bawden. 1973. *The World Wheat Economy: An Empirical Analysis.* University of California, Giannini Foundation Monograph No. 32.

Schmitz, A., and A. McCalla. 1979. "The Canadian Wheat Board." In *Agricultural Marketing Boards: Prices, Profits and Patterns,* edited by S. Hoos, ch. 4. Cambridge, Mass.: Ballinger Publishing Co.

Thompson, S.R., and R. P. Dahl. 1979. "The Economic Performance of the U.S. Grain Export Industry." Department of Agricultural and Applied Economics, University of Minnesota.

Thurston, S.K.; M.J. Phillips; J.E. Haskell; and D. Volkin. 1976. *Improving the Export Capability of Grain Cooperatives.* U.S. Department of Agriculture, Farmer Cooperatives Service, Press Report 34.

U.S. Department of Agriculture. 1971. *World Demand Prospects for Grain in 1980 with Emphasis on Trade by the Less Developed Countries.* Economic Research Service, Foreign Agricultural Economics Report 75.

Warley, T.K. 1976. "Agriculture in International Economic Relations." *American Journal of Agricultural Economics* 58 (December): 820–830.

3 QUANTITATIVE CHARACTERISTICS OF INTERNATIONAL GRAIN MARKETS

International trade in grains has grown rapidly over the postwar period, and this growth has been accompanied by significant changes in market structure. Fewer exporters provide grain to a growing and diverse set of importers. Given the prevalence of state trading and protective domestic agricultural policies, trade is heavily influenced by the decisions of national governments. In order to give a better understanding of some of the implications of a grain export cartel, this chapter focuses on such key quantitative characteristics of grain markets as exports, imports, market shares, and the nature of demand.

COMMODITY COVERAGE AND REGIONAL BREAKDOWNS

Commodity Coverage

Most discussions of exporter association price enhancement schemes are limited to wheat; the "bushel for a barrel" or "wheat OPEC" scenarios are examples. However, there are strong reasons why considering wheat alone is inappropriate. Wheat and coarse grains (corn, barley, oats, sorghum, and rye), crops of the temperate and semiarid tropics, are relatively close substitutes in production. Thus, significant changes in the price of wheat relative to that of coarse (feed) grains would lead to significant shifts in planted acreages in both exporting and importing countries. Similarly, there is substantial substitution in consumption, particularly in terms of feed use of grains. The cross elasticities in consumption are asymmetrical, wheat being a strong substitute for feed grains whereas coarse grains are poorer substitutes for food grains. What these consumption cross-elasticities seem to preclude is a significant enhancement of coarse grain prices without an adjustment in wheat prices. Finally, most countries pursue domestic agricultural policies which include both wheat and coarse grains as closely connected components. This is especially true in the United States and the EEC-9, both major participants in both trades. Therefore, this analysis includes both wheat and coarse grains.

Significant additional interrelationships could also be considered. Rice, the other widely produced food grain, is nevertheless excluded from this study for at least two reasons. First, most of the rice grown is consumed in the country of production. Stated conversely, less than 5 percent of rice production enters international trade. Secondly, rice is not a close production substitute for the other grains, although it is in consumption in some countries; further, the marketing channels, both domestic and international, are distinctly separated. Similarly, the increasing practice of feeding high-concentrate feeds to livestock has led to rapid growth in oilseeds and the oilseed products trade. Given the important interface between the feed grain and livestock sectors, the role of trade in high-protein concentrates is closely intertwined with that of coarse grains. High-protein feed sources have been excluded from the study, however, for two important reasons. First, trade in oilseeds and oilseed products such as soybeans is relatively free of trade barriers in both exporting and importing countries. With virtually free trade, the potential gains from an exporter association are less than with commodities such as wheat and coarse grains that have trade restrictions. The importance of import trade barriers to cartel rents will be apparent later. Secondly, there is a wide array of close substitutes such as copra, fish meal, and cottonseed meal—to name but a few—which are readily available if significant changes in relative prices occur. For these reasons, the study concentrates on wheat and coarse grains.

Exporter and Importer Regional Breakdown

A grain cartel can take many different forms. Prices could be set at many levels; for example, low-income countries could be charged a price substantially below that of high-income importing nations. Thus, it is important in this section to divide the world trade in grain into subregions. In addition, this breakdown is required since some countries will respond differently to a cartel than will others due to different internal government policies, available technologies, and currency constraints.

Export Regions. Unlike grain production, which is widely dispersed over the world, grain exports originate in a limited number of countries. Thus, data are presented for each of the exporters. For wheat, these are Argentina, Australia, Canada, and the United States. France is increasingly a surplus producer of wheat with the result that the EEC-9 in recent years has been a net exporter of wheat. These five countries consistently supply over 80 percent of wheat exports. In past years, the USSR was a major exporter of both wheat and coarse grains, but during the 1970s it became a consistent importer. In the case of coarse grains, two additional countries (Thailand and South Africa) are added to the four major grain exporters (Argentina, Australia, Canada, and the United States); these six now account for over 80 percent of world coarse grain exports. Since 1972, the United States alone has exported over 50 percent of total coarse grain exports. The exporter regions (groupings) used are listed in Table 3–1.

Import Regions. The selection of regions on the import side of the grain market is more difficult. Well over 100 countries, ranging in size from China and India to Grenada, import grain. Their levels of per capita gross national product (GNP) range from those of Kuwait and Sweden to those of Bangladesh and Ethiopia. Some are rich in foreign exchange [for example, the Organization of Petroleum Exporting Countries (OPEC)]; others are in extreme difficulty in terms of international liquidity. This book adopts as a starting point the now widely used triparite division of developed market economies (referred to as DCs), centrally planned economies (CPs), and developing economies (LDCs). However, these classifications are still too diverse to be useful in examining, for example, the

Table 3-1. Basic classification of grain exporters and importers

Region Name	*Commodities*	*Countries Included*
Exporting Regions		
Exporters-4	A[a], B[b]	Argentina, Australia, Canada, USA
Exporters-5	A	Argentina, Australia, Canada, USA, France
Exporters-6	B	Argentina, Australia, Canada, USA, South Africa, Thailand
Importing Regions		
DC—Developed country importers	A, B	EEC-9, Japan, OWE, New Zealand, South Africa (A only), Israel
EEC-9	A, B	Belgium and Luxembourg, Denmark, France, Ireland, Italy, Netherlands, United Kingdom, West Germany.
OWE—Other Western Europe	A, B	Austria, Finland, Greece, Iceland, Malta, Norway, Portugal, Spain, Sweden, Switzerland
Japan	A, B	Japan
CP—Centrally planned importers	A, B	USSR, China, Eastern Europe
USSR	A, B	USSR
China	A, B	People's Republic of China
EE—Eastern Europe	A, B	Albania, Bulgaria, Czechoslovakia, East Germany, Hungary, Poland, Romania, Yugoslavia
LDC—Developing country importers		LDC-1, LDC-2
LDC-1	A, B	LDC-OPEC, LDC-nonOPEC-Middle Income
OPEC—middle income	A, B	Algeria, Equador, Indonesia, Iraq, Iran, Kuwait, Libya, Nigeria, Saudi Arabia, Venezuela

NonOPEC—middle income	A, B	Brazil, Hong Kong, Mexico, Singapore, South Korea, Taiwan
LDC-2—All others (low income)	A, B	Costa Rica, Cuba, Dominican Republic, El Salvador, Guatemala, Haiti, Honduras, Jamaica, Nicaragua, Panama, Trinidad and Tobago, Bolivia, Chile, Colombia, Paraguay, Peru, Uruguay, Venezuela, Guyana, Ethiopia, Morocco, Sudan, Tunisia, Egypt, Somali Republic, Angola, Camaroon, Dahomey, Ghana, Guinea, Ivory Coast, Kenya, Malawi, Malagasy Republic, Mozambique, Niger, Rhodesia, Rwanda, Senegal, Tanzania, Upper Volta Uganda, Zaire, Zambia, Cyprus, Jordan, Lebanon, Syria, Turkey, So. Yemen, Afghanistan, Bangladesh, India, Nepal, Pakistan, Sri Lanka, Burma, Cambodia, Indonesia, Malaysia, Philippines, Vietnam, North Korea, Outer Mongolia, Thailand (A only)

[a]A = Wheat.
[b]B = Coarse grains.

economic characteristics of import demand—a component crucial for the analytical study of alternative market arrangements. The principal criterion used for further subdivision is the degree of similarity in response to price changes.

A detailed breakdown according to this criterion is presented in Table 3–1. The DCs are further subdivided into the EEC-9, Other Western Europe, and Japan. While all of these countries are high-income market economies, significant policy differences exist. Obviously, the EEC-9 must be treated as a unit because of the Common Agricultural Policy (CAP). The remainder of Europe, while exhibiting geographic diversity, pursues similar kinds of domestic food policies, making their interface with world markets similar. Finally, Japan is such a large importer of both wheat and coarse grains that it warrants treatment as a separate region.

The subdivisions within the CPs are reasonably obvious. The USSR and China are so large and important in terms of grain production and trade that each is treated as a separate region. The third subregion is Eastern Europe, a region which in earlier years relied on the USSR for grain imports. However, as the USSR has become a perennially deficit area, this region has become a major world importer. In addition, all of the Eastern block countries pursue domestic food subsidy programs which have divorced internal prices from world prices. Note that other CPs—such as Vietnam, Cuba, North Korea, Cambodia, and Laos—are included in the LDC category because their demand characteristics in terms of international commercial purchases are more akin to those of low-income, foreign-exchange-short countries than to those of the further advanced, ideologically similar countries.

The most difficult problem is confronted in categorizing the approximately ninety countries that remain. To separate these into further subdivisions, two major variables that contribute to commercial demand are used—level of per capita income and availability of foreign exchange. These criteria are similar to those used by the International Food Policy Research Institute (IFPRI) in its long-term projections. The LDC region is first subdivided into two subregions. LDC-1 consists of those developing countries with middle-level per capita GNP (above $300 per capita) or significant availability of foreign exchange. This group is further subdivided into the members of OPEC, where foreign exchange resources are significant, and a small group of developing countries that are experiencing rapid economic growth, which is partly based on exports, and therefore have foreign exchange. This latter group includes South Korea, Taiwan, Hong Kong, and Singapore in Asia and Mexico and Brazil in the Americas.[a]

The second major LDC subregion (LDC-2) contains the remaining countries of the world which are low-income countries or suffer foreign exchange shortages. This group contains a large number of diverse countries which are becoming increasingly important in the world wheat market. For purposes of this discussion, subregions based on similarities of demand-influencing economic characteristics seemed preferable to using more commonly used geographic or ideological groupings.

WORLD GRAIN PRODUCTION AND TRADE

World grain production and trade grew significantly over the period 1960–1978. In order to provide a background for subsequent discussion, this section presents basic historical data on production, trade, exports and imports, net imports, and exporter and importer market shares. Two special cases, the EEC-9 and the USSR, are reviewed in particular detail.

Global Production and Trade Trends

World production and trade data are presented in Table 3–2. World wheat production increased by 65 percent over the nineteen-year period, while the harvested area increased by about 10 percent. Therefore, most of the growth in production results from yields which increased from below 1.2 to over 1.7 tons per hectare. World trade in wheat grew less rapidly than production, showing slightly over a 50 percent increase. Therefore, the percentage of production traded has been stable, ranging from 15 to 20 percent of production.

World coarse grain production increased 57 percent over the period, while the harvested area increased less than 10 percent. A 45 percent growth in yields (1.45 to 2.2 tons per hectare) accounts for most of the increase. Trade in coarse grains grew rapidly over the

[a]In subsequent analysis it may be desirable to include Chile and Colombia in this set.

Table 3-2. World grain production and trade—1960–1978

	Wheat					*Coarse Grains*				
Year	*Area Harvested (Million Hectares)*	*Production Million Metric Tons (mt)*	*Yield mt/hec*	*Trade Million m Tons (Exports)*	*Trade as % of Production*	*Area Harvested (Million Hectares)*	*Production Million Metric Tons (mt)*	*Yield mt/hec*	*Trade Million m Tons (Exports)*	*Trade as % of Production*
1960	202.9	239.4	1.18	49.0	18.3	278.3	420.1	1.58	25.8	6.1
1961	202.4	226.4	1.12	47.1	20.8	271.4	402.6	1.48	33.8	8.4
1962	207.1	255.8	1.24	45.8	17.9	268.9	424.0	1.58	32.5	7.7
1963	206.6	237.8	1.15	58.4	24.6	274.6	432.6	1.57	36.1	8.3
1964	215.8	274.7	1.27	54.8	19.8	272.3	439.9	1.60	37.6	8.6
1965	216.2	264.3	1.22	60.7	22.7	267.8	450.4	1.65	47.1	10.5
1966	214.6	308.7	1.44	58.0	18.8	270.3	464.5	1.72	43.2	9.3
1967	219.3	297.3	1.36	53.2	18.0	278.6	509.0	1.86	44.0	8.6
1968	224.2	328.6	1.47	49.9	15.1	274.3	513.7	1.87	39.9	7.8
1969	217.8	309.8	1.42	55.7	17.8	277.2	534.4	1.93	47.8	8.9
1970	207.0	315.7	1.52	56.2	17.9	278.4	531.9	1.91	53.2	10.0
1971	212.9	348.7	1.64	56.0	16.1	280.9	586.4	2.09	56.4	9.6
1972	210.8	343.2	1.63	71.6	20.9	278.5	570.7	2.05	68.9	12.1
1973	216.8	372.4	1.72	73.0	19.6	290.1	624.8	2.15	81.1	13.0
1974	219.9	357.2	1.62	68.4	19.1	289.7	588.2	2.03	69.1	11.7
1975	225.2	350.4	1.56	73.9	21.9	296.4	604.2	2.04	88.2	14.6
1976	232.3	415.1	1.79	70.6	17.0	300.1	661.7	2.20	88.5	13.4
1977	225.7	382.7	1.70	75.7	19.8	301.8	668.4	2.21	95.0	14.2
1978	225.9	438.5	1.94	81.6	18.6	299.7	713.8	2.38	99.4	13.9

Source: U.S. Foreign Agricultural Service. 1980. *Foreign Production, Supply, and Distribution of Agricultural Commodities* (computer tape).

period, reflecting rapid increases in livestock feeding by DC importers. The nearly 400 percent increase in trade resulted in an increase in the proportion of production traded from 6 to 14 percent.

The data have important implications for the success of an exporter association. The apparent continual rate of growth of trade in both wheat and coarse grains is significant since cartel gains partly depend on the volume of trade. Similarly, the data also point out the limited land base available to support importers' supply response to a high cartel price.

Degree of International Market Dependence

Global averages obscure the fact that the importance of the international market is different for exporters and importers and among importers. Among the four major exporters, Canada and Australia export, on the average, well over two-thirds of their production, while the United States in most years exports over 50 percent of production and Argentine exports are highly variable, ranging from 20 to 50 percent of production. Thus, for the major wheat exporters, the international market represents a significant component of total production (Table 3–3).

On the import side, interesting trends emerge. The EEC-9 shifted from a significant net importer of wheat to an exporter in three of the last four years analyzed. (More details on the EEC-9 are presented in a subsequent section.) Other Western European countries followed a trend similar to that of the EEC-9, with the region now being a net exporter in three of the last five years. In both cases, high internal support prices have stimulated increased production. Japanese dependence on international sources is increasing and has now reached 90 percent of its consumption needs. The USSR has shifted from being a net exporter of wheat to being a consistent importer over the last four years; however, the proportion of total consumption imported is relatively small. Chinese imports, as a percentage of total consumption, fluctuate between 5 and 20 percent depending on domestic production; no discernible trend in international dependence is evident. Eastern Europe's dependence on imported wheat has declined, however, and has been transferred to western supplies rather than the USSR as in the 1960s. OPEC

Table 3-3. Degree of dependence on international markets—wheat

	Exporters				Importers								
	Net Exports as Percentage of Production				*Net Imports as Percentage of Total Consumption*								
Year	*USA*	*Canada*	*Aus-tralia*	*Argen-tina*	*EC-9*	*Japan*	*Other Western Europe*	*USSR*	*China*	*Eastern Europe*	*OPEC*	*NonOPEC Mid-Y LDC*	*LDC-2*
1960	49.3	68.1	86.5	27.6	25.0	66.4	20.4	-7.5[a]	8.5	22.5	26.1	59.8	28.9
1961	58.2	126.0	73.6	47.5	23.9	64.6	21.6	-7.9	22.9	24.1	30.7	64.2	29.9
1962	57.9	58.4	73.6	31.5	13.9	58.7	16.8	-8.6	19.0	25.6	20.2	65.1	27.4
1963	73.7	82.2	78.6	38.7	14.6	86.1	11.8	12.9	18.5	29.2	21.3	67.2	28.4
1964	55.3	66.9	73.2	55.8	7.6	73.6	10.2	0.0	16.3	27.6	30.0	50.1	32.2
1965	63.7	89.8	67.1	91.9	9.9	72.1	11.4	7.9	19.9	22.6	24.2	56.4	34.3
1966	58.3	62.2	66.9	48.0	12.5	84.2	5.3	-1.8	15.3	14.0	33.2	62.6	39.4
1967	50.0	56.5	74.8	29.6	8.7	77.1	-6.1	-5.0	12.8	8.9	27.9	69.7	36.7
1968	34.0	46.9	43.0	36.7	9.5	79.4	-1.7	-6.5	12.2	8.1	23.6	61.3	27.1
1969	40.8	51.6	76.4	29.7	3.9	82.9	3.8	-5.6	15.8	12.1	28.1	55.8	26.8
1970	53.8	131.1	116.4	19.7	15.8	92.6	10.9	-6.6	10.5	19.9	34.9	51.0	27.6
1971	37.0	95.1	90.5	28.7	6.1	92.7	6.5	-2.4	8.8	12.4	46.3	52.8	26.7
1972	72.2	108.3	65.4	39.1	0.4	97.8	2.2	14.5	12.8	10.7	48.8	69.9	21.9
1973	72.3	70.4	58.3	24.1	0.1	95.3	9.1	-0.5	14.1	10.5	46.4	62.3	28.8
1974	60.0	80.4	75.4	29.9	-5.6	96.5	-1.9	-1.6	13.3	8.4	53.1	60.7	30.7
1975	55.2	71.3	72.3	36.9	-6.0	101.9	-1.8	11.1	5.2	11.2	50.2	54.7	32.0
1976	44.2	56.8	81.2	53.6	-2.6	95.6	-1.4	4.1	6.6	10.6	43.7	48.4	27.1
1977	55.0	80.4	90.3	31.6	0.0	98.3	2.6	5.5	17.3	8.0	55.2	58.6	23.7
1978	66.2	62.1	57.4	46.2	-8.5	93.3	4.3	3.4	14.7	6.9	51.6	60.5	21.9

[a]A minus (-) sign indicates exports.

Source: U.S. Foreign Agricultural Service. 1980. *Foreign Production, Supply, and Distribution of Agricultural Commodities* (computer tape).

countries are increasing their dependence on international wheat supplies and now import over 50 percent of their needs. The middle-income, non-OPEC LDCs with foreign exchange (South Korea, Taiwan, Hong Kong, Singapore, Brazil, and Mexico) consistently depend on the international market for over 50 percent of their supplies. Finally, the remaining low-income LDCs consistently depend on the international market for between 20 and 30 percent of their consumption needs. The rapid population growth of the LDCs means that total imports are rising rapidly.

Table 3–4 presents comparable data for trade in coarse grains, where exporter dependence on international markets is variable. Thailand exports virtually all of its coarse grain production. Australia, Argentina, and South Africa export in the neighborhood of 50 percent of production, while Canada exports less than 20 percent of its production. The proportion of the U.S. production exported has grown steadily to over 25 percent. The domestic market, however, remains of crucial importance to the United States.

On the import side, the EEC-9 dependence on world markets for coarse grain supplies has declined to less than 20 percent in most years. On the other hand, Japan is nearly completely dependent on imports. When all DC importers are considered, a fairly stable level of 25 percent of consumption imported is evident. The USSR has shifted to become a significant net importer, and Eastern Europe's dependence on international supplies has increased to a level of over 10 percent. Coarse grain exports in the LDC category go principally to middle-income OPEC and nonOPEC LDCs, whose dependence on the international market is steadily growing.

These market dependence data are extremely important for a cartel because they point out the strength of the exporters' position. There is only a handful of exporters, upon whose production and trade the entire world is dependent.

Exporter Market Shares

The following market share data are important for at least two reasons. First, they suggest that there might be little difficulty in forming a cartel because of the small number of countries which make up the export trade. In the case of coarse grains, for example, most of the exports are in the hands of one country. As the

Table 3-4. Degree of dependence on international markets—coarse grains

	Exporters			*Importers*					
	Net Exports as Percentage of Production			*Net Imports as Percentage of Total Consumption*					
Year	*USA*	*Exporter–4*	*Exporter–6*	*EC–9*	*Japan*	*DC – Imp*	*USSR*	*Eastern Europe*	*LDC–1*
1960	7.6	9.3	10.3	23.4	43.2	23.5	-3.4[a]	0.4	1.8
1961	11.6	13.5	15.0	28.5	52.1	27.2	-5.7	3.3	1.8
1962	11.6	12.7	14.4	28.7	58.0	30.0	-4.6	3.8	1.3
1963	11.7	13.9	14.7	25.3	83.6	28.8	-4.0	5.0	1.1
1964	15.7	16.8	17.1	24.5	78.5	28.5	-3.0	2.8	-3.6
1965	17.6	19.0	19.2	29.1	78.8	33.6	-4.2	6.2	-4.0
1966	13.7	14.9	16.4	25.8	84.7	32.7	-1.0	0.6	-3.7
1967	12.5	13.8	15.5	23.6	87.5	30.1	-1.0	0.9	-4.2
1968	9.7	12.0	12.4	19.0	88.5	26.7	-1.0	2.6	-1.0
1969	11.5	14.5	15.2	17.5	93.5	27.0	-1.4	3.2	-0.8
1970	12.4	18.3	19.7	23.5	94.6	31.0	-1.1	6.1	1.5
1971	12.6	15.0	16.7	17.1	91.1	25.3	4.6	8.9	6.1
1972	21.0	23.0	22.9	17.2	100.8	27.6	8.6	3.8	12.7
1973	21.6	23.2	23.4	17.3	102.2	26.9	5.5	4.3	9.0
1974	23.5	25.1	26.3	19.0	98.5	26.1	1.8	9.2	12.5
1975	26.8	29.2	29.5	18.4	95.8	25.8	18.7	10.1	11.2
1976	25.9	28.2	28.7	30.7	101.2	35.2	3.3	11.6	14.3
1977	27.5	29.2	29.3	14.3	101.2	26.8	10.1	11.0	22.6
1978	27.5	30.0	30.7	12.4	100.1	25.6	8.1	16.8	22.6

[a] A minus (–) sign indicates exports.

Source: U.S. Foreign Agricultural Service. 1980. *Foreign Production, Supply and Distribution of Agricultural Commodities* (computer tape).

concentration of grain-exporting countries increases, the organizational problems of forming a cartel become less severe. Secondly, these data shed light on the problems associated with effectively implementing an export cartel. For example, an argument can be made that the more instability which market shares exhibit through time, the greater is the difficulty of major exporters agreeing on a marketing strategy.

Wheat. Actual gross exports and percentage market shares for major wheat exporters are presented in Table 3–5. The United States is consistently the largest wheat exporter, accounting for approximately 40 percent of world exports; its market share declined in the middle 1960s but increased rapidly in 1972 and 1973 to regain levels comparable to those of the early 1960s. Canada's share fluctuates between 15 and 25 percent. Australia's share fluctuates, generally with production, between 10 and 15 percent of the market. Argentina's share is the most unstable; it is sometimes as low as 2 percent but never higher than 10 percent. The market share of the four traditional exporters (Exporters-4) declined in the middle 1960s from 80 percent to 63 percent in 1968, and then rose slowly to about 75 percent. France's market share has steadily increased so that French exports now account for over 10 percent of the market, and it is accordingly included with the other nations as a significant exporter of wheat. These largest five exporters account for over 85 percent of gross world exports. (A fuller discussion of the EEC-9 follows in a subsequent section; here it is sufficient to note that the question of how to deal with the EEC-9 in an exporter association is a difficult one.)

Coarse Grains. Table 3–6 shows actual exports for the six largest coarse grain exporters; it also shows the market shares of the United States and the four traditional as well as the six largest grain exporters. Trade in coarse grains quadrupled over the nineteen-year period; the United States increased its dominance of coarse grain markets with its market share rising from about 40 percent to over 60 percent of the market in 1978. No other of the six largest exporters approaches the size of the United States' market share. In order of descending importance, they are Argentina, Canada, Australia, South Africa, and Thailand, the first three collectively accounting for between 15 and 20 percent of the market, and

Table 3-5. Exporter market shares—wheat

	Actual Exports (Million Metric Tons)						*Market Shares (%)*						
Year	*Total Exports*	*USA*	*Canada*	*Aus-tralia*	*Argen-tina*	*France*	*USA*	*Canada*	*Aus-tralia*	*Argen-tina*	*Exporters –4*	*France*	*Exporters –5*
1960	43.9	17.9	9.6	6.5	1.1	1.5	40.8	21.8	14.8	2.5	79.9	3.4	83.3
1961	47.2	19.7	9.7	4.9	2.7	1.8	41.7	20.6	10.4	5.7	78.3	3.8	82.2
1962	45.8	17.3	9.0	6.1	1.8	3.0	37.8	19.6	13.3	3.9	74.6	6.6	81.2
1963	58.4	23.1	16.2	7.0	3.5	2.7	39.6	27.7	12.0	6.0	84.8	4.6	89.4
1964	54.5	19.3	10.9	7.3	6.3	4.6	35.4	20.0	13.4	11.6	80.4	8.4	88.8
1965	60.6	22.9	15.9	4.7	5.6	4.8	37.8	26.2	7.8	9.2	81.0	7.9	90.2
1966	58.0	20.7	14.0	8.5	2.2	3.0	35.7	24.1	14.7	3.8	78.3	5.2	83.5
1967	53.5	20.5	9.1	5.6	2.2	4.2	38.3	17.0	10.5	4.1	69.9	7.8	77.7
1968	49.8	14.4	8.3	6.4	2.5	6.3	28.9	16.7	12.8	5.0	63.6	12.6	76.0
1969	55.2	16.1	9.4	8.0	2.3	5.5	29.2	17.0	14.5	4.2	64.9	10.0	74.9
1970	56.4	19.8	11.8	9.1	1.0	3.2	35.1	20.9	16.1	1.8	73.9	5.7	79.6
1971	55.6	16.3	13.7	7.8	1.6	5.8	29.3	24.6	14.0	2.9	70.8	10.4	81.2
1972	71.6	30.4	15.7	4.3	3.2	8.4	42.9	22.2	6.1	4.5	75.7	12.0	87.7
1973	73.0	33.1	11.4	7.0	1.6	8.9	45.3	15.7	9.6	2.2	72.8	12.2	85.0
1974	68.4	27.7	10.7	8.5	1.8	8.5	40.5	15.6	12.4	2.6	71.1	12.5	83.6
1975	73.9	31.9	12.2	8.6	3.2	8.7	43.2	16.5	11.6	4.3	75.6	11.8	87.4
1976	70.6	25.8	13.4	9.5	5.9	6.8	36.5	19.0	13.5	8.4	77.4	9.6	87.0
1977	75.7	30.6	16.0	8.4	1.8	8.0	40.4	21.1	11.1	2.4	95.0	10.6	85.6
1978	81.6	32.5	18.1	10.5	3.8	9.6	39.8	16.0	12.9	4.7	73.4	11.8	85.2

Source: U.S. Foreign Agricultural Service. 1980. *Foreign Production, Supply, and Distribution of Agricultural Commodities* (computer tape).

Thailand and South Africa accounting for about 5 percent of the market. Collectively, the four traditional exporters now account for about 75 percent of the market, while the largest six account for over 80 percent. However, the most obvious result of the market share analysis is the growing dominance of the United States, a fact significant for a possible exporter association.

Imports and Importer Market Shares

Wheat. Actual wheat imports by the three major market subdivisions, as well as three components of each of those subdivisions, are presented in Table A3–1 in the Appendix. Figure 3–1 clearly shows the major import trends in the wheat market. Total imports have risen over the period as has interyear instability, and the behavior of the three major market components seems to explain this aggregate outcome. The DC market is stable in quantity and declining in relative importance: Japanese imports have steadily risen to double their level in 1960; imports to Other Western Europe countries have steadily declined from 2-1/2 million metric tons to less than 2 million; EEC-9 imports are more unstable but do not seem to exhibit a secular trend up or down. The source of the wheat market's instability is the CP countries, whose imports have fluctuated between 8 and 25 million tons. Virtually all of that instability comes from the behavior of the USSR, as imports by China and Eastern European countries are more stable and show a slightly upward trend. The source of the market's growth is the LDC market, whose imports have more than doubled over the period. OPEC demand for wheat has more than tripled (from 2 million to 8 million metric tons), while the middle-income LDCs with foreign exchange have more than doubled their imports, making this subregion (LDC-1) the most rapid growth component of the international wheat market. Low-income LDCs have also increased their demand, from 12 million to over 20 million metric tons, and this increase is even more significant due to the fact that, since 1972, the vast majority of these imports have been under commercial terms. This is in contrast to the 1960s when Public Law 480 sales were significant to this group of countries; for example, the peak in total imports in 1966 is explained by massive U.S. Public Law 480 shipments to India.

Table 3-6. Exporter market shares—coarse grains, 1960-1978

	Actual Exports—Million Metric Tons							Market Shares—Percentage		
Year	*Total Gross Exports*	*USA*	*Canada*	*Australia*	*Argentina*	*Thailand*	*S. Africa*	*USA*	*Exporters[a] –4*	*Exporters[b] –6*
1960	26.1	11.2	1.0	1.3	2.6	0.5	1.7	42.9	61.7	70.1
1961	33.8	15.2	1.0	0.8	3.9	0.6	2.6	45.0	61.8	71.3
1962	32.5	15.2	0.9	0.6	3.3	0.7	2.8	46.7	61.5	72.3
1963	36.1	16.6	1.3	0.6	5.2	0.9	1.2	46.0	65.6	71.5
1964	37.9	19.6	1.1	0.7	3.7	0.9	0.7	51.7	66.2	70.4
1965	47.4	25.7	1.2	0.7	5.5	1.2	0.5	54.2	69.8	73.4
1966	43.1	20.1	1.3	0.7	4.8	1.3	3.0	46.6	64.0	74.0
1967	44.5	20.7	1.0	0.5	4.7	1.3	2.9	46.5	60.4	69.9
1968	39.7	16.3	0.6	0.9	5.5	1.3	0.8	41.0	58.7	64.0
1969	47.1	18.9	1.7	1.2	7.4	1.6	1.2	40.1	62.0	67.9
1970	53.4	18.6	4.3	2.9	8.8	1.7	2.9	34.8	64.8	73.4
1971	55.5	24.1	4.9	2.8	2.7	2.2	3.7	43.4	62.1	72.8
1972	69.0	38.7	3.9	1.4	7.9	1.1	0.2	56.1	75.2	77.1
1973	81.1	40.7	2.7	2.5	9.1	2.3	3.4	50.4	67.6	74.6
1974	69.2	35.9	3.2	2.8	5.9	2.2	3.4	51.9	69.1	77.2
1975	88.2	50.0	5.0	3.6	6.9	2.6	1.5	56.7	74.3	78.9
1976	88.5	50.6	4.4	2.7	9.6	2.3	2.6	37.2	76.1	81.2
1977	95.0	56.2	4.0	1.6	10.9	1.3	3.4	59.1	76.5	81.4
1978	99.4	60.2	3.9	4.0	9.5	2.2	2.4	60.1	78.1	82.7

[a]Exporters-4—USA, Canada, Argentina, Australia.
[b]Exporters-6—USA, Canada, Argentina, Australia, S. Africa, Thailand.
Source: U.S. Foreign Agricultural Service. 1980. *Foreign Production, Supply, and Distribution of Agricultural Commodities* (computer tape).

Figure 3–1. Wheat imports—total, DC, LDC, CP (1960–1978)

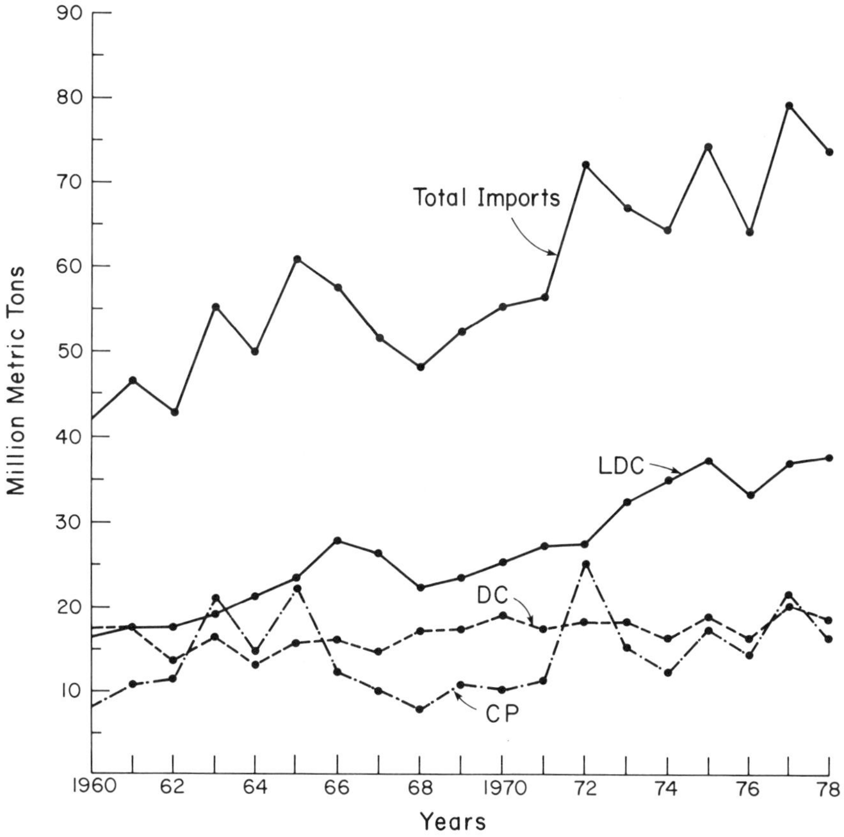

Source: U.S. Department of Agriculture, Foreign Agricultural Service. 1980.

Coarse Grains. Comparable data for coarse grains are presented in Table 3A–2 and Figures 3–2, 3–3, 3–4, and 3–5. As Figure 3–2 clearly shows, coarse grain imports have increased rapidly over the period. Increases in DC imports accounted for nearly all the growth in the 1960s, but in the 1970s rapid increases in imports occurred in the CP and LDC countries. As shown in Figure 3–3, the most rapid increase in coarse grain imports has taken place in Japan, followed by Other Western Europe, while imports into the EEC-9 have been more unstable and exhibit less rapid growth. The rapid

Figure 3–2. Coarse grain imports (1960–1978)

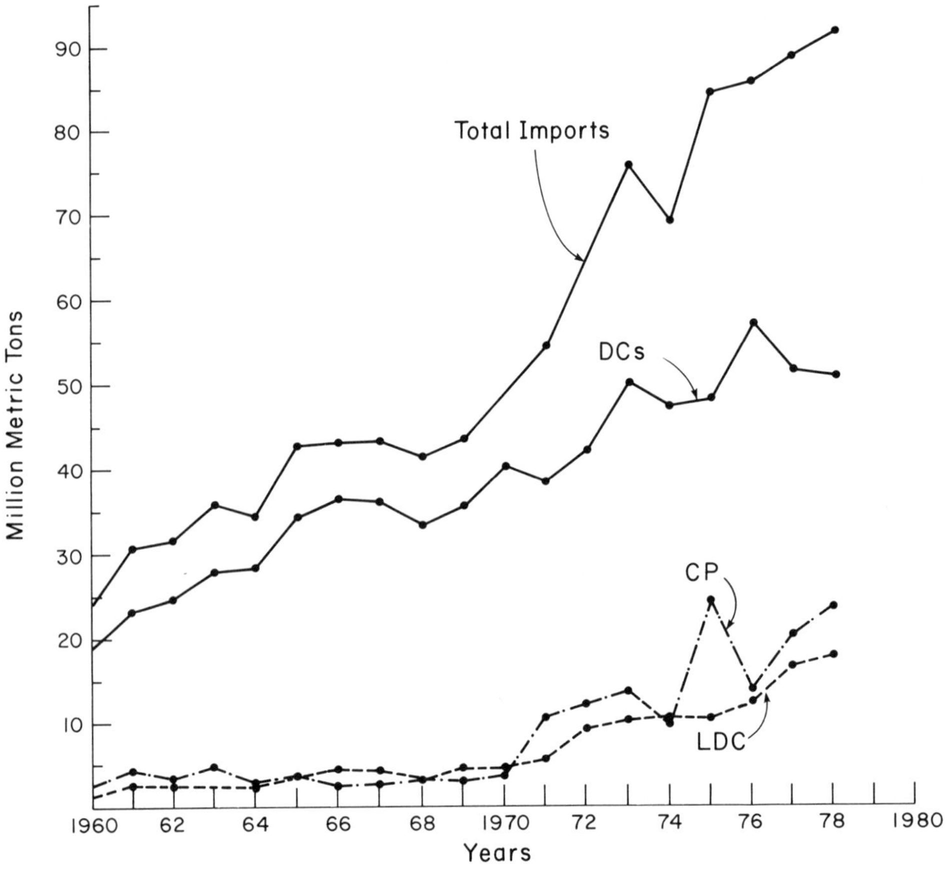

Source: U.S. Department of Agriculture, Foreign Agricultural Service. 1980.

growth in imports by the CP countries in the 1970s (Figure 3–4) is accounted for primarily by steady increases in Eastern Europe; growth has been sporadic in the USSR, and China is insignificant in the coarse grain market. Imports by LDCs also grew in the 1970s (Figure 3–5). The principal source of that growth has been the middle-income LDCs with foreign exchange, particularly South Korea, Taiwan, and Mexico. There has also been significant growth in OPEC imports, although the aggregate quantity is still less than

Figure 3–3. Coarse grain imports—developed countries (1960–1978)

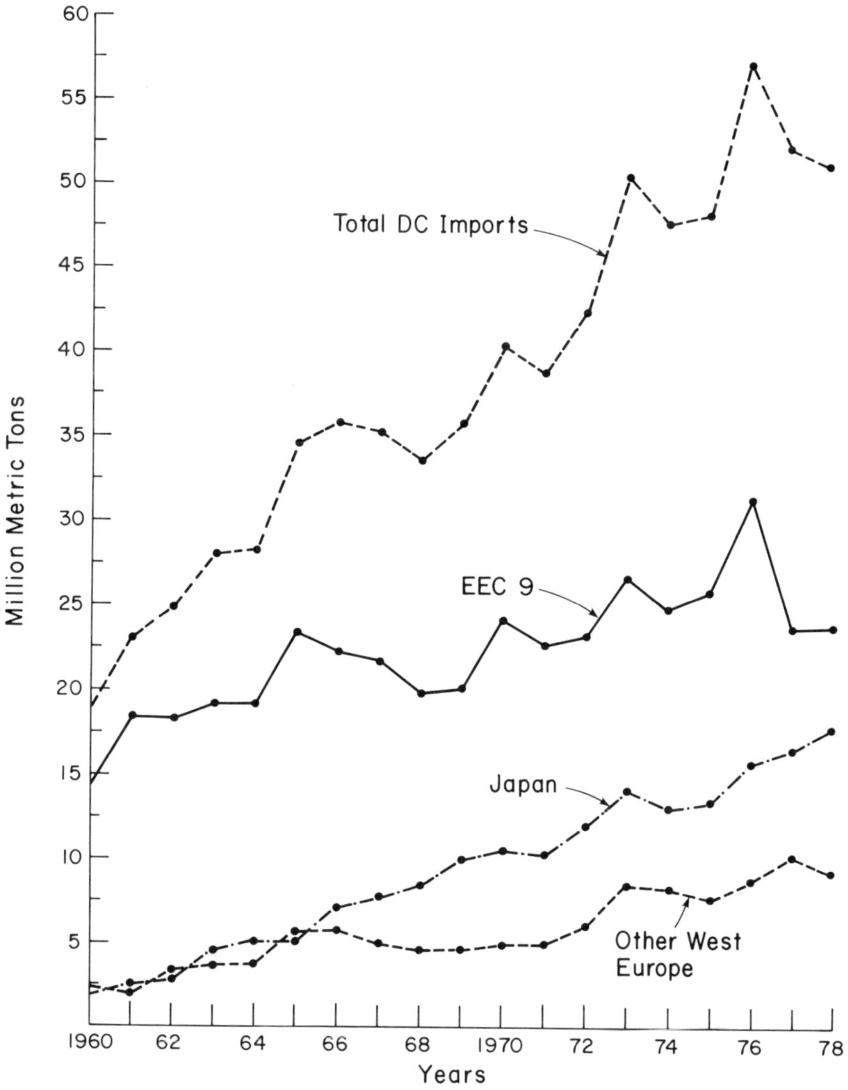

Source: U.S. Department of Agriculture, Foreign Agricultural Service. 1980.

Figure 3–4. Coarse grain imports—centrally planned countries, (1960–1978)

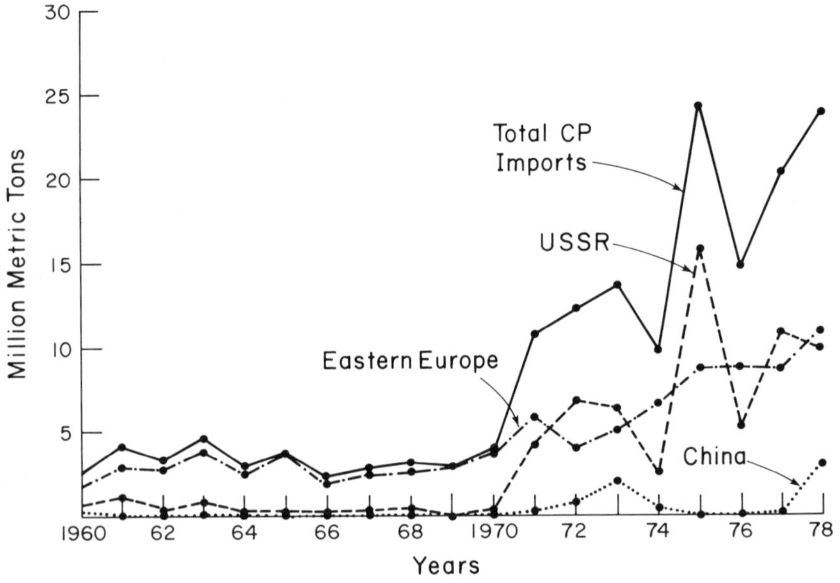

Source: U.S. Department of Agriculture, Foreign Agricultural Service. 1980.

three million metric tons. Imports to low-income LDCs are relatively stable and small.

Market Shares. Wheat market shares by major market subdivisions are presented in Table 3–7. These data show that the relative importance of the DC wheat market has fallen from 40 to 26 percent. Furthermore, these numbers overstate the importance of the market because the EEC-9 also is a significant exporter of wheat. The importance of CP importers is highly variable, ranging from 20 to 35 percent of the market for wheat. The market share of the LDCs has risen steadily from 40 percent to over 50 percent of the market, and virtually all of that increase has come from middle-income LDCs (LDC-1).

In the coarse grain market, the market share of DC importers has also declined (80 percent to less than 60 percent), but this still remains the dominant part of the market (Table 3–7). The market share of the CP countries has risen steadily since its low in 1966 to

Figure 3–5. Coarse grain imports—LDCs (1960–1978)

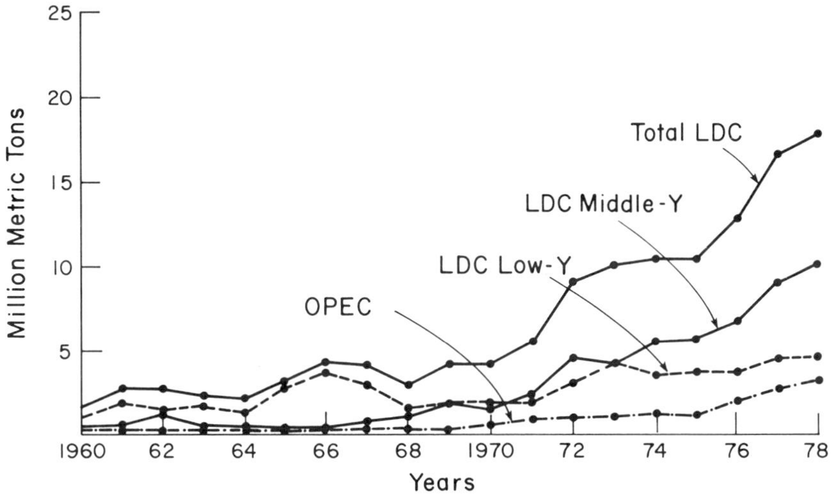

Source: U.S. Department of Agriculture, Foreign Agricultural Service. 1980.

nearly a quarter of the market. The LDC market share has also increased to over 15 percent of the market.

In sum, divergent trends are occurring in the two markets. The LDCs are becoming increasingly dominant in the world wheat market, while the traditional DC market is declining in importance and the CP economies contribute to instability. In the coarse grain market, the DC market still dominates, but rapid increases in imports by CPs and LDCs are causing significant structural changes. In view of these trends one must recognize that a joint wheat-coarse grains cartel could have an interesting pricing structure. For both wheat and coarse grains an international multiple price system seems reasonable because some low-income countries could be charged lower prices. However the degree of price discrimination for importers would be greater in wheat because relatively more poor nations import wheat than feedgrains.

Net Exports and Imports by Region

The above data have been aggregated in terms of gross exports and imports. These data, in a sense, double-count regions that both

Table 3-7. Market shares—imports—percentage (1960-1978)

Year	Wheat					Coarse Grains		
	DC	CP	LDC	LDC-1	LDC-2	DC	CP	LDC
1960	40.7	19.3	39.5	10.7	28.8	79.4	10.5	6.7
1961	38.8	23.5	38.6	11.4	27.1	74.8	13.3	8.7
1962	32.2	26.9	41.1	11.7	29.4	78.8	10.4	8.5
1963	28.3	37.8	34.4	9.9	24.5	78.2	13.1	6.7
1964	28.2	29.4	42.8	10.4	32.4	82.8	8.4	6.1
1965	26.0	36.1	38.6	9.0	29.6	80.8	9.1	7.5
1966	28.6	23.5	48.8	11.1	37.6	82.9	5.1	10.2
1967	28.8	20.3	51.6	13.3	38.3	81.3	6.7	9.7
1968	36.4	16.6	46.8	14.3	32.4	81.4	7.7	7.3
1969	34.0	21.0	45.7	14.1	31.5	81.5	6.9	9.6
1970	34.8	19.5	46.2	14.4	31.8	82.2	8.0	8.8
1971	31.5	20.6	48.7	17.8	30.9	69.7	19.0	10.1
1972	26.1	35.3	38.6	14.4	24.2	65.1	18.7	14.0
1973	28.2	22.5	48.8	17.4	31.8	66.4	18.0	13.3
1974	26.1	19.1	54.0	18.9	35.2	68.5	14.1	15.1
1975	25.9	24.3	49.3	17.2	31.9	56.9	28.7	12.9
1976	25.8	21.5	52.2	19.5	32.7	66.8	17.0	15.0
1977	25.9	26.5	47.6	20.4	22.3	57.9	22.6	18.6
1978	25.3	22.6	51.5	21.5	30.0	54.4	25.4	19.1

Source: U.S. Foreign Agricultural Service. 1980. *Foreign Production, Supply, and Distribution of Agricultural Commodities* (computer tape).

export and import. Thus, the data in Tables 3A–3 and 3A–4 and in Figures 3–6 and 3–7 show net exports or imports by region. From Figure 3–6 it is clear that the DC region is of declining importance in the world wheat market: net imports are less than 5 million tons, and the EEC-9 and Other Western Europe are now virtually self-sufficient. This conclusion, of course, ignores the quality differences in wheat, for while Western Europe continues to import hard wheat, it has at the same time increased exports of soft wheat, leading to the EEC-9 becoming a net exporter. A look at the net wheat imports for the CP countries, which range from zero in 1968 to 23.3 million tons in 1972, clearly shows their impact on market stability. LDC net imports rose consistently and by 1977 accounted for nearly 60 percent of net imports. These data simply accentuate the trends noted earlier.

Figure 3–6. Net exports and imports—wheat (1960–1978)

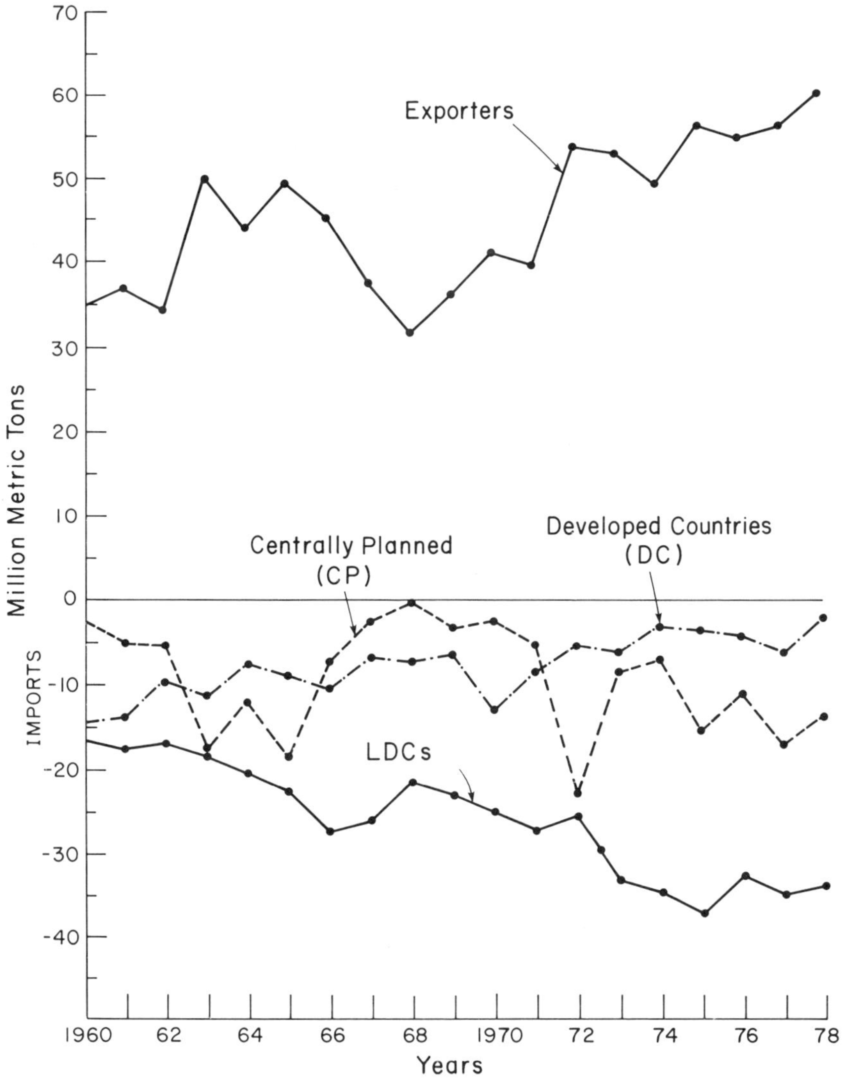

Source: U.S. Department of Agriculture, Foreign Agricultural Service. 1980.

From Figure 3–7, it is clear that net imports of coarse grains have increased in all regions. However, there has been considerable instability since 1970 in the CP region, and the DCs continue to be the dominant factor in this market.

Figure 3–7. Net exports and imports—coarse grains (1960–1978)

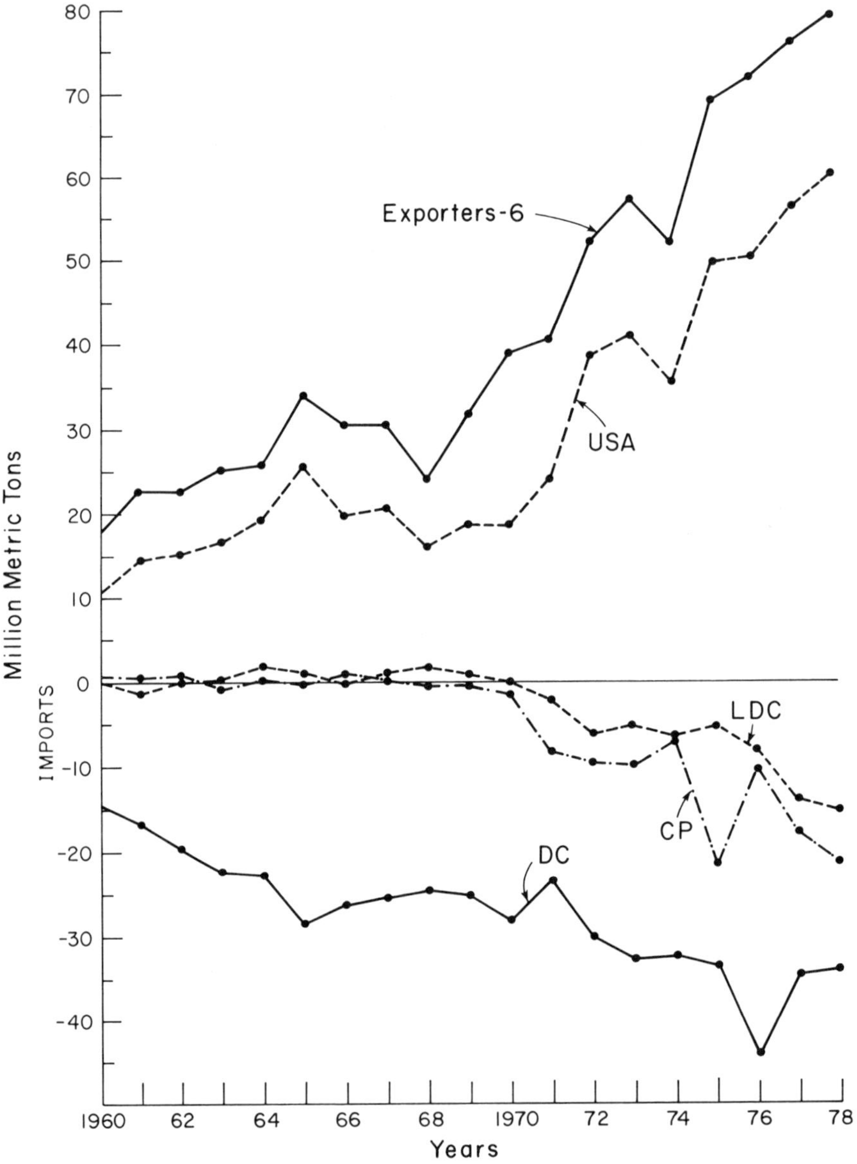

Source: U.S. Department of Agriculture, Foreign Agricultural Service. 1980.

Origin-Destination Trade Flows

Some additional insights into world grain markets can be gained from Table 3A–5, which presents data for wheat origin-destination flows in four selected years between 1971–72 and 1976–77, and from Table 3A–6, which presents data for coarse grains in three selected years between 1973–74 and 1976–77. For example, in the wheat market, Canada's exports are roughly divided into thirds between the three major market segments, with the largest single destination being the EEC-9. The United States and Australia, however, in most years ship over 60 percent of their exports to LDCs. Similarly, Argentina ships over 50 percent to LDC markets. It can also be observed that most of the exports in the "other" category come from France, and that when intracommunity trade is excluded, virtually all of French exports go to the LDCs.

There are a few surprises in the coarse grain matrix. The United States dominates all markets, with Canada, Australia, and Argentina being small and somewhat unstable exporters.

The Special Cases of the EEC-9 and the USSR

The regional analysis of the international grain market using basic country data causes problems for any discussion of cartels if regions or subregions are major participants in the market both as exporters and as exporters and importers. This is clearly the case for the EEC-9 and the USSR.

EEC-9. Wheat production, consumption, feed use, exports, imports, and net imports are charted in Figure 3–8. The chart shows that EEC-9 wheat production has risen steadily, though sporadically, so that since 1973 production has exceeded consumption. Exports have also grown steadily while imports are constant, resulting in the already noted fact that the EEC-9 is now a net exporter of wheat. The increases in production have been stimulated by high prices under the CAP and by protection against low-priced imports via the variable levy. The significance of these developments for a possible exporter association is that, if these trends continue, some countries in the EEC-9 could gain from a cartel via the "free rider" phenomenon.

Figure 3–8. EEC-9—wheat production, consumption, feed use, exports, imports, net imports (1960–1978)

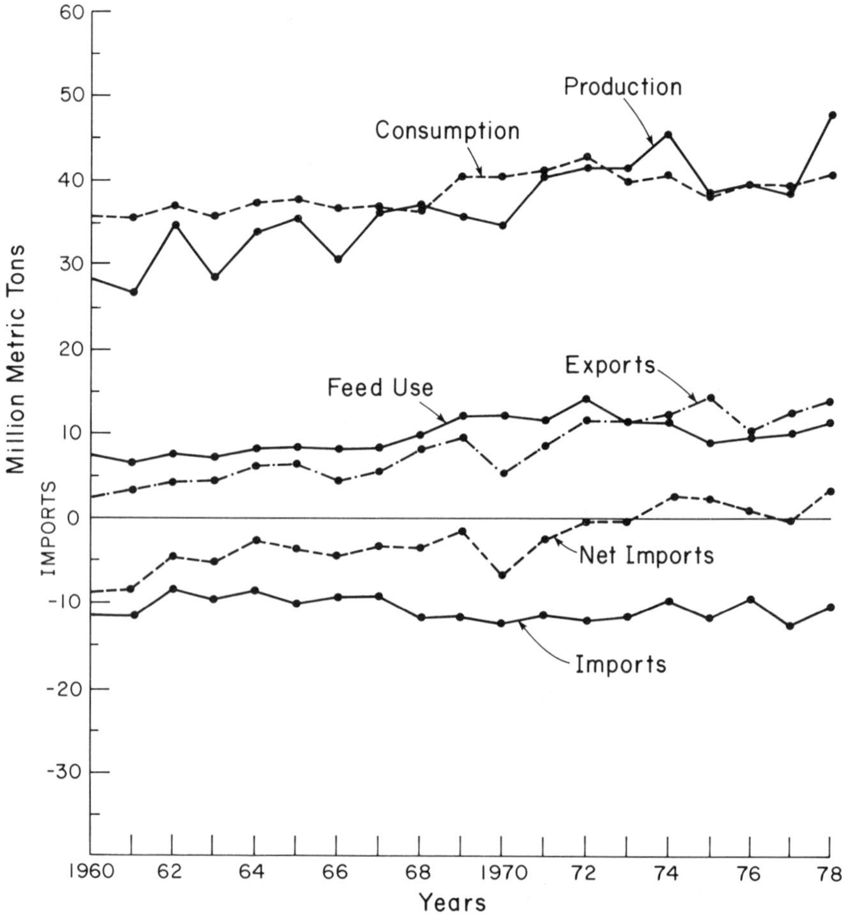

Source: U.S. Department of Agriculture, Foreign Agricultural Service. 1980.

Comparable data for coarse grains are shown in Figure 3–9, which shows rapid increases in total consumption and feed use in the EEC-9. Production has also increased rapidly. Both imports and exports of grains have grown. Net imports are unstable and move closely with production fluctuations within the community. Thus, the CAP appears to be exporting domestic production instability.

Figure 3–9. EEC-9—coarse grains production, consumption, feed use exports, imports, net imports (1960–1978)

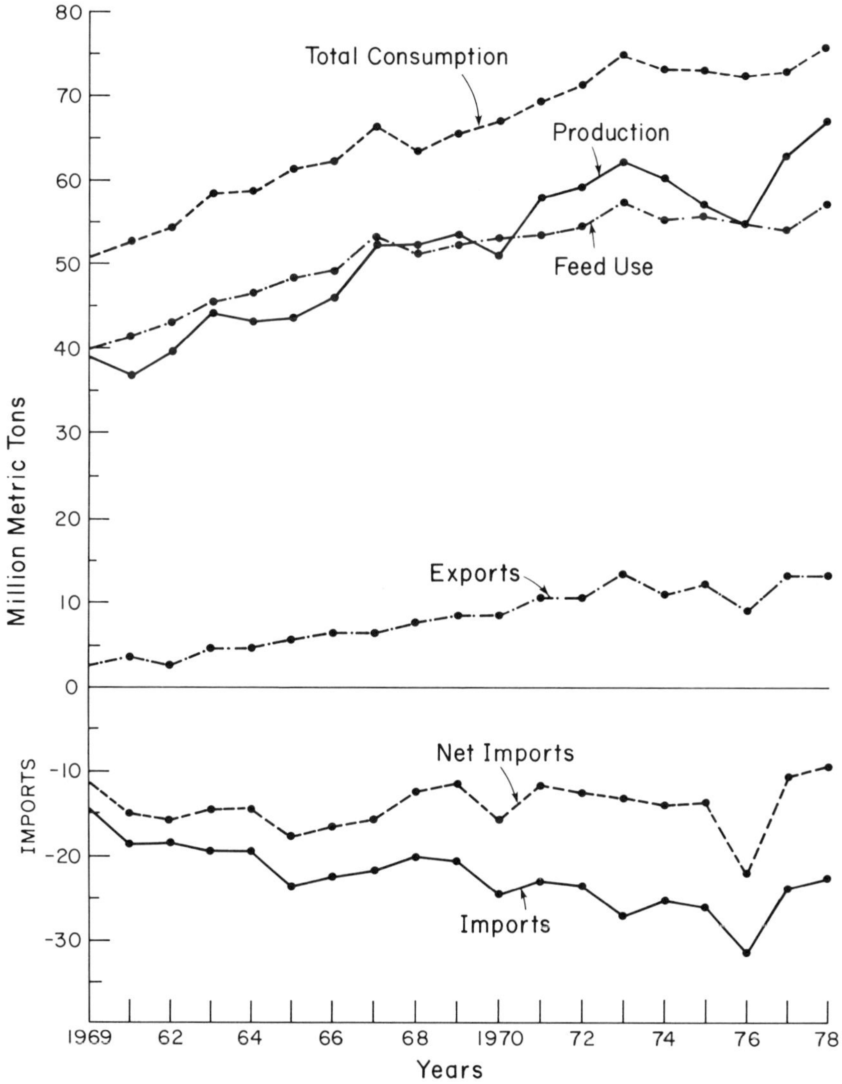

Source: U.S. Department of Agriculture, Foreign Agricultural Service. 1980.

Clearly, however, the EEC-9 must be treated as a major importer of coarse grains.[b]

The USSR. The USSR is the most unstable and, at the same time, the most interesting component of the international grain market. Figure 3–10 provides basic data for wheat. USSR wheat production is extremely variable; in the 1970s, production reached a low of 66 million metric tons in 1975 and peaked at 120 million metric tons in 1978. In earlier years, consumption seemed to adjust to production, but in the 1970s greater stability occurred in consumption, the difference being purchased in the international market. The rapid increase in feed use of wheat, beginning in the early 1960s, reflects increased livestock feeding. The bottom of the figure graphically illustrates the variable behavior of the USSR in the world market. In the eighteen years under review, it was a net exporter for twelve years and an importer for six years, with rapid swings back and forth. For example, in 1970 the net exports of the USSR were 5.5 million metric tons, but by 1972 net imports totaled 14.3 million metric tons, a swing of nearly 20 million tons in a total market of 60 million metric tons. Such data support the often-stated view that the USSR is a destabilizing element in world markets.

Figure 3–11 presents data for coarse grains. Production instability seems greater in the 1970s; however, consumption of coarse grains more closely approximates production than for wheat. The USSR has become a net importer of feed grains only in the 1970s, with its principal foray into the market occurring in 1975 when production fell sharply. Increases in feed use of coarse grains has been rapid, except for a drop in 1975, reflecting increased livestock feeding to satisfy rising consumer demands for meat.

The USSR's participation in the world grain market remains a major question mark in the future. The best prognosis is that it will continue to be a net importer of both wheat and feed grains but will buy only enough to meet domestic shortfalls. Given extreme

[b]The data presented above for the EEC-9 come from individual country data and, therefore, include intracommunity trade. The USDA, in a recent publication (1980), has presented alternative net trade data which use EEC reporting of third-country trade based on import levies and export restitutions. Both data sets point out that the EEC's net impact on world markets is to create instability. At the same time, a declining net import position seems apparent.

Figure 3–10. USSR—wheat production, consumption, feed use, exports, imports, net imports (1960–78)

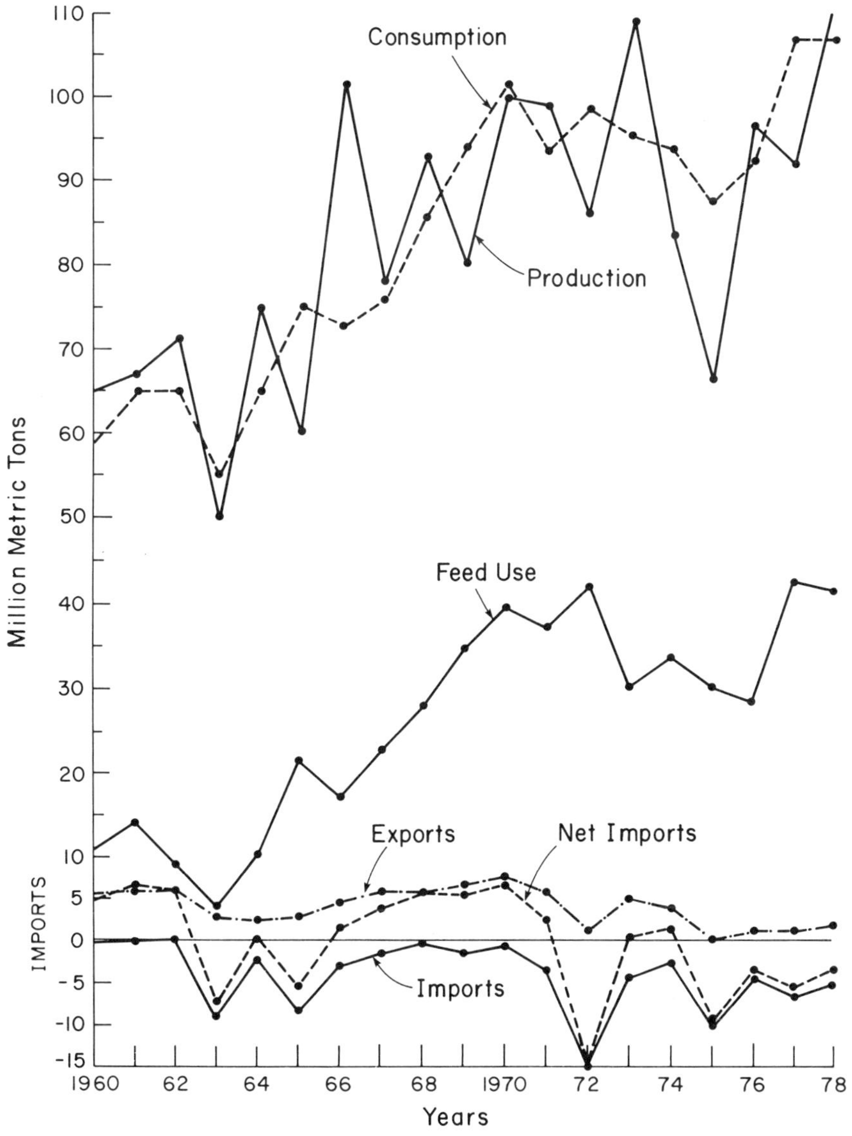

Source: U.S. Department of Agriculture, Foreign Agricultural Service. 1980.

Figure 3–11. USSR—coarse grains production, total consumption, feed use, and net imports (1960–78)

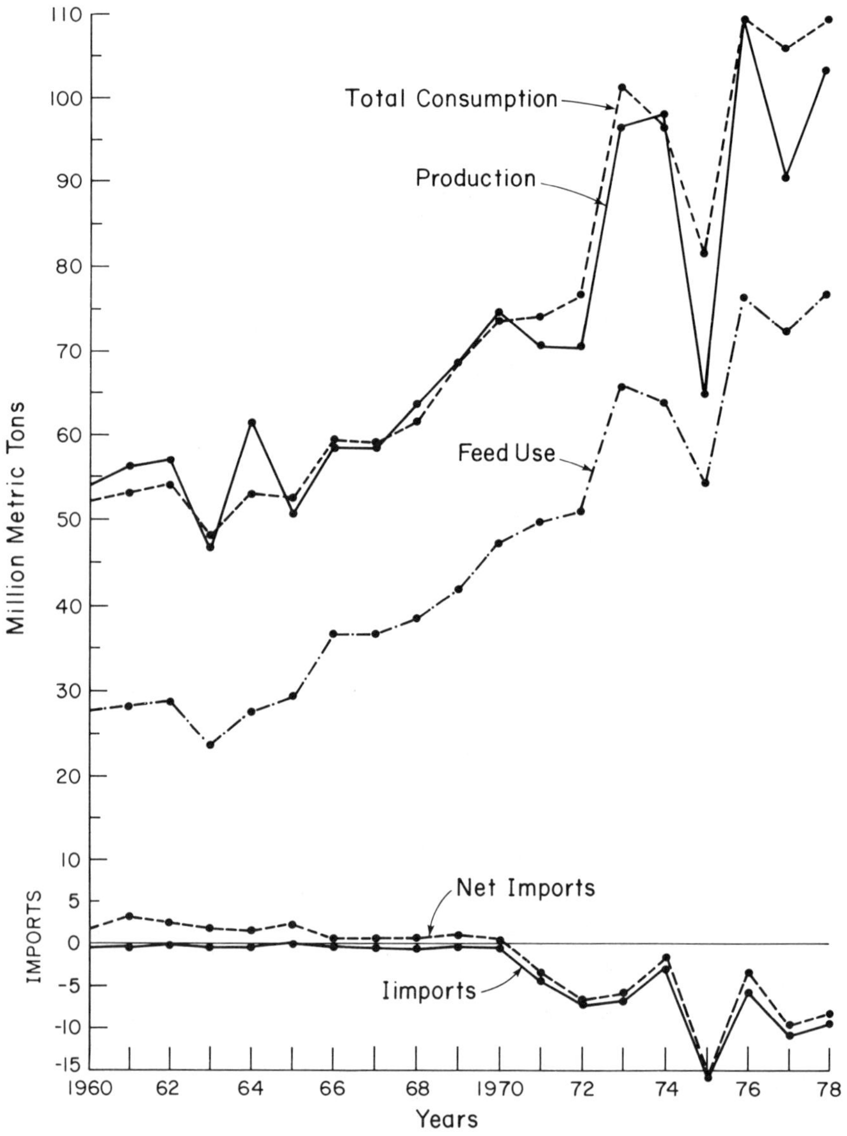

Source: U.S. Department of Agriculture, Foreign Agricultural Service. 1980.

production instability, the USSR is likely to remain an unstable element in world markets.

Because of these conditions, an export cartel has interesting implications. The major grain exporters individually would no longer be subject to the erratic and divisive buying behavior of the USSR. Instability could be reduced, for example, if the cartel bargained minimum prices and quantities in the form of longer term agreements.

CONCLUSIONS

This chapter has focused on key quantitative characteristics of international grain markets. It shows that there has been a significant increase in the volume of grain traded in the past twenty years. The LDCs have come to dominate imports in the wheat market, while the DCs are still the major buyers of coarse grains. There are very few grain exporters.

These data have been presented primarily for two reasons. The first is to give the reader a basic understanding of grain production, consumption, and trade flows. The second is to attempt to draw some implications which historical patterns of production, market shares, and trade would have for a grain cartel. A cartel will have to recognize these historical patterns and structure its price and trade practices accordingly.

APPENDIX A

Tables showing General Quantitative Characteristics of the World Grain Trade.

Table 3A–1. Wheat imports—1960–1978 (million metric tons)

Year	EC–9	Japan	Other Western Europe	DC[a]	USSR	Eastern Europe	China	CP[b]	LDC-OPEC	LDC-Mid Y	LDC-Low Y	LDC[c]
1960	11.6	2.8	2.5	17.4	.6	5.5	1.9	8.1	1.8	2.7	12.1	16.6
1961	11.7	2.8	2.8	17.8	.2	5.8	4.9	10.9	2.1	3.4	12.6	17.9
1962	8.3	2.7	2.2	13.8	.2	6.4	4.9	11.5	1.5	3.5	12.6	17.6
1963	9.6	3.9	1.6	15.7	9.7	6.0	5.2	21.0	1.5	4.0	13.6	19.1
1964	8.7	3.5	1.7	14.4	2.2	7.4	5.0	14.7	2.2	3.0	16.2	21.4
1965	10.1	3.5	1.7	15.9	8.5	7.2	6.3	22.1	1.8	3.7	18.1	23.6
1966	9.3	4.3	1.6	16.4	3.1	5.4	5.0	13.5	2.6	3.8	21.6	28.0
1967	9.1	4.0	1.2	14.9	1.5	4.9	4.2	10.5	2.5	4.4	19.8	26.7
1968	11.7	4.2	1.2	17.5	.2	4.3	3.5	8.0	2.5	4.4	15.6	22.5
1969	11.4	4.4	1.5	17.8	1.1	4.7	5.1	11.0	2.7	4.7	16.5	23.9
1970	12.2	4.5	1.6	19.3	.5	6.7	3.7	10.8	3.4	4.6	17.6	25.6
1971	11.2	5.0	1.2	17.9	3.5	5.2	3.0	11.7	5.2	4.9	17.6	27.7
1972	12.0	5.5	1.1	18.9	15.6	4.6	5.3	25.5	3.9	6.5	17.5	27.9
1973	11.7	5.4	1.5	18.9	4.5	4.8	5.6	15.0	5.8	6.0	20.7	32.5
1974	9.9	5.4	1.2	16.9	2.5	4.0	5.7	12.8	6.8	5.3	22.4	34.5
1975	11.9	5.9	1.0	19.2	10.1	5.7	2.2	18.0	6.8	6.1	23.6	36.5
1976	9.5	5.5	1.2	16.8	4.5	6.3	3.1	14.0	6.9	5.8	21.3	34.0
1977	12.5	5.8	1.5	20.4	6.9	5.0	8.6	20.8	8.8	7.1	21.5	37.4
1978	10.5	5.7	2.0	18.7	5.1	3.9	7.7	16.7	8.1	7.8	22.1	38.0

[a]Developed economies.
[b]Centrally planned economies.
[c]Developing economies.
Source: U.S. Foreign Agricultural Service. 1980. *Foreign Production, Supply, and Distribution of Agricultural Commodities* (computer tape).

Table 3A-2. Coarse grain imports—1960–1978 (million metric tons)

Year	*EC-9*	*Japan*	*Other Western Europe*	*DC*[a]	*USSR*	*Eastern Europe*	*China*	*CP*[b]	*LDC-1*	*LDC-2*	*LDC*[c]	*World Imports*
1960	14.4	1.9	2.2	18.9	0.2	1.7	0.7	2.5	0.6	1.0	1.6	23.8
1961	18.3	2.4	2.0	23.1	0.0	2.9	1.2	4.1	0.8	1.9	2.7	30.9
1962	18.3	2.9	3.3	24.9	0.0	2.9	0.4	3.3	1.3	1.4	2.7	31.6
1963	19.1	4.6	3.8	28.0	0.1	3.8	0.8	4.7	0.7	1.7	2.4	35.8
1964	19.1	5.1	3.7	28.4	0.0	2.6	0.3	2.9	0.8	1.3	2.1	34.3
1965	23.4	5.2	5.6	34.6	0.0	3.9	0.1	3.9	0.5	2.7	3.2	42.8
1966	22.2	7.2	5.8	35.8	0.2	2.0	0.1	2.2	0.6	3.8	4.4	43.2
1967	21.7	7.7	5.1	35.2	0.4	2.5	0.1	2.9	1.1	.1	4.2	43.3
1968	19.8	8.5	4.7	33.6	0.5	2.7	0.0	3.2	1.5	1.5	3.0	41.3
1969	20.1	10.0	4.7	35.6	0.1	2.9	0.0	3.0	2.2	2.0	4.2	43.7
1970	24.1	10.5	5.0	40.3	0.3	3.6	0.0	3.9	2.3	2.0	4.3	49.0
1971	22.7	10.3	5.0	38.8	4.3	5.9	0.4	10.6	3.5	2.1	5.6	55.7
1972	23.2	12.0	6.1	42.2	6.9	4.2	0.9	12.1	5.8	3.3	9.1	64.8
1973	26.8	14.1	8.5	50.4	6.5	5.1	2.1	13.7	5.5	4.6	10.1	75.9
1974	25.0	13.1	8.4	47.6	2.7	6.6	0.5	9.8	6.9	3.6	10.5	69.5
1975	25.9	13.5	7.7	48.2	15.6	8.8	0.0	24.3	7.1	3.8	10.9	84.7
1976	31.7	15.8	8.8	57.5	5.7	8.9	0.0	14.6	9.0	3.9	12.9	86.1
1977	23.8	16.9	10.2	52.0	11.7	8.7	0.1	20.4	12.2	4.6	16.8	90.0
1978	23.8	17.8	9.3	51.2	10.0	10.9	3.1	23.9	13.4	4.6	10.0	94.1

[a]Developed economies.
[b]Centrally planned economies.
[c]Developing economies.
Source: U.S. Foreign Agricultural Service. 1980. *Foreign Production, Supply, and Distribution of Agricultural Commodities* (computer tape).

Table 3A-3. Net exports and imports by region—wheat, 1960-1978 (million metric tons)

Year	Exporters—4 mmt[a]	DCs[b] Importers mmt	EC-9	CP[c] mmt	USSR	LDC-1	LDC-2	LDC[d]
1960	34.9	-14.4[e]	-8.9	-2.5	4.4	-4.4	-11.9	-16.4
1961	36.9	-13.9	-8.4	-5.0	5.9	-5.2	-12.5	-27.6
1962	34.1	-9.2	-4.8	-5.3	5.5	-4.9	-12.1	-17.0
1963	49.6	-10.8	-5.2	-17.9	-7.9	-5.2	-13.2	-18.4
1964	43.8	-7.4	-2.6	-12.0	0.0	-4.6	-15.7	-20.8
1965	49.0	-8.9	-3.7	-18.5	-5.9	-4.9	-17.7	-22.6
1966	45.3	-10.5	-4.6	-7.3	1.3	-6.1	-21.3	-27.5
1967	37.4	-7.0	-3.2	-2.8	3.8	-6.5	-19.7	-26.2
1968	31.2	-7.7	-3.4	-0.2	5.6	-6.6	-15.3	-21.9
1969	35.8	-6.7	-1.6	-3.3	5.3	-7.0	-16.4	-23.4
1970	41.8	-13.1	-6.5	-2.8	6.7	-7.8	-17.5	-25.3
1971	39.4	-8.6	-2.5	-5.8	2.3	-9.9	-17.5	-27.5
1972	53.1	-5.8	-0.2	-23.3	-14.3	-10.1	-15.9	-26.0
1973	52.6	-6.2	-0.1	-8.8	0.5	-11.6	-21.8	-33.4
1974	48.4	-3.4	2.3	-7.2	1.5	-11.9	-22.3	-34.2
1975	55.9	-3.7	2.3	-16.0	-9.6	-12.7	-23.6	-36.3
1976	54.6	-4.5	1.0	-11.7	-3.6	-12.6	-21.1	-33.7
1977	56.7	-6.3	-0.1	-17.4	-5.9	-15.8	-19.9	-35.7
1978	59.8	-2.9	3.5	-14.1	-3.6	-15.6	-19.2	-34.8

[a] Million metric tons.
[b] Developed economies.
[c] Centrally planned economies.
[d] Developing economies.
[e] Minus sign indicates net imports.
Source: U.S. Foreign Agricultural Service. 1980. *Foreign Production, Supply, and Distribution of Agricultural Commodities* (computer tape).

Table 3A-4. Net exports and imports by region—coarse grains, 1960–1978 (million metric tons)

Year	USA	Exporters –6	DC[a] Importers	EC–9	Japan	CP[b]	USSR	Eastern Europe	LDC[c]	LDC–1	LDC–2
1960	10.8	17.6	14.4[d]	-11.8	-1.9	0.9	1.8	-0.6	0.3	-0.5	0.8
1961	14.8	22.9	-16.6	-15.0	-2.4	0.6	3.0	-1.3	-1.0	-0.5	-0.5
1962	15.1	22.7	-19.1	-15.6	-2.9	0.7	2.5	-1.5	0.1	-0.4	0.5
1963	16.4	25.0	-22.1	-14.8	-4.6	-0.9	1.9	-1.7	0.3	-0.3	0.6
1964	19.2	25.7	-22.8	-14.4	-5.1	0.3	1.6	-1.9	1.7	1.1	0.6
1965	25.4	33.9	-28.3	-17.8	-5.2	-0.3	2.2	-1.7	1.0	1.3	0.3
1966	19.8	30.4	-26.2	-16.0	-7.2	0.4	0.6	-0.3	-0.5	1.2	1.7
1967	20.4	30.1	-25.5	-15.6	-7.7	0.1	0.6	-0.4	0.8	1.4	0.6
1968	16.0	23.9	-24.8	-12.1	-8.5	-0.6	0.6	-0.8	1.5	0.4	1.1
1969	18.6	31.1	-25.1	-11.5	-10.0	-0.5	1.0	-1.6	-0.8	0.3	0.5
1970	18.2	38.6	-28.2	-15.6	-10.5	-2.0	0.8	-2.9	-0.3	-0.6	0.3
1971	23.8	40.0	-23.1	-11.9	-10.3	-8.7	-3.4	-4.9	-2.1	-2.6	0.5
1972	38.3	51.9	-30.0	-12.3	-12.0	-9.7	-6.6	-2.2	-1.1	-5.3	-0.8
1973	40.4	56.6	-32.8	-13.0	-14.1	-10.0	-6.0	-2.4	-5.1	-3.9	-1.2
1974	35.4	51.9	-32.3	-13.9	-13.1	-7.8	-1.7	-5.6	-6.6	-5.7	-0.9
1975	49.6	68.5	-33.7	-13.5	-13.5	-21.8	-15.5	-6.4	-5.7	-5.6	0.1
1976	50.3	71.2	-44.7	-22.2	-15.8	-11.1	-3.7	-7.4	-8.1	-7.6	-0.5
1977	56.0	76.3	-34.8	-10.4	-16.9	-13.8	-10.7	-7.0	-14.4	-12.2	-2.4
1978	59.9	81.2	-34.5	-9.7	-17.8	-21.7	-8.9	-9.7	-15.5	-13.7	-1.8

[a] Developed economies.
[b] Centrally planned economies.
[c] Developing economies.
[d] Minus sign indicates net imports.
Source: U.S. Foreign Agricultural Service. 1980. *Foreign Production, Supply, and Distribution of Agricultural Commodities* (computer tape).

Table 3A-5. World wheat and flour trade matrix—1971-72, 1973-74, 1975-76, 1976-77 (million metric tons)

	Importer Destinations by Region									
Exporter Origin	*EC-9*	*Other Western Europe*	*Japan*	*Total DCs*[a]	*USSR*	*China*	*Eastern Europe*	*Total CP*[b]	*Total LDC*[c]	*Total Exports*
USA										
71-72	1.8	.4	2.2	4.4	0	0	.03	.03	12.2	16.9
73-74	2.5	.7	3.0	6.2	2.7	3.2	.8	6.7	18.1	31.1
75-76	3.7	.4	3.3	7.4	4.0	0	.9	4.9	19.2	31.5
76-77	1.7	.5	3.1	5.3	2.9	0	1.0	3.9	16.4	25.7
Canada										
71-72	2.7	.2	1.4	4.3	2.8	3.0	.1	5.9	3.5	13.7
73-74	2.3	.3	1.7	4.3	1.6	1.4	.3	3.3	4.2	11.7
75-76	2.1	.2	1.6	3.9	3.1	1.2	.8	5.1	3.0	12.1
76-77	2.5	.2	1.3	4.0	1.2	1.9	1.3	4.4	4.5	12.9
Australia										
71-72	.9	.2	1.4	2.5	.5	0	.2	.7	5.3	8.7
73-74	0	0	.4	.4	.02	1.2	0	1.22	3.6	5.4
75-76	.1	0	1.1	1.2	1.3	1.0	.02	2.32	4.2	7.9
76-77	.1	0	1.2	1.3	.4	.8	0	1.2	5.9	8.5
Argentina										
71-72	.3	0	0	.3	0	0	0	0	.8	1.3
73-74	.4	.01	.03	.44	.03	0	0	.03	.6	1.1
75-76	.5	0	0	.5	1.2	0	0	1.2	1.5	3.2
76-77	.7	.2	0	.9	.1	.5	1.0	1.6	2.9	5.6
Other										
71-72	5.8	.4	0	6.2	0	0	.6	.6	4.1	11.1
73-74	6.7	.4	0	7.1	.02	.03	.1	.15	4.7	12.0
75-76	6.9	.4	0	7.3	0	0	1.0	1.0	6.7	15.4
76-77	5.7	.3	0	6.0	0	0	.8	.8	4.3	11.4
Total imports										
71-72	11.5	1.1	5.0	17.6	3.3	3.0	.9	7.2	26.1	51.7
73-74	11.6	1.3	5.2	18.1	4.4	5.8	1.2	11.4	31.1	61.4
75-76	13.3	1.0	6.1	20.4	9.6	2.2	2.7	14.5	34.5	70.2
76-77	10.8	1.1	5.6	17.5	4.6	3.2	4.2	12.0	33.7	64.2

[a]Developed economies.
[b]Centrally planned economies.
[c]Developing economies.
Source: U.S. Department of Agriculture, Foreign Agricultural Service. 1978. *Grain Exports by Selected Exporters.* Foreign Agriculture Circular, FG 5-78.

Table 3A-6. World coarse grain trade matrix—1973-74, 1975-76, 1976-77 (million metric tons)

Exporter Origin	EC-9	Other Western Europe	Japan	Total DCs[a]	USSR	China	Eastern Europe	Total CP[b]	Total LDC[c]	Total Exports
	Importer Destinations by Region									
USA										
73-74	12.3	4.8	10.2	27.3	5.0	1.8	1.3	8.1	8.7	44.3
75-76	14.0	4.5	8.0	26.5	9.9	0	2.7	12.6	6.6	46.4
76-77	19.9	5.4	10.1	35.4	4.6	0	2.7	7.3	7.2	50.6
Canada										
73-74	.7	.02	.9	1.6	.2	0	.3	.5	.6	2.8
75-76	1.2	.02	1.0	2.2	1.4	0	.5	1.9	.4	4.9
76-77	2.0	0	1.0	3.0	.3	0	.4	.7	.6	4.6
Australia										
73-74	.1	0	1.2	1.3	.1	0	0	.1	.3	1.9
75-76	.2	0	1.5	1.7	.9	0	0	.9	.4	3.3
76-77	.5	0	1.6	2.1	.2	0	.04	.24	.3	3.3
Argentina										
73-74	4.0	1.6	.7	6.3	.3	.3	.1	.7	1.5	8.5
75-76	2.2	1.0	.7	3.9	.2	0	.1	.3	1.1	5.4
76-77	2.9	1.6	2.0	6.5	.2	0	.8	1.0	1.7	9.3
Other										
73-74	10.1	1.2	.1	11.4	.5	0	.6	1.1	.6	13.9
75-76	10.8	1.4	1.3	13.5	1.2	0	.9	2.1	1.3	17.5
76-77	8.7	1.0	.5	10.2	.4	0	.2	.6	1.0	12.2
Total imports										
73-74	27.3	7.6	13.1	48.0	6.1	2.1	2.4	10.6	11.8	71.4
75-76	28.4	7.0	12.5	47.9	13.7	0	4.2	17.9	9.8	77.5
76-77	34.0	8.0	15.4	57.4	5.6	0	4.2	9.8	10.9	80.0

[a]Developed economies.
[b]Centrally planned economies.
[c]Developing economies.
Source: U.S. Department of Agriculture, Foreign Agricultural Service. 1978. *Grain Exports by Selected Exporters.* Foreign Agriculture Circular, FG 5-78.

REFERENCES

U.S. Department of Agriculture, 1978. *Grain Exports by Selected Exporters.* Foreign Agricultural Circular FG 5–78.

———. 1979. *World Grain Situation Outlook for 1979–80.* Foreign Agricultural Circular FB 15–79, September 14.

———. Foreign Agricultural Service. 1980. *Foreign Production, Supply, and Distribution of Agricultural Commodities.* Computer tape.

4 THE THEORY OF CARTELS

This chapter presents the theory of export cartels as it relates to the grain trade. Little has been written on cartel theory as it applies to grains, a renewable resource; most of the literature focuses instead on nonrenewable resources such as oil.[a] This chapter focuses only on the theory relevant to the grain trade which, along with the data given earlier, provides the basis for the empirical results presented later.

In order to derive estimates of the possible gains from forming an exporter association in grains, more is needed than the discussion in the previous chapters. A theoretical analysis is also necessary in order to focus on such an issue as whether the cartel is supposed to enhance producer welfare or reduce food prices in exporting countries. Other issues which the theory deals with include (1) the pricing of grains to poor countries relative to high-income nations, (2) the free-rider problem, (3) the rents or economic gains to be obtained from a cartel, (4) the problem of cheating among cartel

[a]Those interested in nonrenewable resource cartel theory should see the following: Comanor and Schankerman 1976; Cremer and Weitzman 1976; Eckbo 1976; Gilbert and Goldman 1978; Hryilicza and Pindyck 1976; Nichols and Zeckhauser 1977; Orr and McAvoy 1965; Osborne 1976; Page and Kymn 1978; Patinkin 1947; Pindyck 1978, 1979; Salant 1976; and Duyne 1975.

members, and (5) the role of the public and private sectors in cartel formation.

In simplest terms, a producer cartel is an association of producers or suppliers of a product who jointly determine levels of output and prices so as to maximize a commonly agreed-upon objective function. On the other hand, a government cartel is an association made up of government exporters who consider the interests of both producers and consumers in setting export prices and quantities. In general, characteristics similar to monopoly are necessary prerequisites for the success of each form of cartel—namely, control of supply, sloping demand functions, blocked entry, noncountervailing power, and a single-valued objective function. However, additional conceptual issues arise because a cartel is a special kind of monopoly: it is an association of previously independent suppliers (countries) who collude for mutual benefit.

THE SIMPLE CARTEL MODEL[b]

The simplest of cartel models is demonstrated in Figure 4–1. The foreign (importing country) demand curve for the product is D_f, and the supply curve in the exporting country is S_d. Under competition the exporter supplies Q^* of the product at price P^*. Suppose now that an export cartel is formed so that *all* firms in the industry belong to the cartel. To maximize profits for the cartel, it equates MR_f (the marginal revenue to D_f) with S_d and charges price P_c and sells only Q_c of the good. Note that in this model under the time period considered, the cartel has to restrict output in order to maximize profit for the cartel.

In the simplest of all possible worlds, only one firm would make up the industry, or the industry producing Q could be owned by a single government. In this case there is no problem of allocating the restricted output Q_c among countries or among several or more firms. This assumption eliminates the free-rider problem, where firms produce and sell the product but do not belong to the cartel. In addition a quota rule to allocate Q_c among producers would not have

[b]The analysis contained in this chapter rests partly on the concept of economic surplus; for a review of this subject, see Currie, Murphy, and Schmitz (1971).

Figure 4–1. The simple cartel model

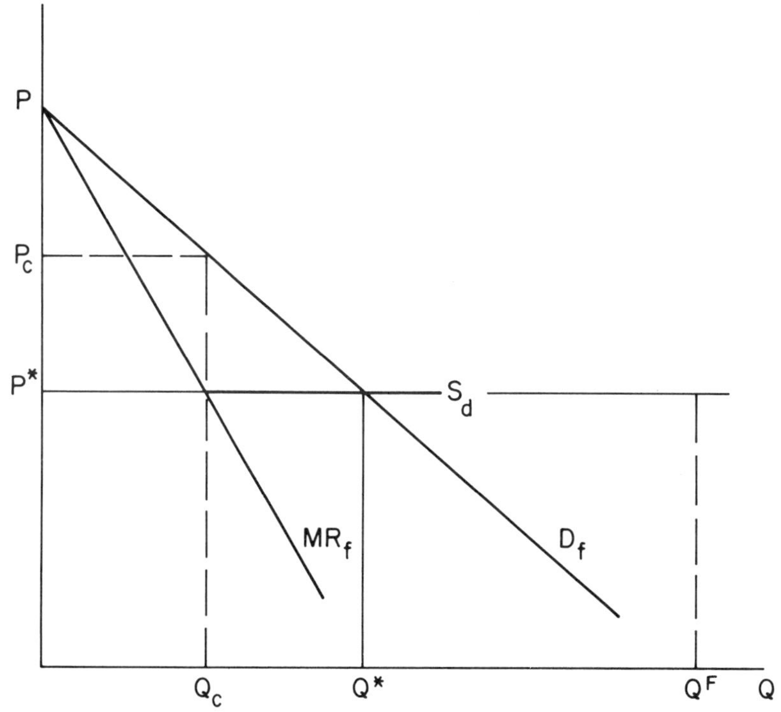

to be established. However, the problem of substitutes coming into the market still exists.

Why, theoretically, can a cartel gain by restricting output? A precondition for the success of a cartel is that there must be monopoly rents for it to obtain. Figure 4–2 shows two such cases where monopoly rents are not present. First, if the foreign demand curve is D_f and S_d is the domestic supply for exporters, the cartel could not do better than remain at the competitive price P^* and sell Q^* of the good. Second, if D_f^1 is the foreign demand and S_d^1 is the domestic supply, interestingly, a cartel could not gain over a free trade competitive solution, P_1Q_1 given quantity Q. The marginal revenue schedule MR^1 cuts S_d^1 at the same quantity as S_d^1 cuts the demand curve D_f^1. Thus, for an export cartel to be beneficial for exporters, it is necessary for the foreign demand curve to be downward sloping. However, this is not a sufficient condition. The

Figure 4–2. The no-gain export cartel

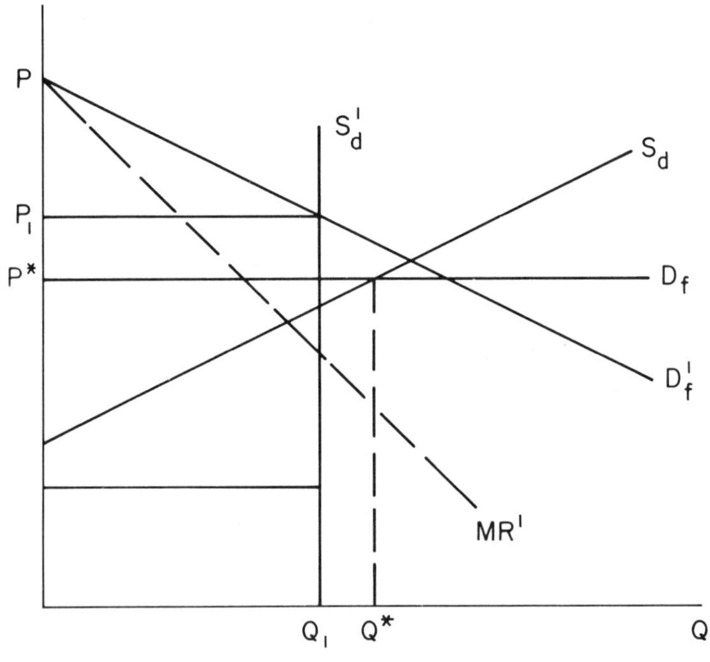

domestic supply curve (that is, the one in the exporting country) cannot be completely price inelastic within the relevant range. The flatter the domestic supply and the steeper the foreign demand, the greater are the gains from an export cartel.

With reference to the models in Figures 4–1 and 4–2, if the cartel has more than one member, the problem of allocating quotas among cartel participants arises whether the commodity is oil or wheat. However, if, unlike wheat, the resource is a nonrenewable one, its quantity is of a fixed stock and is given. For example, in Figure 4–1, suppose Q^F is the total amount of the resource available and S_d represents the marginal cost of extracting the resource. Then, ignoring the discounting factor, each period the cartel would sell Q_c until Q^F is exhausted, given that D_f is a single period demand curve. (The way Q^F is positioned in Figure 4–1, the supply of the resource would be depleted in four periods.) For a renewable resource, however, the price charged for all time periods would be P_c, and quantities would be available for all periods into infinity. Of course, in a real world situation, supply and demand would change through time; hence, the optimal cartel price and quantities would also adjust.

There are at least two issues where the distinction between renewable and nonrenewable resources is crucial: domestic demand in the case of renewable resources and pricing by the cartel in the case of "fringe firms" (that is, those not belonging to the cartel). A discussion of these issues follows.

CARTEL MODEL WITH DOMESTIC DEMAND

Unlike commodities such as oil, there is a relatively large domestic demand for grains in exporting countries. When this is the case, a distinction has to be made between a government export cartel and a producer export cartel. The two have different objectives: the government maximizes "social welfare" from a cartel, taking into account both producers and consumers, while the producer cartel maximizes producer welfare only. In the single cartel model (Figure 4–1), this distinction does not have to be made since demand in the exporting country was assigned as nonexistent. A producer cartel and a government export cartel in this case are the same thing.

The model in Figure 4–3 is important for understanding the implications of a grain export cartel. In Figure 4–3, the demand and supply curves for the exporter of good X are D_C and S_C, while for the importer the corresponding schedules are D_D and S_D. The excess demand curve for the importer is *ED*, the excess supply curve for the exporter is *ES*, and the free-trade price is P_F. The optimal export tax (that is, the optimal government export cartel) imposed by the government in the exporting country is computed simply by determining where the *ES* schedule crosses the marginal revenue curve (*MR*) pertaining to *ED*. Due to the tax, the price in the importing country becomes P_C (for both consumers and producers), and the price in the exporting country for both producers and consumers becomes P_D. The tax revenue is *abcd*. Note that the producer's loss in economic rent is *defg*, while the gain in the consumer's surplus is the crosshatched area. The net gain to the exporters is the crosshatched area plus *abcd* minus *defg*. The difference has to be positive under the large-country assumption used in this model.

Figure 4–3. Optimal government export cartel

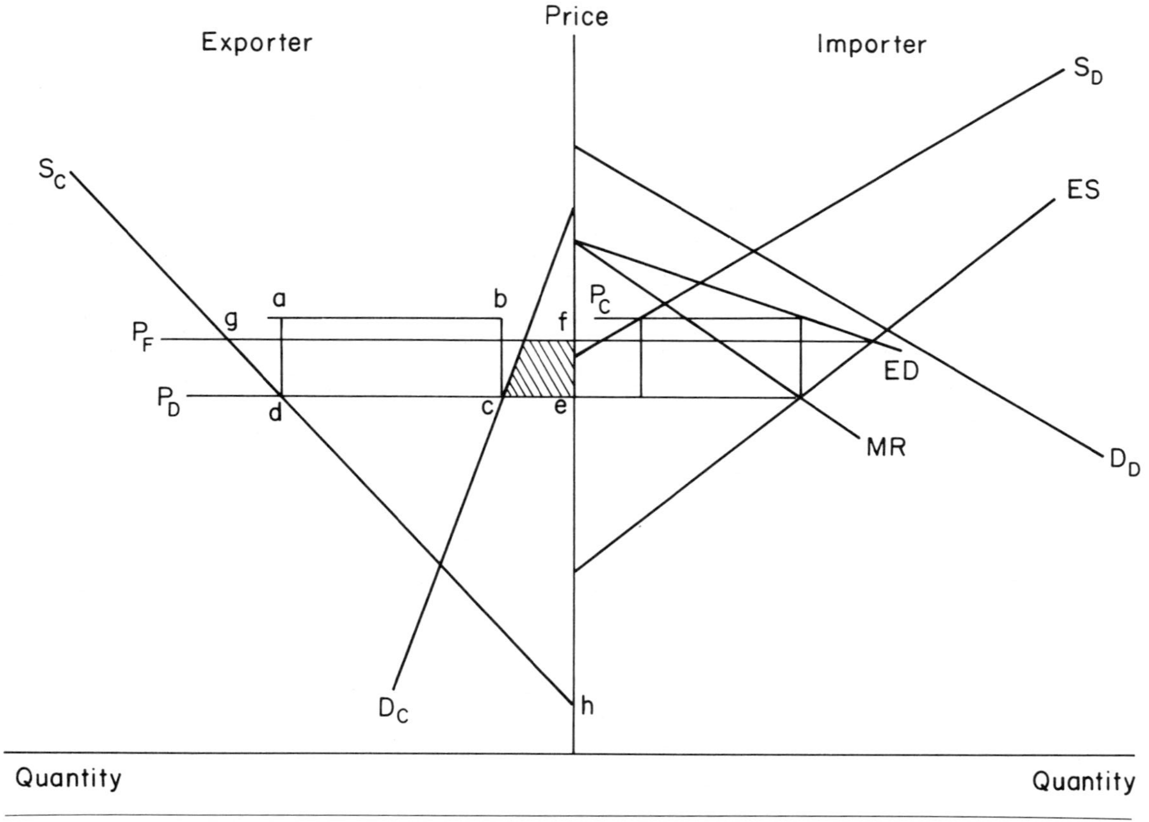

The simple model above points out that a sharp distinction must be made between an export cartel established to maximize welfare in aggregate for the exporting countries (a government cartel) and a producer export cartel which maximizes producer welfare. The government cartel always results (except for the conditions in Figure 4–2 and in the absence of retaliation) in a net welfare gain for the exporting country since the welfare of both consumers and producers is considered. However, the interesting point is that the producers in the exporting country can be made worse off from the cartel arrangement imposed by the government.

Stated in a different way, if the producers organized to form a cartel and used the pricing and output solution of a government cartel, they could be worse off. Figure 4–3 also illustrates this case. In this figure, note that—with an optimal export tax—the gain to consumers in the exporting country is the crosshatched area. There is a loss to producers in the form of economic rent of *defg* and a gain in tax revenue of *abcd,* but the loss in rent (*defg*) is greater than the gain in the tax revenue (*abcd*). Hence, there is a net loss to producers even if all the tax revenue is given to them.[c] Note further that the reason the government cartel leads to a net improvement in welfare for the exporting country is that, in addition to the tax revenue, there is a gain to consumers since domestic prices fall as a result of the export tax. In the above case, if a government cartel were formed, part of the consumer gain would have to be taxed and given to the producers in addition to the export tax revenue if everyone in the exporting country is to be made better off by the cartel arrangement.

On the other hand, a producer cartel which maximizes producer returns would yield a different solution. The producer cartel would take into account the marginal revenue schedule to the domestic demand curve. The solution is illustrated in Figure 4–4. For the importers, only the excess demand is represented. The demand in the exporting region is D_d, the domestic supply is S_d, and the free-trade price is P_f. The government export cartel price is not shown; only the solution for the producer export cartel is given. Note that, unlike the case with the government export cartel, the "true" supply price in the exporting country and the domestic demand price are not the same (P^* is the supply price, and P_d is the demand price).

[c]The conditions under which a government export cartel leads to a welfare loss to producers have been worked out rigorously in (Carter, Gallini, and Schmitz 1980).

Figure 4–4. Optimal government export cartel and optimal producer export cartel compared

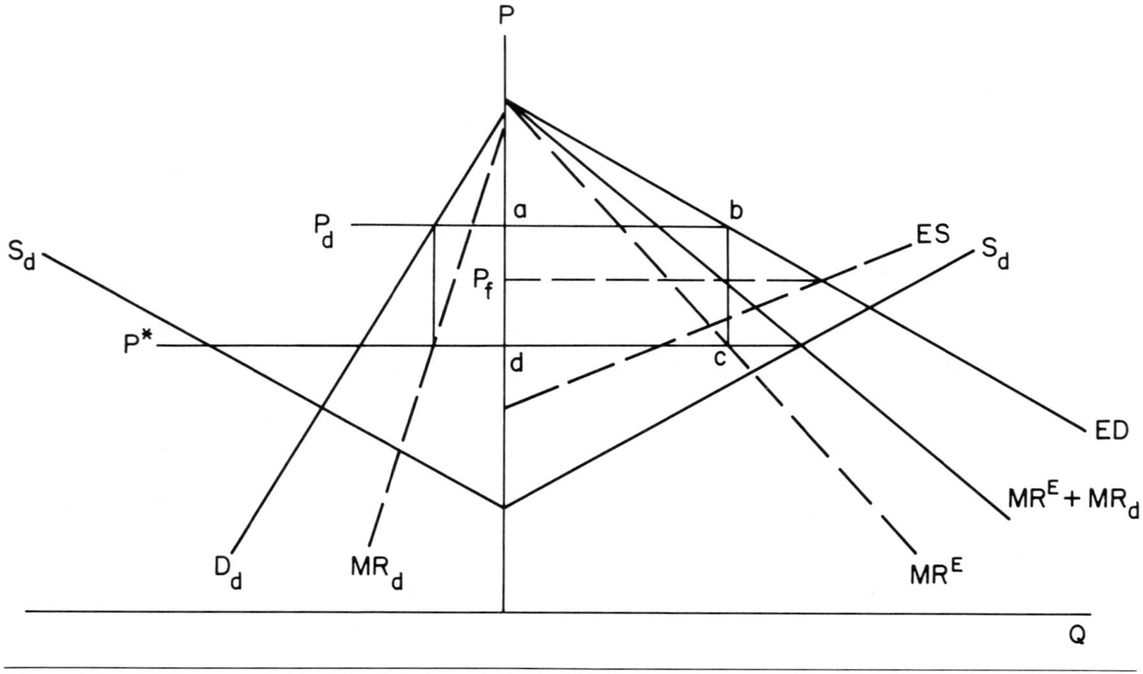

Also, note that the free-trade price is between these two prices whereas, with the government cartel, the free-trade price is above the home price. In this model, one can easily show that if the export tax revenue (*abcd* in Figure 4–4) is given to producers, they are always better off with a producer export cartel than with free trade.

Note that in the above models of cartels, output has to be reduced in the exporting country in order for the cartel to be effective. However, along with this reduced output is associated a higher price, due to the export tax revenue, which is not the price needed to bring forth the cartel output. The cartel price is much higher. Increased production accompanied by increased prices is an inconsistency in this model. Thus, there is the problem (to be discussed in a later section) of how to redistribute the higher earnings to producers without stimulating increased production.

FRINGE SUPPLIERS

The preceding models have assumed that only one firm or country is involved in producing the good. This assumption is now relaxed in order to consider the free-rider problem where one or several countries producing a product for export do not join the countries which have formed a cartel. The countries outside the cartel are fringe suppliers.

Figure 4–5 presents a model of a renewable resource cartel where some firms and countries are in the cartel and others are not. Suppose *D* is the demand for a single time period and *S* is the supply of the export cartel members. Given the supply of the competitive fringe members (which is also upward sloping and is shown on the right-hand side of the diagram), the excess demand curve *ED* facing the cartel members can be drawn.[d] The marginal revenue to *ED* is MR^E. The cartel will equate MR^E with the supply curve *S* and charge price P_1. At this price the fringe suppliers will provide Q_1Q_2, and the market will be cleared. Note that the fringe supplier price is higher, as are the returns, than in the absence of a cartel. Without the cartel group, the fringe would only receive price P_f. It is clear why the fringe suppliers receive a free ride, for they can increase price and

[d]Note that the difference between *ED* and *D* represents at each price the supply forthcoming from the fringe supplies.

Figure 4–5. A model of the competitive fringe for renewable resources

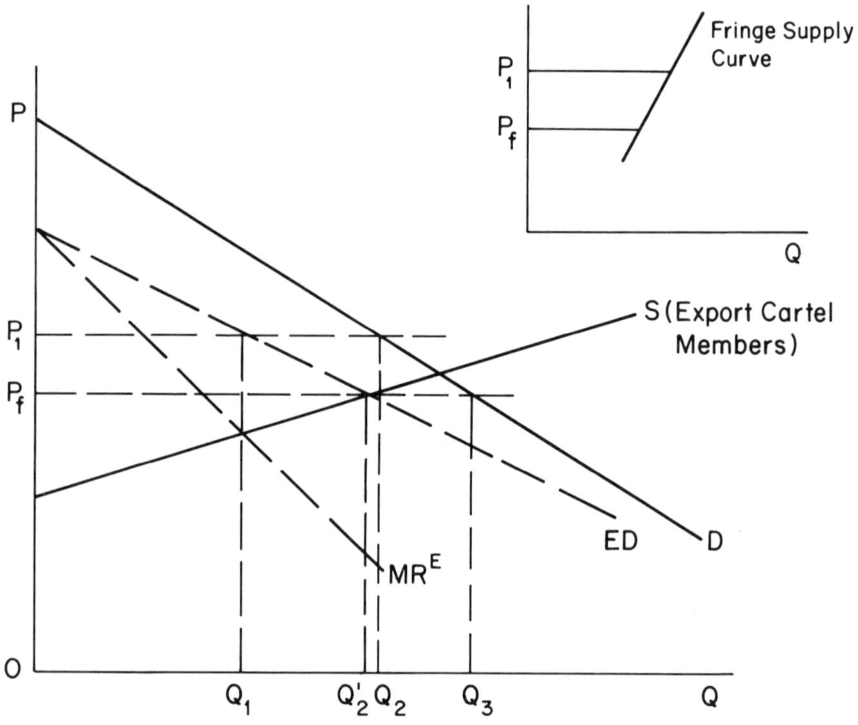

returns simply by pricing at the cartel price P_1. Note that in the model the cartel provides OQ_1. Also, note how the relative shares have changed. At the free-trade price P_f, the fringe suppliers sell $Q_2'Q_3$ while those in the potential cartel sell OQ_2^1. Under the cartel, the fringe sells Q_1Q_2 while the cartel sells only OQ_1. Thus, the fringe s uppliers gain proportionally more from the cartel than the members of the cartel because, due to the higher price, the fringe suppliers increase output while the members within the cartel reduce output.[e] How much of the market the cartel members need before it is worth their while to form a cartel if free riders exist has been worked out (Duyne 1975; LaFrance, Schmitz, and Zilberman 1980),

[e] Note that the general conclusions do not change even if the supply curve for the fringe is completely price inelastic. In this case, *ED* would be drawn parallel to *D*.

and it is surprising to discover that cartel members can still gain even if they have less than 50 percent of the market prior to their establishing a cartel.

The case of the nonrenewable resource is not so straightforward to solve (Salant 1976). The pricing problem is discussed in Figure 4–6. The demand for the product is *D*, and *MC* is the marginal cost of extracting the resource for the cartel members. The total stocks of the resource are known and are given by S^*. The amount owned by the fringe firms is $S_1\bar{S}$. If the cartel members know that the fringe firms will sell $S_1\bar{S}$ in the first period (*D* representing the demand for each period through time), then the cartel can compute both *ED* and MR^E. The cartel would price at P_1 and sell OQ^* from its stocks. The fringe at P_1 would sell its entire stock, $S_1\bar{S}$, at that price. Then, in the next period, the cartel would be the only supplier. It would then price by using the marginal revenue curve MR^D and act as a monopolist. It would charge price P_2 and sell Q_2. Eventually, all of

Figure 4–6. The fringe and a cartel for nonrenewable resources

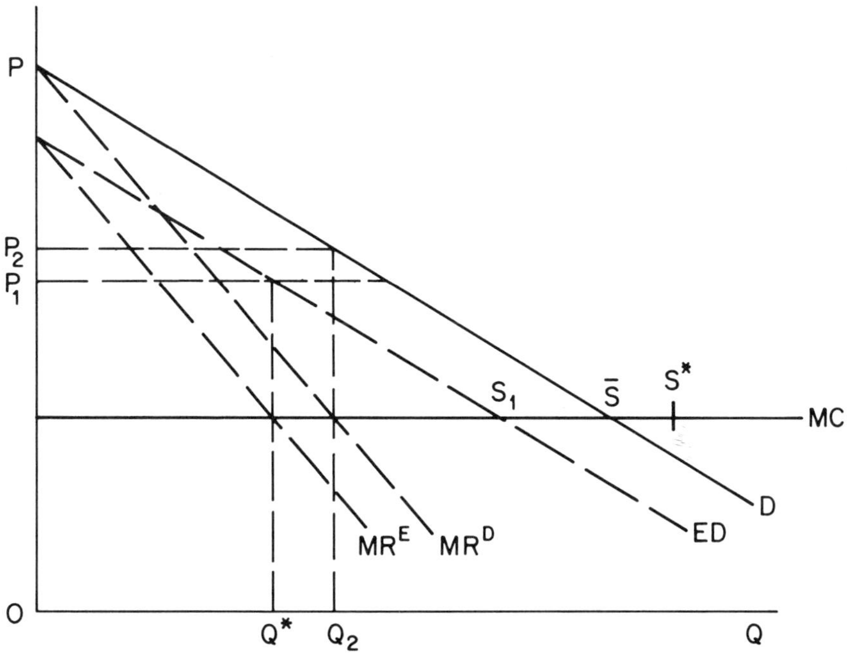

the stock would be depleted (in the model it is depleted in two periods). Note that in one period both the cartel and the fringe supplied the product; then the fringe dropped out, and only the cartel remained in existence.

In the above model the cartel could compute *ED* since it was assumed that the cartel knew that the fringe would sell all of its product in the first period. (In the renewable resource case, this is not a problem.) If the cartel does not know in which period the fringe will sell its supplies, however, the pricing problem becomes complex since there is no easy way for the cartel members to compute *ED*. The problem of uncertainty with respect to fringe suppliers is always a problem for cartel members.[f]

THE PURE THEORY OF TRADE AND MARKET INTERMEDIARIES

The previous cartel models are partial equilibrium models in that only one good is considered and balance-of-payment constraints are not included. Often both partial and general equilibrium models are useful in economic analysis, and so the theory of cartels is discussed in a general equilibrium context in Figure 4–7.

The production possibility curve for the country forming the cartel in PP_1. The no-trade production point is *a*, while the free-trade point is *b* (*bx* is exported for imports *xy*). The free-trade terms of trade are P_1/P_2. It is also the domestic price line (that is, the relative price for both producers and consumers). In the movement from no trade to free trade, the nation as a whole gains, but some factors of production gain more than others from the opening up of trade, while some may actually lose. As an example, if X_1 is land-intensive and trade opens up, the real returns to land increase absolutely.

The country, however, can be made better off than under free trade, if the trading partner does not retaliate by imposing an optimal export tax as demonstrated earlier in the partial models. When the

[f]It is interesting to read Mead (1979) who argues that the current pricing strategy by OPEC does not follow any of the theoretical models developed. He argues that the main reason for high prices is a change in the discount rate. It has been lowered because more and more resources now are in the control of government. A lower discount rate means that relatively less oil will be drilled in the short run which results in a higher short-run price than would exist at a high discount rate. Also, Adelman (1978) argues that the oil-pricing method by OPEC does not fit either a cartel model or a dominant firm price model.

Figure 4–7. The optimal cartel in general equilibrium

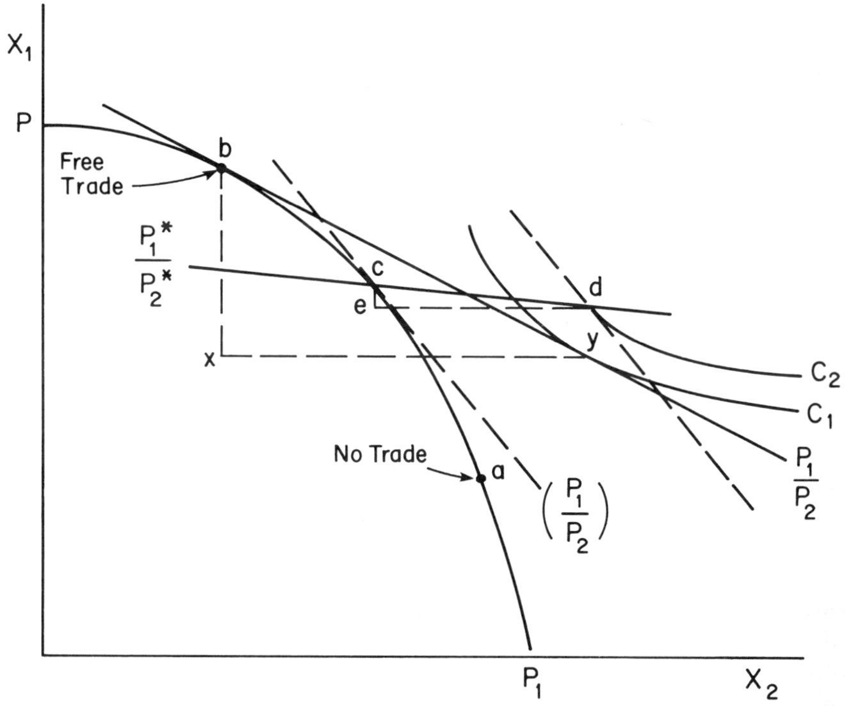

government imposes the optimal export tax, it drives a wedge between export and domestic prices (note that this was also the case in partial models). The tax solution is illustrated in Figure 4–7. The production point is *c* (between the no-trade and free-trade points). Domestic consumption is at *d*. The internal price is (P_1/P_2) along which domestic production and consumption occur. The international terms of trade, however, are P_1^*/P_2^*. The country now exports *ce* for *ed*. It is clear that the country's terms of trade have improved due to the export tax which is essentially the reason why the country can be made better off than under free trade.

An interesting question is: How are the factors of production affected? If the revenue is not given back to landowners, they become worse off than under free trade. Note that if it is given back to them, it is not used to increase production of X_1 beyond *c*. The true supply price is (P_1/P_2).

The above discussion raises the issue of the various implications of a cartel under different institutional arrangements. Batra (1976) recently argued that the model in Figure 4–7 is appropriate for a centrally planned economy trading with a market economy.[g] The central planner will act analogously to a profit-maximizing monopolist-monopsonist and thus pursue the optimal cartel policy. Batra argues that the centrally planned country has an advantage over the market economy and thus will not want to pursue a free-trade policy because it can set the optimal export tax (that is, optimal export cartel) implicitly by simply changing the quantities of exports and imports it is willing to trade. The market economy does not know what the centrally planned economy's offer curve looks like because the monopolist's supply curve is not well defined. Batra concludes convincingly that in the presence of market power possessed by a centrally planned economy, the market economy should introduce a state-trading corporation to deal with this type of economy; he suggests that in response to OPEC, the United States should stockpile oil and form a federal corporation to import oil from the OPEC countries.

This discussion opens up the subject of the role of institutions in international trade. As discussed in earlier chapters, both the private and public sectors are involved in trade on a day-to-day basis; and the question of whether a cartel can function with both types of intermediaries involved in trade is the topic of a later chapter. If the exporters use private firms to negotiate and carry out trade with importers who use government importing agencies, could an export cartel ever be successful?

QUOTA RULES, DETERRING, AND CHEATING

In the early simple model, the issue of allocating quotas among cartel members did not arise since only one country or one firm was assumed to produce and export the good. For most commodities, this assumption is unrealistic. For example, in the case of OPEC, many countries are engaged in oil production, and this is also true for grains.

The internal problems of a cartel (that is, problems internal to cartel members) are to locate the contract surface, choose a point on

[g]Wolf (1978) recently argued that while Batra's theoretical results appear correct, the application of this model to the East-West trade is not appropriate.

that surface (the sharing problem), detect cheating, and deter cheating. If an enforceable contract is available, the cartel can pool revenues and share them according to some negotiated rule (Bain's [1948] perfect cartel, the theory of which was given by Patinkin [1947]).

Osborne (1976) recently argued that the problems of sharing and deterring are easily solved if the locating and detecting problems are solved. He concludes that it would be a mistake for oil-importing countries to create a cental international buying agency to deal with OPEC since such an agency would solve the detecting problem for the cartel.

Optimal Quota Rule for a Cartel

Consider Figure 4–8 where, for simplicity, only two members make up the cartel. I_1's represent the isoprofit contours for member 1 and

Figure 4–8. Joint profit maximization and quota rules

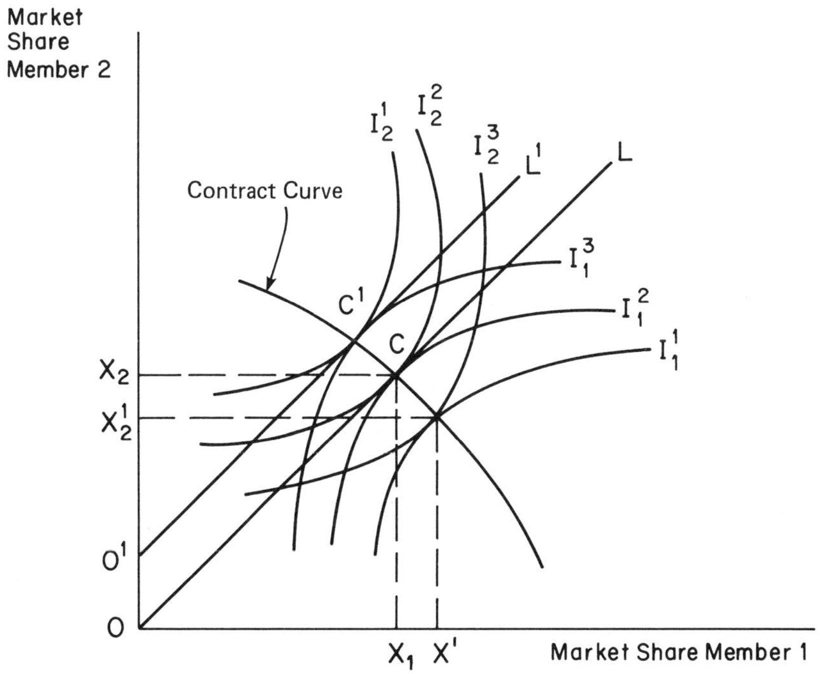

I_2's, the contours for member 2. A contract curve is formed from points of tangency from the isoprofit curves; movement along such a curve raises one member's profits and lowers the other's. Where do the members operate along the contract curve in order that the rule used to allocate quotas among members will lead to a stable cartel arrangement? It can be established that a point of stable market shares for the cartel is C because OL has the "ray property"; it is a line drawn through the origin which is tangent to an isoprofit contour of each member where the tangency point is on the contract curve. (Note, for example, that O^1L^1 does not possess the ray property; hence, quotas allocated at C^1 would lead to an unstable cartel.)

At C the output quota for member 1 is OX_1, and for member 2 it is OX_2. Note that if member 1 wanted to increase its quota to X^1, thus attaining a higher profit, member 2 would have to lower its quota to X_2^1, thus reducing its profit. To avoid cheating, the cartel must assign each member a quota rule—an operating rule incorporating a deterrent to cheating. One cannot allow the cartel to deviate from OL.

One such rule to deter cheating and to solve the sharing problem is discussed below. Let $s_i = x_i^o / \Sigma_{j=1}^{n} x_j^o$ be member i's market share at the cartel point. The quota rule for member i is to produce

$$max \quad x_i^o, x_i^o + \frac{s_i}{s_j} \Delta x_j$$

where Δx_j is the amount by which member j's output deviates from his quota x_j^o.

Upon discovering that member j cheats, member i increases his output so that when all the other loyal members increase their outputs according to the quota role, all market shares are preserved. This rule operates to keep the output vector x on the ray OL. If all observe the quota rule, no member can gain by a unilateral departure of any kind from his assigned quota rule. It is also important to recognize that member j has every reason to expect that all the other members will retaliate to his cheating since they can be made better off than by staying with their original quota.

A distinction has to be made between a cartel where only one country supplies the good and a cartel involving more than one country. In the case of a one-country cartel, there is a quota problem (that is, output has to be restricted and shared among the producers in the industry) only if the tax revenue is given back to producers. (The quota problem for internal producers can easily be solved by using delivery quotas which is the current practice of the Canadian Wheat Board.) If it is not, the price system solves the problem since the price that producers receive is the true supply price. In the general equilibrium model presented in Figure 4–7, that is what happens. The tariff revenue is distributed to all of society, and fewer exports are produced because relative prices change in favor of the nonexport good. There is no quota problem since adjustments occur via the price system.

If more than one country is involved in the cartel, there can be problems, especially if the tax revenue goes back to producers. The problem arises in maintaining cartel output so as to maximize joint profits for all countries in the cartel—not just allocating production among producers in a single country. This is essentially the problem discussed earlier, and to solve it, the members of the cartel have to restrict output jointly. Once this is done, they will have only *internal* supply management problems with which to deal.

While the problem of quota allocation is discussed later, one way to allocate quotas among countries is to use past export market share data. If, for example, a ten-year average were used and illustrated that the United States had an average of 30 percent of the export market, it would have 30 percent of the cartel output. Internally, a number of schemes, such as acreage controls and production quotas, could be used to keep exports at that level. One of the problems of allocating quotas among countries is that costs of production, as well as government policies, may be quite different.[h] Consider two exporters in Figure 4–9 where the higher cost producer has supply S_1 and the lower cost producer has supply S_2. Aggregate export demand is D. Without government policy, country 1 would export OX_1 and country 2 would export X_1X_2. Suppose, however, that due to subsidies (for example,a fertilizer subsidy), the supply curve for country 1 is S^1 instead of S_1. Now the picture becomes quite different in terms of market shares since each would export the same amount. In this case, would the cartel assign quotas on the basis of the true supply curve S_1 or the government-induced supply curve S^1?

[h]Empirical results suggest that in wheat, for example, costs of production are similar among Canada, Australia, and the United States.

Figure 4–9. Export cartels and different supply conditions

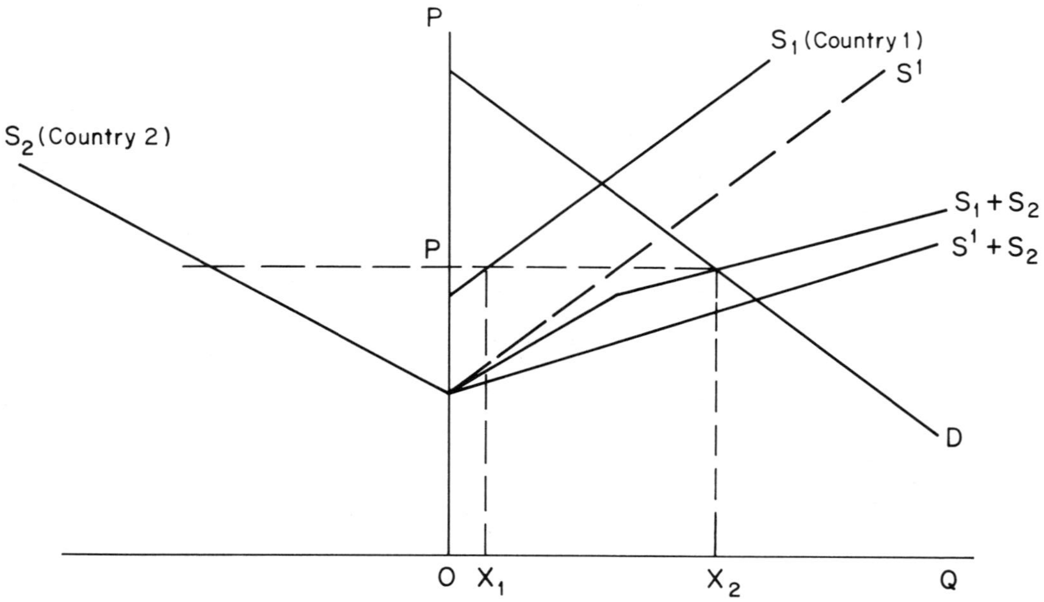

Figure 4–10. Multiple price cartel

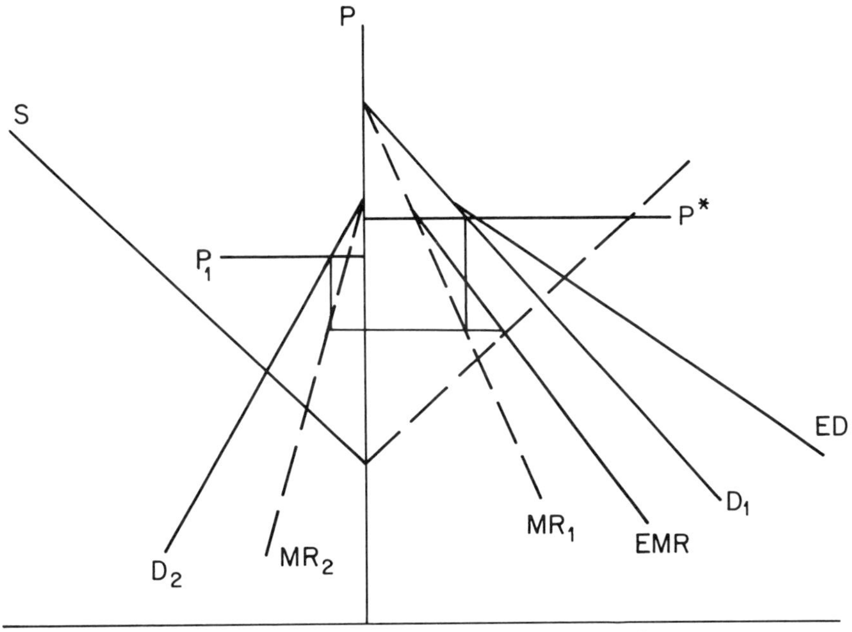

This is an issue which could only be solved by government negotiations.

MULTIPLE PRICE CARTEL

It is not necessary for an export cartel to charge the same price to all of the importers.Consider two importers which are high-income countries. In Figure 4–10, D_1 is the demand curve for one importer and D_2 is the demand for the other. The export supply curve is S. In this case the export cartel would charge two different prices—P_1 to one country and P^* to the other.[i]

THE PROBLEM FOR POOR COUNTRIES

It may well be that the export cartel members may not want to charge the true cartel price to all importers.In the wheat market at

[i]The problem of resale will be discussed in the next section.

the moment, through Public Law 480 and other means, a uniform price is not charged all importers. One such model, where importers are charged different prices according to ability to pay, is illustrated in Figure 4–11. The excess demand for the rich country importers is ED^r. The excess demand for the poor nations is ED^p. The domestic demand for the cartel nations is D_d, and the cartel supply curve is S. The solution shown is where the cartel charges the same price to the poor countries as to its own consumers. The solution to this problem is where the excess supply (excess to S and $D_d + ED^p$) crosses MR^r. The cartel will charge P^* to its domestic consumers and to the poor-country importers. It will export OX to these countries and OX^1 to the rich importers at a price P^r which is higher than P^*—the price charged to poor-country importers. The tax revenue collected is in the crosshatched area and is only collected from rich importers.

Clearly, this is *not* the short-run solution that maximizes welfare for the cartel. There is also the possibility of resale from the poor to the wealthy, and a scheme would have to be worked out to detect cheating. If ED^p is the true excess demand curve for the poor-country importers and ED^r the true excess demand for the rich, in a cheating situation the "cheating" excess demand for the poor would be to the left of ED^p and that for the rich would be to the left of ED^r. These would only be, of course, the excess curves facing the cartel.

STOCKS AND INTERRELATED COMMODITIES

In contrast to a commodity such as oil, grain production is stochastic in nature. Thus, the models above have to include stocks. This is no problem theoretically; it can be handled along the lines of Hueth and Schmitz (1972) and Bieri and Schmitz (1973). The problem in reality is to have a good prediction model so as to know when to build up stocks and when to release them. With perfect information, stocks can be used essentially to create a supply situation (in the marketplace) that is nonstochastic.

The above models also have to be complicated to incorporate more than one commodity. This has to be done in two directions. Wheat, feed grains, and other crops compete in some areas for the same acreage; thus, a cartel in wheat only, for example, has effects on feed grain production, while a cartel in both wheat and feed grains would imply different land uses. As well, livestock producers use

Figure 4–11. Nonuniform pricing among less developed and developed country importers

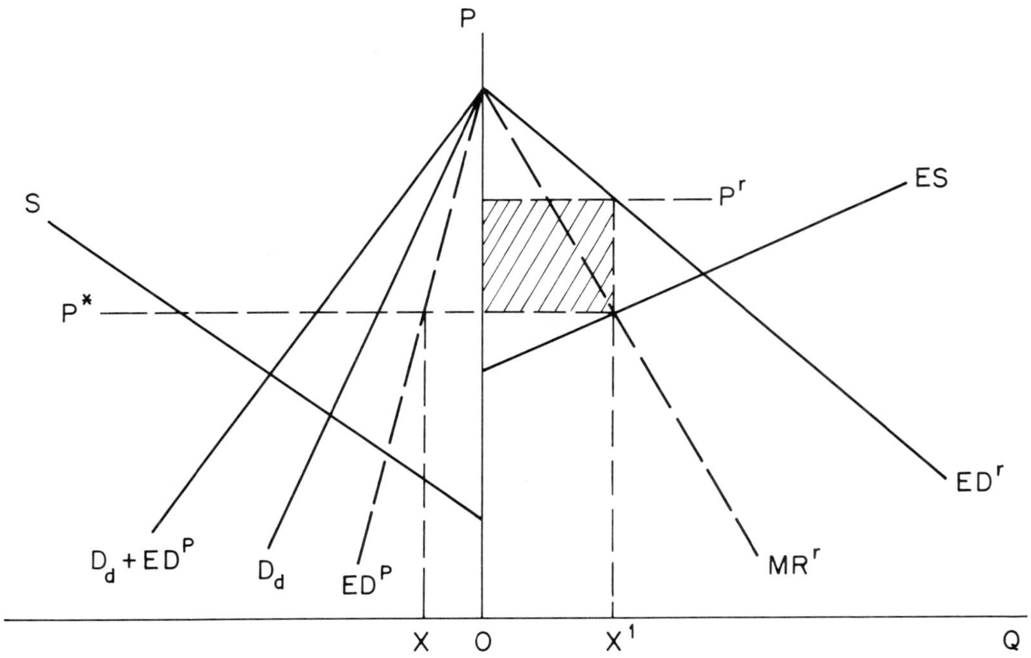

feed grains; hence, any change in the pricing of these grains directly due to an export cartel affects livestock producers. Whether prices would go up or down depends critically on the type of export cartel formed and on the way benefits are distributed. The theory developed earlier can easily incorporate these dimensions. This, however, does not solve the practical problems of forming and sustaining an export cartel.

THE CRUCIAL NATURE OF THE ASSUMPTIONS

In the above models it is assumed that the cartelists would be able to impose their price solution on previously existing competitive international markets. However, it may be unrealistic to start from such a premise. The grain trade may already be oligopolistic as suggested by McCalla (1966, forthcoming) and Alaouze, Watson, and Sturgess (1978). Both of these approaches are implicit cartel models in a seller's market, but they do not assume profit-maximizing behavior. A recent paper by Carter and Schmitz (1979) suggests that importing countries may be exerting some degree of monopsony power in international trade. Let us assume for the moment that the hypothesis of Carter and Schmitz is correct. What, then, would be the effect of an export cartel? Consider Figure 4–12 where, for simplicity, S is the export supply curve, D is the importer's demand curve, and P_f is the free trade price. Suppose the importer is exerting monopsony power in trade through a tariff and is paying exporters only P_p and charging consumers price P^*. The tariff revenue collected is the crosshatched area. Now if the exporters form a cartel and the importer does not retaliate, neither exports nor prices would change. The only difference would be that now the exporter would collect the revenue in the form of an export tax. (This would be true only if importers did not adjust their variable levies or quotas to counteract the export cartel. It is clear that the market structure prevailing at the beginning of the cartel could significantly influence outcomes.) Eventually, the two countries may agree on a free-trade policy (the joint welfare maximization solution). Thus, since the threat of an export cartel may well bring about an expansion of trade through trade liberalization, the ideal cartel, from an exporter's point of view, may never be implemented.

Figure 4–12. Export tax versus variable levy

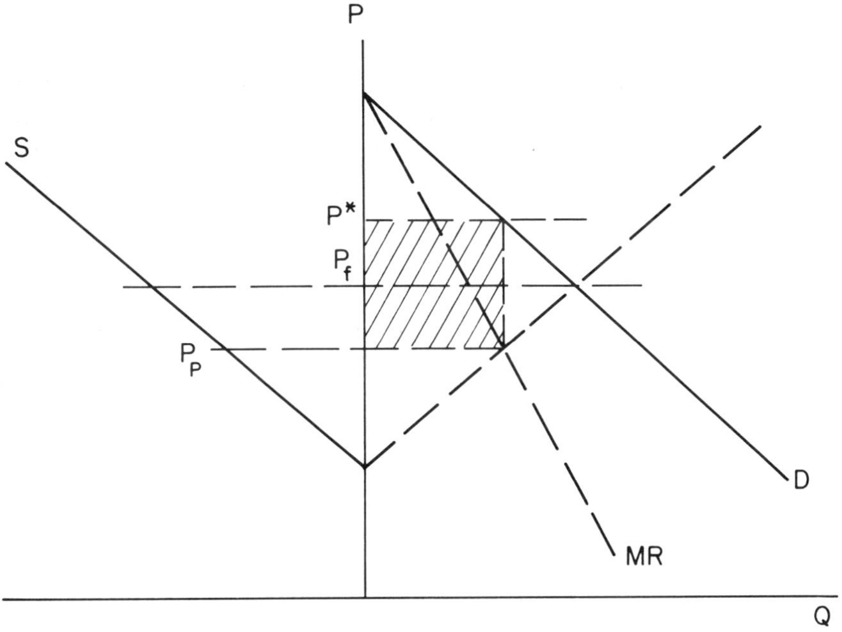

CONCLUSIONS

This chapter has focused on the theory of export cartels. On the basis of theory alone, one cannot determine whether a cartel in grains could become a reality, but theoretically it can be supported. For example, Caves (1979) recently argued that cartels in themselves are not unstable if rules are properly laid out before the cartel is formed. Penalties for cheating have to be present and enforced. The theory points out the problems which must be overcome before an export cartel would work and indicates some of the possible economic gains from an "effective" cartel. Also, the theory points out the possible forms that export cartels can take and who gains and who loses from such arrangements.

A crucial part of the theory is the demonstration that consumers in exporting countries can actually be made better off with an export cartel if the latter is of a government type rather than organized solely to maximize producer incomes. Consumers then should not oppose a government cartel arrangement. Producers may, however, oppose a government export cartel since they may actually lose from such an arrangement. Also, depending on the assumptions made about the existing market structure of the grain trade, under a cartel arrangement the volume traded and the prices charged in importing countries need not change a great deal from the present; only the tariff revenue now collected by importers would go to exporters. Theoretical considerations reveal that the assumptions made about the current structure of the market are crucial to determining the qualitative effects of implementing an export cartel.

An important point which emerges from this discussion is that if products are freely traded prior to the cartel's formation and if the cartel is to be effective, output has to be restricted and quota rules among exporters have to be established. If products are not freely traded, the mere threat of a cartel could result in an expansion of the volume of trade and increase producer prices and production in exporting countries by forcing importers to reduce trade barriers.

REFERENCES

Adelman, M.A. 1978. "Constraints on the World Oil Monopoly Price." *Resources and Energy* 1 (June): 3–19.

Alaouze, C.M.; A.S. Watson; and N.H. Sturgess. 1978. "Oligopoly Pricing in the World Wheat Market." *American Journal of Agricultural Economics* 60 (May): 173–185.

Bain, J.S. 1948. "Output Quotas in Imperfect Cartels." *Quarterly Journal of Economics* 62 (August): 617–622.

Batra, R.N. 1976. "The Theory of International Trade with an International Cartel or a Centrally Planned Economy." *Southern Economic Journal* 42 (January): 364–376.

Bieri, J., and A. Schmitz. 1973. "Export Instability, Monopoly Power, and Welfare." *Journal of International Economics* 3 (November): 389–396.

Carter, C., and A. Schmitz. 1979. "Import Tariffs and Price Formation in the World Wheat Market." *American Journal of Agricultural Economics* 61 (August): 517–522.

Carter, C.; N. Gallini; and A. Schmitz. 1980. "Producer-Consumer Trade-Offs in Export Cartels." *American Journal of Agricultural Economics.* 62 (November): 812–818.

Caves, R.E. 1979. "International Cartels and Monopolies in International Trade." In *International Economic Policy: Theory and Evidence,* edited by Dornbusch and J.A. Frenkel. Baltimore: Johns Hopkins University Press.

Comanor, W.S., and M.A. Schankerman. 1976. "Identical Bids and Cartel Behavior." *Bell Journal of Economics* 7 (Spring): 281–286.

Cremer, J., and M.L. Weitzman. 1976. "OPEC and the Monopoly Price of World Oil." *European Economic Review* 8 (August): 155–164.

Currie, J.M.; J.A. Murphy; and A. Schmitz.1971. "The Concept of Economic Surplus and Its Use in Economic Analysis." *Economic Journal* 81 (December): 741–799.

Duyne, C.V. 1975. "Commodity Cartels and the Theory of Derived Demand." *Kyklos* 28 (January): 597–612.

Eckbo, P.L. 1976. *The Future of World Oil.* Cambridge, Mass.: Ballinger Publishing Company.

Gilbert, R.J. and S.M. Goldman. 1978. "Potential Competition and the Monopoly Pricing of an Exhaustible Resource." *Journal of Economic Theory* 17 (April): 319–331.

Hryilicza, E., and R.S. Pindyck. 1976. "Pricing Policies for a Two-Part Exhaustible Resource Cartel: The Case of OPEC." *European Economic Review* 8 (August): 139–154.

Hueth, D., and A. Schmitz. 1972. "International Trade in Intermediate and Final Goods: Some Welfare Implications of Destabilized Prices." *Quarterly Journal of Economics* 86 (August): 351–365.

LaFrance, J.; A. Schmitz; and D. Zilberman. 1980. "The Small Dominant Firm." Giannini Foundation Working Paper No. 150, University of California, Berkeley. September.

McCalla, A.F. 1966. "A Duopoly Model of World Wheat Pricing." *Journal of Farm Economics* 48 (August):711–727.

———. "Structural and Market Power Considerations in Imperfect International Agricultural Markets." *Imperfect Markets in Agricultural Trade* A.F. McCalla, and T. Josling pp. 9–28 Montclair, N.J.: Allanheld Osmun and Co.

Mead, W.J. 1979. "An Economic Analysis of Crude Oil Price Behavior in the 1970s." *Journal of Energy and Development* 4 (Spring): 212–228.

Nichols, A.L., and R.J. Zeckhauser. 1977. "Stockpiling Strategies and Cartel Prices." *Bell Journal of Economics* 8 (Spring): 66–96.

Orr, D., and P.W. MacAvoy. 1965. "Price Strategies to Promote Cartel Stability." *Economica* 32 (May): 186–197.

Osborne, D.K. 1976. "Cartel Problems." *American Economic Review* 66 (December): 835–844.

Page, W.P., and K.O. Kymn. 1978. "Cartel Rivalry and the World Price of Oil: An Explanation." *Energy Communications* 4 (September): 129–141.

Pindyck, R.S. 1978. "Gains to Producers from Cartelization of an Exhaustible Resource." *Review of Economics and Statistics* 60 (May): 238–251.

———. 1979. "The Cartelization of International Commodity Markets." *American Economic Review* 69 (May): 154–158.

Salant, S.W. 1976. "Exhaustible Resources and Industrial Structure: A Nash-Cournot Approach to the World Oil Market." *Journal of Political Economy* 84 (October): 1079–1093.

Wolf, T.A. 1978. "The Theory of International Trade with an International Cartel or a Centrally Planned Economy: Comment." *Southern Economic Journal* 44 (April): 987–991.

5 THE ESTABLISHMENT AND OPERATION OF A GRAIN EXPORT CARTEL

In this chapter it is assumed that there are potential gains to grain exporters from the establishment and operation of a grain export cartel. That is, the conditions which yield monopoly rent, as discussed in the preceding chapter, are assumed to be satisfied. The purpose of this chapter is to discuss some of the issues involved in establishing and operating a grain export cartel. It focuses on the successes and failures of past cartels and highlights the importance of quota allocation and market share rules among exporters. Supply management is also discussed along with the types of institutions implied by an export cartel. For example, it may well be that different pricing institutions than currently exist are needed in order for an export cartel to be successful. Concerning cartels generally, there exists a small body of literature on the role of institutions. Osborne (1976), argues that a central purchasing agency cannot deal successfully with a cartel such as OPEC, largely because the central agency provides too much information to the cartel and thus helps keep the cartel together by avoiding cheating among members. Batra (1976), on the other hand, maintains that once an exporter or importer state trades by using a state-trading agency, the trading partners should also do so. This hypothesis raises the question as to whether or not the combination of private and public marketing used by grain exporters is optimal since, as pointed out earlier, most major importers state trade.

In discussing the outcome of a cartel, one must be careful not to fall into the habit of assuming that free trade currently exists in the grain trade. Understanding trade barriers and other market imperfections is very important. First, the potential gains from cartelization increase if prior to its formation, high barriers to trade and other market imperfections are present. Secondly, the existence of barriers affects the pricing strategy used by an exporter association.

SUCCESS AND FAILURE OF PAST CARTELS

It is customary for people to assume that cartels have not worked and will not work in the future. Many believed that OPEC would not work, but they were clearly wrong. In this section we briefly review cartels that have worked and those which have not and present reasons why some have failed—important insights if one is to avoid past mistakes.

There is a small but growing literature which has analyzed the actual experience of cartels. Eckbo (1976), in a comprehensive study of OPEC, includes a review of the analysis of fifty-one cartels. He found that nineteen of the fifty-one arrangements were "successful" in raising prices 200 percent above costs of production and distribution. The median duration of successful cartels was 4.0 years and the average duration, 6.6 years. Eckbo concluded:

> Cartels were able to raise prices for four years or more, where *concentration* of production was high, *demands inelastic,* the cartel's *market share* was high, the membership had *cost advantages* over outsiders, and governments did not get involved in the cartel (1976:26).

Behrman (1977), in reviewing the work of Eckbo and others, concluded:

> The successful efforts seemed to be sustained longer where concentration of production was high, demand was price inelastic, the members' market share was high, the members had cost advantages over outsiders, and governments were not involved in operations. Successful agreements broke down most often due to competition among members, with competition from nonmembers being the second most common cause (1977:23).

Finally Behrman, in his own simulation analysis of commodity agreement proposals of the United Nations Conference on Trade and Development (UNCTAD), concludes that price stabilization is a more easily accomplishable objective than a price increase. In the latter case, he argues that it would be extremely difficult for a cartel to materially change long-term secular price trends. Contrary to Eckbo's finding, Behrman suggests that strong government commitment to a cartel should improve its chances.

The early literature on cartels developed in the 1930s and 1940s was almost always couched in terms of manufactured products where control over production was possible because production units were large and output was not subject to random variability. More recent literature has devoted emphasis to primary product cartels (Pindyck 1978; Salant 1976). This literature differentiates between nonrenewable resource cartels (for example, OPEC) and renewable resource cartels. Clearly, it is much easier to deal with the former where one can assume a fixed supply of a resource, thereby leaving the basic problem as the time rate of exploitation. Salant (1976), in a recent article, has presented a theoretically complete analysis of exhaustible resource cartels. The additional difficulties of a renewable resource cartel where supply is variable, particularly in the long run, are not easily solved. Geer (1971), in an analysis of the world coffee market, finds it difficult to determine long-run conditions for a successful cartel. If one now adds the two additional factors relevant to grains—namely, that there are thousands of small, independent producers and that the vast majority of production is domestically consumed—the problems of organizing a cartel are theoretically more complicated.

The question of enforcement is equally difficult. It is frequently argued that successful cartels contain the seeds of their own destruction. If a cartel is formed and succeeds in raising prices by restricting output, presumably for the collective benefit of members, the temptation to defect is great. If one member leaves an effective cartel, presumably he is able to benefit from higher prices without the cost of supply reduction. Therefore, he is better off outside the cartel provided that the cartel remains in force and members do not retaliate. But if it is profitable for one to leave, it must also be profitable for others to do so; thus, the cartel breaks down. This is the so-called free-rider problem.

In a recent comprehensive review of cartels and monopolies in international trade, however, Caves (1979) argues that the breakdown of a cartel because of the free-rider problem is not inherent in the nature of cartels but, rather, represents an incomplete cartel arrangement from the outset. He maintains that it is theoretically possible to design a cartel agreement so that the explicit penalties for desertion always make it preferable for a member to stay in the cartel, but some of the conditions suggested, such as firm takeover and punitive pricing, may not be possible when the cartel members are sovereign states.

Caves' principal reference in this regard is Osborne (1976), discussed earlier, who argues that, if a cartel is able to locate the contract surface and pick up a point on the contract curve (the sharing problem), it is possible to devise a quota retaliation rule which makes it unprofitable for a member to cheat, provided that the market-sharing vector selected exhibits "the ray property." If these conditions are met, Osborne asserts, the basic problem remaining for the cartel members is the detection of cheating.

MARKET SHARES AND QUOTA ALLOCATION

As suggested above, successful cartels require the restriction and proper management of output; the cartel has to devise enforceable quota rules which allocate supplies among cartel members. The successful cartels, such as OPEC, seem to have resolved this problem.

Table 5–1 gives data on wheat market shares for the major exporters—the United States, Canada, and Australia. Notice how the U.S. share increased during the early 1970s. The factors giving rise to this have been discussed by McCalla and Schmitz (1979). The reasons included differences in government policy among countries, varying degrees of investment in grain transportation facilities, and weather.

It is important to interpret the data in a historical perspective because of its direct bearing on the issue of quota allocation among countries. In the past, partly in response to existing trade barriers, countries such as Canada and the United States have generally managed and curtailed grain production. For example, Canada has limited grain production via production quotas, and acreage controls have been used in the United States. These policies have been used

Table 5-1. World wheat market shares, 1965-66 to 1976-77

Year	*Total World Exports (mmt)*[a]	*Market Shares*[b] *Australia*	*Canada*	*U.S.*	*Total of Three*[b]
1965-66	62.0	9.2	23.9	37.7	70.8
1966-67	55.8	12.5	26.5	35.8	74.8
1967-68	51.2	13.7	17.4	39.5	70.6
1968-69	45.7	11.8	19.0	32.2	63.0
1969-70	50.7	14.4	17.8	32.5	64.7
1970-71	54.3	17.5	21.4	36.5	75.4
1971-72	52.5	16.6	26.1	32.2	74.9
1972-73	68.3	8.2	22.8	46.9	77.9
1973-74	63.1	8.7	18.5	49.3	76.5
1974-75	63.4	12.6	17.7	44.6	74.9
1975-76	66.5	12.2	18.2	47.4	77.8
1976-77 (prelim.)	61.8	13.6	20.9	42.7	77.2

[a]Million metric tons.

[b]All figures given in percentages.

Source: Computed from International Wheat Council. 1978. *World Wheat Statistics.* Geneva.

without explicit agreement among the countries on what type of policy to use and the extent to which production should be reduced. Thus, in part, the data in Table 5–1 reflect differences in government policy aimed at reducing grain supplies.

Note how the market-share percentages change from year to year in large part due to the differences in production because of weather. Even though the percentages change, there is no reason why an agreement on shares could not be reached among exporters once the export price was agreed upon and, with it, the corresponding exports. For example, if exports had to be reduced below the past five-year average, the three countries could determine market shares on the basis of using a percentage of the past five-year average of shares. Adjustments would have to be made, as alredy pointed out, for weather phenomena. More elaborate quota rules could be devised along the lines recently suggested by Osborne (1976).

The issue of quota allocation among counties also has been

discussed in the context of the existing structure of the international grain market. Part of the historical supply management problem discussed above was a result of the large trade barriers existing in grain markets. Thus, the extent to which supplies have to be managed among exporters partly depends on how importers respond to a cartel. The threat of a cartel may cause them to remove or lower trade barriers if the exporters promise not to impose their ideal cartel, with the result that both the volume of trade and production would increase. This would result in less of a supply management problem among exporters than has often existed in the past.

To illustrate the above point, consider Figure 5–1 where ES is the excess supply curve of the export cartel members and ED is the excess demand by importers. Suppose that under the current system importers are pricing internally at price P_1, paying exporters P_2, and collecting the crosshatched area as tariff revenue. Supply had to be managed among exporters at Q_1 when the importers were buying at P_2 by the use of import tariffs. At the other extreme, an export cartel would price at P_1 and collect the crosshatched area as an export tax—

Figure 5–1. Supply management under a cartel

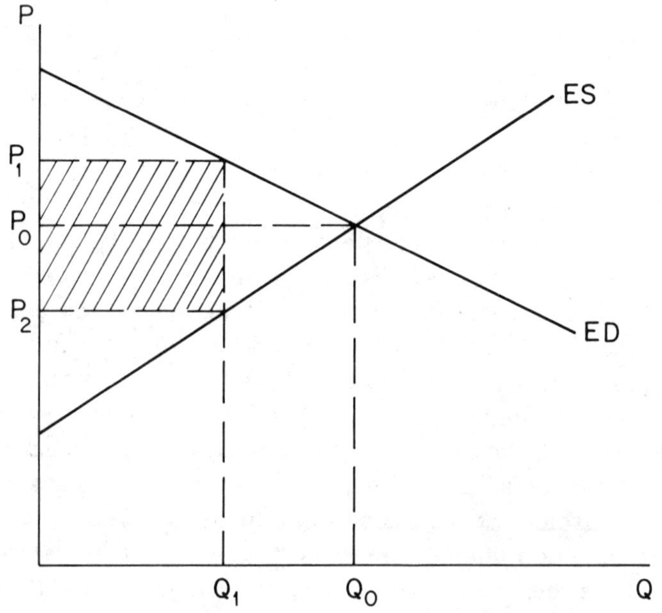

reversing the power in the marketplace. Notice that the quantity exported has not changed, so neither would the supply management mechanism have to change. However, the countries might agree on free trade or close to it (Q_0 in Figure 5–1) if the importers feel that the exporters are serious about a cartel. If this is the case, it seems probable that the supply management problem for exporters would be less severe than in the past, especially during the 1960s. To repeat, the severity of the quota allocation problem among exporters, depends to a large extent on how the importers would respond to an export cartel. This subject, discussed in the next chapter, should be seriously studied before proposing a grain export cartel. There is no reason, a priori, why the problem of allocating supplies among members needs to pose a serious threat to a grain export cartel.

From Table 5–1, we see that the United States, Canada, and Australia account for nearly 80 percent of world wheat exports. In feed grains, (shown in Table 5–1) the United States alone accounts for well over 60 percent. In either case, an export cartel effective in raising prices would bring about a gain to those exporters who would not join the cartel—the free-rider problem.[a] There is probably no way of getting all exporters to form a cartel, but, on the basis of the experience of past cartels, if 80 percent of exports are sold through cartel members, the free-rider problem does not pose a serious difficulty to the success of an export cartel. It appears that on the basis of past market shares, the United States, Canada, and Australia have a sufficient market share to form a cartel that would yield potential gains, and that the United States alone could probably manage a cartel in feed grains.[b]

SUPPLY MANAGEMENT

As already suggested, one of the key issues surrounding an export cartel is the management of supplies among exporters. This section deals with some of the important features of this problem but leaves to a later section the discussion of the type of institution or mechanism needed to handle these aspects of the cartel.

[a]As discussed in Chapter 3, France may be such a country with respect to wheat.

[b]One must remember that in industrial organization theory, once four-firm concentration in an industry approaches 70 percent, price leadership and imperfect competition are suggested.

Exports to Poor Countries

For political and other reasons, exporters might want to sell to poor countries at a price below what they would charge developed country importers. The solution to this problem has been worked out theoretically in Chapter 4. Such a model can be viewed as one which contains a commercial market along with a Public Law 480 component.

A problem which may arise with a multiple-price export cartel is that the poor countries may resell the product to the wealthy nations at a higher price than that which they paid for it—the resale problem. However, some experts consider that the size of ships now carrying grain would ensure that ships traveling from poor to rich countries could be easily spotted.[c] In addition, exporters could attach severe penalties for cheating which would deter low-income countries from attempting resale.

In 1980, the United States blocked grain shipments to the Soviet Union in response to the invasion of Afghanistan. Some have argued that the embargo was only mildly effective because the Soviet Union obtained grain from other major exporters. If so, however, the issue concerns other exporters not going along with the embargo rather than the resale issue discussed above. An export cartel, of which the embargo would be a component, requires cooperation among exporters. In an effective cartel, cheating could be detected easily because all the major exporters, through a common bookkeeping scheme, would know whether or not abnormally large purchases were being made by allies of the Soviet Union for resale.

Perhaps the most important factor which stands in the way of operating an effective cartel is politics. Historically, Canada has traded with the Soviet Union and mainland China when the United States has been unwilling to do so. On this issue, some agreement would have to be worked out among cartel members.

External Versus Internal Management

Once exporters agree on the volume to export and the prices to charge, they have essentially solved the external supply management

[c]Dr. L. Kristjanson of the Canadian Wheat Board pointed out to the authors that the current mode of ocean grain shipping would, in his opinion, deter cheating by poor countries.

problem. Internally, however, the exporters may pursue different supply management strategies; some may use acreage controls, while others may use production quotas if, in fact, they are needed. Also, some countries might want to pursue a feed grain policy which maintained low grain prices for the livestock sector. In this case, production controls may not have to be implemented.

The livestock sector, as emphasized in earlier chapters, is an integral part of any proposal to establish a grain cartel. The grain and livestock sectors are closely intertwined since the livestock sector is a substantial user of feed grains. In the past, many government policies have only focused on the grain sector, though indirectly the livestock sector has been affected. (For instance, large reserves in the 1960s, unlike the 1970s, created stability for the livestock sector.) Because of the importance of meat in terms of food expenditures by consumers in exporting countries, a substantial increase in feed grain prices in the export market without an accompanying policy to hold down prices domestically is politically unfeasible. In this connection, a government export cartel, discussed earlier, or some variation of it (where the domestic sector is protected) has more appeal than does a producer cartel.

Consider Figure 5–2 where the optimal export cartel is established but optimal internal supply management for the domestic market demand is not followed. In Figure 5–2, the domestic demand and supply are given by D_d and D_s. The foreign demand and supply are D_f and S_f. The free-trade price is P_f. First, consider the export tax solution where the price charged to importers increases to P^*. If the importer does not retaliate and *if* the crosshatched area is not given to domestic producers, producer price drops to P_p and output drops by ΔX. Here there is *no* quota or allocation problem among growers since P_p is the true supply price: the supply management problem arises when the export tax revenue is distributed to producers. This is because the "real" price that producers receive is higher than P_p. In this case the only way output can be maintained at $0X$ is through the use of acreage controls or production quotas. If not, production would expand beyond $0X$. However, the market could still be cleared. An export tax could still be charged, but prices domestically would have to fall below P_P to clear the market. For example, rather than price at P_P on the demand curve, the clearing price in the absence of quotas might be P_0 which is below P_P. As a result, an export cartel can work even if it is not accompanied by supply management for the domestic market,

Figure 5–2. Internal supply management

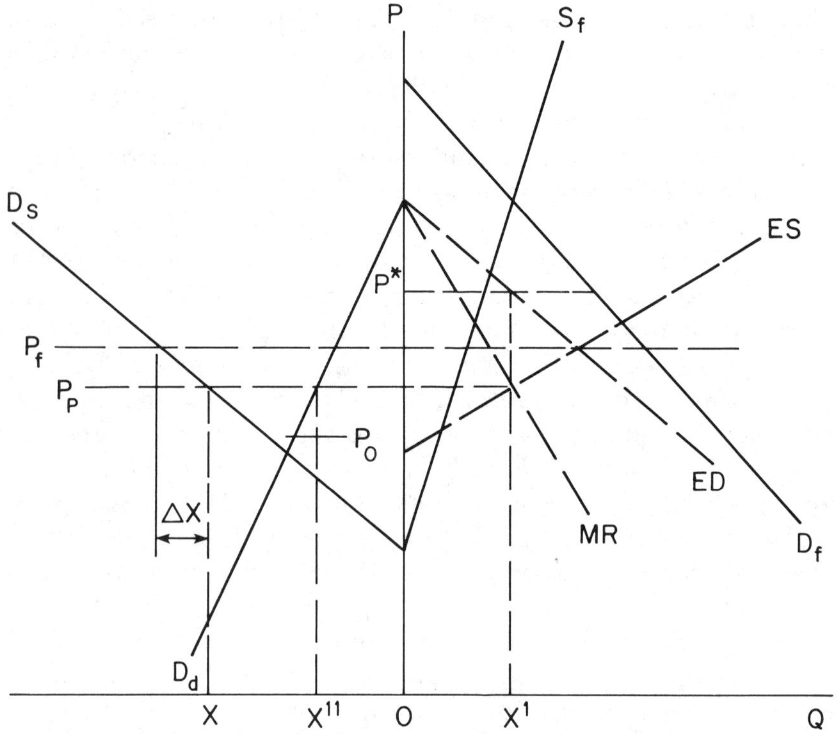

although the ideal cartel also requires regulating production for the domestic market.

The distinction between internal and external supply management is crucial since each country in the cartel may want to pursue different internal pricing policies. Currently, Canada—with its feed grain policy and two-price system—operates differently from the United States. This is also true in the use of production quotas.

In summary, the export cartel management problem is to export $0X^1$ in Figure 5–2 and collectively charge price P^*. How $0X^1$ is allocated among exporters depends on the quota rule established and is the external management problem. A cartel must resolve that problem in order to be minimally successful. Supply sold in the domestic market (that is, the internal markets in the exporting countries) does not have to be restricted to $0X^{11}$ for the cartel to be successful even though $0X^{11}$ is the ideal quantity to sell domestically.

Exporters can vary the degree of output control for the internal market. This would partly depend on, among other things, the relative importance of the livestock sector.

Stocks

Another relevant issue is the management of stocks. An initial distinction must be made between stocks that result from weather phenomena and stocks that build up because of excess production. The latter can occur without changes in weather patterns if the supply price is greater than what the market can absorb at that price. Figure 5–2 clarifies this distinction. If the cartel exports $0X^1$ and the producers are paid P_P plus the tariff revenue, there will be an excess supply situation if consumers are charged P_P and output is not restricted by any means; this excess supply occurs even if all the demand and supply relationships are nonstochastic. The problem for the cartel is to agree on output and to try to meet this target by the use of stocks. In certain years, due to the stochastic nature of production, output will be greater than the ideal cartel output, and in other years it will be less. If stocks are to be used, they should be used to create price stability—not as a means of taking excess production off the market. They should be used in addition to production controls if the latter are needed to make the cartel effective.

Before arguing that stock management is a needed and vital component of a successful export cartel, however, one must consider carefully the controversial issue of who gains and who loses from stability. Hueth and Schmitz (1972) and Just, Lutz, Schmitz, and Turnovsky (1977, 1978) have recently researched the question of why stocks should be used at all to create price stability, and the results are not clearcut. Generally, countries taken together gain from stability, but importers seem to gain more than exporters, while producers in exporting countries may have the most to lose from price stabilization policies.

Members of the cartel would have to have some stock rule built into their quota allocation procedure. As an example, suppose that in a given year the United States, which is to provide 50 percent of the export volume, has an extremely bad crop that cannot be offset by its stocks on hand. If Canada, for example, has a good crop, part of the deficit in the U.S. share could be made up with extra shipments from Canada. Thus, when devising a quota rule for sharing output among export members, stocks have to be considered explicitly.

A Multiple-Commodity Cartel

How one manages supply depends partly on the nature of the cartel. One could envision a wheat cartel only, a feed grain cartel only, or a cartel that combines both. Clearly, a combined cartel would look quite different from one that focuses only on wheat or feed grains. As an example, suppose a cartel in wheat only were established. In the absence of tight production controls, there would be an increase in feed grain utilization both from wheat production and from expanded feed grain production on unused wheat acreage. This would cause an expansion in trade in feed grains due to the lower price and expanded production. However, if a cartel were formed in both wheat and feed grains, theoretically, at least, exports of *both* wheat and feed grains would contract.

The impact that either type of cartel would have on the domestic livestock sector largely depends on the internal supply management policy pursued. Feed grain prices could actually drop domestically even with a feed grain export cartel if internal supply were not controlled. At this juncture, it is important to recall the distinction between a producer export cartel and a government export cartel, which was discussed in detail in a theoretical paper on cartels by Carter, Gallini, and Schmitz (1980). If an export cartel were set up by grain producers for their own interest, they would restrict domestic supply so that domestic grain prices for livestock users would actually increase over what they would be in a free-trade situation with no production controls. On the other hand, the organization of a government export cartel would result in lower domestic feed grain prices than under free trade because supply would be managed differently under a government export cartel than under a producer export cartel.

THE ROLE OF STATE AND PRIVATE SECTORS

The role of the state and private sectors in the grain trade cannot be overemphasized in a discussion of grain export cartels. Trade takes place within a society in which there are producers, consumers, government, and marketing entities—both private and public. The extent to which private and public agencies are involved in the grain trade has been discussed in general terms in Chapter 2. As illustrated, state trading (in terms of overall price setting) is becoming increasingly important, although state-trading exporters almost never become directly involved in the logistical problems of grain handling. Thus, the private sector not only negotiates and carries out sales but is also involved in carrying out the shipping and other logistical features (not the overall pricing) for such marketing boards as the Canadian Wheat Board; this has recently been documented in a marketing system comparison study by McCalla and Schmitz (1979). Thus, the private sector is involved in more of the world grain trade than that which emanates directly from the United States.

Studies by Bieri and Schmitz (1973) and Just, Schmitz, and Zilberman (1979) have shown that pricing policies and welfare implications can be quite different under various types of marketing institutions. This is especially true if a marketing board organized for producers maximizes producer returns while the private sector seeks to obtain the greatest return to shareholders. One of the key differences between the two outcomes is that the private sector prefers price instability, while the marketing board arrangement favors price stability. Carter, Gallini, and Schmitz (1980) as well have recently shown that the private grain trade opposes a grain export cartel because of the reduced volume of exports likely to result and the increased role of state trading in the actual pricing of the commodity. With regard to institutions involved in international trade, Batra (1976) suggests that exporters which are market economies cannot adequately deal with state-trading monopolies due to the latter having superior information. This would imply that for a cartel to be formed among exporters, the U.S. government would have to set up a marketing export board or central selling agency which would have, at a minimum, the power to negotiate prices. This solves the problem of the imposition of export taxes which are, at least for the United States, perhaps unconstitutional. Such an agency, by cooperating with those in Canada and Australia, could also negotiate with the Japanese and the EEC, for example, to remove barriers to trade so perhaps at least a free-trade regime could be agreed upon rather than the trade arrangement that currently exists. (In this case, neither the export cartel solution nor the current import tariff solution would be in effect.)

To motivate the institutional issue further, suppose one starts with the assumption presented in Chapter 2 that some of the major importers are exerting monopsony power in trade by imposing such devices as tariffs. If this is true, how did it come about? How did the importers get the upper hand? What it says is that the exporters were generally "price takers" through time, and that prices were set by importers. The pricing mechanism seems to run something like this: the EEC offers to buy a certain quantity of wheat at a certain C.I.F. (cost, insurance, and freight) price which is below its threshold price. The private grain trade or boards, such as the Canadian Wheat Board, either offer to sell at that price or counteroffer. Except for unusual circumstances, the offer price accepted by the exporters is well below the EEC target price. Why does this have to be the case? Why could the exporters not set a minimum price which would be, for example, the EEC threshold price? Do exporters lack economic know-how, or is there a problem due to the pricing mechanism among exporters?

One hypothesis is that since the private firms are interested in margins and the volume of trade—not in absolute prices—and since they dominate the marketing scene, there is no reason for them to hold out for higher prices. For example, if the private sector can buy wheat from producers at $3.00 per bushel and sell to the EEC at $4.50 per bushel at a volume of 100 million bushels, this is a better arrangement for them than having a cartel restrict trade (or have volume restricted regardless of the type of institutions due to higher export prices) to, say, 75 million bushels and have the margin stay the same.

In view of the above, is it because of the private sector that the importers have obtained an upper hand in the pricing of grains? Obviously, this is a complex issue as is the related subject concerning the type of institutions needed for a cartel to work.

CARTEL INSTRUMENTS AND INSTITUTIONS

There are several types of institutions which could be used to implement an export cartel. The type of cartel instrument to use depends on many factors, among which are: (1) the degree of competitiveness in international grain markets; (2) political acceptability; (3) the objective of the cartel; (4) anticipated response by importers; and (5) the time horizon of the export cartel. An example of the importance of these will suffice. Suppose, for example, policymakers perceive that markets are highly imperfect partly due to trade barriers, and they expect that importers would remove these barriers if they thought exporters were serious about implementing a cartel. In this case, if satisfied with the free-trade outcome, it is likely that only minimum government intervention among exporters would be required. The governments would set a uniform minimum price below which the EEC, Japan, and other importers could not buy.

There is also involved in the choice of instruments the question of short-run versus long-term strategy. For example, even though initially a particular cartel instrument is chosen, it does not mean that it should not be changed through time. In fact, it should be changed if "learning by doing" in response to dealing with importers is properly incorporated into the process of optimally choosing cartel instruments.

Three specific cartel instruments or institutions are now presented in Table 5–2 and discussed. The export tax is probably the easiest to implement. The revenue would be collected by the government, pooled, and paid to producers on a monthly or bimonthly basis according to their sales during that time period.[d] In the United States, pricing would be handled by the private trade, while the boards in Australia and Canada could still price by the methods they currently use. The governments would set the export tax and manage internal supplies. As previously discussed, the extent to which output would be restricted would depend on, among other things, how low exporters wanted internal prices to fall.

The question of the legality of forming an export cartel has recently been discussed by Tredennick (1978). In addition, Groenewegen and Cochrane (1980) have discussed the legality of the export tax in reference to their recent proposal for increasing stability:

> Export levies are a form of export tax and the latter are considered unconstitutional. Article 1, Section 9, Clause 5 of the U.S. Constitution

[d]One equitable way to distribute the tax revenue is to have a record of the total bushel sales of each producer and pay a higher price on the aggregate percentage of sales that go to export. As an example, suppose a producer sold 15,000 bushels of wheat, and 50 percent of the total U.S. wheat crop was sold in the export market. In this case the farmer would receive a higher price on 7,500 bushels. The above problem, which is important to keep in mind, will occur only if government sets the export tax and leaves the private trade to carry out the actual marketing.

Table 5-2. Cartel institutions, production controls, and prices

Type of Institution	*Role of the Private Trade*	*Production Controls*	*Prices*	*Producer or Government Cartel*
Export tax	Pricing and logistical function, including transportation	Government-imposed (e.g., acreage controls)	Fluctuate daily making marketing decisions crucial	Government cartel
Producer marketing board	Logistical function, including transportation	Board-imposed (e.g., production and delivery quotas)	Pooled prices; the timing of marketing not crucial	Producer cartel
Government central selling agency	Logistical function, including transportation	Government-imposed (e.g., acreage controls)	Pooled prices or daily pricing	Government cartel

> states that "No Tax or Duty shall be laid on Articles Exported from any State" (U.S. Code, Annotated). Where there was a proper exercise by Congress of its power to regulate commerce, it has been held that the export clause did not limit such power (American Law Reports). The case of Moon (Appellent) v. Freeman (Secretary of Agriculture) et al., exemplifies the point. Moon contended that the purchase of export wheat marketing certificates (under the Agricultural Act of 1964) was analogous to an export tax and prohibited by the Constitution. "Overruling Moon's contention, the court interpreted the Statute (Agriculture Act of 1964) as an exercise by Congress of its power to regulate commerce under the Constitution, which is not to be limited by the constitutional prohibition against taxation of exports. The court stated that the purpose of the statute was to induce producers to comply with crop controls and to regulate the price of wheat reaching both the domestic and foreign markets" (American Law Reports). Export controls which have a similar effect as export taxes on prices and amount exported are not prohibited by the Constitution. Under the auspices of the Export Administration Act of 1969 the Congress declared that it is "the policy of the United States to use export controls to the extent necessary to protect the domestic economy from the excessive drain of scarce materials and to reduce the inflationary impact of abnormal foreign demand" (U.S. Code Service). The purpose of the export levy in this proposal is to regulate domestic price and to reduce the inflationary impact of abnormal foreign demand. The ruling on the case of Moon v. Freeman and the legality of export controls to protect domestic interests serves as a precedent for arguing that the export levies in this proposal should not be considered unconstitutional (1980: 809–810).

Given that a cartel, if properly designed, would reduce instability for the U.S. market by, for example, placing some of the instability burden on the EEC, Japan, and the Soviet Union, the optimal export tax form of a cartel may well be legal. The courts, however, would have to decide.

The establishment of a marketing board would be a drastic departure from existing institutions in the United States, even though it is the system used by Canada and Australia. The private sector would then carry out only the logistical aspects of the trade but would not negotiate the initial buyer–seller price. The board would impose delivery quotas, as is now done by the Canadian and Australian boards, and collect the export tax which is built into the board's asking price. Prices would be pooled on a yearly basis. Thus, unlike the case of export taxing, the timing of sales by producers is not crucial.

If a government central selling agency were instituted, it would, at a minimum, set a price below which the private trading companies could not buy. At the extreme, it would negotiate the initial buyer–seller price. The government, furthermore, would also manage internal supplies. The central selling agency could "pool" prices for an entire year, as in the board case, or have producers' receipts fluctuate daily. In the latter case, as with export taxes, the timing of sales by producers is critical.

Of the three institutions discussed, the producer marketing board would probably come closest to the theoretical producer export cartel, while the other two alternatives would yield outcomes resembling the theoretical government export cartel. However, we are not implying that a change in the way grain is currently marketed by exporters will necessarily alter the bargaining power of buyers and sellers. For example, it may well be a necessary condition for the successful operation of a grain export cartel that the United States introduce a marketing board or central selling agency or, at a minimum, set some floor below which export prices cannot fall. The sufficient condition is, however, that the exporting countries cooperate in their export pricing policies; if they do not, then changing only the marketing institutions in a given country will not bring about an effective export cartel.

In the previous discussion, two of the cartel models involved either a producer marketing board or a government central selling agency as the key element in the price formation process. In either case, the private sector would carry out transactions once the initial or minimum prices were determined by the nonprivate sector. The impact of such a system on the efficiency of the current marketing situation is difficult to assess since it raises the familiar debate concerning the relative performances of the private and public sectors. This subject was addressed by McCalla and Schmitz (1979) in a comparison of the U.S. and Canadian systems, but no conclusive results were reached.

Some points worth keeping in mind when comparing the marketing efficiency of the public and private sectors are demonstrated in Figure 5–3. Suppose that under the public system, the price and quantity are $P_O Q_O$ where S is the supply curve including marketing costs. Now suppose that the private sector is more efficient, which shifts the supply to S^1. It is clear that even if the private sector behaves as a monopolist, producers and consumers need not be

Figure 5–3. Public marketing and the private system

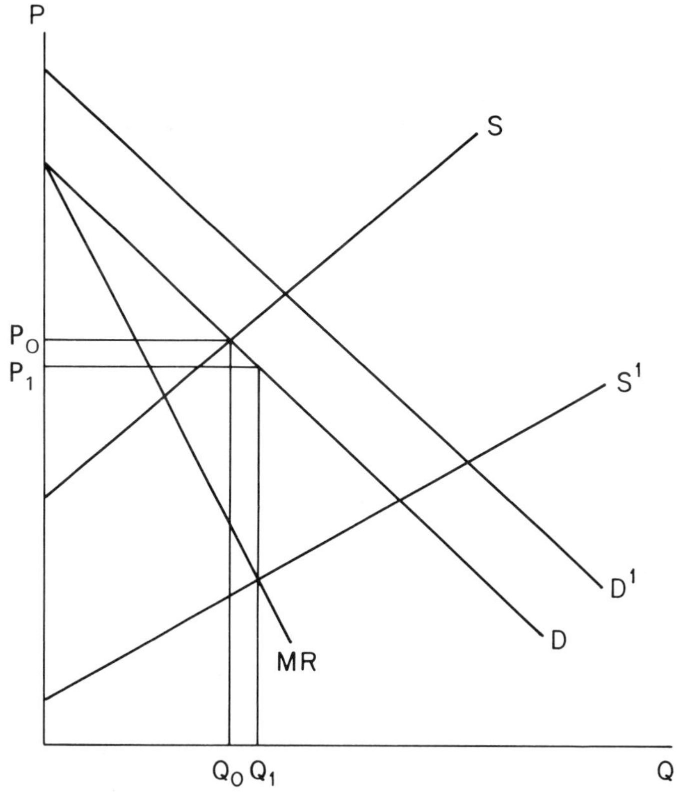

worse off. Also, if the private sector is more aggressive in marketing (so that under the private system, demand is D^1 instead of D), this is an added gain for producers, which makes them better off than under a board arrangement even if the private sector is noncompetitive. If the opposite is true (that is, D and S are the schedules under the private sector), clearly the public system is preferable.

These points are worth considering since it is quite possible that if the private sector were no longer able to price grain, it would shift resources out of the grain business into other areas of activity. At the extreme, this would mean that government would have to take over the shipping and other logistical features of the trade, and there is no a priori way of knowing how efficient such a system would be. At least it should be remembered that while the board system works reasonably well for Canada, the volume and number of different types of grains shipped are much less than in the United States. This difference may or may not cause serious problems for the operation of a marketing board or central selling agency in the United States.

The above discussion of cartel instruments ignores the effects of exchange rates on the real income of the agricultural sector. The cartel instruments are possible devices to improve the position of agriculture and the general economy in grain-exporting countries where the improper use of monetary policy and its effects on exchange rates could well be a reason why export cartels have been seriously proposed. (Some reasons have already been given, including the use of monopsony power by importers.) In an interesting paper, Schuh (1974) has argued that the farm problem (that is, low farm incomes) during most of the 1950s and 1960s was partly due to overvaluation of the U.S. dollar. An overvalued dollar reduces exports and stimulates imports.

Table 5–3 presents data on the overvalued dollar phenomenon. Note how since 1952 the parity ratio generally declined (indicating a loss of purchasing power by farmers) until 1973. The value of commodity credit corporation stocks increased at least during the 1960s as did acreage diversion. Also, government support payments increased rapidly during the 1960s. Schuh (1974) contends that policies such as price supports during parts of the 1950s and 1960s were partly in response to an overvalued dollar. In other words, had the dollar been devalued, the need for such programs would have been greatly reduced.

In view of the above, one could add exchange rates as another possible cartel instrument in that it should be adjusted first before export taxes, central selling agencies, and the like are used. The standard outcomes of cartel theory improve exporters' welfare as does devaluing the dollar when it is overvalued.

CONCLUSIONS

This chapter has presented some of the issues relevant to the establishment and operation of a grain export cartel. Clearly, there is no way a priori that one can dismiss the notion of a cartel as unworkable. One thing, though, is clear from the chapter: interest groups, such as private traders, will try to block an export cartel in

Table 5-3. Selected data on U.S. agriculture, 1952-1978

Year	*CCC Stocks Owned by Government (Millions of Dollars)*	*Government Payments*	*Acreage Diversion (Million Acres)*	*Parity Ratio*
1952	946	275		100
1953	2,415	213		92
1954	3,951	257		89
1955	5,604	229		84
1956	5,323	554	13.6	83
1957	4,791	1,016	27.8	82
1958	4,692	1,089	27.1	85
1959	6,408	682	22.5	81
1960	6,079	702	28.7	80
1961	5,248	1,493	53.7	79
1962	5,271	1,747	64.7	80
1963	5,023	1,696	56.1	78
1964	4,611	2,181	55.5	76
1965	4,110	2,463	57.4	77
1966	2,340	3,277	63.3	80
1967	1,005	3,079	40.8	74
1968	1,064	3,462	49.3	73
1969	1,784	3,794	58.0	74
1970	1,594	3,717	57.1	72
1971	1,118	3,145	37.2	70
1972	830	3,961		74
1973	394	2,607		91
1974	188	531		85
1975	402	809		76
1976	634	734		72
1977	1,104	1,819		66
1978	1,186	3,030		70
1979	1,237	4697		71
1980	2,802	6349		64

Sources: U.S. Department of Agriculture. *Agricultural Statistics* (various issues). Also: Schuh, G.E. 1974. "The Exchange Rate and U.S. Agriculture." *American Journal of Agricultural Economics* 56 (February): 6.

grains since such an arrangement would not appear to be in their best interests.

A problem of supply management among cartel members often is discussed as the key barrier to the success of a cartel. This does not seem to pose serious threats because under a cartel arrangement the volume of exports may not change a great deal since free trade currently does not exist in grains. Also, the United States has a large share of the feed grain exports; and the United States, Canada, and Australia have a large share of the wheat market. Hence, a cartel in grains is relatively easy to form because a few countries make up a large percentage of exports. Also, the livestock industry is a heavy user of feed grains in exporting countries. Opposition from this group to a grain export cartel can be avoided if pricing strategies are pursued by the cartel which recognize this sector. An export cartel in grains need not adversely affect the livestock sectors in the exporting countries; its effect depends on the type of policy the exporters want to follow with regard to pricing grains for internal demand.

In theorizing about cartels, perhaps the most important issue for exporters is what they want the cartel to accomplish. Do they want the cartel to help grain producers, livestock producers, or consumers in general? The distinction between a government export cartel and a producer export cartel has to be made since the type of pricing and supply management for a government cartel can be quite different from that of a producer export cartel. This problem is not relevant to an oil cartel because domestic demand for oil is relatively unimportant. This issue over the trade offs between producers and consumers could become problematic, for example, between the United States and Canada. In the United States "consumerism" is relatively more pervasive than in Canada. As a result, a producer cartel would likely be pursued by Canada and a government cartel pursued by the United States. If this were the case, substantial compromises would have to be made among the exporting nations.

REFERENCES

Batra, R.N. 1976. "The Theory of International Trade with an International Cartel or a Centrally Planned Economy."*Southern Economic Journal* 42 (January): 364–376.

Behrman, J.R. 1977. *International Commodity Agreements: An Evaluation of the UNCTAD Integrated Commodity Program.* Monograph No. 9. Washington, D.C.: Overseas Development Council.

Bieri, J., and A. Schmitz. 1973. "Export Instability, Monopoly Power, and Welfare." *Journal of International Economics* 3 (November): 389–396.

Carter, C.; N. Gallini; and A. Schmitz. 1980. "Producer-Consumer Trade-Offs in Export Cartels." *American Journal of Agricultural Economics* 62 (November): 812–818.

Caves, R.E. 1979. "International Cartels and Monopolies in International Trade." In *International Economic Policy: Theory and Evidence,* edited by R. Dornbusch and J.A. Frenkel. Baltimore: Johns Hopkins University Press.

Eckbo, P.L. 1976. *The Future of World Oil.* Cambridge, Mass.: Ballinger Publishing Company.

Geer, T. 1971. *An Oligopoly: The World Coffee Economy and Stabilization Schemes.* New York: Dunellen Publishing Company.

Groenewegen, J.R., and W.W. Cochrane. 1980. "A Proposal to Further Increase the Stability of the American Grain Sector." *American Journal of Agricultural Economics* 62 (November): 806–811.

Hueth, D., and A. Schmitz. 1972 "International Trade in Intermediate and Final Goods: Some Welfare Implications of Destabilized Prices." *Quarterly Journal of Economics* 86 (August): 351–365.

Just, R.; E. Lutz; A. Schmitz; and S. Turnovsky. 1977. "The Distribution of Welfare Gains from International Price Stabilization Under Distortions." *American Journal of Agricultural Economics* 59 (November): 652–661.

———. 1978. "The Distribution of Welfare Gains from Price Stabilization: An International Perspective." *Journal of International Economics* 8 (November): 551–563.

Just, R.; A. Schmitz; and D. Zilberman. 1979. "Price Controls and Optimal Export Policies Under Alternative Market Structures." *American Economic Review* 69 (September): 706–714.

McCalla, A.F., and A. Schmitz. 1979. "Grain Marketing Systems: The Case of the United States Versus Canada." *American Journal of Agricultural Economics* 61 (May): 199–212.

Osborne, D.K. 1976. "Cartel Problems." *American Economic Review* 66 (December): 835–844.

Pindyck, R.S. 1978. "Gains to Producers from Cartelization of an Exhaustible Resource." *Review of Economics and Statistics* 60 (May): 238–251.

Salant, S.W. 1976. "Exhaustible Resources and Industrial Structure: A Nash-Cournot Approach to the World Oil Market." *Journal of Political Economy* 84 (October): 1079–1093.

Schuh, G.E. 1974. "The Exchange Rate and U.S. Agriculture." *American Journal of Agricultural Economics* 56 (February): 1–13.

Tredennick, J., Jr. 1978. "The Webb-Pomerene Act: A Reexamination of Export Cartels in World Trade." *Virginia Journal of International Law* 19 (Fall): 151–182.

6 IMPORTERS' RESPONSE

Importers' response to a cartel is an important and interesting subject. This chapter considers such issues as the importers' domestic demand and supply relationships, the aggregate import demand for grain, and the question of changing government policies in importing regions in response to an export cartel association. As the theoretical chapter pointed out, determining these factors is crucial to any analysis of the probable success of a grain export cartel.

Studies which have used trend analyses to project the long-term supply and demand potential for grain are discussed first. These results give a dynamic picture of the international grain market, and they indicate which world regions will likely become the most important grain importers. In the second section, some estimated supply and demand elasticities of the major importers are presented. This discussion is then tied in with descriptive hypotheses regarding grain importers' price responsiveness. Government policies and actions by private firms are also important factors explaining importers' responses; they are discussed in the final section of this chapter.

LONGER TERM DEMAND PROSPECTS FOR WHEAT AND COARSE GRAINS

In recent years, several long-term projections of cereal production, consumption, and trade have been completed. Carter (1976) summarized studies through 1976; his results are reproduced in Table 6–1. All studies reviewed project large food deficits in the LDCs in the year 1985, ranging from a low of 22.5 million metric tons to a high of 118 million metric tons, depending on projection procedures and assumptions about income and population growth.

Two additional studies have been completed since Carter's review. An updated USDA study by Rojko, Regier, O'Brien, Coffing, and Bailey (1978) projects world production, consumption, and net trade of cereal grain to 1985 under alternative assumptions, grouping the world into three categories: DCs, CPs, and LDCs. Under all scenarios, the DCs are significant net exporters with exports ranging from 52 to 98 million metric tons. CPs are projected to be deficit regions, but only under one scenario (high rate of income growth) do imports exceed the levels of 1973–1976 (21 million metric tons). LDCs are projected under all scenarios except one (high productivity and high-income growth) to have significant increases in import requirements (41, 49, and 70 million metric tons compared with 34 million metric tons in 1973–1976). The more recent study of the International Food Policy Research Institute (IFPRI) (1977) projects LDC needs to 1990. According to this study, under low-income growth assumptions, food-deficit LDCs are projected to have import needs of 116 million metric tons, while under high-income growth assumptions, the net deficit is 139 million metric tons.

All of these projection models have as their dominant elements projections of demand based on assumptions about population growth rates, income growth rates, and estimated income elasticities of demand. Given that the LDCs have the majority of the world's population, are experiencing rapid rates of population growth, and have relatively high income elasticities of demand for food, these countries tend in long-run projection models to dominate outcomes. These studies also generally project supply by assuming land area approximately constant and by using linear projections of historical yield data. The supply projection, therefore, reinforces the demand outcome, making net trade deficits large.

Despite the simplicity of the projection models, however, the results all confirm the trends already evident in the historical data regarding shifts in the import demand for food grains. Therefore, it seems likely that in the near future import demand by the LDCs will continue to grow; the major limitation, in the absence of concessional sales, would appear to be foreign exchange earnings. Demand for wheat imports by the CPs based on the USDA model remains about constant, and net import demand in the DCs will presumably grow less slowly, if at all.

These long-range projection models have much less to say about future prospects for coarse grain imports. However, past evidence, as well as a priori expectations, suggest that income elasticities of demand for meat products is high, particularly in middle-income countries experiencing rapid income growth (CPs and LDC-1). Thus, one would expect the derived demand for feed grains to grow rapidly in these regions. This increased demand for feed grains will be further strengthened by low and constant retail food prices in most CPs and many LDCs.

In sum, the available evidence suggests: (1) the DC importers will become relatively less important in both the wheat and coarse grain markets; (2) the demand for coarse grains and, to a lesser extent, wheat will grow in the CPs although, in part, demands will continue to be highly variable principally because of USSR production fluctuations; (3) the LDCs will become an even larger component of the wheat market with foreign exchange availability being the major constraint; and (4) the middle-income LDCs with foreign exchange (OPEC and nonOPEC middle-income countries) will increase imports of coarse grains, but their population relative to that of the low-income LDCs will limit aggregate quantities.

PRICE RESPONSIVENESS OF MARKET SEGMENTS

Most of the projection models discussed above are either constant price models or price equilibrium models. Thus, price plays a limited role in longer term projections; but, in the shorter run, price responsiveness is a major issue for any contemplated exporter association. In simplest terms, the elasticity of import demand indicates whether significant monopoly rents exist to be exploited. In this section, a sampling of elasticity estimates is reviewed.

One's first reaction upon reviewing the literature is bewilderment at the array of techniques and outcomes. For purposes of this discussion, the studies are divided into two categories: those which include estimates of domestic or import demand elasticities in importing regions and those which estimate the elasticity of import demand for a particular exporter's products.

Table 6-1. Comparison of cereal projections to 1985[a] (million metric tons)

Item	*FAO Base 1969–71*	*FAO 1985*	*USDA Base 1969–71*	*USDA-I[f] 1985*	*USDA-II[g] 1985*	*USDA-III[h] 1985*	*USDA-IV[i] 1985*	*ISU 1985*	*UC 1985*	*IFPRI 1985–86*
World										
Demand	1,207	1,725	1,062.6	1,548.5	1,618.7	1,501.8	1,643.9	1,145.5	1,777.2	
Production	1,239	NS	1,081.8	1,550.4	1,620.6	1,503.6	1,645.7	1,187.3 (L)[j] 1,191.7 (H)[j]	1,176.6 -0.6	
Balance[b]	+32	NS	19.2	1.9	1.9	1.9	1.9	41.8 (L)[j] 46.2 (H)[j]		
Developing countries										
Demand	590	929	466.6	691.2	726.2	678.6	743.5		954.5	
Production	585	853	443.1	632.4	648.7	626.2	721.0		917.9	
Balance	-5	-76	-23.5	-58.8	-77.5	-52.4	-22.5		-36.6	
Developing market economies[c]										
Demand	386	629	299.7	479.4	512.6	466.7	529.1	524.7	210.2	534.2 (H)[k] 517.1 (L)[k]
Production	370	544	279.2	424.7	441.0	418.7	513.3	411.0 (H)[j] 406.6 (L)[j]	206.5 -3.7	451.6
Balance	-16	-85	-20.5	-54.7	-71.6	-48.0	-15.8	-113.7 (H)[j] -118.1 (L)[j]		-82.6 (H)[k] -65.5 (L)[k]
Asian centrally planned countries[d]										
Demand	204	300	166.9	211.8	213.6	211.9	214.4		744.3	
Production	215	309	163.9	207.7	207.7	207.7	207.7		711.4	233.4
Balance	+11	+9	-3.0	-4.1	-5.9	-4.2	-6.7		-32.9	

Developed countries[e]									
Demand	617	796	596.0	857.3	892.5	823.2	900.4	403.4	822.7
Production	654	NS	635.7	918.0	971.9	877.4	924.7	574.0	855.8
Balance	+37	NS	42.7	60.7	79.4	54.2	24.3	170.6	36.1

Note: FAO = Food and Agriculture Organization: USDA = U.S. Department of Agriculture; ISU = Iowa State University; IFPRI = International Food Policy Research Institute.

[a]The data for FAO and USDA are not comparable because FAO carries rice as paddy, USDA carries rice as milled.

[b]Imbalances for USDA between demand and production in base are due to stock buildup, timing of shipments, and missing data on a number of small importers. Projected equilibrium does not allow for building or reducing stocks.

[c]UC developing market economies include Africa and Latin America. IFPRI includes Asia, North Africa, Middle East, Sub-Sahara Africa, and Latin America.

[d]UC, FAO, and IFPRI; Asian centrally planned includes the People's Republic of China and other Asian centrally planned countries (North Korea, North Vietnam, etc.). UC also includes Japan.

[e]Includes the USSR and Eastern Europe.

[f]USDA-I—Assumes economic growth temporarily slowed, but resumes strong expansion in late 1970s. Limited expansion of world trade.

[g]USDA-II—High world import demand situation. Larger income growth rate than USDA-I in both developing and developed countries.

[h]USDA-III—Low demand situation that assumes economic stagnation would continue in the late 1970s and recovery does not occur until the 1980s.

[i]USDA-IV—Developing countries' import needs are reduced. Have assumed that they have increased their investment in food production by increasing the inputs used.

[j]Projections designated (L) are made under a low variant upper bound on cropland expansion. Those designated (H) are made under a high variant bound on cropland expansion.

[k]Projections designated (L) are made under a low variant upper bound on income growth. Those designated (H) are made under a high variant bound on income growth.

Source: U.S. Department of Agriculture, Economic Research Service. 1974. *The World Food Situation and Prospects to 1985.* Foreign Agricultural Economic Report, No. 98 (December): 35; University of California Food Task Force Report. 1974. *A Hungry World: The Challenge to Agriculture.* Berkeley: University of California; and International Food Policy Research Institute. 1976. *Meeting Food Needs in the Developing World: The Location and Magnitude of the Task in the Next Decade.* Research Report No 1. Washington, D.C.: International Food Policy Research Report.

Foreign Demand Elasticities

Table 6–2 presents a sampling of demand elasticity estimates. Four categories of estimates are identified, principally on the basis of estimation techniques.

Two studies present estimates of domestic demand elasticities in importing countries and regions. The USDA (Rojko et al. 1978) GOL global projection model included elasticity estimates from various sources. These estimates for the DCs range from –.1 to –.45 for wheat and from –.5 to –.6 for feed grains. The only elasticity used for CPs is –.25 for corn in Eastern Europe, while LDC estimates range from –.1 to –.6. The Lattimore and Zwart (1978) study uses econometric techniques to estimate domestic demand elasticities for wheat. Except for the EEC-9, these estimates are uniformly lower than the USDA estimates. In both of these studies, additional computations would be required to estimate import demand elasticities. Since this conversion would require using supply elasticities and an estimate of the degree of self-sufficiency (McCalla 1967; McCalla and Learn 1967), these estimates represent the minimum possible level of import demand elasticities.

Two studies are examples of direct estimation of import demand elasticities: the Michigan State model (Mitchell 1979), which contains estimates for the three major importing regions, and the Zwart and Meilke (1979) simulation model, which contains estimates for wheat only. In all cases the estimates are extremely low and, therefore, seem to capture the effect of protective policies isolating domestic markets from world prices.

A newer approach uses transmission elasticities (the elasticity of domestic price with respect to changes in world prices) to adjust traditional net import demand estimations derived from domestic supply and demand estimates. Two recent studies have used this approach. The Bredahl, Meyers, and Collins work (1979) inserts a priori estimates of transmission elasticities into a model to estimate the elasticity of import demand facing U.S. exporters. These a priori estimates in most instances are zero leading to perfectly inelastic demands for imports.[a] (Their results for U.S. exporters are discussed in the next section.) Abbott (1979) attempts to estimate import

[a]A recent article by Collins (1980) attempts empirical estimates of the transmission of price and exchange rate changes. Also, see Paarlberg and Thompson (1980) for recent estimates for both wheat and corn.

Table 6-2. Estimated elasticities of foreign demand for grains

	Elasticity of Domestic Demand			*Internally Estimated Import Demand Elasticities*			*Assumed Transmission Elasticities*		*Elasticity of Substitution Model*		
Model	*Rojko, Regier, O'Brien, Coffing, and Bailey (1978)*		*Lattimore and Zwart (1978)*	*MSU*	*Mitchell (1979)*	*Zwart and Mielke (1979)*	*Bredahl, Meyers, and Collins (1979)*		*Grennes, Johnson, and Thursby (1978)*		*Capel and Rigaux (1974)*
Commodity	*Wheat*	*Corn*	*Wheat*	*Wheat*	*Coarse Grains*	*Wheat*	*Wheat*	*Feed Grains*	*Wheat*	*Feed Grains*	*Wheat*
Region											
Developed countries				-.79							
EEC-9						-0.0004	0	0	-2.87	-2.79	
EEC-6[a]	-.2	-.5	-0.634								-1.76 (UK)
EEC-3	-.1	-.5	-0.040								
Other Western Europe	-.25	-.5	-0.053			-0.053	0	0			
Japan	-.45	-.6	-0.270			-0.093	0	1	-2.060	-2.50	
Centrally planned countries				-1.23	-1.47						
USSR			-0.030			0	0	0			-13.19
China						0					
Eastern Europe		-.25	-0.008			0	0	0			
Developing countries			-0.085 to -0.634	-0.06	-1.26	0 to -.15					
LDC-1	-.25 to -.6	-.3 to -.5									-4.86 (Taiwan)
LDC-2	-.1 to -.4	-.1 to -.4									

[a]First countries to join.

demand functions with government policies included explicitly through a transmission elasticity. Although his results are difficult to interpret and his estimation results are often statistically insignificant, Abbott is prepared to conclude that for the vast majority of importing countries, the import elasticity of demand is less than the domestic demand elasticities used in the USDA GOL model. For only four wheat importers and two feed grain importers do his results suggest that world prices are transmitted to domestic producers and consumers. For a much longer list including the EEC, Japan, the USSR, and many DCs, he concludes that import demand has a low level of response to changes in international prices because of isolationist domestic policies.

Thus, at least three recent studies (Abbott 1979; Bredahl, Meyers, and Collins 1979; and Zwart and Meilke 1979) all suggest strongly that in major import markets, price changes in international markets have limited effects on import demand.

In sharp contrast to these estimates are two studies (Capel and Rigaux, 1974; Grennes, Johnson, and Thursby 1978) which use the elasticity of substitution approach. Their results, although covering only a limited number of countries, suggest that demand is very price elastic. However, it should be noted that these estimates are of the elasticity of import demand facing particular exporters and are, therefore, more akin to the next set of studies discussed.

Elasticity of Import Demand for a Particular Exporter's Product

Tweeten (1967) estimated the elasticity of demand for U.S. agricultural export products. Basically, he estimated domestic supply and demand elasticities in importing countries an then weighted them by the proportion of U.S. production to world production. His estimated elasticities are –6.42 and –6.9. Johnson (1977) challenged Tweeten's methodology but achieved a similar empirical estimate (–6.69). The Bredahl, Meyers, and Collins study (1979) also attempted to estimate this elasticity by using three different assumptions regarding the degree of trade restrictions. Comparative results for these three studies are presented in Table 6–3, which

Table 6-3. Elasticity of demand for U.S. agricultural products

	Tweeten (1967)	Johnson (1977)	Bredahl, Meyers, and Collins (1979) Restricted Case 1	Restricted Case 2	Free Trade Case 3
All agricultural products	-6.42 and -6.9	-6.69			
Wheat		-6.72	0.00	-1.67	-5.50
Feed grains		-10.18			
Corn			-0.09	-1.31	-3.13
Sorghum			-0.29	-2.36	-2.55

demonstrates the extreme sensitivity of results to assumptions about domestic policies.

This incomplete sampling of recent studies is presented not to criticize any particular author but rather to show that there is little convergence in empirical estimates. One can pick a result, depending on methodology and assumptions, where elasticities range from perfectly inelastic to very elastic for almost any region or country; hence, it is small wonder that there are strongly differing opinions regarding the effects of price increases in international grain markets. If there is any agreement in the recent literature, it is that protective food and agricultural policy tends to make import demand insensitive to price. However, empirical attempts to measure that impact by modeling government behavior yield poor statistical results more often than not (Abbott 1979). Thus, it seems reasonable to review policy in the major importing regions to see what a priori hypotheses can be made about price responsiveness.

A PRIORI HYPOTHESES REGARDING PRICE RESPONSIVENESS

This section presents our best judgment of demand characteristics in the various importing regions.

The Developed Countries

EEC. The EEC-9 isolates domestic prices from world prices by the variable levy. As many authors have argued (Abel 1966; Josling 1977; McCalla 1967), this makes the demand for wheat and coarse grain imports by the EEC perfectly inelastic with respect to world price, as long as world price is below the threshold price (which can also vary from time to time); the empirical results of Zwart and Meilke (1979), Abbott (1979), and Hurtado (1976) tend to support this view. For world prices above the threshold level, one would expect the import elasticity of demand to be quite high.

Japan. Japan's use of import quotas on wheat and barley, accompanied by its practice of purchasing at world prices and reselling at much higher internal prices, has the same analytical outcome as the variable levy. Therefore, one would expect the import demand for wheat and barley to be perfectly inelastic for world prices below the internal resale price. The elasticity of demand for other coarse grains and for wheat and barley for world prices above the resale price would be more price elastic. However, Japan's extreme dependence on international markets for both wheat and coarse grains means that it has few options and, therefore, would be practically price unresponsive.

Other Western Europe. Most countries in Western Europe outside the EEC-9 state trade in wheat, and many pursue low and subsidized domestic food programs. In view of these policies, the import demand elasticity is very low, if not zero. One would expect the elasticity of demand for coarse grains to be larger but still well within the inelastic range.

The Centrally Planned Economies

USSR. One would expect the USSR import demand for wheat and coarse grains to be nearly perfectly price inelastic for the following reasons: (1) the USSR appears to have decided to maintain domestic consumption levels despite extreme variations in domestic production; (2) rising real incomes coupled with stable consumer prices are causing dramatic increases in the demand for meat; and (3) having decided on its import needs, the country state-trades and tends to bargain on prices. Thus, the conclusion is that USSR imports are largely unrelated to price. A recent Central Intelligence Agency (CIA) report (1979) projects that USSR imports will be at least 15 million tons and possibly as high as 25 million tons into the 1980s. This report does suggest that after 1980, foreign exchange could be a constraint, which would tend to make its demand more elastic. However, as long as gold prices remain high, the foreign exchange cost of Western grain is low since the USSR has both large gold reserves and is a large gold exporter. Thus, one may continue to assume that world prices have limited (if any) impact on Soviet grain purchases.

China. A similar set of arguments can be made regarding China. A recent CIA study (1979) projects that Chinese imports will increase to about 10 million tons in the 1980s largely because of domestic policy commitments; it views transportation capacity as a greater constraint than foreign exchange. Thus again, the expectation is for a highly, if not perfectly, inelastic demand.

Eastern Europe. Eastern Europe has been a grain deficit area throughout the period reviewed. During the 1960s, its major source of supply was the USSR; but, with the USSR's shift to importer status, this area turned to traditional Western suppliers. All countries in the Eastern bloc pursue domestic food subsidy programs by maintaining low and relatively constant consumer prices. In Poland, for example, real incomes have doubled since 1966 while retail prices, by political necessity, have remained constant. The result is that per capita meat consumption has doubled and that, despite rapid increases in producer prices, Poland is increasingly deficit in grains and feedingstuffs. This set of domestic policies forces Poland, like the other Eastern European countries, to buy regardless of price. The only factor that might moderate a perfectly price-inelastic demand would be an absolute foreign exchange constraint.

The Developing Countries

The number and diversity of LDCs make a priori hypothesizing a very hazardous business. Thus, what follows should be viewed as, at best, a set of working hypotheses. In general, the LDCs are caught in the race between rapidly growing populations, rising incomes and expectations, and less rapidly growing and unstable production. Domestic policies which maintain low urban food prices and the lack of resources to increase producer prices have increased their dependence on external food sources; Egypt is a case in point. Foreign exchange availability, therefore, appears to be the major limiting factor on food purchases. If this is the case, then one would expect the elasticity of import demand to be at least –1. Hence, we see the appropriateness of the earlier division of the LDCs into two groups used principally on income levels and foreign exchange availability.

LDC-1. In this group of countries, two subdivisions were included: OPEC countries and middle-income LDCs with foreign exchange. In general, this group does not suffer a foreign exchange constraint. In fact, in the case of OPEC countries, one can anticipate that food grain demand could soon become saturated. However, rising incomes are causing increases in the demand for meat. To the extent that meat production can be expanded, demand for feed grains should increase, although large increases in grain prices could lead these countries to import meat rather than feedstuffs. Nevertheless, one would expect the import demand for grains to be price inelastic.

In the non-OPEC,middle-income countries such as South Korea, Taiwan, Mexico, and Brazil, one would expect a rapid increase in the demand for feed grains. This increase in demand could be tempered by price increases, but one would still expect the absolute value of the elasticity of demand to be less than one.

LDC-2. This large and diverse set of countries, now the dominant importer of wheat, is relatively unimportant in the coarse grain market. Their common characteristics are poverty and extreme limitations on foreign exchange, which would lead to an a priori expectation that their elasticity of import demand is at least –1. Clearly, that is the appropriate elasticity for that portion of their food imports accounted for by concessional sales (Public Law 480). If foreign exchange is not the most binding constraint, divergent hypotheses result. On the one hand, the existence of policies of low urban food prices, mainly because of political necessity (recall the food riots in Cairo and Bangkok), would tend to force grain imports regardless of price and, in turn, to suggest inelastic demands. On the other hand, high world prices make incentive producer prices relatively less expensive and tend to encourage domestic production. Thus, if India's pattern were followed so that LDCs built stocks during low price periods and contracted consumption during high price periods, the demand would tend to be quite elastic. Since it is not known how to attach weights to these divergent factors, a working hypothesis is that the elasticity of import demand in the low-income LDCs is in the range of –1 to –1.5.

AGGREGATION, SUPPLY RESPONSE, AND NET IMPORT DEMAND

Many of the empirical estimates made are based on data which covered several periods of time when prices did not vary a great deal from week to week. The first major shock in at least twenty years in the grain trade was in 1972–73. During such short-crop years, price responsiveness becomes very critical. When one agggregates the different wheat demands together and feed grain demands together, the aggregate response is quite different from many of the individual region's responses. For example, in wheat, during the 1973–1975 period, high-income countries imported relatively more than did poor countries (even though to meet basic food needs the opposite should have been the case). This was because, as prices rose, the poor nations, because of foreign exchange constaints, could not compete with countries such as the Soviet Union. However, based on many of the empirical estimates, one would not have necessarily expected this since many of the studies showed that demands are price unresponsive even for poor countries. This may well be true over the data range estimated when prices did not move a great deal, but it is not the case for large price changes. At any given point in time, there is only a fixed quantity of grain to be exported; and how it is distributed depends on the relative buying strengths of major importers. These differences in buying power are clearly brought out during periods of tight grain supplies.

In terms of feed grains, the aggregate demand may well be similar to that of individual regions since most of the import demand comes from high-income regions. As a result, as prices go up due to shortages, the distribution of purchases among importers need not change.

In the hypotheses discussed above, most of the attention was given to demand variables. However, net import demand is a function of both domestic demand and supply; therefore, the question of world supply potential and the supply responses of particular countries must be raised. Two variables are critical to this discussion: domestic supply responsiveness and the degree to which international prices are transmitted to domestic producers. If the transmission elasticity is zero, domestic supply elasticity is irrelevant as long as world prices are below internal support levels, and it was on this basis that the DC and CP regions were hypothesized as having very low or zero elasticities of import demand. In the LDCs, however, supply response may be an issue because, as noted above, higher world prices lessen the internal costs of raising producer prices. However, most estimates of short-run domestic supply elasticities for grains are very low and so, in the short run, it seems likely that income and population variables will dominate in the import demand function.

The a priori expectations for import demands which considers both domestic demand and supply outlined above are summarized in Table 6–4. These should be viewed as best guesses in the absence of convergent empirical estimates.

It is unfortunate that one is not able to pin down more precisely what supply response is likely to be if importers face higher prices. Certainly, countries such as Brazil and Turkey have experienced enormous increases in grain production in recent years. However, on the other hand, increased production in countries such as Japan is limited.

Not only is import demand important in determining grain prices in exporting countries but supply response in exporting countries is also crucial. It is important to keep in mind that part of the increase in U.S. production of grains in the 1970s was due to bringing land into production which was in the government set-aside program and, in addition, some pasture land was broken up and seeded to grain. If one is at full capacity in the 1980s in that there are no more acres available to plant wheat and feed grains unless they are taken from other crops, then the only way to increase production further is to rely on new technologies. However, one has to keep in mind that already heavy amounts of fertilizer are being used as well as other modern inputs. Also, there is the problem of soil deterioration as farming practices become more intensive. Because of the above phenomena, experts in the field of supply response disagree. The Canadian government, for example, has taken the stand that Canada

Table 6-4. A priori import demand elasticities

	Wheat	*Coarse Grains*	
Developed countries			
EC-9	0	0	for Wp < Threshold
	>-1	>-1	for Wp > Threshold
Japan	0	low -.1 to -.25	for p < internal price
	-.25 to -.5		for p > resale price
Other Western Europe	0	low	
Centrally planned countries			
USSR	0	0	
China	0	0	
Eastern Europe	0	0	
Developing countries			
LDC-1			
OPEC	0	low	
NonOPEC	low	low	
LDC-2	-1 to -1.5	high	if foreign exchange constraint
	elastic	elastic	if no foreign exchange constraint

can increase its grain production by at least 25 percent. USDA estimates also support increased productivity through time. In our opinion, however, further research on the issue of productivity change is still needed. What would happen if new technologies of major significance could not be found?

GOVERNMENT AND PRIVATE TRADERS' RESPONSES

A Movement Toward Freer Trade?

Governments in importing countries influence the level of grain imports through trade policy and support for domestic producers. The EEC's use of variable levies, for example, results in less consumption and greater production, the latter because producer prices are supported above the free-trade level; hence, imports are below what they would be under free trade. This point is clearly illustrated in Table 6–5. In addition, note that Japanese producer prices are occasionally at least three times the U.S. export price.

Importers may react to a possible grain export cartel with attempts to increase production of grains by direct subsidies or investment in new technologies. This could, in effect, act as a supply shifter (that is, at a given price the new supply function would lie to the right of the old one). How such attempts would succeed depends on the

Table 6-5. World wheat prices, 1966-67 to 1976-77

	Export Prices ($U.S./Metric Ton)				*Basic Support Levels*[d]	
Crop Year	*Argentina Trigo Pan*	*Australia*[a]	*Canada*[b]	*United States*[c]	*Japan*	*EEC*
1966-67	59	63	72	67	140	e
1967-68	62	58	66	63	145	99
1968-69	58	58	68	63	152	99
1969-70	56	54	64	57	153	99
1970-71	57	58	67	63	164	99
1971-72	62	58	65	62	175	101
1972-73	86	91	92	92	217	114
1973-74	f	195	202	178	282	128
1974-75	163	167	198	170	334	148
1975-76	144	147	174	161	354	163
1976-77	104	113	130	118	401	183
Mean 1966-73 + 1976-77	68	69	78	73	193	113

[a]Australian Wheat Board selling price (f.o.b.). Australian Standard White.

[b]Canadian Wheat Board official "in store" price converted to f.o.b. at current fobbing rates (price basis Thunder Bay). Canada Western Red Spring.

[c]F.o.b. Gulf. U.S. No. 2. Hard Winter.

[d]These prices are those used for government-guaranteed prices.

[e]No data available.

[f]Due to the limited trading in this wheat in the 1973-74 crop year, no representative average export price is available.

Source: International Wheat Council.

availability of land that is now submarginal and on the possibilities of technological advances such as high-yielding varieties, variables which are largely a function of the resources available in each region. Assessing the production possibilities of each major grain importer is beyond the scope of this book, and the partially unresolved issue of producer supply response in importing countries may be a major weakness in the empirical estimates presented later.

Among the most important issues is how policies by importing countries toward trade barriers might change. Given production technologies, will imports increase, decrease, or stay the same in response to an export cartel? What will happen is largely conjecture on our part. However, we feel that for regions such as the EEC and Japan, imports would not decrease a great deal; in fact, they might even increase. This has been suggested in earlier chapters but, because of its importance, is reemphasized here. During the 1973–74 period of extremely high world grain prices, the EEC variable levy was at times zero or negative (Carter and Schmitz 1979). The internal target prices were not raised significantly during this period, and grain imports into the EEC were not decreased. On the other hand, Japan raised its internal support price levels to extremely high levels in 1973–74, without reducing the normal volume of grain imports. The behavior of these major importers during this period of abnormally high grain prices lends some support to our argument that these regions may not cut back on imports after the formation of a grain cartel. Only after a cartel raised the price above the threshold level (in the EEC) or the support level (in Japan) might these regions begin reducing imports. The 1973–74 prices were just approaching these critical points so unfortunately we do not have any data on prices and imports to allow us to reach strong conclusions. On the question of government response consider Figure 6–1 where S and D are supply and demand for grains in the importing region. The free-trade price is P_f. With tariffs, the price in the importing country is I_p, and the exporter's price is P_F. The tariff revenue is *abcd*. Suppose now that exporters respond to the tariff by raising price to I_p. Producers in the importing country would be unaffected, and consumers would pay the same price that they paid when the importers imposed the tariff. The government, however, would lose *abcd* in tariff revenue, which would now go to exporters in the form of an export tax. (Note that part of the supply response argument revolves around whether or

Figure 6–1. Government response to tariffs and taxes

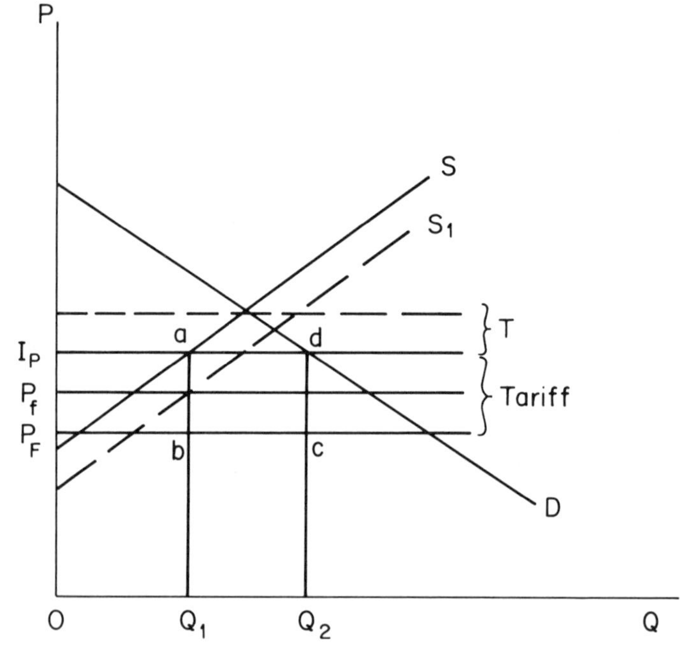

not supply would shift from S to S_1 if, for example, I_p became the export asking price rather than P_F.)

Consider these possible responses by importers in response to exporters raising their price from P_F to I_p:

1. The importers might impose a tariff on top of price I_p, say, T.
2. On the other hand, the importing country might reduce its tariff if it knew that the exporter was threatening to charge price I_p. It might agree on free trade and price at P_f. The exporter would be better off than with the import tariff in place, and the importer would be better off than being charged price I_p. (Free trade is the optimum joint solution.) If the latter occurs, the exporter may use the ideal cartel solution (discussed in Chapter 4) only as a threat and, in reality, pursue free trade. Thus, a cartel may, in fact, raise prices and increase the volume of trade. While the theory of optimal cartels assumes no retaliation, the optimal theoretical export tax may, in fact, never be implemented if trade liberalization occurs because of fear of importers' retaliation.

3. Importers may well invest in new technologies which, if effective, would shift supply from S to S_1, thus reducing the importers' dependence on trade.

This issue is worth pursuing further and in a broader context. As an example, it has been suggested within the American farm movement that, if the price of grain to the Japanese were increased, Japan would switch to Brazil for its supplies. Such an argument ignores the fact that to buy grain, Japan needs a source of foreign exchange. Brazil is not a large purchaser of such Japanese exports as cars and television sets, and the issue is thus one of barter, where a certain amount of grain trades for an automobile. This is clearly shown in Figure 6–2. In equilibrium, Japan exports *OX* of cars for *OY* of wheat. For Japan to offer cars and ignore the U.S. offer curve for wheat would result in major cutbacks in food consumption and a decline in Japan's real income. It is clear then that one cannot consider only grains when discussing the current terms of trade between Japan and the United States since there is an offer curve not only for U.S. exports of grain but also for Japanese exports; equilibrium is determined where these offer curves intersect. In the broad context of international trade, the Japanese might have no other choice than to import grain from the proposed cartel even at

Figure 6–2. The offer curve of wheat for cars

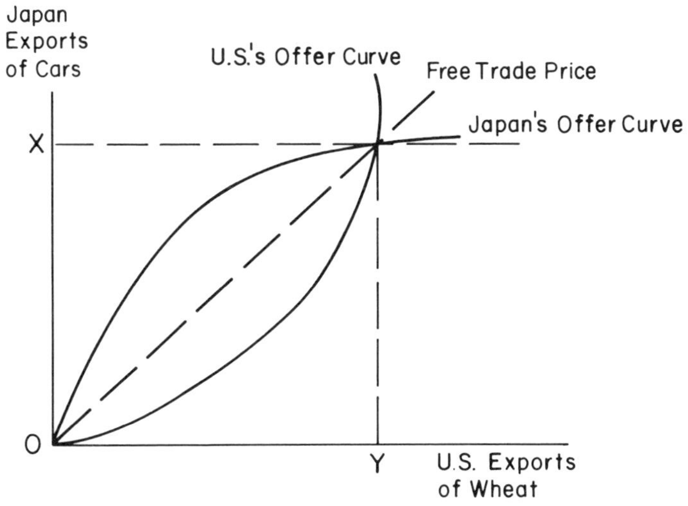

higher prices than currently exist; depending on the strategies used by exporters, Japan might be willing to reduce barriers on grain imports.

This example also serves as a reminder of the fact that the proposed cartel deals with food, a much more basic item than a television set. This is an important fact in gauging possible reactions to the cartel especially in discussions of trade with high-income but food-deficit countries where, largely because of land constraints, food production can seldom be increased substantially at any price.

Strategic Planning by Importers

How importers respond to grain exporters in terms of strategic planning by importers unfortunately has never been studied in detail by economists located in exporting countries. What do the price elasticities estimated by American economists mean when viewed from a planning agency located, for example, in the Soviet Union? Perhaps we provided a correct interpretation earlier partly on the basis of observed past response. Even if we have, forces may be at work which make the use of past estimates of demand price elasticities for analysis of future events questionable. For example, consider grain stock piling policies by both exporters and importers and how they might change through time. This phenomenon is not uncommon as, partly to offset the economic power of OPEC, the United States is now actively stockpiling petroleum. Since the major grain importers do not currently practice stockpiling in a major way, this may well become an important policy objective if they are faced with the threat of a grain cartel. The importers have, until now, viewed stockholding as a cost which the exporters have been willing to bear (see Carter and Schmitz 1979). The importance of stocks and the cost of holding stocks would take on a new meaning in the face of a cartel, however, since it is likely that the largest volume of stocks would be held by importers rather than by exporters. Members of the cartel would have to be careful to ensure that the importers did not build up sufficient stocks to "break up" the cartel in the short run. Stockpiling by food importers during rising periods of uncertainty, which they would face as a result of a cartel, can also be supported on theoretical grounds (see Feder, Just, and Schmitz 1977).

Consider further the case of Japan as a concrete example. It may well be already engaged in stockpiling strategies, perhaps in an anticipation of tighter grain markets; and yet, stock data on Japan suggest this is not the case. It appears that Japan, either through its public food agency or through the private sector, is engaged in the Chicago futures market. This allows it to remove some of the risk in the grain-importing business (see Feder, Just, and Schmitz 1980). Secondly, Japanese grain firms are beginning to establish grain-trading firms in the United States and, thus, are partly bypassing the use of such old established companies as Cargill, Inc., and Continental Grain, Inc. The Japanese companies buy directly from U.S. country elevators for shipment to Japan. This strategy allows the Japanese to be close to the source of supply, thus enabling them to make better use of futures markets and storage facilities. Japanese companies located in the United States could well store grain for final destination (Japan), but it would not show up as stocks held by the Japanese. If such activities continue to grow, it may well be that the effective short-term import demand for grains by the Japanese could become quite price responsive. Properly designed import strategies make the import demand more price elastic through time which reduces potential gains from a cartel.

To what extent many poor countries use import strategies is not known. Because of foreign exchange constraints and lack of storage facilities, import buying is likely done on a short-term, nonplanned basis. This seems to be consistent with the many arguments that have been put forward for a world food security system in order to avoid massive starvation due to droughts.

We have already emphasized the power of importers, such as the EEC-9, that results from their trading as a bloc of countries and their optimal use of trade policies allowing them to operate in a buyer's market most of the time. Storage policies are also part of this package.

The two large grain importers (which at any point in time seem to be able to play havoc with grain exporters), mainland China and the Soviet Union, present a mystery to analysts in exporting nations. Because of their size and economic power, these nations surely have a long-term strategy for importing grains. One such strategy may be that of manufacturing price instability which has been suggested in a different context by Bieri and Schmitz (1974). This strategy enables a large importer to buy large quantities of grain at relatively low prices. Then prices rise, world supply increases, prices drop, and once again importers buy large quantities. In essence, importers create false price signals to producers in exporting countries. If this hypothesis is correct, then a grain cartel, to be effective, has to prevent this type of buying behavior. To say the least, more work is needed on this subject before exporters can deal effectively with large state traders such as the above.

CONCLUSIONS

This chapter has explored the question of the response of importers to the cartelization of grain. Long-term trend projections and elasticity estimates provide some but not all of the answers. The estimates of government policy behavior are as important as the statistical estimates. Much uncertainty remains on this topic of importer response, but we have attempted to provide as many insights as possible.

In the next two chapters several cartel models, incorporating different import response functions, are evaluated empirically. We try first to estimate the effects of the ideal export cartel, where importers remove all barriers to trade and the export tax is imposed, and then to estimate the gains, assuming that the threat of a cartel would lead to free trade and no export tax would be imposed. The sensitivity of the results, in view of the different price elasticities presented earlier, is also discussed. As well, we run additional cartel models discussed in the theoretical chapter—for example, a two-price cartel, where the price charged to poor-country importers is much less than the price facing high-income importers. The discussion also includes feed grain cartels and the implications for the livestock sector.

REFERENCES

Abel, M.E. 1966. "Price Discrimination in the World Trade of Agricultural Commodities." *Journal of Farm Economics* 48 (May): 194–208.

Abbott, P.C. 1979. "Modeling International Grain Trade with Government Controlled Markets." *American Journal of Agricultural Economics* 61 (February): 22–31.

Bieri, J., and A. Schmitz. 1974. "Market Intermediaries and Price Instability: Some Welfare Implications." *American Journal of Agricultural Economics* 56 (May): 280–285.

Bredahl, M.E.; W.H. Meyers; and K.J. Collins. 1979. "The Elasticity of Foreign Demand for U.S. Agricultural Products: The Importance of the Price Transmission Elasticity." *American Journal of Agricultural Economics* 61 (February): 58–63.

Capel, R.E., and L.R. Rigaux. 1974. "Analysis of Export Demand for Canadian Wheat." *Canadian Journal of Agricultural Economics* 22 (July): 1–14.

Carter, C., and A. Schmitz. 1979. "Import Tariffs and Price Formation in the World Wheat Market." *American Journal of Agricultural Economics* 61 (August): 517–522.

Carter, H.O. 1976. "World and U.S. Food Trends: A Current Perspective for Policy." In *Contemporary Economic Problems,* edited by W. Fellner, pp. 293–322, Washington, D.C.: American Enterprise Institute.

Central Intelligence Agency. 1979. "China: Demand for Foreign Grain." Washington, D.C.: National Foreign Assessment Center.

———. 1979. "U.S.S.R.: Long-Term Outlook for Grain Imports." Washington, D.C.: National Foreign Assessment Center.

Collins, H.C. 1980. "Price and Exchange Rate Transmission." *Agricultural Economics Research* 32 (October): 50–55.

Feder, G.; R. Just; and A. Schmitz. 1977. "Storage and Price Uncertainty in International Trade." *International Economic Review,* 18 (October): 553–568.

———. 1980. "Futures Markets and the Theory of the Firm Under Price Uncertainty." *Quarterly Journal of Economics* 94 (March): 317–328.

Grennes, T.; P.R. Johnson; and M. Thursby. 1978. *The Economics of World Grain Trade.* New York: Praeger Publishers.

Hurtado, H. 1976. "EC Import Demand for Grains: Some Implications of the Common Agricultural Policy for U.S. Imports." Ph.D. dissertation, University of California, Davis.

International Food Policy Research Institute (IFPRI). 1977. *Food Needs of Developing Countries: Projections of Production and Consumption to 1990.* Washington, D.C.: IFPRI.

Josling, T. 1977. "Government Price Policies and the Structure of International Trade." *Journal of Agricultural Economics* 28 (September): 261–276.

Johnson, P.R. 1977. "The Elasticity of Foreign Demand for U.S. Agricultural Products." *American Journal of Agricultural Economics* 59 (November): 735–736.

Lattimore, R., and A.C. Zwart. 1978. "Medium Term World Wheat Forecasting Model." In *Commodity Forecasting Models for Canadian Agriculture,* Vol. 2. Ottawa: Agriculture Canada.

McCalla, A.F. 1967. "Pricing in the World Feed Grain Market." *Agricultural Economics Research* 19 (October): 93–102.

McCalla, A.F., and E.W. Learn. 1967. "Nonequilibrium Fixed-Price Schemes in Agricultural Trade." *Agricultural Economics Research* 19 (October): 111–116.

Mitchell, D. 1979. "The MSU Agricultural Trade Model." Unpublished paper, Department of Agricultural Economics, Michigan State University.

Paarlberg, P.L., and R.L. Thompson. 1980. "Interrelated Products and the Effects of an Import Tariff." *Agricultural Economics Research* 32 (October): 21–32.

Rojko, A.D.; D. Regier; P. O'Brien; A. Coffing; and L. Bailey. 1978. *Alternative Futures for World Food in 1985, Volume 1, World GOL Model Analytical Report.* U.S. Department of Agriculture, Foreign Agricultural Economic Report No. 146.

Tweeten, L.G. 1967. "The Demand for United States Farm Output." *Stanford Food Research Institute Studies* 7: 343–369.

Zwart, A.C., and K.D. Meilke. 1979. "The Influence of Domestic Pricing Policies and Buffer Stocks on Price Stability in the World Wheat Industry." *American Journal of Agricultural Economics* 61 (August): 434–447.

7 THE GRAIN EXPORT CARTEL: A QUANTITATIVE ASSESSMENT

The objective of this chapter is to provide an aggregate quantitative assessment of the effects of introducing a grain export cartel. It presents an analysis of the cartel's impact on the producing and consuming sectors of the exporting countries and estimates optimal price and quantity solutions for the cartel.

The chapter provides a static computation of potential monopoly profits in the world grain market for both a wheat and a combined wheat-coarse grain (barley, sorghum, and corn) cartel. It presents empirical estimates of gains and losses for the two alternative cartel arrangements. It is clear from the results that within the exporting countries there is likely to be a producer–consumer conflict of interest over the grain cartel question.

First, previous studies are reviewed which have estimated the effects of attempts at forming cartels in other primary products; the failure of past cartels is also discussed. Consistent with the theory presented earlier, mathematical solutions are presented for both the government export cartel and the producer export cartel. Finally, the effects of cartels are quantified and discussed.

It should be emphasized that past attempts at forming cartels are reviewed in order to demonstrate that even if there are potential gains from a cartel consistent with the theory discussed earlier, it does not immediately follow that these can become actual gains. For example, if exporters do not cooperate in export pricing and market share allocation, the chance that a cartel will succeed is slight even though the gains could be large if they did cooperate (see Bickerdike, 1906). Our empirical results should be interpreted in this light; they are derived for different types of cartels where it is assumed that the organizational difficulties of introducing a cartel and keeping it running, once organized, have been overcome. Again, even though the results show that large gains are possible from a cartel, this in no way is a sufficient condition, although it is a necessary one, for a grain export cartel to be effective.

PREVIOUS RELATED STUDIES

Underwood (1976:5) states that "in spite of all the discussion of the liklihood of O.P.E.C. imitators, very few attempts have been made to actually measure the potential gain from collusion by producers of other primary commodities." In fact, he cites only two pieces of work (one by Kofi [1972] and the other by Gorouex, Kendrick, and Kim [1974]), neither of which actually looks at potential cartel gains. Kofi calculates the potential net gain to cocoa producers from the ratification of the 1968 International Cocoa Agreement, while Gorouex, Kendrick, and Kim study the empirical implications of stabilizing the world cocoa market. The implications of a tea and copper cartel are assessed dynamically in the Underwood study; his results give a tea cartel a borderline chance of success and a copper cartel even less than that.

Pincus (1965) has considered the possibility of increasing export earnings through international commodity agreements in sugar, coffee, tea, cocoa, and bananas. He crudely estimated that monopoly pricing of these five commodities would have raised export earnings in 1961 by 15.7 percent to $5 billion.

Harry G. Johnson (1967, 1968) slightly modified Pincus's procedure, calculating the maximum monopoly profit that could have been extracted by international commodity agreements in the same crops. His results indicated that producers could have extracted $2.6 billion in monopoly profits.

The implications of charging a monopolistic price in the world cocoa market were examined by Behrman (1968) for 1964. He simply calculated total revenue changes for the cocoa-exporting group under different price and quantity scenarios. The revenue increase from the formulation of a cocoa cartel was found to be marginal, and Behrman suggested that the costs of implementing such an arrangement could possibly outweigh the benefits.

Paul Johnson (1965) recognized the potential monopoly position of the United States in the world tobacco market. He was able to show that the world price increasing feature of the domestic U.S. tobacco program created international monopoly rents which more than offset domestic welfare losses associated with the program.

Wong (1978) argued that in the international rice market, Thailand faces a downward sloping demand curve. He calculated the static welfare effect of the export tax imposed by Thailand and found it to be substantial.

Shei and Thompson (1978) have shown that the United States and other major wheat-exporting countries may gain in the short run by imposing export controls (such as quotas). They estimate that export revenue accruing to the United States in the short run could increase by $2.2 billion with a 26 million metric ton quota on wheat exports.

More recently, Pindyck (1978) has empirically estimated the gains to producers from the cartelization of three exhaustible resources: bauxite, copper, and petroleum. To serve as a base from which to measure the potential cartel gains, he draws on a model of exhaustible resource pricing. He points out that a simple static computation of potential monopoly profits, given elasticity estimates, might be quite realistic and quite sufficient for markets where supply and demand can adjust quickly to price and where resource exhaustion is not a problem.

In other recent studies, Eckbo (1976) reviewed the operation of fifty-one cartels and found that nineteen of those arrangements were "successful" in raising prices 200 percent above costs of production and distribution.[a] As reported in Chapter 5, the median duration of successful cartels was 4.0 years, and the average duration, 6.6 years (Behrman 1977).

EFFECTS OF TRADE LIBERALIZATION

The problem of empirically estimating gains from cartelization can be viewed as the counterpart to the problem of estimating the effects

[a]In an analysis of the world coffee market, Geer (1971) finds much difficulty in determining long-run conditions for an export cartel.

of a tariff reduction (that is, trade liberalization). This is so because, as the previous chapters pointed out, an export cartel results in economic gains to exporters—the opposite effect from tariffs imposed by importers. Also, as pointed out, given that free trade in grains does not exist due to tariff barriers and the like, one result of a cartel may be to liberalize trade.

Analyses of trade liberalization, which are fairly abundant, are thus relevant. Table 7–1 reports results of three of the more comprehensive studies on agricultural trade liberalization. Even though the alternative studies give substantially different estimates of the effects of eliminating trade barriers, the results are important and consistent in that even the smallest estimate suggests large gains from trade liberalization.

CARTEL SOLUTIONS

Consistent with the theory presented earlier, two forms of cartels are discussed: a government cartel and a producer cartel.

The Government Cartel Solution

Once formed, a government cartel may aim to maximize the joint profit of its members; in so doing, its behavior will be similar to that of a monopolist exercising monopoly power in the export market only, with the price and output decision rules being straightforward. If marginal costs are decreasing for each member in the cartel, then the correct profit-maximixing procedure would be to choose one member and allocate the total cartel output to him. If the marginal costs of all cartel members are increasing, output for the cartel as a whole should be allocated among members so as to equalize their marginal costs. Then, in order to obtain the profit-maximizing output for the cartel as a whole, the members' equalized marginal costs must be set equal to the marginal revenue for the cartel.

Assuming we can horizontally sum the cartel members' cost functions to give an aggregate supply and the rest of the world's demand functions to give an aggregate demand function, then the procedure in this chapter for estimating potential profits for a

Table 7-1. Alternative estimates of increased imports resulting from complete removal of agricultural trade barriers (millions of dollars)

Importing Area and Products	*USDA*	*FAO*	*Cline and Others (1978)*[b]
EEC-9			
Beef	1,022	n.a.[a]	135
Wheat	646	1,275	411
Feed grains	1,935	1,322	843
Soybeans	1,005	n.a.	0
Total, four products	4,608	n.a.	1,389
Japan			
Beef	6,199	n.a.	42
Milk, dairy products	5,109	169	50
Wheat	90	80	234
Feed grains	1,623	n.a.	45
Soybeans	889	n.a.	0
Total, five products	13,910	n.a.	371
United States			
Beef	-189	n.a.	98
Dairy products	929	1,420	76
Total, two products	740	n.a.	174
Total, three importing areas	19,258	n.a.	1,934

[a] n.a. = not available.

[b] Cline, W.R., Kawanabe, N.; Kronsjo, T.O.M.; and Williams, T., 1978. *Trade Negotiations in the Tokyo Round: A Quantitative Assessment.* Washington, D.C.: The Brookings Institution, p. 181.

Source: For USDA, calculated from U.S. Department of Agriculture, Foreign Agricultural Service. 1973. *Agricultural Trade and the Proposed Round of Multilateral Negotiations,* pp. 153–54, 158–59. For FAO, calculated from Food and Agricultural Organization. 1975. *Agricultural Protection and Stabilization Policies: A Framework of Measurement in the Context of Agricultural Adjustment.* C75/Lim/2. Rome: FAO, Table 3-6. Physical quantity trade changes for 1971 are converted to value changes by using 1971 unit import values as reported in FAO, *Trade Yearbook 1974,* and for dairy products, the producer price net of subsidy as shown in FAO, *Agricultural Protection and Stabilization Policies,* Appendix A. These values are converted to 1974 long-term prices by a uniform 50 percent increase above the 1971 value levels. For this study, project calculations (referring to imports from nonbloc suppliers for the EEC); Table 5-5 (expanded by 50 percent to arrive at 1974 long-term prices); Table 5-10; "beef" includes other meats.

government cartel will be one that draws directly on monopoly profit maximization rules.

The internationally earned profits, π of a cartel are

$$\pi(q) = p_f(q_f)q_f - c(q_s) \tag{7.1}$$

where $p_f(q_f)$ and $c(q_s)$ are excess demand and supply (cost) functions and where it is assumed that

$$p_f' < 0 \text{ and } c' > 0.$$

That is, the cartel faces a downward sloping excess demand function and is armed with an upward sloping excess supply function.

The first-order condition for profit maximization is

$$p_f(q_f^*) + p_f'(q_f^*)q_f^* = c'(q_s^*). \tag{7.2}$$

This is a necessary condition for maximum profits, and a sufficient condition is that the second derivative of profits with respect to output be negative. The second-order conditions will be satisfied as long as the usual concavity assumptions associated with the production function hold.

The Producer Cartel Solution

Domestic grain producers could lose from the government cartel relative to a free-trade situation. Therefore, grain producers would (if allowed) choose to form a producer cartel which, to maximize their welfare, would discriminate against domestic as well as foreign consumers.

The profits of a producer cartel selling q_d domestically and q_f internationally are

$$\pi(q) = p_d(q_d)q_d + p_f(q_f)q_f - c(q_d + q_f) \tag{7.3}$$

where $p_d(q_d)\, q_d$ and $p_f(q_f)\, q_f$ are the revenue functions and $c(q_d + q_f)$ is the cartel's cost function. Assuming that these revenue and cost functions have the usual shapes, to maximize profits the first-order conditions are

$$p_d(q_d^*) + p_d'(q_d^*)q_d^* - c'(q_d^* + q_f^*) = 0 \tag{7.4}$$

$$p_f(q_f^*) + p_f'(q_f^*)q_f^* - c'(q_d^* + q_f^*) = 0. \tag{7.5}$$

These conditions imply that the marginal revenue in both the domestic and foreign markets must equal the marginal cost of the total output of the cartel.

Alternatively, the producer cartel might treat domestic and foreign consumers on an equal basis and charge them the same monopoly price. This arrangement would avoid problems associated with discriminating between consuming markets and might prove to be a superior arrangement even though revenue would be slightly less than under the market discrimination solution in (7.4) and (7.5).

The profits of a nondiscriminating cartel are

$$\pi(q) = p_c(q_c)q_c - c(q_c) \qquad (7.6)$$

where $q_c = q_d + q_f$ and $p_c = p_f + p_d$.

The first-order condition is

$$p_c(q_c^*) + p_c'(p_c^*)q_c^* = c'(q_c^*). \qquad (7.7)$$

A QUANTITATIVE ASSESSMENT OF CARTEL EFFECTS

The Equations

The highly aggregate market models described by equations (7.1), (7.3), and (7.6) have never been directly estimated for the grain market. Several econometric models that might be appropriate for our analysis in this chapter do exist in a more disaggregated form, however, and an excellent review of these is given by Thompson (forthcoming).

For the empirical analysis in this chapter, the model by Rojko, Urban, and Naive (1971) (hereafter referred to as the ERS model) will be used to compute the optimal grain cartel solutions and to draw some aggregate welfare implications.[b] The ERS model has estimated national supply and demand equations for wheat (all uses) and coarse grains. The grain model, based on average data for 1964–1966, divides the world into twenty-two regions and contains

[b]The World Food Model (Rojko et al. 1978) was also used, but the results are not presented. In addition, other estimates of supply and demand are available (P.R. Johnson 1971).

supply and demand equations for each commodity in each region. The parameters of these equations are not all econometrically estimated; some are synthesized from economic theory and statistical findings. Table 7–2 lists the trading regions of the model for coarse grains and wheat and also some of the corresponding base data on production and consumption.

From the estimates of the ERS study, aggregate supply and demand functions were computed for the major wheat and coarse grain exporters and importers. The aggregate supply and demand curves were obtained by a horizontal summation of the country's individual supply and demand curves. Although time constraints influenced this study, its estimates are probably as good as one can realistically derive for the world grain economy due to data problems.

By substituting 1964–1966 average data for the wheat, coarse grain, and rice prices and quantity variables, the intercept terms of the ERS supply and demand equations were adjusted and expressed as functions of own price and quantity only. These adjusted aggregate equations serve as the basis for the empirical estimates of the welfare effects of a grain cartel that follow.

The approach used here is similar to that contained in an empirical analysis of the world wheat economy by Schmitz and Bawden (1973) and in many of the quantitative studies found in Judge and Takayama (1973). Econometrically estimated supply and demand equations for each major trading region are used as the basis of the analysis (that is, a demand and supply curve for each region is estimated directly rather than a net import demand or export supply). It is from these "domestic" demand and supply equations that excess supply and excess demand curves are derived by an algebraic procedure which, after aggregation, result in a total import demand and a total export supply equation (or, consistent with the theoretical chapter, total excess demand and total excess supply for the aggregate of all regions). These are presented in equation (7.8) below. It should be clear that in this model excess supply and demand equations are not estimated directly but are derived from estimated domestic demand and supply equations.

The net or excess equations of the wheat model are

$$
\begin{aligned}
Q_{ESW_t} &= 30{,}411.4 + 434.9\, P_{W_t} \\
Q_{EDW_t} &= 159{,}603.5 - 1102.6\, P_{W_t}
\end{aligned}
\tag{7.8}
$$

Table 7-2. Trading regions used in the ERS model and production and consumption data for these regions (1964-66 average)

Coarse Grains			*Wheat*		
Region	*Production*[a]	*Consumption*[a]	*Region*	*Production*[a]	*Consumption*[a]
		Developed			
Importers			Importers		
E.C.	30.9	43.0	E.C.	28.8	27.7
United Kingdom	9.5	13.0	United Kingdom	3.8	8.2
Other W. Europe	19.4	24.9	Other W. Europe	10.2	11.5
Japan	1.4	7.5	Japan	1.2	4.8
Exporters			South Africa	0.8	1.1
United States	136.6	124.5	Exporters		
Canada	14.1	13.5	United States	35.5	18.6
Australia &			Canada	18.8	4.2
New Zealand	3.1	2.4	Australia &		
South Africa	5.1	4.6	New Zealand	10.2	2.7
Central Plan			Central Plan		
E. Europe	44.0	44.4	E. Europe	20.8	26.6
USSR	51.6	51.3	USSR	63.1	65.5
Com. Asia	46.9	46.8	Com. Asia	22.9	28.6
		Less Developed			
Importers			Importers		
Central America			Central America		
& Mexico	11.1	10.5	& Mexico	1.9	2.9
W. South America	2.8	2.9	E. South America	0.8	3.8
W. Africa	11.1	11.1	W. South America	1.6	2.8
N. Africa	6.5	6.5	E. Africa	0.5	0.8
W. Asia	8.3	8.8	W. Africa	0	0.7
S. Asia	25.8	27.2	N. Africa	4.1	7.7
E. Asia	6.4	6.8	W. Asia	12.5	14.4
			S. Asia	17.3	26.7
Exporters			So.E. Asia	0	0.3
Argentina	9.0	3.9	E. Asia	0.3	2.4
E. South America	11.6	11.3			
E. Africa	12.1	12.2	Exporters		
So. E. Asia	1.4	0.2	Argentina	7.9	3.9
		Developed and Less Developed			
World total:	468.7	477.0	World total:	263.1	265.7

[a] In millions of tons.

where

Q_{EDW_t} = total annual import demand for wheat (× 1,000 tons)

Q_{ESW_t} = total annual export supply of wheat (× 1,000 tons)

and

P_{W_t} = price of wheat (dollars per ton) in constant 1964–1966 dollars.

The net equations of the coarse grain model are

$$Q_{ESC_t} = -78{,}566.5 + 2561.4\, P_{C_t}$$
$$Q_{EDC_t} = 213{,}035.2 - 2149.1\, P_{C_t} \tag{7.9}$$

where

Q_{EDC_t} = total annual import demand for coarse grain (× 1,000 tons)

Q_{ESC_t} = total annual export supply of coarse grain (× 1,000 tons)

and

P_{C_t} = price of corn (dollars per ton) in constant 1964–1966 dollars.

Using the parameter estimates and projections of the ERS model for a present-day analysis involves two obvious problems, the first due to a structural change that has taken place in the world grain market since the model was estimated. During the 1970s, Russia and China were fairly consistent net importers of large volumes of both wheat and coarse grains, whereas in the 1960s their net trade in these commodities was almost zero. For the purpose of the current analysis, the first modification of the model was, therefore, to drop the supply and demand equations for the Soviet Union and China. The annual net trade of these two centrally planned economies was then treated exogenously by increasing the intercept of the importers' excess demand function for wheat by 15 million tons per annum and for coarse grains by 8 million tons per annum to correspond approximately to 1980 imports.

The second problem is with some of the model's projections. It predicts that wheat production in the major developed grain-exporting countries will increase at an annual rate of 1 percent, but actual data from the 1970s reveal that this estimate is too low and should be adjusted to at least 2 percent per annum. Similarly, wheat production in the developed importing countries has tended to grow at approximately 1.8 percent per annum and not 1.2 percent as predicted by the model. The production of coarse grains, on the other hand, has not grown as rapidly in the 1970s as was predicted by the model, which projected that production of coarse grains in the developed exporting countries would increase 2.6 percent per annum from 1964–1966 through to 1980; the growth rate has been closer to a modest 1 percent per annum. The growth of production in the developing countries has been close to 2 percent per year over this period, while this model predicted a growth rate of 3.3 percent. The second modification, then, was the adjustment of the ERS model to correspond to 1980 prices and quantities, according to the approximate rates presented in Table 7–3.

Treating Russia and China as exogenous to the model and inflating the variables in the supply and demand functions by the rates in Table 7–3 yields the consequent net wheat equations:

$$Q_{ESW_t} = 45{,}472.3 + 434.9\, P_{W_t}$$
$$Q_{EDW_t} = 189{,}763.2 - 684.8\, P_{W_t} \qquad (7.10)$$

Table 7-3. Rates used to inflate base variables of the ERS model to reflect 1980 prices and quantities

Variable	*Assumed Growth Rate Over the 1964-66 to 1980 Period (in Percentages)*
Wheat production in developed countries	30
Wheat production in developing countries	52.5
Coarse grain production in developed exporting countries	15
Coarse grain production in developed importing countries	45
Coarse grain production in developing countries	30
Wheat consumption in developed countries	15
Wheat consumption in developing countries	60
Coarse grain consumption in developed countries	45
Coarse grain consumption in developing countries	60
Wheat prices	105
Coarse grain prices	105

The consequent net equations of the coarse grain model are

$$Q_{ESC_t} = -179{,}968.1 + 2561.4\, P_{C_t}$$
$$Q_{EDC_t} = 280{,}300.4 - 1490.7\, P_{C_t}. \qquad (7.11)$$

Wheat Cartel Gains and Losses

The impact analysis in this chapter is based on the parameterized models described above. The demand and supply equations in (7.8) and (7.10) yield the wheat cartel price and quantity results shown in Table 7–4 and the economic effects shown in Tables 7–5 and 7–6.

From Table 7–4, the optimal producer cartel price in 1980 is estimated to be approximately \$362 per ton (or \$9.86 per bushel). The optimal price is higher and the quantity traded internationally is lower than it would be with a government wheat cartel. This scenario represents a price increase of 37 percent above the competitive level and a reduction in annual foreign sales of 32 percent, from 101.5 million tons to 68.7 million tons.

The formation of a government wheat cartel and the consequent imposition of the optimal export tax would restrict the amount of wheat traded to 73 million tons per annum, raise the world price

Table 7-4. Competitive and Cartel Price and Quantity Solutions in the World Wheat Market

Variable	*Base Period (1964-66)*	*Nominal Period (1980)*
Competitive price (\$/tonne)	84.0	264.1
Competitive quantity traded (X 1,000 tonnes)	66,952	101,511
Government cartel world price (\$/tonne)	96.7	349.2
Government cartel domestic price (\$/tonne)	51.7	130.3
Government cartel quantity traded (X 1,000 tonnes)	52,920	73,116
Producer cartel price (\$/tonne)	101.1	362.5
Producer cartel quantity traded (X 1,000 tonnes)	48,073	68,674

Note: Table figures were computed from equations (7.8) and (7.10).

from $264 to $349 per ton, and increase domestic consumption in the major exporting countries by roughly 24 percent per annum. Table 7–5 shows the gain accruing to the consumers of wheat for all uses in the exporting nations to be $5.4 billion per annum. This interesting empirical result makes it clear that consumers in the exporting countries have the most to gain from an optimal export government cartel because the domestic price falls substantially under such an arrangement. The estimates in Table 7–5 also show that even if producers in the exporting countries receive the entire export tax revenue, they are worse off with a government wheat cartel vis-a-vis free trade. Their loss is estimated at $1 billion per year.(Keep firmly in mind that the government export cartel is compared to free trade).

Table 7–6 indicates that producers in the exporting countries would support a producer wheat cartel while consumers in the exporting countries would oppose its formation. Producers as a group would stand to gain approximately $6.9 billion annually, and consumers would lose roughly $3.6 billion.

Marketing firms which act as intermediaries in the market have not been considered in any of the above models. Besides the exporting and importing nations, however, the intermediary firms and marketing boards play an important role in price discovery in the

Table 7-5. Welfare effects of the formation of a government wheat cartel, 1980

	Welfare Effects (Million $ U.S.)
Major exporters	
1. Gain to consumers[a]	$5,361
2. Loss to producers[a]	17,049
3. Export tax revenue	16,003
4. Net Gain (1 + 3 - 2)	4.315
5. Loss to producers net of tax revenue (2 - 3)	1,046
Major importers	
1. Loss to consumers[a]	$25,202
2. Gain to producers[a]	17,780
3. Net Loss (1 - 2)	7,422

[a]Based on estimates of consumers' surplus and economic rents.

Table 7-6. Welfare effects of the formation of a producer wheat cartel, 1980

	Welfare Effects (Million $ U.S.)
Major exporters	
1. Loss to producers[a]	$23,315
2. Export tax revenue	30,186
3. Net gain to producers (2 - 1)	6,871
4. Loss to consumers[a]	3,634
Major importers	
1. Loss to consumers[a]	$29,016
2. Gain to producers[a]	20,651
3. Net loss (1 - 2)	8,365

[a]Based on estimates of consumers' surplus and economic rents.

international grain market. This point has been discussed by McCalla (1979) and Morgan (1979). Carter and Gallini (1979) have demonstrated theoretically that the intermediary firms will oppose the formation of a grain cartel as it would result in lost revenue for them. This theoretical result showed that the marketing margin charged by the revenue-maximizing intermediary is insensitive to the formation of a cartel. The estimates in Table 7–5 suggest that the quantity of wheat traded internationally would decline by 28 percent under a government cartel and by 32 percent under a producer cartel. If the intermediary firms choose to hold their marketing margins constant under a cartel structure (as Carter and Gallini suggest), then they would undoubtedly oppose a 28 to 32 percent reduction in trade.

Interpretation of the Estimates of Cartel Effects

Estimates of gains and losses presented should be interpreted with caution. The empirical results and all of the accompanying discussion rest on the assumption that the market was in competitive equilibrium when the ERS parameter estimates were made and, more importantly, that the formation of a grain cartel is done vis-a-vis an

Table 7-7. Estimated effects to wheat-importing nations from the imposition of the optimal import tariff

Economic Effects	*Net Gain*[a]
1. Loss to consumers[b]	$-9,439
2. Gain to producers[b]	5,971
3. Import tariff revenue	7,202
4. Net gain (3 + 2 - 1)	3,734

[a] $ U.S. millions (1964-66).
[b] Based on estimates of consumers' surplus and economic rents.
Source: Carter, C., and Schmitz, A., 1979. "Import Tariffs and Price Formation in the World Wheat Market." *American Journal of Agricultural Economics* 61 (August): 517-22.

initial competitive free trade market situation. However, as Carter and Schmitz (1979) have argued, it is highly doubtful that the current marketplace is anywhere near equilibrium in the normal competitive sense. They demonstrated that the importing nations are currently earning abnormal "rents" in the wheat market; as shown in Table 7–7 the major importers are estimated to be earning $7.2 billion (1964–1966) annually in tariff revenue.

Consistent with the results from Table 7–1 on trade liberalization, our results suggest that major wheat exporters would gain roughly $5 billion from removing trade barriers in the wheat trade.[c] Thus, if the only effect of a cartel were to remove or reduce trade barriers, producers in exporting countries would gain while consumers would lose in the absence of internal compensation schemes. However, if the exporters were also able to impose the ideal cartel solution (the government or producer cartel discussed earlier), the gains would be greater than $5 billion. In the producer cartel case, one has to add on the gains to producers in Table 7–6 of roughly $7 billion, which brings the total to roughly $12 billion. In the government cartel case, the producers would still gain, but this would be due to the trade liberalization effect. The gain from both liberalization and imposing the export tax would be roughly $4 billion. (Note from Table 7–5 that producers lose from a government export cartel.)

[c] The loss to producers in exporting nations is roughly two-thirds of the tax revenue earned by importers.

Coarse Grain Cartel Gains and Losses

The demand and supply equations in (7.9) and (7.11) provide the results shown in Tables 7–8, 7–9, and 7–10 for the coarse grain market. It is estimated that a government cartel in coarse grains should set the export price at approximately $292 per ton, which represents a 25 percent increase over the competitive price. A producer grain cartel would raise the price an additional 7 percent above the government cartel price to $307 per ton.

As with the wheat cartel, users of feed grains in the exporting countries have the most to gain from a government cartel arrangement in coarse grains. Their welfare gain is estimated at $11.3 billion under a government cartel and their welfare loss at $21.7 billion under a producer cartel. Conversely, producers in the exporting countries stand to lose $11.2 billion under a government coarse grain cartel, but they should expect to gain approximately $15.8 billion under a producer cartel arrangement.

These estimates are more useful when they are combined with those associated with a wheat cartel. A coarse grain cartel has little or no appeal to the exporting nations unless it is combined with a wheat cartel. The same does not hold true for a wheat cartel, however, since feed grains are not a substitute for wheat in human consump-

Table 7-8. Competitive and cartel price and quantity solutions in the world coarse grain market

Variable	*Base Period (1964–66)*	*Nominal Period (1980)*
Competitive price ($/tonne)	61.9	232.8
Competitive quantity traded (X 1,000 tonnes)	79,997	110,975
Government cartel world price ($/tonne)	75.0	291.9
Government cartel domestic price ($/tonne)	50.9	198.4
Government cartel quantity traded (X 1,000 tonnes)	51,819	67,994
Producer cartel price ($/tonne)	81.2	306.7
Producer cartel quantity traded (X 1,000 tonnes)	38,547	57,242

Note: Table figures were computed from equations (7.9) and (7.11).

Table 7-9. Economic effects of the formation of a government coarse grains cartel, 1980

	(Million $ U.S.)
Major exporters	
1. Gain to consumers[a]	$11,277
2. Loss to producers[a]	14,356
3. Export tax revenue	3,101
4. Net gain (1 + 3 - 2)	22
5. Loss to producers net of tax revenue (2 - 3)	11,255
Major importers	
1. Loss to consumers[a]	$26,537
2. Gain to producers[a]	21,248
3. Net loss (1 - 2)	5,289

[a]Measures of consumers' surplus and economic rent.

tion. If the wheat–coarse grain price ratio remains relatively constant, then the welfare implications of a joint wheat–coarse grain cartel can be roughly estimated by summing the relevant figures in Tables 7–6 and 7–9 and Tables 7–8 and 7–10. For instance, a government joint coarse grain–wheat cartel would accrue gains to domestic consumers (and users) in the order of $16.7 billion and losses to producers of approximately $12.3 billion. Alternatively, a

Table 7-10. Welfare effects of the formation of a producer coarse grains cartel, 1980

	(Million $ U.S.)
Major exporters	
1. Loss to producers[a]	$62,412
2. Export tax revenue	78,219
3. Net gain to producers (2 - 1)	15,807
4. Loss to consumers[a]	21,670
Major importers	
1. Loss to consumers[a]	$32,906
2. Gain to producers[a]	26,691
3. Net loss (1 - 2)	6,215

[a]Measures of consumers' surplus and economic rent.

producer's joint coarse grain–wheat cartel would yield them welfare benefits in the neighborhood of $22.7 billion and would inflict a loss of approximately $25.3 billion on consumers in the exporting nations.

As in our discussion with respect to wheat, it is important to keep in mind when interpreting these results that they are derived by assuming that initially free trade exists. Clearly, this is not the case. As Table 7–1 shows, sizable gains could be had if trade liberalization occurred in feed grains, and these gains would have to be added to the economic effects presented in Tables 7–9 and 7–10 if an ideal cartel would be put into effect. Again, in terms of our chapter on importer responses to a cartel, perhaps the best that exporters could hope for is freer trade in response to a cartel threat, in which case the results in Table 7–1 are more relevant. However, the distribution effects are quite different than if an ideal cartel solution is reached. Unless exporters implemented a two-price system to put a ceiling on feed grain prices, feed grain prices would increase from trade expansion, resulting in welfare losses to the livestock sector.

It is clear from the empirical results that the gains from a feed grain cartel would be much greater than for a wheat cartel, and the feed-grain component would make up the largest percentage of gains from a joint wheat-feed grain exporter cartel. Thus, in terms of exporting countries, the United States has the most to gain from a cartel both absolutely and relatively since it is by far the largest exporter of feed grains.

These numbers not only point out the possible magnitude of the effects of a cartel in both wheat and feed grains; they also illustrate the important relationship between the feed grain and livestock sectors. In trade policy discussions, grains are often discussed without reference to the effect an expansion or contraction in feed grain exports has on the livestock sector. An increase in feed grain prices from trade expansion has a generally negative economic effect on hog producers, poultry growers, cattle ranchers, and the like, as was evident in the rapid grain export expansion in the 1973–74 period (Figure 1–3). This relationship is borne out by the results derived above for a grain export cartel. A government cartel could help the livestock sector in the grain exporting sectors by lowering feed grain prices,[d] but a grain producer cartel could cause feed grain

[d]We use the area under the derived demand for feed grains as the effect on livestock producers.

prices to rise in exporting nations and create economic losses for livestock growers.

Robustness of the Results

Calculated at the free-trade equilibrium, the estimated models employed in this chapter are a reflection of the elasticities shown in Table 7–11. The point elasticity estimates in Table 7–11 are roughly consistent with those in other empirical studies of the international grain market reviewed in Chapters 3 and 6. If we had employed an alternative set of estimated excess supply and demand equations, our results would not have been changed substantially. In absolute value, P.R. Johnson's (1971) estimates of both excess supply and demand elasticities are higher than those in Table 7–11. On the other hand, estimates provided by Shei and Thompson (1978)are both lower (in absolute value).

The optimal cartel prices computed in this chapter would be higher if the excess supply functions of the cartel members were more elastic than assumed and lower if they were less elastic. Similarly, the optimal cartel prices would be lower if the excess demand functions were more elastic than assumed here and higher if they were less elastic.

Table 7-11. Elasticities of excess supply and demand equations: wheat and coarse grains

Equations	*Elasticity at Free Trade Equilibrium*
Wheat	
Excess supply (7.8)	.54
Excess demand (7.8)	-1.38
Excess supply (7.10)	1.13
Excess demand (7.10)	-1.78
Coarse grains	
Excess supply (7.9)	1.98
Excess demand (7.9)	-1.66
Excess supply (7.11)	5.37
Excess demand (7.11)	-3.12

CONCLUSIONS

The empirical anaylsis in this chapter provides estimates of the welfare effects of the implementation of a grain cartel. Based on ERS supply and demand equations, the estimates strongly suggest that a grain cartel could yield substantial net welfare gains to the major grain-exporting nations. They also point out that within the exporting countries, there are producer-consumer distributional implications. These suggest that a cartel arrangement should be combined with an income redistribution scheme.

The reader is cautioned that the estimates presented are at best approximations and are based on explicit assumptions. At certain points, some of these assumptions are relaxed. For example, while the text notes that the market is not in a competitive state at present, it also suggests modifications to account for this situation.

An important question raised is the impact of a grain cartel on the livestock sector, which would lose from a producer grain cartel. A combined government wheat–coarse grain cartel, however, would probably increase the total revenue of meat producers by approximately 20 percent per annum—a substantial gain.

The fact that the gains from cartelization appear large in no way ensures that a grain export cartel will, in fact, work. But our estimates should provoke policymakers to consider the issue seriously. Nevertheless, the implementation and operation of a cartel involve more than merely showing that gains would accrue if it were properly functioning.

REFERENCES

Behrman, J.R. 1968. "Monopolistic Cocoa Pricing." *American Journal of Agricultural Economics* 50 (August): 702–720.

———. 1977. *International Commodity Agreements: An Evaluation of the UNCTAD Integrated Commodity Program.* Monograph No. 9. Washington, D.C.: Overseas Development Council.

Bickerdike, C.F. 1906. "The Theory of Incipient Taxes."*Economic Journal* 16 (December): 121–132.

Carter, C., and N. Gallini. 1979. "Wheat Cartelization in the Presence of a Market Intermediary." Paper presented at the AAEA annual meeting, Pullman, Washington.

Carter, C., and A. Schmitz. 1979. "Import Tariffs and Price Formation in the World Wheat Market." *American Journal of Agricultural Economics* 61 (August): 517–522.

Eckbo, P.L. 1976. *The Future of World Oil.* Cambridge, Mass.: Ballinger Publishing Company.

Geer, T. 1971. *An Oligopoly: The World Coffee Economy and Stabilization Schemes.* New York: Dunellen Publishing Company.

Gorouex, L.; D. Kendrick; and H. Kim. 1974. "Feedback Control Rule for Cocoa Market Stabilization." Discussion paper, Department of Economics, University of Texas.

Johnson, H.G. 1967. *Economic Policies Toward Less Developed Countries.* Washington, D.C.: The Brookings Institution.

———. 1968. "The Gain from Exploiting Monopoly or Monopsony Power in International Trade." *Economica* 35 (May): 151–156.

Johnson, P.R. 1965. "The Social Cost of the Tobacco Program." *Journal of Farm Economics* 47 (May): 242–255.

———. 1971. *Studies in the Demand for U.S. Exports of Agricultural Commodities.* Economic Research Report No. 15, North Carolina State University.

Judge, G.G., and T. Takayama. 1973. *Studies in Economic Planning over Space and Time.* Amsterdam: North Holland Publishing Company.

Kofi, T.A. 1972. "International Commodity Agreements and Export Earnings, Simulation of the 1968 'Draft International Cocoa Agreement'." *Food Research Institute Studies* 2: 177–201.

McCalla, A.F. 1979. "Strategies in International Agricultural Marketing: Public Versus Private Sector." In *International Trade in Agriculture: Theory and Practice,* edited by J. Hillman and A. Schmitz. Boulder, Colo.: Westview Press.

Morgan, D. 1979. *Merchants of Grain.* New York: Viking Press.

Pincus, J.A. 1965. *Economic Aid and International Cost Sharing.* Baltimore: Johns Hopkins University Press.

Pindyck, R."Gains to Producers from Cartelization of an Exhaustible Resource." *Review of Economics and Statistics* 60 (May): 238–251.

Rojko, A.D.; D. Regier; P. O'Brien; A. Coffing; and L. Bailey. 1978. *Alternative Futures for World Food in 1985, Volume 1, World GOL Model Analytical Report.* U.S. Department of Agriculture, Economics, Statistics, and Cooperatives Service, Foreign Agricultural Economics Report 146.

Rojko, A.D.; F.S. Urban; and J.J. Naive. 1971. *World Demand Prospects for Grain in 1980 with Emphasis on Trade by Less Developed Countries.* U.S. Department of Agriculture, Economic Research Service, Foreign Agricultural Economics Report 75.

Schmitz, A., and D.L. Bawden. 1973.*The World Wheat Economy: An Empirical Analysis.* Giannini Foundation Monograph No. 32, University of California, Berkeley.

Shei, S.Y., and R.L. Thompson. 1978. "The Short Run Welfare Effects of Export Controls." *Canadian Journal of Agricultural Economics* 26: 29–34.

Thompson, R.L. Forthcoming. "Survey of Recent Developments in Agricultural Trade Modeling and Forecasting." In *New Directions in Econometric Modeling and Forecasting in U.S. Agriculture,* edited by G.C. Rausser. New York: Elsevier North Holland, Inc.

Underwood, J. 1976. "Optimization Rules for Producer Groups in a Stochastic Market Setting with Application to the Copper and Tea Markets." Ph.D. dissertation, University of Minnesota.

Wong, C.M. 1977. "A Model for Evaluating the Effects of Thai Government Taxation of Rice Exports on Trade and Welfare. *American Journal of Agricultural Economics*.60 (February): 65–73.

8 A DYNAMIC SIMULATION OF ALTERNATIVE GRAIN CARTEL POLICIES

As the theoretical chapter has suggested, a grain cartel could take many different forms: it could involve only wheat or include coarse grains as well; prices could be set at many levels; the market could be allocated among exporting countries in different ways. This chapter attempts to review some of the more likely scenarios by employing a dynamic, econometric simulation model of world wheat and coarse grain production, consumption, trade, and prices for major world regions.

This model differs from the one presented in Chapter 7 in terms of both its structural characteristics and its ability to compute the optimal export cartel solution. Unlike the results in Chapter 7, those presented here in no way suggest that optimality is achieved; that is, the results presented are derived from a variety of assumptions about prices, quantities, and trade flows and do not attempt to determine what the outcome of an "ideal" cartel would be.

MODEL DESCRIPTION

The model used for this analysis is the Michigan State University (MSU) agriculture trade model—an annual econometric simulation model which generates production, consumption, net trade, stock levels, livestock units, and world price estimates for major world regions for wheat and coarse grains. It has eighty endogenous equations estimated by ordinary least squares from 1960–1976 annual data. This chapter presents an overview of the model; a full description of the model, its data sources, estimation procedures, and model performance will be available in a forthcoming MSU research report.

The MSU agriculture trade model defines nine trade regions, four designated as exporting regions and five as importing regions. The exporting regions are the United States, Canada, Australia, and Argentina. The importing regions include all remaining world countries and are defined as the Soviet Bloc (USSR and Eastern Europe), the developed market economies (Western Europe, Japan, Israel, South Africa, and New Zealand), and the less developed market economies (Caribbean, Central and South America, Africa, Asian Middle East, East, and South East). The final two regions are China and a residual region, referred to as Undesignated, which includes all other countries.

Production for both importing and exporting regions is determined from an estimated area harvested equation and from crop yields. Area harvested is estimated as a function of land availability and relative crop prices from the previous year. Crop yields are projected into the future by a linear trend.

In general form, the three equations that determine production for each region are as follows:

Planted Hectares

$$PH_{i,t} = \beta_{0_i} + \beta_1 CLB_{i,t} + \beta_2 P_{i,t-1} + \beta_3 P_{j,t-1}$$

where: $PH_{i,t}$ is planted hectares of commodity i in year t;

$CLB_{i,t}$ is the total cropland planted to wheat and coarse grains in year t

$P_{i,t-1}$ is the lagged price of commodity i

$P_{j,t-1}$ is the lagged price of substitute commodity j

Yields

$$Y_{i,t} = \beta_0 + \beta_1 T$$

where: $Y_{i,t}$ is yields measured in metric tons per hectare for commodity i in year t

T is a linear trend

Production

$$PROD_{i,t} = PH_{i,t} * Y_{i,t}$$

where: $PROD_{i,t}$ is production measured in metric tons of commodity i in year t

Net imports of wheat and coarse grains for each importing region are estimated directly. All import equations are specified on a per capita basis, and the explanatory variables include grain prices (deflated by exchange rates), per capita income, and per capita domestic grain supplies. Exchange rates are defined relative to the U.S. dollar and are weighted by volume of net imports. In general form, the estimated equation for net imports is:

Net Imports

$$NI_{i,t} = \beta_0 + \beta_1 S_{i,t} + \beta_2 GDP_{i,t} + \beta_3 P_{i,t} + \beta_4 P_{i,t-1} + \beta_5 Z_t$$

where: $NI_{i,t}$ is per capita net imports of commodity i in year t

$S_{i,t}$ is per capita domestic supply (production + beginning stocks) or commodity i in year t

$GDP_{i,t}$ is per capita gross disposable product of the importing region in year t

$P_{i,t}$ is the world price of commodity i in year t deflated by the exchange rate of the importing region

$P_{i,t}$ is the world price of commodity i in year $t - 1$

Figure 8–1. Net import relationships

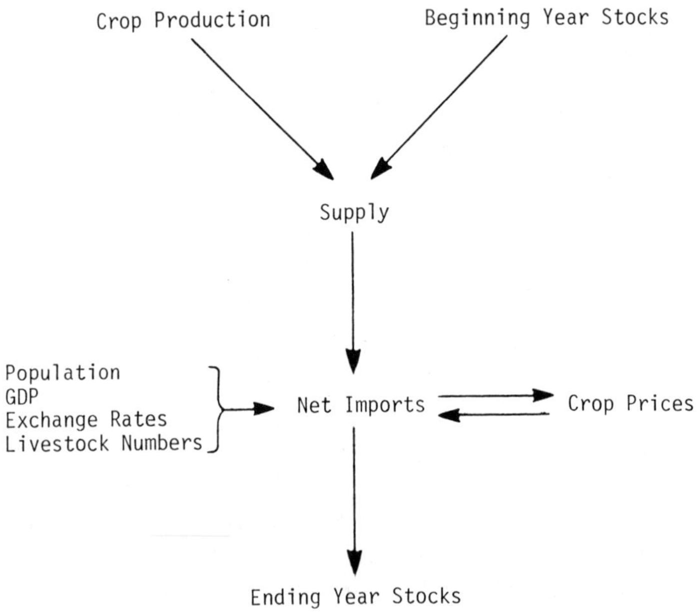

deflated by the exchange rate of the importing region

Z_t is other variables which affect imports such as livestock numbers

The net import relationships are illustrated in Figure 8–1. Ending year stocks are estimated for the importing regions according to stock equations of the general form:

Beginning Year Stocks

$$ST_{i,t} = \beta_0 + \beta_1 S_{i,t-1} + \beta_2 P_{i,t-1}$$

where: $ST_{i,t}$ is per capita beginning year stocks of commodity i in year t

$S_{i,t-1}$ is the per capita domestic supplies of commodity i in year $t - 1$

$P_{i,t-1}$ is the world price of commodity i in year $t - 1$

Net supplies available for export from each of the four exporting countries are computed as grain supplies which remain after domestic consumption and minimum stock demand are satisfied. Domestic demand in each exporting country is estimated by several equations which include feed, seed, and food uses. In turn, feed demand is estimated as a function of grain prices and the number of grain-consuming animal units, which are endogenously determined; per capita food demand is estimated as a function of per capita income and prices and seed demand as a function of cropland area. Grain stocks are defined as the residual supplies which remain after domestic demand and net exports are satisfied. A minimum stock balance, equal to the recent low stock levels from the 1970–1976 period, is incorporated as a constraint. When supplies of grain are not sufficient to satisfy both domestic and export demand while maintaining the minimum stock requirements, exports are reduced until the minimum stock level is reached. An illustration of the model structure is shown in Figure 8–2.

We can represent net import demand as:

$$QIW = \sum_{i=1}^{5} QIW_i$$

$$QICG = \sum_{i=1}^{5} QICG_i$$

where *QIW* and *QICG* are world net import demand for wheat and coarse grain, respectively, and QIW_i and $QICG_i$ are net import demand for each region. Similarly, we can represent net export supply as:

$$QEW = \sum_{i=1}^{4} QEW_i$$

$$QECG = \sum_{i=1}^{4} QECG_i$$

where *QEW* and *QECG* are world net export supplies for wheat and coarse grain, respectively, and QEW_i and $QECG_i$ are net export supplies for each region.

Figure 8–2. Structure of the model

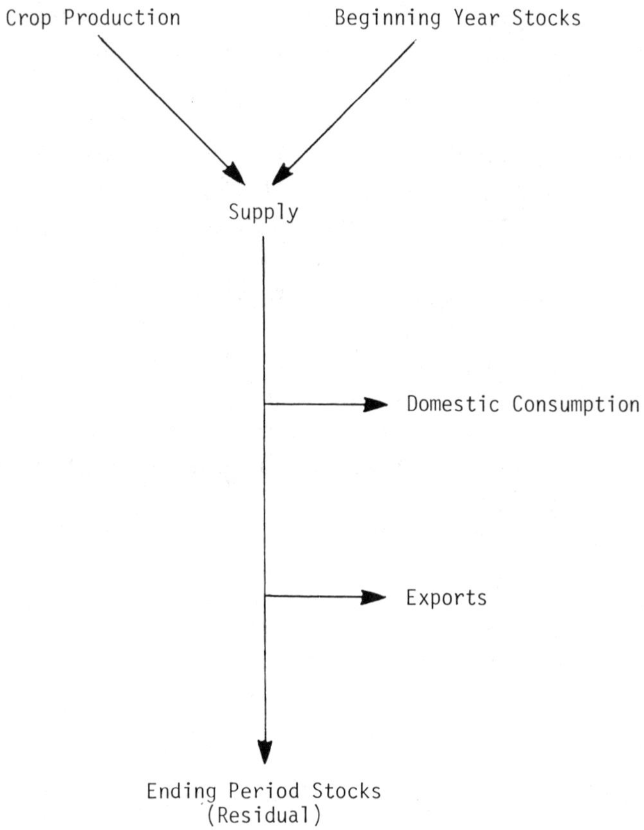

The model solution determines world price, net import demand, and net export supply simultaneously. A single world price, the U.S. export price, is determined. Trade flows between specific regions are not identified; however, quantities traded for both exporting and importing regions are determined. The model assumes that trade flows are determined by availability of grain for export and marketing behavior—not by transportation costs as a spatial equilibrium model would imply. Net exports from each of the four regions are determined after net import demand for each region, price, and world exports have been determined. Given the total world net import demand, *QIW* and *QICG*, the model allocates these quantities among the four exporting regions based on available supplies and an estimated hierarchy which allows Argentina and Australia to sell as much grain as desired. Canada and the United States then share the remaining market based on their available supplies.

The model obtains desired exports for each country from an estimated econometric equation based on world price, available export supplies, and world demand. Estimation results show that Argentina acts in an export dumping-like manner; after satisfying its domestic consumption and stock requirements, it has historically dumped remaining supplies on the world market regardless of price. Australia acts in a similar manner but has shown an increased willingness in recent years to store grain when prices are low. Both countries are allowed to export as much grain to the world market as they desire, while the remaining world import demand is allocated between the United States and Canada, based on relative availability of grain for export and the export price as obtained from estimated equations. Finally, U.S. and Canadian exports are adjusted proportionately to balance world exports with world imports.

Stocks which remain at the year end are estimated econometrically in the importing regions and calculated from an identity in the exporting regions. Since net import demand and net consumption is estimated in the importing regions, stocks are estimated from prices, production levels, and the previous year's stocks. Ending stocks in the exporting regions are calculated as the residual of domestic supply minus domestic demand and net exports.

SCENARIOS ANALYZED[a]

Eighteen scenarios are analyzed to investigate alternative marketing arrangements under two sets of assumptions. The two sets of assumptions are denoted as "base" and "low income-high yields." See Appendix 8B for a description of these assumptions. A table describing each scenario is included for each of the two sets of model assumptions (Tables 8–1 and 8–2).

This chapter considers three pricing policies. The first alternative, which is to allow the model to determine the market equilibrium prices, is designated as a "no-price policy" and provides a basis for comparison. The second and third price policies represent two levels

[a]Validation of the model used is discussed in data sources and in Appendices 8A and 8B.

Table 8-1. Scenarios analyzed using Base Assumptions[a]

Price Policy: *Marketing Arrangements*	*No Price Policy (Model determines equilibrium wheat and coarse grain prices)*	*WP ≥ \$5.45, FP ≥ \$4.30 (Wheat price floor is set at \$5.45 and coarse grain price floor is \$4.30)*	*WP ≥ 6.80, FP ≥ \$5.37 (Wheat price floor is set at \$6.80 and coarse grain price floor is \$5.37)*
Current market conditions No cartel exists	Run 1		
Producer cartel—historical market shares All consumers and producers face the cartel grain prices. Exporting countries share export market based on historical market shares.		Run 2	Run 3
Producer cartel—U.S. residual supplier All consumers and producers face the cartel grain prices. The United States acts as the residual supplier.		Run 4	Run 5
Price discrimination cartel All importing nations are charged high prices and exporters receive market equilibrium prices. The United States acts as the residual supplier.		Run 11	Run 12
Price discrimination cartel Developed market economies and Soviet Bloc are charged high import prices and Less Developed countries and exporters receive market equilibrium prices. The United States acts as the residual supplier.		Run 13	Run 14

[a]WP = Wheat price, FP = Coarse Grain price.

Table 8-2. Scenarios analyzed using low income-high yields assumptions[a]

Price Policy: / Marketing Arrangements	No Price Policy (Model determines equilibrium wheat and coarse grain prices)	WP ≥ \$5.45, FP ≥ \$4.30 (Wheat price floor is set at \$5.45 and coarse grain price floor is \$4.30)	WP ≥ 6.80, FP ≥ \$5.37 (Wheat price floor is set at \$6.80 and coarse grain price floor is \$5.37)
Current market conditions No cartel exists	Run 6		
Producer cartel—historical market shares All consumers and producers face the cartel grain prices. Exporting countries share export market based on historical market shares.		Run 7	Run 8
Producer cartel—U.S. residual supplier All consumers and producers face the cartel grain prices. The United States acts as the residual supplier.		Run 9	Run 10
Price discrimination cartel All importing nations are charged high prices and exporters receive market equilibrium prices. The United States acts as the residual supplier.		Run 15	Run 16
Price discrimination cartel Developed market economies and Soviet Bloc are charged high import prices and Less Developed countries and exporters receive market equilibrium prices. The United States acts as the residual supplier.		Run 17	Run 18

[a]WP = Wheat price, FP = Coarse Grain price.

of cartel prices. In each case, a price floor for wheat and course grains is specified. For example, one scenario specified a wheat export price of $5.45 per bushel and $4.30 per bushel for coarse grains. Export prices cannot fall below these levels but will rise above them if the market equilibrium prices exceed the price floors. In addition to the export price floors, market equilibrium prices are also determined within the model. In the scenarios analyzed, it is common to have two prices: the export price determined by the price floors and the market equilibrium price. This allows price discrimination policies which charge high prices for exports and lower market equilibrium prices to consumers in the exporting countries.

The relationship between the wheat and coarse grain export price floors is based on the average ratio of wheat and coarse grain prices over the 1970–1977 period, while the price floors chosen were based on a wheat price of $200 and $250 per metric ton. Coarse grain prices were then set equal to the 1970–1977 average ratio of coarse grain to wheat price.

Two market share policies are also considered. The historical share of world wheat and coarse grain exports for each exporting country, based on the 1970–1977 period, was calculated and used as the cartel share. Production in excess of each country's share of the world market is considered available for domestic consumption or storage. A second policy, based on the historical behavior of the four exporting countries, identifies the United States as the residual grain supplier to the world. The United States is forced to hold stocks when world demand is not sufficient to equal desired exports.

Runs 1 and 6 (Tables 8C–1 and 8C–6 of Appendix 8C) are the current market conditions runs for the base assumptions and low income–high yields assumptions, respectively. No cartel price policy is assumed; and no market shares or export restrictions are placed on Canada, Australia, or Argentina. These runs correspond with a free market scenario under alternative model assumptions. The assumptions for run 1 represent the most likely outcomes over the 1979–1983 period, while the assumptions for run 6 are intended to represent a series of events unfavorable to the success of a world grain cartel. Accordingly, run 6 is thought to represent a reasonable lower bound on the success of a world grain cartel.

Runs 2 and 3 (Tables 8C–2 and 8C–3) for the base assumptions and runs 7 and 8 (Tables 8C–7 and 8C–8) for the low income–high yields assumptions consider two levels of cartel prices and historical market shares. The United States, Canada, Australia, and Argentina are assumed to share the export market based on the average market share over the 1970–1977 period. All consumers and producers in both exporting and importing nations face the single world price. No production controls are imposed and, since price floors are set for both producers and consumers at levels above equilibrium, a buildup of stocks is expected.

Runs 4 and 5 (Tables 8C–4 and 8C–5) for the base assumptions and runs 9 and 10 (Tables 8C–9 and 8C–10) for the low income–high yields assumptions represent a producer cartel which sets a single world price for consumers of both importing and exporting nations under two levels of prices. These runs differ from the historical market share scenarios above because no restriction is placed on the behavior of other exporting countries. The United States is assumed to allow Canada, Australia, and Argentina to export as much wheat and coarse grains as they desire, an assumption which places the U.S. in the role of the dominant firm and price leader. Other firms are allowed to receive the price determined by the dominant firm but are not forced to limit sales. These scenarios are useful because they indicate the consequences of an effort on the part of the United States alone to raise export prices.

Runs 11 and 12 (Tables 8C–11 and 8C–12) for the base assumptions and runs 15 and 16 (Tables 8C–15 and 8C–16) for the low income–high yields assumptions represent a price-discriminating cartel. The market is separated into all exporting and all importing countries, and a high price is charged importing countries, while the lower equilibrium price is available to consumers of the exporting countries. The lower price in the exporting countries protects the consumer and prevents high grain prices from feeding back into the livestock sectors. These scenarios are particularly interesting when we recall the impact that the U.S. livestock sector had on the high grain prices of 1972–1976.

The final set of scenarios is shown by runs 13 and 14 (Tables 8C–13 and 8C–14) for the base assumptions and runs 17 and 18 (Tables 8C–17 and 8C–18) for the low income–high yields assumptions. These four runs represent a price-discriminating cartel in which the exporting countries and the less developed market economies receive low market prices, and the developed market economies and the Soviet Bloc countries receive high prices. As in the previous set of runs, domestic consumers in the exporting countries are protected from high grain prices. In addition, the less developed market economies are allowed to buy wheat and coarse grain at market prices which are below those of the cartel. This scenario has the desirable characteristic of market differentiation based on income.

SIMULATION RESULTS

Eighteen computer simulations were run to explore the implications of a world grain cartel. The full results of each simulation are presented in Appendix 8C. Only a summary will be presented here, emphasizing the implications of each alternative marketing arrangement for the United States. The interested reader, however, can easily compare the simulations to obtain results for other countries.

The eighteen computer simulations are analyzed in three groups: (1) the simulations based on the current market structure; (2) those which assume that the United States is the residual supplier of world exports; and (3) those which assume a marketing arrangement that allocates market share among exporting countries based on historical market shares.

Current Market Structure

Two of the eighteen simulations assume the current market structure. Run 1 forecasts production, consumption, trade, stock levels, prices, and grain-consuming animal units with the base assumptions; and run 6 incorporates the low income–high yields assumptions. These two simulations provide a benchmark by which other results can be measured since they are free from any price policy and represent the currently existing market structure.

Run 1 projects that U.S. net wheat and coarse grain exports will grow to 44.1 and 71.2 million metric tons, respectively, by 1983. These exports are substantially above the 1975–1978 averages of 30.1 and 51.8 million metric tons but are not significantly above the expected 1979 exports of 39.0 and 67.1 million metric tons.

Prices under run 1 are projected to increase substantially from current levels, with wheat price expected to reach $6.09 by 1983 and coarse grain price to equal $4.13. Both prices are expressed in nominal U.S. dollars per bushel and are U.S. export prices. Compared with an estimated 1978 price of $3.63 and $2.50 for wheat and coarse grains, respectively, prices would increase approximately 65 to 70 percent by 1983.

The results from run 1 suggest that the world wheat and coarse grain markets are entering a period of high prices and large U.S. exports. Stock levels will be drawn down, and prices will rise substantially. The first signs of these changes began to appear in 1979, with U.S. wheat exports projected to be 39.4 million metric tons and coarse grain exports estimated at 67.6 million metric tons, representing values of 20 to 22 percent above the 1978 levels.

The market projected by run 1 is dependent upon the base assumptions. If we use lower growth rates in world income and higher yields of wheat and coarse grains which correspond with favorable weather, we obtain the results projected by run 6. Specific details of the low income–high yields assumptions used for run 6 are presented in Appendix 8B.

Run 6 projects that U.S. wheat net exports will equal 35.0 million metric tons in 1979 and 35.2 million metric tons by 1983. Compared with 1978 levels, this increase is approximately 9 percent. Coarse grain exports are projected to equal 58.3 million metric tons by 1983 compared to 56.0 and 59.1 million metric tons for 1978 and 1979, respectively.

Wheat export price is projected to decrease from $3.81 per bushel in 1979 to $3.42 per bushel by 1983. Coarse grain export price is projected to remain at the government support level of $2.50 per bushel over the entire 1979–1983 period. This level is obtained by adding the historical export marketing margin to the loan rate.

Run 6 projects that ending-year wheat and coarse grain stocks held in the United States will increase over the 1979–1983 period. By the end of 1983, U.S. wheat stocks are projected to reach 37.6 million metric tons compared with 25.1 million metric tons in 1978. U.S. coarse grain ending-year stocks are projected to equal 65.0 million metric tons by 1983 compared with 45.6 million metric tons in 1978.

The two benchmark scenarios, runs 1 and 6, thus yield substantially different results based on world economic growth and crop yields. The conditions specified as high yields in run 6 would be met if the world has five years of crop yields which are free of any major shortfalls. Reduced world economic growth, as assumed in run 6, could probably be accounted for by substantially higher energy costs. Together, these two conditions would result in low grain prices and a buildup of grain stocks.

Cartel Alternatives with the United States As the Residual Supplier of Exports

The United States is often described as the residual grain supplier to the world. Other grain exporting countries—such as Canada, Australia, and Argentina—export as much wheat and coarse grains as desired, and the United States exports to the remaining market. Twelve simulations are presented in this section to determine the implications of alternative marketing arrangements under this structure. The simulations assume that the United States receives the residual demand for wheat and coarse grains after other exporting countries have sold their desired amounts as indicated by their historical behavior.

U.S. Wheat and Coarse Grain Net Exports

Tables 8–3 and 8–4 show projected U.S. wheat and coarse grain net exports for the 1979–1983 period. Alternative export pricing policies are represented by each of seven runs under the two sets of assumptions. The first set of assumptions is denoted as the base assumptions and corresponds to a "most likely" outcome. The second set of assumptions is denoted as low income–high yield assumptions and assumes a growth of world income and yields unfavorable to a cartel marketing arrangement. Specific details of both sets of assumptions are presented in Appendix 8B.

Under the base assumptions, U.S. wheat exports are projected to grow from 39.1 million metric tons in 1979 to 44.1 million metric tons in 1983 for run 1. U.S. coarse grain exports are projected to grow from 67.1 million metric tons in 1979 to 71.5 million metric tons in 1983. No restrictions are placed on quantities of exports from Canada, Australia, or Argentina. The growth of U.S. exports shown under run 1 represents the projected outcomes under the current market structure with no pricing arrangements or cartel. Six additional runs for the base assumptions represent three types of cartel arrangements and two levels of prices.

Table 8–3. Projected U.S. wheat net exports, 1979–83[a]

Run	Policy Description[a]	1979	1980	1981	1982	1983
			(Million Metric Tons)			
Base assumptions						
Run 1	No price policy	39.1	38.3	41.9	44.0	44.1
Run 4	WP ⩾ 5.45, FP ⩾ 4.30, all regions	39.3	39.4	43.6	43.5	43.5
Run 5	WP ⩾ 6.80, FP ⩾ 5.37, all regions	38.4	37.5	41.9	44.7	46.1
Run 11	WP ⩾ 5.45, FP ⩾ 4.30, for SB, DM, and LD only	39.8	36.6	39.0	45.2	45.0
Run 12	WP ⩾ 6.80, FP ⩾ 5.37, for SB, DM, and LD only	39.3	34.5	36.8	41.5	46.1
Run 13	WP ⩾ 5.45, FP ⩾ 4.30, for SB and DM only	40.7	38.6	41.2	45.0	44.2
Run 14	WP ⩾ 6.80, FP ⩾ 5.37, for SB and DM only	41.0	38.4	40.7	45.3	44.9
Low income-high yields						
Run 6	No price policy	35.0	30.7	31.8	33.6	35.2
Run 9	WP ⩾ 5.45, FP ⩾ 4.30, all regions	35.1	31.2	32.4	32.7	34.3
Run 10	WP ⩾ 6.80, FP ⩾ 5.37, all regions	34.1	29.3	30.6	30.6	32.1
Run 15	WP ⩾ 5.45, FP ⩾ 4.30, for SB, DM, and LD only	35.6	28.7	29.0	30.5	32.0
Run 16	WP ⩾ 6.80, FP ⩾ 5.37, for SB, DM, and LD only	35.1	26.5	26.7	28.1	29.5
Run 17	WP ⩾ 5.45, FP ⩾ 4.30, for SB and DM only	36.5	31.1	32.0	33.8	35.4
Run 18	WP ⩾ 6.80, FP ⩾ 5.37, for SB and DM only	36.8	30.9	31.8	33.6	35.2

[a]WP = Wheat price, FP = Coarse grain price, SB = Soviet Bloc, DM = Developed market economies, and LD = Less developed market economies.

Runs 4 and 5 in Table 8–3 show projected U.S. wheat exports when a single wheat and coarse grain price floor is set for all regions; U.S. producers and consumers, as well as all exporting and importing regions, face the higher prices. U.S. wheat exports are projected to increase slightly for 1979–1981 and then decline for 1982 and 1983 for run 4 relative to the no-price policy of run 1. For run 4, a floor on

Table 8–4. Projected U.S. coarse grain net exports, 1979–83[a]

Run	Policy Description[a]	1979	1980	1981	1982	1983
		(Million Metric Tons)				
Base assumptions						
Run 1	No price policy	67.1	66.0	64.1	66.6	71.2
Run 4	WP ≥ 5.45, FP ≥ 4.30, all regions	59.0	49.9	51.6	57.8	65.6
Run 5	WP ≥ 6.80, FP ≥ 5.37, all regions	55.3	41.8	41.9	45.2	50.4
Run 11	WP ≥ 5.45, FP ≥ 4.30, for SB, DM, and LD only	62.1	59.4	61.6	61.2	69.6
Run 12	WP ≥ 6.80, FP ≥ 5.37, for SB, DM, and LD only	60.0	54.9	57.6	59.3	62.1
Run 13	WP ≥ 5.45, FP ≥ 4.30, for SB and DM only	64.9	61.5	61.9	63.5	70.2
Run 14	WP ≥ 6.80, FP ≥ 5.37, for SB and DM only	64.1	58.8	59.9	60.3	66.7
Low income–high yields						
Run 6	No price policy	59.1	54.8	54.5	56.2	58.3
Run 9	WP ≥ 5.45, FP ≥ 4.30, all regions	51.2	36.9	35.7	37.0	38.2
Run 10	WP ≥ 6.80, FP ≥ 5.37, all regions	47.4	28.4	26.2	26.9	27.5
Run 15	WP ≥ 5.45, FP ≥ 4.30, for SB, DM, and LD only	54.2	46.6	46.1	47.4	49.2
Run 16	WP ≥ 6.80, FP ≥ 5.37, for SB, DM, and LD only	52.1	42.1	41.2	42.3	44.0
Run 17	WP ≥ 5.45, FP ≥ 4.30, for SB and DM only	57.1	50.0	49.9	51.5	53.6
Run 18	WP ≥ 6.80, FP ≥ 5.37, for SB and DM only	56.4	47.1	46.8	48.4	50.5

[a]WP = Wheat price, FP = Coarse grain price, SB = Soviet Bloc, DM = Developed market economies, and LD = Less developed market economies.

wheat price is placed at $5.45 per bushel, and coarse grain price is constrained to at least $4.30 per bushel. Run 5 also assumes a single world price for all world regions, with a wheat price floor of $6.80 per bushel and a coarse grain price floor of $5.37 per bushel. This price policy results in slightly lower exports, compared to run 1, for 1979 and 1980 and slightly higher exports for 1981, 1982, and 1983.

Taken in isolation, these results contradict expected outcomes—U.S. wheat exports increase with higher export prices. To understand fully the interactions which cause these results, however, we must also consider coarse grain price and exports.

Table 8–4 demonstrates that the price floors on wheat and coarse grains result in large decreases in U.S. coarse grain exports when either run 4 or run 5 is compared to run 1. Coarse grain exports are projected to decrease from 67.1 million metric tons in 1979 under run 1 to 59.0 and 55.3 for runs 4 and 5, respectively. Further decreases occur in 1980 as coarse grain exports fall from 66.0 million metric tons in run 1 to 49.9 and 41.8 million metric tons in runs 4 and 5, respectively. The large decreases in coarse grain exports are caused by several factors which also contribute to the increases in wheat exports.

Under the pricing policy of runs 4 and 5, coarse grain prices increase significantly compared to run 1. Wheat price, on the other hand, increases by a much smaller percentage because it is already relatively high under run 1. This difference results in a substitution away from coarse grain consumption to wheat consumption and partially accounts for the increased wheat exports under runs 4 and 5. Under run 1, coarse grain price in 1979 is $2.50 per bushel; when the price policies of runs 4 and 5 are implemented, coarse grain price increases to $4.30 and $5.37, an increase of 72 and 115 percent, respectively. Wheat price for 1979 is $3.88 under run 1 and is increased to $5.45 and $6.80 for runs 4 and 5, respectively; the increase in wheat price is 40 percent and 75 percent for runs 4 and 5, respectively. The relatively greater price increase for coarse grains results in a shift in demand for wheat which exceeds the decrease caused by the higher wheat price.

A second factor accounting for the significant decrease in coarse grain exports under runs 4 and 5 is the higher level of exports from competing exporters. As shown in Appendix 8C and summarized in Table 8–5, Canada, Australia, and Argentina decrease consumption and increase exports for coarse grains more than for wheat. Table 8–5 shows 1979 wheat and coarse grain exports for Canada, Australia and Argentina for runs 1, 4, and 5. In response to the higher prices imposed by runs 4 and 5, combined wheat exports from Canada, Australia, and Argentina increase from 29.09 million metric tons for run 1 to 29.92 and 30.14 for runs 4 and 5, respectively. Coarse grain exports for the three countries combined

Table 8-5. Wheat and coarse grain exports for Canada, Australia, and Argentina for 1979

	Wheat Exports			*Coarse Grain Exports*		
Region	*Run 1*	*Run 4*	*Run 5*	*Run 1*	*Run 4*	*Run 5*
Canada	15.51	15.62	15.21	2.66	4.97	6.01
Australia	10.88	11.44	11.93	3.69	4.52	4.88
Argentina	2.70	2.86	3.00	8.90	9.25	9.46
Total	29.09	29.92	30.14	15.25	18.74	20.35

increase from 15.25 million metric tons under run 1 to 18.67 and 20.35 million metric tons under runs 4 and 5, respectively. This greater willingness to curtail domestic coarse grain consumption and increase exports results in a greater decline in U.S. coarse grain exports than wheat exports under similar price changes.

To consider the sensitivity of these results to the model assumptions, an alternative set of assumptions was used. Runs 6, 9, and 10, as shown in Tables 8–3 and 8–4, contain the same price policies as runs 1, 4, and 5 but incorporate the low income–high yields assumptions. A comparison of run 6 with run 1 shows the effect of the alternative assumptions when a no-price policy is implemented. Run 6 projects that U.S. wheat exports will equal 35.0 million metric tons in 1979 compared to 39.1 million metric tons under run 1. Coarse grain exports for 1979 are projected to reach 67.1 million metric tons under run 1, compared to 59.1 million metric tons under run 6. By 1983, U.S. exports for wheat and coarse grains for run 6 are 25 percent and 22 percent below run 1 levels.

Runs 9 and 10 result in significantly lower U.S. wheat and coarse grain exports compared to runs 4 and 5. Tables 8–3 and 8–4 show that U.S. wheat exports for runs 9 and 10 are 34.3 and 32.1 million metric tons, respectively, for 1983, while U.S. wheat exports for runs 4 and 5 are 43.5 and 46.1, respectively, for 1983. U.S. coarse grain exports are also significantly lower for runs 6, 9, and 10 compared to runs 1, 4, and 5. They fall from a 1983 level of 50.4 million metric tons in run 5 to 27.5 million metric tons in run 10. This difference is attributed completely to the different assumptions about growth in world income and yields.

Runs 11–14 and 15–18 consider two types of price discrimination, two levels of export prices, and two sets of model assumptions. A wheat export price floor of $5.45 or $6.80 per bushel is combined with a price floor of $4.30 or $5.37 on coarse grain exports. Prices for consumers in the exporting countries are determined by the market but are generally below the price floors. High export prices are charged to all importers in runs 11, 12, 15, and 16, while runs 13, 14, 17, and 18 charge high export prices only to the Soviet Bloc and developed market economies.

A summary of runs 11–14 indicates that price discrimination would increase U.S. wheat exports but decrease U.S. coarse grain exports by 1983 compared to the benchmark results of run 1. The higher U.S. wheat exports result from decreased wheat exports from Canada, Australia, and Argentina as domestic consumption responds to the lower domestic prices. Increased wheat imports also occur in most importing regions as they are substituted for coarse grain imports, which show a relatively greater price increase. Two factors account for the decrease in U.S. coarse grain exports: first, imports decrease in response to the higher prices; and secondly, slightly higher domestic prices in Canada, Austalia, and Argentina reduce domestic consumption and slightly increase the exports of these countries.

The price discrimination cartel combined with the low income–high yields assumptions incorporated in runs 15–18 results in lower U.S. wheat and coarse grain exports over the entire 1979–1983 period when compared to run 6. These results are caused primarily by decreased imports.

Wheat and Coarse Grain Prices

Tables 8–6 and 8–7 show wheat and coarse grain prices. Both an export price and a market equilibrium price are shown for each run for the 1979–1983 period. The export prices, the top row of prices for each run, are the prices charged for grain exports. If no cartel policy is implemented, as in runs 1 and 6, then the export price and the market equilibrium price, the lower row of prices, are the same. When a cartel policy is in effect, the export price will have a floor, and the market equilibrium price will often be lower. Run 11 shows that the export price of wheat in 1979 is $5.45 per bushel and that the market equilibrium price is $3.92 per bushel. The export price of

Table 8-6. Projected nominal U.S. wheat export and domestic prices, 1979-83[a]

Run	Policy Description[b]	1979	1980	1981	1982	1983
		(U.S. $/Bu.)				
Base assumptions						
Run 1	No price policy	3.88	4.04	4.69	5.78	6.09
		3.88	4.04	4.69	5.78	6.09
Run 4	WP ⩾ 5.45, FP ⩾ 4.30,	5.45	5.45	5.51	6.45	6.39
	all regions	5.45	5.45	5.51	6.45	6.39
Run 5	WP ⩾ 6.80, FP ⩾ 5.37,	6.80	6.80	6.80	6.80	7.57
	all regions	6.80	6.80	6.80	6.80	7.57
Run 11	WP ⩾ 5.45, FP ⩾ 4.30,	5.45	5.45	5.45	5.45	6.09
	for SB, DM, and LD only	3.92	3.92	4.19	5.44	6.09
Run 12	WP ⩾ 6.80, FP ⩾ 5.37,	6.80	6.80	6.80	6.80	6.80
	for SB, DM, and LD only	3.90	3.81	3.91	4.46	5.84
Run 13	WP ⩾ 5.45, FP ⩾ 4.30,	5.45	5.45	5.45	5.85	6.02
	for SB and DM only	3.97	4.08	4.57	5.85	6.02
Run 14	WP ⩾ 6.80, FP ⩾ 5.37,	6.80	6.80	6.80	6.80	6.80
	for SB and DM only	3.99	4.07	4.46	5.75	6.06
Low income-high yields						
Run 6	No price policy	3.81	3.52	3.43	3.41	3.42
		3.81	3.52	3.43	3.41	3.42
Run 9	WP ⩾ 5.45, FP ⩾ 4.30,	5.45	5.45	5.45	5.45	5.45
	all regions	5.45	5.45	5.45	5.45	5.45
Run 10	WP ⩾ 6.80, FP ⩾ 5.37,	6.80	6.80	6.80	6.80	6.80
	all regions	6.80	6.80	6.80	6.80	6.80
Run 15	WP ⩾ 5.45, FP ⩾ 4.30,	5.45	5.45	5.45	5.45	5.45
	for SB, DM, and LD only	3.84	3.48	3.36	3.32	3.31
Run 16	WP ⩾ 6.80, FP ⩾ 5.37,	6.80	6.80	6.80	6.80	6.80
	for SB, DM, and LD only	3.82	3.43	3.30	3.26	3.23
Run 17	WP ⩾ 5.45, FP ⩾ 4.30,	5.45	5.45	5.45	5.45	5.45
	for SB and DM only	3.89	3.56	3.45	3.43	3.43
Run 18	WP ⩾ 6.80, FP ⩾ 5.37,	6.80	6.80	6.80	6.80	6.80
	for SB and DM only	3.90	3.55	3.45	3.42	3.42

[a]Both the export price and domestic price are presented for each computer run. The top row of prices for each run is the price charged for wheat exports, and the second row of prices for each run is the equilibrium domestic price. When no-price policy is implemented, a single price exists for all countries. When the equilibrium price exceeds the targeted exported price, then the export price will rise to the equilibrium.

[b]WP = Wheat price, FP = Coarse grain price, SB = Soviet Bloc, DM = Developed market economies, and LD = Less developed market economies.

Table 8-7. Projected nominal U.S. coarse grain export and domestic prices, 1979-83[a]

Run	*Policy Description*[b]	*1979*	*1980*	*1981* (U.S. $/Bu.)	*1982*	*1983*
Base assumptions						
Run 1	No price policy	2.50	2.91	3.51	3.67	4.13
		2.50	2.91	3.51	3.67	4.13
Run 4	WP ⩾ 5.45, FP ⩾ 4.30,	4.30	4.30	4.30	4.30	4.30
	all regions	4.30	4.30	4.30	4.30	4.30
Run 5	WP ⩾ 6.80, FP ⩾ 5.37,	5.37	5.37	5.37	5.37	5.37
	all regions	5.37	5.37	5.37	5.37	5.37
Run 11	WP ⩾ 5.45, FP ⩾ 4.30,	4.30	4.30	4.30	4.30	4.34
	for SB, DM, and LD only	2.50	2.53	3.37	3.30	4.34
Run 12	WP ⩾ 6.80, FP ⩾ 5.37,	5.37	5.37	5.37	5.37	5.37
	for SB, DM, and LD only	2.50	2.50	2.85	3.25	3.62
Run 13	WP ⩾ 5.45, FP ⩾ 4.30,	4.30	4.30	4.30	4.30	4.30
	for SB and DM only	2.50	2.72	3.49	3.52	4.25
Run 14	WP ⩾ 6.80, FP ⩾ 5.37,	5.37	5.37	5.37	5.37	5.47
	for SB and DM only	2.50	2.62	3.40	3.39	4.18
Low income–high yields						
Run 6	No price policy	2.50	2.50	2.50	2.50	2.50
		2.50	2.50	2.50	2.50	2.50
Run 9	WP ⩾ 5.45, FP ⩾ 4.30,	4.30	4.30	4.30	4.30	4.30
	all regions	4.30	4.30	4.30	4.30	4.30
Run 10	WP ⩾ 6.80, FP ⩾ 5.37,	5.37	5.37	5.37	5.37	5.37
	all regions	5.37	5.37	5.37	5.37	5.37
Run 15	WP ⩾ 5.45, FP ⩾ 4.30,	4.30	4.30	4.30	4.30	4.30
	for SB, DM, and LD only	2.50	2.50	2.50	2.50	2.50
Run 16	WP ⩾ 6.80, FP ⩾ 5.37,	5.37	5.37	5.37	5.37	5.37
	for SB, DM, and LD only	2.50	2.50	2.50	2.50	2.50
Run 17	WP ⩾ 5.45, FP ⩾ 4.30,	4.30	4.30	4.30	4.30	4.30
	for SB and DM only	2.50	2.50	2.50	2.50	2.50
Run 18	WP ⩾ 6.80, FP ⩾ 5.37,	5.37	5.37	5.37	5.37	5.37
	for SB and DM only	2.50	2.50	2.50	2.50	2.50

[a]Both the export price and domestic price are presented for each computer run. The top row of prices for each run is the price charged for wheat exports, and the second row of prices for each run is the equilibrium domestic price. When no-price policy is implemented, a single price exists for all countries. When the equilibrium price exceeds the targeted exported price, then the export price will rise to the equilibrium.

[b]WP = Wheat price, FP = Coarse grain price, SB = Soviet Bloc, DM = Developed market economies, and LD = Less developed market economies.

wheat for this simulation has a floor of $5.45 by 1983, the market equilibrium price of wheat exceeds the lower bound designated by the cartel policy, and both the export price and the equilibrium price increase to $6.09 per bushel.

The price discrimination cartel simulation, runs 11–14 and 15–18, allows a two-price solution. The export price, determined by the cartel arrangement, applies to selected importing countries, and the market equilibrium price applies to all exporting countries and designated importing countries. For example, run 11 sets an export price floor for wheat at $5.45 per bushel for all importing regions, while all exporting countries receive the market equilibrium price. This results in a lower price in the exporting countries than is the case under a no-cartel arrangement because the higher-than-equilibrium export price dampens import demand, increases supplies, and drives market price down.

The result of the two-price market created by the price discriminating cartel is to lower the market equilibrium price below the no-cartel solution. Consumers in the exporting countries and, for runs 11 and 12 and runs 15 and 16, in the less developed market economies are being subsidized by the high prices charged to the Soviet Bloc and developed market economies. A comparison of the two-price discrimination cartel arrangements—runs 11 and 12, and runs 13 and 14—to run 1 shows that the lowest prices in exporting regions result from charging all importing regions the cartel price. Excluding the less developed market economies from the cartel prices results in slightly higher prices to consumers in exporting countries, but prices are still below the no-cartel solution.

U.S. Wheat and Coarse Grain Export Revenue

Tables 8–8 and 8–9 show revenue earned from U.S. wheat and coarse grain exports, respectively. Total revenue is shown in Table 8–10. Run 1 projects a 1979 U.S. wheat export revenue of $5.57 billion and coarse grain export revenue of $6.60 billion. Combined revenue is projected to equal $12.17 billion for 1979; by 1983, combined export revenue is projected to reach $21.45 billion. This rapid growth in export revenue reflects both higher grain prices and increased export sales. When the low income–high yields assumption is used, export revenue is projected to decrease from $10.71 billion in 1979 to $10.16 billion in 1983.

Table 8-8. Projected U.S. wheat export revenue, 1979-83[a]

Run	Policy Description[a]	1979	1980	1981 (Billion Dollars)	1982	1983
Base assumptions						
Run 1	No price policy	5.57	5.68	7.22	9.34	9.87
Run 4	WP ⩾ 5.45, FP ⩾ 4.30, all regions	7.87	7.89	8.81	10.31	10.22
Run 5	WP ⩾ 6.80, FP ⩾ 5.37, all regions	9.58	9.37	10.46	11.17	11.51
Run 11	WP ⩾ 5.45, FP ⩾ 4.30, for SB, DM, and LD only	7.97	7.32	7.81	9.05	10.07
Run 12	WP ⩾ 6.80, FP ⩾ 5.37, for SB, DM, and LD only	9.81	8.61	9.19	10.36	11.52
Run 13	WP ⩾ 5.45, FP ⩾ 4.30, for SB and DM only	8.14	7.72	8.25	9.67	9.76
Run 14	WP ⩾ 6.80, FP ⩾ 5.37, for SB and DM only	10.23	9.59	10.18	11.33	11.22
Low income-high yields						
Run 6	No price policy	4.90	3.96	4.01	4.21	4.43
Run 9	WP ⩾ 5.45, FP ⩾ 4.30, all regions	7.03	6.25	6.48	6.55	6.86
Run 10	WP ⩾ 6.80, FP ⩾ 5.37, all regions	8.53	7.33	7.64	7.65	8.01
Run 15	WP ⩾ 5.45, FP ⩾ 4.30, for SB, DM, and LD only	7.13	5.74	5.81	6.11	6.41
Run 16	WP ⩾ 6.80, FP ⩾ 5.37, for SB, DM, and LD only	8.77	6.63	6.67	7.01	7.37
Run 17	WP ⩾ 5.35, FP ⩾ 4.30, for SB and DM only	7.32	6.23	6.41	6.76	7.09
Run 18	WP ⩾ 6.80, FP ⩾ 5.37, for SB and DM only	9.20	7.72	7.94	8.39	8.79

[a]WP = Wheat price, FP = Coarse grain price, SB = Soviet Bloc, DM = Developed market economies, and LD = Less developed market economies.

Table 8-9. Projected U.S. coarse grain export revenue, 1979-83[a]

Run	Policy Description[a]	1979	1980	1981 (Billion Dollars)	1982	1983
Base assumptions						
Run 1	No price policy	6.60	7.55	8.85	9.62	11.58
Run 4	WP ≥ 5.45, FP ≥ 4.30, all regions	9.99	8.45	8.73	9.97	12.81
Run 5	WP ≥ 6.80, FP ≥ 5.37, all regions	11.68	8.83	8.85	9.56	9.74
Run 11	WP ≥ 5.45, FP ≥ 4.30, for SB, DM, and LD only	10.50	10.05	10.42	10.36	11.89
Run 12	WP ≥ 6.80, FP ≥ 5.37, for SB, DM, and LD only	12.67	11.61	12.18	12.53	13.12
Run 13	WP ≥ 5.45, FP ≥ 4.30, for SB and DM only	10.98	10.40	10.47	10.74	11.87
Run 14	WP ≥ 6.80, FP ≥ 5.37, for SB and DM only	1.356	12.44	12.65	12.74	14.10
Low income–high yields						
Run 6	No price policy	5.81	5.39	5.36	5.53	5.73
Run 9	WP ≥ 5.45, FP ≥ 4.30, all regions	8.66	6.25	6.05	6.26	6.47
Run 10	WP ≥ 6.80, FP ≥ 5.37, all regions	10.02	6.01	5.55	5.69	5.81
Run 15	WP ≥ 5.45, FP ≥ 4.30, for SB, DM, and LD only	9.17	7.89	7.80	8.02	8.32
Run 16	WP ≥ 6.80, FP ≥ 5.37, for SB, DM, and LD only	11.01	8.89	8.71	8.95	9.30
Run 17	WP ≥ 5.35, FP ≥ 4.30, for SB and DM only	9.66	8.46	8.44	8.71	9.07
Run 18	WP ≥ 6.80, FP ≥ 5.37, for SB and DM only	11.92	9.96	9.90	10.23	10.67

[a]WP = Wheat price, FP = Coarse grain price, SB = Soviet Bloc, DM = Developed market economies, and LD = Less developed market economies.

Table 8-10. Projected U.S. total wheat and coarse grain export revenue, 1979-83[a]

Run	Policy Description[a]	1979	1980	1981 (Billion Dollars)	1982	1983
Base assumptions						
Run 1	No price policy	12.17	13.23	16.07	18.96	21.45
Run 4	WP ⩾ 5.45, FP ⩾ 4.30, all regions	17.86	16.34	17.54	20.28	23.03
Run 5	WP ⩾ 6.80, FP ⩾ 5.37, all regions	21.26	18.20	19.31	20.73	21.25
Run 11	WP ⩾ 5.45, FP ⩾ 4.30, for SB, DM, and LD only	18.47	17.37	18.23	19.41	21.96
Run 12	WP ⩾ 6.80, FP ⩾ 5.37, for SB, DM, and LD only	22.48	20.22	21.37	22.89	24.64
Run 13	WP ⩾ 5.45, FP ⩾ 4.30, for SB and DM only	19.12	18.12	18.72	20.41	21.63
Run 14	WP ⩾ 6.80, FP ⩾ 5.37, for SB and DM only	23.79	22.03	22.83	24.07	25.32
Low income-high yields						
Run 6	No price policy	10.71	9.35	9.37	9.74	10.16
Run 9	WP ⩾ 5.45, FP ⩾ 4.30, all regions	15.69	12.50	12.53	12.81	13.33
Run 10	WP ⩾ 6.80, FP ⩾ 5.37, all regions	18.55	13.34	13.19	13.34	13.82
Run 15	WP ⩾ 5.45, FP ⩾ 4.30, for SB, DM, and LD only	16.30	13.63	13.61	14.13	14.73
Run 16	WP ⩾ 6.80, FP ⩾ 5.37, for SB, DM, and LD only	19.78	15.52	15.38	15.96	16.67
Run 17	WP ⩾ 5.35, FP ⩾ 4.30, for SB and DM only	16.98	14.69	14.85	15.47	16.16
Run 18	WP ⩾ 6.80, FP ⩾ 5.37, for SB and DM only	21.12	17.68	17.84	18.62	19.46

[a]WP = Wheat price, FP = Coarse grain price, SB = Soviet Bloc, DM = Developed market economies, and LD = Less developed market economies.

Runs 4 and 5, which charge high cartel prices to all exporting and importing countries, would generate combined export revenue earned of $23.03 and $21.25 billion, respectively, for 1983. Runs 11 and 12, which discriminate between all importing and all exporting countries, would generate 1983 export revenue of $21.96 and $24.64 billion, respectively. Runs 13 and 14, which charge high prices to the Soviet Bloc and developed market economies and low prices to all other countries, would generate export revenues of $21.63 and $25.32 billion, respectively, by 1983.

The highest export revenue of the seven simulations incorporating the base assumptions is generated by run 14, which discriminates between the Soviet Bloc and developed market economies, on the one hand, and all other countries, on the other. The former are charged cartel prices of $6.80 per bushel of wheat and $5.37 per bushel of coarse grains imported. Exporting countries and the less developed market economies receive the market equilibrium prices, which are below the cartel prices. Total 1979 wheat and coarse grain export revenue for run 14 is $23.79 billion compared to $12.17 billion for run 1. By 1983, combined export revenue for run 14 is $25.32 billion compared to $21.45 billion for run 1. Over the 1979–1983 period, the increased U.S. export revenues for run 14, in comparison to run 1, are $11.62, $8.80, $6.76, $5.11, and $3.87 billion. The difference decreases because market equilibrium prices grow under run 1, while cartel prices are constant.

The price-discriminating cartel that excludes the less developed market economies from the cartel prices results in larger U.S. export revenue than the cartel which includes these countries. This can be seen by comparing the U.S. export revenue of runs 12 and 14 from Table 8–10.

U.S. WHEAT AND COARSE GRAIN ENDING-YEAR STOCKS

Tables 8–11 and 8–12 show ending-year stocks of wheat and coarse grains for the United States. With the base assumptions, U.S. wheat stocks decrease for every simulation over the 1979–1983 period. By 1983, U.S. wheat stocks are projected to reach 8.99 million metric tons under the no-price policy scenario of run 1 compared with 21.29 million metric tons projected to be available at

Table 8-11. Projected U.S. wheat ending–year stocks, 1979-83[a]

Run	Policy Description[a]	1979	1980	1981	1982	1983
				(Million Metric Tons)		
Base assumptions						
Run 1	No price policy	21.29	18.81	13.37	10.14	8.99
Run 4	WP ⩾ 5.45, FP ⩾ 4.30, all regions	21.27	17.27	10.60	8.63	8.55
Run 5	WP ⩾ 6.80, FP ⩾ 5.37, all regions	23.61	22.63	17.98	11.92	8.48
Run 11	WP ⩾ 5.45, FP ⩾ 4.30, for SB, DM, and LD only	20.67	20.69	17.38	11.52	8.97
Run 12	WP ⩾ 6.80, FP ⩾ 5.37, for SB, DM, and LD only	21.09	22.81	21.66	16.48	11.47
Run 13	WP ⩾ 5.45, FP ⩾ 4.30, for SB and DM only	19.93	18.21	13.83	9.96	8.73
Run 14	WP ⩾ 6.80, FP ⩾ 5.37, for SB and DM only	19.69	18.44	14.64	10.26	8.65
Low income–high yields						
Run 6	No price policy	25.25	31.49	35.26	37.05	37.59
Run 9	WP ⩾ 5.45, FP ⩾ 4.30, all regions	2.562	31.49	35.82	39.73	42.09
Run 10	WP ⩾ 6.80, FP ⩾ 5.37, all regions	27.97	36.80	43.44	49.49	53.60
Run 15	WP ⩾ 5.45, FP ⩾ 4.30, for SB, DM, and LD only	24.75	33.01	38.95	42.61	44.67
Run 16	WP ⩾ 6.80, FP ⩾ 5.37, for SB, DM, and LD only	25.18	35.28	42.81	47.82	51.01
Run 17	WP ⩾ 5.35, FP ⩾ 4.30, for SB and DM only	23.95	30.25	34.21	36.10	36.73
Run 18	WP ⩾ 6.80, FP ⩾ 5.37, for SB and DM only	23.70	30.27	34.42	36.42	37.15

[a]WP = Wheat price, FP = Coarse grain price, SB = Soviet Bloc, DM = Developed market economies, and LD = Less developed market economies.

Table 8-12. Projected U.S. coarse grain ending-year stocks, 1979-83[a]

Run	Policy Description[a]	1979	1980	1981	1982	1983
				(Million Metric Tons)		
Base assumptions						
Run 1	No price policy	44.10	23.29	15.95	13.29	10.37
Run 4	WP $\geqslant$ 5.45, FP $\geqslant$ 4.30, all regions	70.08	112.10	153.71	187.47	207.11
Run 5	WP $\geqslant$ 6.80, FP $\geqslant$ 5.37, all regions	83.19	161.96	249.61	333.68	406.88
Run 11	WP $\geqslant$ 5.45, FP $\geqslant$ 4.30, for SB, DM, and LD only	49.05	30.00	17.59	15.98	9.69
Run 12	WP $\geqslant$ 6.80, FP $\geqslant$ 5.37, for SB, DM, and LD only	51.22	36.77	23.19	17.06	12.84
Run 13	WP $\geqslant$ 5.45, FP $\geqslant$ 4.30, for SB and DM only	46.10	26.27	16.48	14.39	10.18
Run 14	WP $\geqslant$ 6.80, FP $\geqslant$ 5.37, for SB and DM only	46.75	28.14	17.32	15.46	10.70
Low income-high yields						
Run 6	No price policy	52.69	53.13	57.56	62.11	65.02
Run 9	WP $\geqslant$ 5.45, FP $\geqslant$ 4.30, all regions	78.25	147.52	226.90	308.69	391.44
Run 10	WP $\geqslant$ 6.80, FP $\geqslant$ 5.37, all regions	91.37	198.09	321.47	450.31	582.29
Run 15	WP $\geqslant$ 5.45, FP $\geqslant$ 4.30, for SB, DM, and LD only	57.46	65.76	79.71	95.29	110.67
Run 16	WP $\geqslant$ 6.80, FP $\geqslant$ 5.37, for SB, DM, and LD only	59.63	72.99	93.25	116.14	139.71
Run 17	WP $\geqslant$ 5.35, FP $\geqslant$ 4.30, for SB and DM only	54.46	58.64	66.92	75.48	82.43
Run 18	WP $\geqslant$ 6.80, FP $\geqslant$ 5.37, for SB and DM only	55.08	61.92	73.25	84.98	95.18

[a]WP = Wheat price, FP = Coarse grain price, SB = Soviet Bloc, DM = Developed market economies, and LD = Less developed market economies.

the end of 1979. Under the low income–high yields assumptions, U.S. wheat stock would increase for every simulation over the 1979–1983 period. By 1983, U.S. wheat stocks would range from 37.15 to 53.60 million metric tons depending on the cartel scenario used.

U.S. coarse grain ending-year stocks are shown in Table 8–12. Using the base assumptions, run 1 results in a decrease from a projected 44.10 million metric tons in 1979 to 10.37 million metric tons by 1983. The price-discriminating cartel scenarios result in 1983 U.S. coarse grain stocks which range from 9.69 to 12.84. A producer cartel would result in huge coarse grain stocks, as shown by runs 4 and 5 and Table 8–12; by 1983, U.S. coarse grain stocks would reach 406.88 million metric tons. This projection is not realistic but results from the way the cartel was simulated. Prices available to all producers and consumers are constrained to at least $6.80 bushel of wheat and $5.37 per bushel of coarse grains. No feedback to production is allowed so producers keep producing coarse grains; and this, combined with significantly lower U.S. exports, causes stocks to build. In reality, the buildup of stocks would create a need for a government supply control policy. The seven simulations which incorporate the low income–high yields assumptions indicate that U.S. coarse grain stocks would build under all scenarios. Under the no-price policy, as shown by run 6, a buildup of coarse grain stocks is projected to increase stocks from 52.69 million metric tons in 1979 to 65.02 by 1983. All cartel scenarios would cause stocks to increase significantly from those levels.

U.S. Wheat and Coarse Grain Consumption

Tables 8–13 and 8–14 show U.S. wheat and coarse grain total consumption; all categories of use are included in this single quantity. U.S. wheat consumption (Table 8–13) shows relatively minor response to alternative cartel scenarios. With the base assumption, it ranges from 20.6 to 22.3 million metric tons in 1979 and 21.0 to 23.3 million metric tons in 1983. The low income–high yields assumptions result in a 1979 range of 20.5 to 22.3 million metric tons in 1979 and 22.1 to 26.2 million metric tons in 1983. The higher U.S. wheat consumption accompanying this second set of model assumptions is caused by the lower domestic price which accompanies these scenarios.

Table 8-13. Projected U.S. wheat consumption, 1979-83[a]

Run	Policy Description[a]	1979	1980	1981	1982	1983
				(Million Metric Tons)		
Base assumptions						
Run 1	No price policy	22.3	23.6	23.8	21.7	22.7
Run 4	WP ⩾ 5.45, FP ⩾ 4.30, all regions	22.0	22.5	23.1	21.1	22.1
Run 5	WP ⩾ 6.80, FP ⩾ 5.37, all regions	20.6	20.9	21.7	22.5	21.0
Run 11	WP ⩾ 5.45, FP ⩾ 4.30, for SB, DM, and LD only	22.1	23.1	25.1	21.7	23.3
Run 12	WP ⩾ 5.45, FP ⩾ 5.37, for SB, DM, and LD only	22.2	23.3	24.6	24.6	22.2
Run 13	WP ⩾ 5.45, FP ⩾ 4.30, for SB and DM only	22.0	23.0	24.2	21.1	23.3
Run 14	WP ⩾ 6.80, FP ⩾ 5.37, for SB and DM only	21.9	22.8	24.3	21.1	23.0
Low income-high yields						
Run 6	No price policy	22.3	23.8	24.6	25.2	25.7
Run 9	WP ⩾ 5.45, FP ⩾ 4.30, all regions	21.9	22.2	22.7	23.2	23.8
Run 10	WP ⩾ 6.80, FP ⩾ 5.37, all regions	20.5	20.6	21.0	21.6	22.1
Run 15	WP ⩾ 5.45, FP ⩾ 4.30, for SB, DM, and LD only	22.2	23.9	24.8	25.4	26.0
Run 16	WP ⩾ 6.80, FP ⩾ 5.37, for SB, DM, and LD only	22.3	24.1	24.9	25.6	26.2
Run 17	WP ⩾ 5.45, FP ⩾ 4.30, for SB and DM only	22.1	23.7	24.5	25.1	25.7
Run 18	WP ⩾ 6.80, FP ⩾ 5.37, for SB and DM only	22.1	23.7	24.5	25.2	25.7

[a]WP = Wheat price, FP = Coarse grain price, SB = Soviet Bloc, DM = Developed market economies, and LD = Less developed market economies.

Table 8-14. Projected U.S. coarse grain consumption, 1979-83[a]

Run	Policy Description[a]	1979	1980	1981	1982	1983
		(Million Metric Tons)				
Base assumptions						
Run 1	No price policy	158.9	160.9	156.1	153.9	150.2
Run 4	WP ≥ 5.45, FP ≥ 4.30, all regions	141.0	125.0	124.2	130.8	135.9
Run 5	WP ≥ 6.80, FP ≥ 5.37, all regions	131.6	102.1	97.1	99.7	106.9
Run 11	WP ≥ 5.45, FP ≥ 4.30, for SB, DM, and LD only	159.1	165.2	161.0	160.7	153.1
Run 12	WP ≥ 6.80, FP ≥ 5.37, for SB, DM, and LD only	159.0	165.3	167.2	165.1	164.1
Run 13	WP ≥ 5.45, FP ≥ 4.30, for SB and DM only	159.2	163.4	158.3	157.0	150.6
Run 14	WP ≥ 6.80, FP ≥ 5.37, for SB and DM only	159.3	164.6	160.4	159.9	153.8
Low income-high yields						
Run 6	No price policy	158.4	163.6	168.7	173.7	178.8
Run 9	WP ≥ 5.45, FP ≥ 4.30, all regions	140.7	124.1	122.6	125.7	130.2
Run 10	WP ≥ 6.80, FP ≥ 5.37, all regions	131.2	101.2	95.6	97.5	101.7
Run 15	WP ≥ 5.45, FP ≥ 4.30, for SB, DM, and LD only	158.5	163.5	168.5	173.4	178.4
Run 16	WP ≥ 6.80, FP ≥ 5.37, for SB, DM, and LD only	158.4	163.3	168.3	173.2	178.2
Run 17	WP ≥ 5.45, FP ≥ 4.30, for SB and DM only	158.6	163.7	168.7	173.7	178.8
Run 18	WP ≥ 6.80, FP ≥ 5.37, for SB and DM only	158.6	163.7	168.7	173.7	178.8

[a]WP = Wheat price, FP = Coarse grain price, SB = Soviet Bloc, DM = Developed market economies, and LD = Less developed market economies.

Unlike wheat consumption, U.S. coarse grain consumption (Table 8–14) would vary significantly under alternative cartel arrangements. Run 1 would result in a 1979 U.S. coarse grain total consumption of 158.9 million metric tons. By 1983, it would drop to 150.2 million metric tons, a decrease caused by the increase in coarse grain price from $2.50 in 1979 to $4.13 per bushel in 1983. Run 5 shows that a producer cartel price of $5.37 per bushel for coarse grains would decrease U.S. coarse grain consumption to 106.9 million metric tons by 1983. Although this seems unreasonable, the results are similar to the reduction which occurred in the 1972–1976 period, when U.S. coarse grain price increased from $1.65 per bushel to $3.55 per bushel and consumption dropped from 158.7 to 121.8 million metric tons. For the cartel simulation shown by run 5, coarse grain price will increase from $2.50 in 1978 to $5.37 for 1979–1983; total coarse grain consumption will decrease from 158.9 in 1979 to 97.1 million metric tons in 1981.

U.S. coarse grain consumption is very responsive to coarse grain prices, and an increase in U.S. consumption is expected to accompany those cartel scenarios which reduce domestic prices. In turn, a significant decrease would result from a cartel which increased price to U.S. consumers.

HISTORICAL MARKET SHARES

Historical shares of world grain exports can be used to allocate exports among exporting countries in a cartel marketing arrangement. Runs 2,3, 7, and 8 consider the implications of a producer cartel which allocates exports among the United States, Canada, Australia, and Argentina based on each country's average share of total exports over the 1970–1977 period. Two levels of export prices for wheat and coarse grains and two sets of model assumptions are considered.

Runs 2 and 3 use the base assumptions, and runs 7 and 8 use the low income–high yields assumptions. A producer cartel price floor of $5.45 per bushel of wheat and $4.30 per bushel of coarse grains is assumed in runs 2 and 7; and $6.80 and $5.37 are assumed for wheat and coarse grains, respectively, for runs 3 and 8. Under the assumptions of the producer cartel, all consumers pay the cartel price. A comparison of these four simulations with runs 4, 5,9, and

10 shows the effects of allocating exports using the historical market share as opposed to assuming that the United States is the residual supplier of world exports.

Runs 3 and 5 show the producer cartel with an export price floor of $6.80 per bushel for wheat and $5.37 per bushel for coarse grains. Base assumptions are used for both runs; however, run 3 assumes that grain exports are allocated among the four major exporting countries on the basis of historical market shares, while run 5 assumes that the United States is the residual supplier of grain to the world markets. U.S. wheat exports for run 3 are 37.9 million metric tons in 1979, increasing to 47.6 million metric tons by 1983. For run 5, U.S. wheat exports are 38.4 million metric tons in 1979, increasing to 46.4 million metric tons by 1983. Little difference in U.S. wheat exports is observed because of alternative export market allocation schemes. U.S. coarse grain exports, however, show significant differences. Using the historical market share to allocate exports, run 3, U.S. coarse grain exports are 56.7 million metric tons in 1979. By 1980, they drop to 48.1 and then increase to 59.9 million metric tons by 1983. Run 5, which assumes that the United States acts as the residual supplier of exports to the world market, has U.S. coarse grain exports of 55.3 million metric tons in 1979, 41.8 million metric tons in 1980, and 50.4 million metric tons by 1983. The difference between runs 3 and 5 shows that U.S. coarse grain exports would be substantially higher under an export allocation scheme based on historical market shares than one based on the assumption that the United States is the residual supplier of exports to the world markets.

An examination of both runs using the base assumptions produces similar results. A historical market share allocation scheme would not significantly influence U.S. wheat exports but would significantly increase U.S. coarse grain exports. When the low income–high yields assumptions are used, the importance of the historical market share allocation scheme increases. Both U.S. wheat and coarse grain exports would drop if the United States continues as the residual supplier of exports to the world, but they would not fall as much if the market allocation is based on historical market shares.

A simulation run combining a historical market share allocation scheme with a price-discriminating cartel pricing arrangement was not tried but would be useful. The probable conclusion of such a simulation would be that neither U.S. wheat nor coarse grain exports would be significantly altered when a historical market share allocation system was introduced. This observation is based on the inability of exporting countries to increase exports under the price-discriminating cartel case. Domestic consumption increases, and insufficient supplies are available to increase exports at the same time.

SUMMARY

This chapter has presented eighteen computer simulations to explore the implications for the 1979–1983 period of U.S. participation in a world wheat and coarse grain cartel. The MSU agriculture trade model was used to evaluate alternative model assumptions and cartel scenarios. This model does not determine the optimum cartel arrangement; however, it does estimate the impacts of alternative cartel arrangements on U.S. wheat and coarse grain consumption, production, net exports, prices, and stocks. Results are also presented for Canada, Australia, Argentina, and three world grain-importing regions.

Four types of grain cartels are considered: (1) a producer cartel which increases wheat and coarse grain prices to all world consumers; (2) a price-discriminating cartel which charges high cartel prices to all importing regions and lower market equilibrium prices to the four major exporting countries—the United States, Canada, Australia, and Argentina—a cartel arrangement which also assumes that the United States continues its traditional role as the residual supplier of grain exports to the world; (3) a price-discriminating cartel which charges high cartel prices to the Soviet Bloc and developed market economies and lower market equilibrium prices to the four major exporting countries and the less developed market economies, with the United States again assumed to be the residual supplier of grain exports; and (4) a cartel which combines the producer cartel with a constraint on exports from the four major exporting countries; each exporting country is constrained to export no more than its historical share of world grain exports.

Within the four types of grain cartels, two levels of wheat and coarse grain prices are considered as well as two levels of world economic and crop yield assumptions. Cartel price floors of $5.45 and $4.30 are placed on wheat and coarse grain exports, respectively, under one alternative and $6.80 and $5.37, respectively, for the other. Prices for specified world regions cannot drop below these levels but may increase if market pressure warrants an increase. Two sets of model assumptions are also specified to explore the sensitivity of alternative cartel arrangements on different markets. The first set of assumptions is denoted as the base assumptions and represents the best estimates of growth in income, population, crop yields, exchange rates, and cropland base for all world regions. A second set of assumptions, reducing growth rates in income and assuming a more rapid growth in yields, is used to represent a climate less favorable to U.S. exports and a world grain cartel. This second set is designated as the low income–high yields assumptions; all other assumptions are equivalent to the base assumptions.

A number of conclusions can be drawn from these eighteen scenarios. The increased revenue which the United States could gain from a cartel involving wheat and coarse grains is substantial. Under the base assumptions, the 1979 U.S. export revenue could be increased from a projected $12.17 billion to $23.79 billion under the most favorable alternative analyzed. This is accomplished, with the base assumptions, by the price-discriminating cartel which exports wheat and coarse grains at prices of $6.80 and $5.37, respectively. A market equilibrium price for wheat and coarse grains of $3.99 and $2.50 is available to consumers in the United States, Canada, Australia, Argentina, and the less developed market economies. These prices compare with market equilibrium prices of $3.88 and $2.50, respectively, for wheat and coarse grains without any cartel policy. Consequently, a cost is associated with increased consumer expenditures for wheat and coarse grains. A cost of $.09 billion would accrue to U.S. consumers based on the higher wheat price and the same consumption levels as are observed under the base run, which does not include any cartel scenario. The total direct benefit to the United States from the cartel would be $11.53 billion in 1979. For 1980, the increased U.S. export revenue would be $8.80 billion, and a consumer saving of $1.81 billion would result from lower domestic coarse grain prices. In subsequent years the total direct benefit of this cartel policy, in comparison to a no-cartel scenario, would be $7.64, $6.83, and $3.63 billion for 1981, 1982, and 1983, respectively. The decrease in benefits over the five-year period is caused both by an adjustment in world production, which reduces world grain demand, and by the failure to raise cartel prices as income and population growth increases world demand.

When the same cartel scenario is followed under the low

income–high yields assumptions, the 1979 U.S. export revenue exceeds the no-cartel base run scenario by $10.41 billion. Prices to U.S. consumers are $3.90 and $2.50 per bushel of wheat and coarse grains, respectively, compared to $3.81 and $2.50 in the no-cartel case. The resulting increased cost to U.S. consumers of purchasing quantities identical to the no-cartel case is $.07 billion. A total U.S. benefit of $10.34 billion is obtained for 1979; during the 1980–1983 period, increased U.S. benefits are $8.30, $8.44, $8.85, and $9.30 billion, respectively, when compared to a marketing strategy which does not charge cartel prices. Contrary to the previous case, U.S. benefits do not decrease significantly over the 1979–1983 period. This results from an overall surplus in world supply, caused by the low income–high yields assumptions, which does not increase market price and hence does not require cartel price increases.

The price-discriminating wheat and coarse grain cartel results in a significant increase in U.S. benefits under both the base assumptions and the low income–high yields assumptions. U.S. exports and export revenues drop significantly under the low income–high yields assumptions, but the increased benefits generated from a cartel do not change significantly. We can conclude that the profitability of a wheat and coarse grain cartel is not particularly sensitive to world grain market conditions, although U.S. exports and total export revenues are.

The price-discriminating wheat and coarse grain cartel is profitable for the United States for several reasons. First, world import demand is relatively inelastic, and the higher grain prices cause only a small reduction in imports. Secondly, by establishing a two-price system, the exporting countries continue to consume grain at prices near or below the prices which prevail without a cartel; this encourages domestic consumption and reduces grain available for export. Without this two-price system, exports from Canada, Australia, and Argentina would increase with cartel prices hence reducing the share of the world grain market available to the United States. Finally, the price-discriminating cartel lowers consumer expenditures through lower grain prices. Coarse grain prices for the U.S. consumer will fall as much as 29 cents per bushel. Wheat price will increase by as much as 23 cents per bushel, but the benefit to the U.S. consumer from total wheat and coarse grain expenditures will be positive because of the relatively larger coarse grain consumption.

A comparison to the single-price producer cartel further demonstrates the advantages of the two-price system created by the price-discriminating cartel. Given the base assumptions and the cartel wheat price of $6.80 per bushel and coarse grain price of $5.37 per bushel, the producer cartel generated a total U.S. export revenue of $21.26 billion in 1979. The price-discriminating cartel, which charges cartel prices to all importing countries, generates U.S. export revenue for 1979 of $22.48 billion, a difference of $1.22 billion; by 1980, the difference increases to $2.02 billion. This difference is totally attributable to the two-price cartel which encourages consumption in the exporting countries.

An additional reason to favor a price-discriminating cartel is associated with consumer expenditures for wheat and coarse grains. With a price-discriminating cartel, consumer costs in the United States are approximately half as high as they would be with a producer cartel. For 1979, U.S. consumer expenditures are $18.88 billion for wheat and coarse grains under the most favorable price-discriminating cartel scenario. If a producer cartel were implemented to raise prices to $6.80 and $5.37 per bushel of wheat and coarse grains, respectively, the same level of consumption would cost U.S. consumers $39.14 billion.

An alternative to the price-discriminating cartel would be the imposition of export market share restrictions on each of the four major exporting countries, which would prevent Canada, Australia, or Argentina from obtaining an increased share of the world grain market at the expense of the United States. If each of the four major exporting countries agreed to export no more than its 1970–1977 average historical share of world export markets, U.S. exports would decline only in proportion to the decrease in world imports. U.S. export revenue for 1979 under the historical market share scenario, using the base assumptions and a cartel price of $6.80 and $5.37 for wheat and coarse grains, respectively, would be $21.45 billion This is below the export revenue earned by either of the price-discriminating cartels formulated using the same model assumptions.

A wheat and coarse grain cartel involving the United States, Canada, Australia, and Argentina is economically feasible for the United States. It could raise U.S. export revenues by at least $10 billion per year. Furthermore, the world demand for wheat and coarse grain imports is sufficiently price inelastic to permit a cartel to raise prices without significantly reducing imports. The benefits to be gained by the United States from a grain cartel are not particularly sensitive to world economic conditions. A reduction in the rate of growth in world income, for example, would alter U.S. total export revenues but not the increased revenue which could be earned from a cartel.

CONCLUSIONS

It seems unlikely that an exporter association would charge poor countries the same price for grains that it would charge high-income importers. This issue takes on added significance in the wheat market which, relative to feed grains, is made up of more low-income nations. This chapter has explored the economic impacts of different pricing policies which take income differences among countries into account.

The above model also presents results for export policies which maintain a low domestic price relative to that charged high-income importers.These results are extremely important, especially for feed grains, since they clearly show the interdependence between feed grain prices, usage, and the livestock sector. A two-price policy that keeps a lid on domestic feed grain prices (this is, in a sense, a government export cartel) helps the overall society at the expense of grain producers. On the other hand, a producer grain cartel would attempt to increase both domestic and foreign prices for wheat and feed grains. This may not be in the best interests of livestock producers and consumers generally.

APPENDIX 8A. DATA SOURCES

The primary data sources used in the Michigan State University agricultural trade model are presented here. Numerous other sources have been consulted and some were used, but a complete list is not possible. Data on quantities of wheat, corn, oats, barley, sorghum and rye production, hectares harvested, consumption, imports, exports, feed use, nonfeed use, and stocks are from the *Foreign Production, Supply and Distribution of Agricultural Com-*

modities, a computer tape prepared by the Foreign Agricultural Service of the U.S. Department of Agriculture. Data on approximately 120 countries for the 1960–77 period are available from this tape. Data on population, gross disposable product, and exchange rates come from several sources; however, the primary sources are the *Statistical Yearbook,* published by the United Nations; *International Financial Statistics,* published by the International Monetary Fund; and the *Handbook of Economic Statistics,* published by the Central Intelligence Agency. Data on livestock numbers by country are taken from *Livestock Statistics in Selected Countries, 1960–1975,* Foreign Agricultural Circular FLM 10-78, and *World Livestock Numbers, Red Meat Production, Consumption and Trade, 1974–78,* Foreign Agricultural Circular (FLM 9-78) by the Foreign Agricultural Service, USDA.

APPENDIX 8B
MODEL VALIDATION

Table 8B–1 presents a comparison of actual and forecast values for selected endogenous variables for 1971–1976. These results are generated by the full simulation model when all equations are allowed to interact; they are not individual equation results viewed in isolation. The correlation coefficient for the actual versus predicted values for the entire 1962–1976 period is also presented for each endogenous variable.

The correlation coefficients for actual versus forecast U.S. wheat and coarse grain prices are .917 and .976, respectively. Forecast prices for both wheat and coarse grain correctly capture the rapid increase in 1973 and the price turnaround in 1975.

The comparison of forecast and actual net import and net export values in Table 8B–1 shows that the model captures both the direction and the magnitude of trade for most regions. U.S. coarse grain exports, including the volatile 1972–73 period, are explained. U.S. wheat export quantity forecasts lagged behind the actual ones in 1971 and 1972 but captured the levels of the 1973–1976 period. Net imports of wheat and coarse grains are accurately forecast, with the exception of the Soviet Bloc net wheat imports, which are underestimated in 1972.

Table 8B-1. Forecast and actual values of selected endogenous variables

Variables	Correlation Coefficient[a]	1971 Actual	1971 Estimate	1972 Actual	1972 Estimate	1973 Actual	1973 Estimate	1974 Actual	1974 Estimate	1975 Actual	1975 Estimate	1976 Actual	1976 Estimate
Prices[b]													
Wheat	.917	1.68	1.97	1.98	1.62	4.12	2.89	4.80	5.29	4.27	3.95	3.29	3.69
Coarse grain	.976	1.37	1.58	1.65	1.56	2.71	2.34	3.55	3.83	3.10	2.93	2.80	2.54
Net exports[c]													
U.S. wheat	.893	16284	20688	30355	26193	32824	29251	27334	30851	31598	29754	25393	23209
U.S. coarse grain	.975	23822	24378	38305	38638	40448	38402	35091	40126	49279	54607	49959	51224
Canada wheat	.676	13710	13525	15692	14678	11414	12993	10739	11116	12254	11399	13450	11276
Can. coarse grain	.861	4693	2728	3071	3180	1334	2842	2102	1918	4333	3517	3727	3267
Australia wheat	.826	7788	6974	4309	4211	6789	6806	8526	8043	8229	7904	8500	8020
Aust. coarse grain	.843	2779	3070	1369	1342	2483	2816	2865	3534	3628	3261	2812	2596
Argentina wheat	.864	1629	1133	2700	2711	1582	2731	1784	2170	3160	2701	6000	4448
Arg. coarse grain	.855	2736	4619	7923	8350	8737	9322	6051	6120	7075	6903	9655	10523
Net imports[c]													
Soviet Bloc wheat	.696	2064	3188	17988	7576	3103	2310	1513	7837	13312	12723	9037	5636
Sov. Bloc. coarse grain	.938	7843	3514	10233	10064	6605	7219	6857	9450	19291	17728	10865	10663
Developed mkt. wheat	.923	8625	7511	5931	6822	6366	7260	3382	1997	3975	3684	4457	4622
Developed mkt. coarse grain	.963	23429	24940	29941	30560	32823	30781	32421	33790	33799	36735	44717	45243
Less developed wheat	.969	27867	26939	25575	26019	32303	31151	25571	34035	37623	34670	33106	30248
Less developed coarse grain	.972	2091	2852	6173	4749	4817	6091	6249	5383	4934	6168	6906	7496
U.S. stocks[d]													
Wheat	.895	26807	25993	16302	18003	9226	17271	11703	8852	16071	19903	30264	27105
Coarse grain	.925	46592	40744	31726	39998	21824	22137	15414	14875	17361	21462	30022	29337

[a] Predicted versus actual, 1962–1976.
[b] U.S. export price, imputed, nomina U.S. dollars per bushel.
[c] Million metric tons.
[d] Beginning stocks, million metric tons.

U.S. wheat and coarse grain forecasts versus actual ending stock levels have correlation coefficients of .895 and .925, respectively, for the 1962–1976 period. The model captures the rapid drawdown of stocks in the 1972–1974 period and the accumulation in 1975 and 1976; it also forecasts the magnitude, as well as the direction, of stock accumulation and dispersion.

Numerous other validation criteria, in addition to the ability of the model to track the historical path for the endogenous variables, have been applied. When subjected to various exogenously imposed shocks, the model responds logically both in the direction and magnitude of adjustments. Import demand elasticities have been calculated for all equations and are consistent with other estimated values and our expected magnitudes.

Model Assumptions

The forecasts of trade and related variables generated by the MSU agriculture trade model are dependent on numerous assumptions about how population, income, crop yields, and other key factors will change in the future. These assumptions are so important that moderate changes can significantly alter the simulation results. Two sets of assumptions will be used in this study. The first is referred to as the "base" and represents the most likely set of outcomes, while the second set is developed to represent a less optimistic view of world grain trade. This alternative assumes a slower rate of growth in income for all regions and higher grain yields which correspond with good weather; it is denoted as "low income–high yields." These two sets of assumptions are summarized in Tables 8B–2 and 8B–3. Changes for all variables except wheat and coarse grains are expressed as annual growth rates measured in percent changes. Wheat and coarse grain yields are increases per year measured in metric tons per hectare. The importance of each assumption and the source of the values selected will be outlined next.

Gross Domestic The first variable listed in Tables 8B–2 and 8B–3 is gross domestic product (GDP). The base run growth rates for GDP over the forecast period, 1979–1983, are taken from the *World Development Report* (World Bank 1978b). As detailed there,

Table 8B–2. Annual growth rates for exogenous variables for base forecast

	United States	*Canada*	*Australia*	*Argentina*	*Soviet Bloc*	*Developed Market Economies*	*Less Developed Market Economies*
				(in Percents)			
Gross domestic product	4.200	4.200	4.200	5.700	5.100	4.200	5.700
Population	.726	1.436	1.796	1.265	.864	.836	2.680
Wheat yield[a]	.029	.038	-.005	.010	.047	.071	.029
Coarse grain yield[a]	.104	.054	.011	.063	.046	.067	.016
Crop land base	1.0	0	0	0	0	0	2.0
Exchange rates with U.S.	–	0	0	0	0	0	0

[a]Annual yield increase expressed in metric tons per hectare. Estimated from trend yield equation over 1960–77 period.

Table 8B-3. Annual growth rates for exogenous variables for low income-high yields forecast

	United States	*Canada*	*Australia*	*Argentina*	*Soviet Bloc*	*Developed Market Economies*	*Less Developed Market Economies*
				(in Percents)			
Gross domestic product	3.000	3.000	3.000	4.500	4.000	3.000	4.500
Population	.726	1.436	1.796	1.265	.864	.836	2.680
Wheat yield[a]	.033	.041	.005	.013	.053	.071	.029
Coarse grain yield[a]	.111	.057	.022	.060	.052	.078	.016
Crop land base	1.0	0	0	0	0	0	2.0
Exchange rates with U.S.	—	0	0	0	0	0	0

[a]Annual yield increase expressed in metric tons per hectare. Estimated from trend yield equation over 1960–77 period, with crop-failure years excluded.

the economic interdependence among nations has been growing in importance and will probably continue to do so. Economic growth in the developed market economies is expected to be slower during the 1975–1985 period than during the previous decade due to inflationary pressures, balance-of-payment problems, and continued difficulty in managing aggregate demand. An average annual growth rate of 4.2 percent per year is expected for the 1975–1985 period. The United States, Germany, and France are expected to grow at approximately the average rate for the group, while Japan is expected to grow approximately 6 percent per year and other countries in Western Europe, such as Italy, will experience slower-than-average growth.

The centrally planned economies are projected to grow at an annual real rate of 5.1 percent per year over the decade from 1975–1985. This is significantly below the recent rate of growth but is still more rapid than the expansion expected for the developed market economies. The less developed market economies are projected to grow at an average rate of 5.6 percent per year. Table 8B–4 presents the historical and projected growth rates for GDP.

The alternative growth rates used for the low income–high yields run reflect a pessimistic view of the world economy. The growth rates, as shown in Table 8B–3, are approximately 1 percent lower than for the base run which, in turn, results in a lower growth in the import demand for wheat and coarse grains.

Population. Population growth rates used in both base run and low income–high yields run are shown in Tables 8B–2 and 8B–3. The values used are taken from *World Population Growth: Analysis and New Projections* by the United Nations (Atkinson 1977). The

Table 8B-4. Growth of gross domestic product, 1960-85; average annual percent growth rates at 1975 prices[a]

	1960–70	*1970–75*	*1975–86*
Industrialized countries	4.9	2.8	4.2
Centrally planned economies	6.8	6.4	5.1
Less developed market economies	5.5	5.9	5.7

[a]Source: *World Development Report, 1978.* Washington, D.C.: World Bank, p. 27.

tables show the medium population forecasts taken from the 1975 United Nations forecast. The importance of population on the model forecast depends primarily on the number of years being projected. When only three to five years are being forecast, as is the case here, then population will probably not be a critical source of error due to the relatively well-developed techniques of forecasting population and the small changes in population growth which have historically been observed for large regions such as are included in this study. This is not to imply that population is not important or that it is relegated to a minor role in the MSU agriculture trade model—it is not. All consumption and import relationships for wheat and coarse grains are estimated on a per capita basis, a procedure which ties world demand directly to population.

Yields. Wheat and coarse grain yields are among the most important variables in the model and are usually the source of the greatest error. The growth in yields per year (Tables 8B–2 and 8B–3) is represented in metric tons per hectare. The rates of increase for the base run were obtained from a linear trend regression equation estimated over the 1960–1977 period. A linear trend is a reasonable way to project future yields and—in the absence of specific knowledge about key variables such as fertilizer levels, genetic potentials of seed varieties, irrigated areas, and weather—is probably the best approach. However, a series of unusually high or low yields has the potential to cause either a surplus or a shortage of grain in the world markets, and the result would have dramatic consequences on efforts to operate a world grain cartel. Therefore, an alternative set of yield forecasts, which correspond to a high yield or good weather scenario, was developed. This was done by excluding the years which had unusually low yields and estimating a new trend line.

Cropland Base. The MSU agriculture trade model treats total cropland used for wheat and coarse grain production as a variable. Land used for wheat and coarse grain is constrained to equal the total cropland base. Since cropland has such an important role in world grain production, this variable acts as an explicit constraint on production. The availability of cropland in the future is extremely important to the world grain situation and will strongly influence future market conditions for wheat and coarse grains. Several recent studies have examined the availability of cropland at both a world and U.S. level. Lee (1978) examines the availability and factors which influence cropland in the United States, and Brown (1978) reviews the evidence concerning changes in cropland for the world.

Lee reports that a 1974 unpublished study by the U.S. Economic Research Service estimated that 467 million acres of land were classified as cropland. Of that amount, 363 million acres were used for crops, 20 million acres were idle or used for conservation crops, and 84 million acres were used for pasture. By 1977, an estimated 376 million acres of cropland were used for crop production. Lee concludes that the United States currently has 78 million acres of land with high potential for cropland which are not currently being used for crop production; an additional 33 million acres are classified as having medium potential for development. However, she notes that only 15 of the 78 million acres classified as having high potential are free of limitations such as a high water table, dense forest, flooding, erosion potential, and others. Lee also notes that the United States had 22.9 million acres of cropland converted from agricultural uses to urban and buildup uses between 1967 and 1975. One-third of this was considered prime agricultural land. It seems reasonable to conclude that the United States can add significantly to its cropland base, but high grain prices over a number of years would probably be required to encourage the capital investments needed to expand the area used for crop production.

Brown (1978) raises similar arguments at the world level. He notes that between 1950 and 1978, the area planted to cereals expanded by 23 percent. During this time, two periods of rapid increases in area were observed: the first, from 1951 to 1956, saw an increase of 10 percent (an average of 2 percent per year) while the second, from 1972 to 1976, increased cropland area by 8 percent (also an average of 2 percent per year). The second period of rapid expansion, however, was accompanied by a return to production of some 20 million acres of idle cropland in the United States. This is a one-time change which cannot be repeated. Brown concludes that the growth would have been reduced at least one-third except for special circumstances which will not be repeated.

The Agricultural Committee of the Organization for Economic Cooperation and Development (OECD) reported, according to Brown, that the opportunities for new land reclamation in Western

Europe are negligible. Eastern Europe and the Soviet Union have already extended crop production into highly marginal rainfall areas and are not likely to expand cropland above current levels. Asia, China, and India are reported to have few opportunities to increase land used for crop production. Africa is thought to have some potential for increased cropland, and two other areas which have this potential are Argentina and Brazil. In Argentina, cropland area can be expanded by plowing up some grasslands. Brazil also has the potential to open new lands, but the principal constraint here is low soil fertility. Brown also points out that historically we have seen significantly lower crop yields when new land is added to the cropland base.

Table 8B–5 shows the area of wheat and coarse grains harvested over the 1960–1978 period; the data for the United States also include soybeans since substantial land is devoted to soybean production. Over the 1960–1978 period, the United States has shown significant increases in the area devoted to wheat, coarse grain, and soybean production, most occurring in response to the high grain prices since 1973. The 1970–1972 average was 77.3 million hectares compared to an average of 92.5 million hectares in the 1975–1977 period. Allowing for the approximately 8.1 million hectares of idle cropland during 1970–1972, an additional 7.1 million hectares were added over the 1973–1977 period in response to high grain prices. This suggests a growth in cropland base of approximately 1.2 million hectares or 1.3 percent per year based on new cropland area, a figure which is assumed to represent the maximum growth in land possible in the United States and which would probably not be reached again even if grain prices were at the 1974–75 levels. Since the cartel arrangement being investigated in this study would result in high prices, the growth in cropland base which will prevail in the 1979–1983 period is assumed to be 1 percent per year as shown in Table 8B–1. This growth rate is applied to the 1960–1978 maximum historical area of 93.5 million hectares.

Canada's cropland has responded to the high grain prices since 1972 with higher areas in 1976, 1977, and 1978 when 19.0, 18.6, and 18.8 million hectares of wheat and coarse grains were harvested, respectively. Similar areas were harvested in 1966, 1967, and 1968; and this area seems to represent an upper bound on cropland. Based

Table 8B-5. Cropland harvested area of wheat and coarse grains combined for the 1960-78 period

Year	United States[a]	Canada	Australia	Argentina	Soviet Bloc	Developed Market Economies	Developing Market Economies
	(Million Hectares)						
1960	83.2	17.0	8.3	9.1	139.4	48.2	131.0
1961	75.4	16.3	8.4	9.9	143.2	47.8	129.8
1962	71.2	17.7	9.1	8.0	145.8	48.8	133.3
1963	73.5	17.9	9.1	11.4	143.8	48.3	136.0
1964	73.0	18.0	9.8	11.7	148.4	48.0	137.8
1965	73.8	17.9	9.8	9.9	146.2	48.2	138.0
1966	75.3	18.9	11.5	10.7	143.7	47.8	137.7
1967	81.4	19.1	11.8	12.3	140.8	48.1	141.3
1968	79.1	19.2	14.1	12.3	141.6	48.6	146.3
1969	75.5	17.6	12.9	12.4	142.0	48.5	148.1
1970	76.0	12.7	10.8	11.2	137.9	48.7	150.5
1971	80.6	17.2	11.7	10.3	137.7	49.0	149.3
1972	76.6	17.0	11.6	12.6	139.1	47.8	148.0
1973	86.5	17.9	12.7	11.5	144.3	48.3	151.9
1974	89.5	17.1	11.6	10.5	145.4	48.7	152.8
1975	93.2	17.3	12.5	11.2	146.2	47.8	155.5
1976	91.7	19.0	12.9	13.0	146.2	48.0	160.3
1977	93.5	18.6	14.9	10.5	147.9	46.8	156.8
1978	89.9	18.8	14.7	10.9	146.0	n.a.	n.a.

[a]Includes soybean area.

on this assumption, Canada's cropland base is assumed to remain constant at 19.0 million hectares of wheat and coarse grains over the 1979–1983 period.

Australia has shown significant increases in cropland area of wheat and course grains harvested over the 1960–1978 period. However, most of the gains date back to the early 1960s, and the 14.1 million hectares harvested in 1968 have been exceeded only in 1977 and 1978. The high grain prices during the 1972–1976 period seem to have had almost no effect on harvested area until 1977 and 1978 when large increases were evident. The assumption used in this study is that the harvested area will be constant at the 1977–78 average of 14.8 million hectares.

Argentina probably has the greatest potential of the exporting regions to augment its cropland base but because of its unstable political character, it may not utilize this potential. A review of the historical data shows that the area devoted to wheat and coarse grain production has ranged from 10 to 13 million hectares since the mid-1960s. An assumed 12 million hectares of wheat and coarse grains will be used in this analysis. No growth is projected over the 1979–1983 period.

The Soviet Bloc, which consists of the Soviet Union and Eastern Europe, has demonstrated an upper bound of approximately 148 million hectares of wheat and coarse grains. This level was surpassed in 1964 when the harvested area reached 148.4 million hectares and nearly equaled in 1977 when 147.9 million hectares were harvested. Inability to exceed this level in the last decade implies that little potential for cropland expansion exists. For this analysis, the Soviet Bloc cropland is set at the 1975–1977 average of 146.8 million hectares and is not assumed to grow above this level.

The developed market economies do not show either greater variability or the potential for expansion of their cropland base. The wheat and coarse grain area has ranged from 46.8 million hectares in 1977 to 49.0 million hectares in 1971. The average over the period is 48.2 million hectares and, for this analysis, the cropland base is assumed to remain constant at the 1960–1977 average for the 1979–1983 period.

The less developed market economies show the greatest potential for expansion of the seven regions considered. This region shows a continuing pattern of expansion over the entire period considered and is growing at a rate of approximately 2 percent per year. Based on a cropland base equal to the 1975–1977 average of 157.5 million hectares, the 1978–1983 period is assumed to have a growth of 2 percent per year in the cropland base.

Exchange Rates. The exchange rates among other major currencies and the United States are assumed to remain constant at the values of December 31, 1978. This assumption is not based on any preconceived knowledge of world monetary conditions but, rather, a lack of such knowledge. It is not critical for most regions since exchange rates have remained relatively constant over the last decade and can be assumed to remain nearly constant in the future. Note that this contrasts significantly with the popular view of exchange rates. Most of the changes in exchange rates, however, have occurred in only a few countries, while the majority of countries which engage in grain trade have maintained a relatively stable exchange rate relative to the dollar; and it seems that this may continue.

One region which has not been insulated from changes in the exchange rate is the Soviet Bloc. Since the Soviet Union derives a significant part of its foreign exchange from the sale of gold, the high price of gold should be a very important factor influencing Soviet grain imports. The assumption of a constant exchange rate between the Soviet Bloc and the United States essentially holds the gold price constant at December 31, 1978, levels.

Trade with the People's Republic of China. The People's Republic of China (PRC) is not endogenously represented in the MSU agriculture trade model; its trade levels are exogenously specified. Over the 1979–1983 period, the PRC is assumed to import 8.5 million metric tons of wheat and 2.5 million metric tons of coarse grain per year. These imports are consistent with 1977 and 1978 levels and do not assume significant increases for the 1979–1983 period.

APPENDIX 8C: FORECAST TABLES

In the following runs (Tables 8C–1 through 8C–18) endogenous variables are listed on the left, and historical and forecast results are shown across the page for the 1974–1983 period. Forecasts begin in 1979, and historical values are included for the years from 1974 through 1978 for comparison. Results are presented by country or region.

REFERENCES

Atkinson, L.J. 1977. "World Population Growth: Analysis and New Projections of the United Nations." Foreign Agricultural Economic

Report 129, Economic Research Service, U.S. Department of Agriculture.

Brown, L.R. 1978. "The Worldwide Loss of Cropland." Worldwatch Paper 24, Worldwatch Institute.

L.K. Lee, 1978. "A Perspective on Cropland Availability." Agricultural Economic Report No. 406, Economics, Statistics, and Cooperatives Service, U.S. Department of Agriculture.

———. 1978b. *World Development Report, 1978.* Washington, D.C.: World Bank.

Table 8C-1. Run 1—base assumptions, current market conditions, no price policy[a]

	1974/75	1975/76	1976/77	1977/78	1978/79	1979/80	1980/81	1981/82	1982/83	1983/84
United States										
W Price, Export	4.80	4.27	3.29	3.43	3.63	3.88	4.04	4.69	5.78	6.09
F Price, Export	3.55	3.10	2.80	2.54	2.50	2.50	2.91	3.51	3.67	4.13
W Production	48,879	58,078	58,432	55,139	48,962	57,500	59,439	60,298	62,399	65,651
F Production	150,469	184,926	193,083	201,914	212,070	224,700	206,063	202,886	217,933	218,507
W Consumption	19,068	20,112	21,037	22,800	23,600	22,254	23,626	23,811	21,661	22,691
F Consumption	121,788	133,700	132,385	136,900	153,200	158,938	160,886	156,886	153,921	150,173
W Net Exports	27,334	31,598	25,393	31,000	32,400	39,054	38,298	41,929	43,984	44,115
F Net Exports	35,091	49,279	49,959	51,800	56,000	67,123	65,955	64,099	66,636	71,219
W Ending Stocks	11,703	18,071	30,264	32,300	25,100	21,291	18,809	13,374	10,135	8,986
F Ending Stocks	15,414	17,361	30,022	41,200	45,600	44,095	23,285	15,950	13,287	10,368
GCAU	70	75	76	78	80	81	81	79	79	79
Canada										
W Production	13,295	17,078	23,523	19,651	21,145	17,300	21,432	20,982	20,914	22,427
F Production	17,436	19,987	21,198	22,362	20,016	18,100	21,869	23,436	24,509	23,508
W Consumption	4,607	4,827	4,875	4,800	4,800	4,917	5,072	5,113	4,984	5,081
F Consumption	15,923	16,800	16,953	16,300	17,000	17,199	16,582	15,296	14,566	12,869
W Net Exports	10,739	12,254	13,450	16,000	14,400	15,510	16,298	18,471	16,085	17,347
F Net Exports	2,102	4,333	3,727	3,370	5,396	2,656	4,752	6,635	8,623	9,942
W Ending Stocks	8,038	8,035	13,310	12,100	13,823	10,696	10,757	8,155	8,000	8,000
F Ending Stocks	5,626	4,483	5,188	7,579	6,250	4,500	5,060	6,596	7,950	8,677
GCAU	13,130	12,838	12,838	13,191	13,339	13,391	13,050	12,264	11,558	10,543
Australia										
W Production	11,357	12,024	11,800	9,200	18,300	16,000	12,560	11,863	11,529	11,970
F Production	4,453	5,611	5,334	3,983	7,100	5,900	4,983	5,700	6,080	5,590
W Consumption	3,025	2,764	2,925	2,600	2,800	3,288	3,288	3,161	2,974	2,834
F Consumption	1,717	1,753	2,222	2,351	2,393	2,237	2,058	1,810	1,555	1,473
W Net Exports	8,526	8,229	8,500	8,100	9,762	10,881	10,363	9,992	9,832	9,686
F Net Exports	2,865	3,628	2,812	1,819	3,727	3,687	3,341	3,874	4,336	4,593
W Ending Stocks	1,788	2,819	2,312	800	6,566	8,397	7,308	6,048	4,766	4,217
F Ending Stocks	501	731	787	791	1,036	1,015	602	621	814	741
GCAU	3,025	3,008	2,955	3,005	3,054	3,081	3,030	2,868	2,654	2,335

Argentina										
W Production	5,970	8,570	11,200	5,500	8,100	8,000	7,703	7,231	7,045	7,595
F Production	13,793	12,438	17,261	17,839	17,300	16,678	17,874	19,229	20,102	19,650
W Consumption	4,498	5,382	4,692	4,400	4,500	5,105	5,220	5,241	5,213	5,334
F Consumption	7,465	6,501	6,826	6,881	6,833	7,912	8,310	8,807	9,340	9,644
W Net Exports	1,784	3,160	6,000	1,800	2,218	2,703	2,546	2,148	1,922	2,165
F Net Exports	6,051	7,075	9,655	9,505	10,317	8,896	9,512	10,350	10,731	10,070
W Ending Stocks	714	742	1,400	500	634	826	763	606	517	613
F Ending Stocks	1,359	221	338	324	830	701	757	833	867	807
GCAU	3,928	3,749	3,631	3,948	3,841	3,999	4,123	4,237	4,406	4,555
Soviet Bloc										
W Production	117,869	94,650	131,519	126,603	155,300	111,600	132,914	134,970	136,969	138,912
F Production	156,945	125,439	173,829	146,252	162,300	143,300	170,350	175,268	180,241	185,269
W Net Imports	1,513	13,312	9,037	9,000	4,064	14,393	111,113	12,530	12,144	14,818
F Net Imports	6,857	19,291	10,865	17,805	18,997	24,697	21,708	21,367	22,470	23,067
W Ending Stocks	23,416	14,104	4,528	11,336	16,765	16,261	17,766	18,668	19,272	19,726
F Ending Stocks	4,768	6,487	6,223	4,340	6,858	4,514	7,965	7,161	7,343	7,831
Developed Market Economies										
W Production	58,213	51,205	54,139	50,510	53,739	56,299	57,579	57,270	57,067	59,143
F Production	93,161	87,889	82,189	98,400	101,300	100,722	102,742	106,455	110,049	111,219
W Net Imports	3,382	3,975	4,457	6,400	4,887	3,363	3,455	4,214	3,435	2,579
F Net Imports	32,421	33,799	44,717	35,955	33,500	37,603	39,457	39,902	42,147	44,810
W Ending Stocks	15,083	13,407	13,026	13,063	13,392	13,572	13,598	14,079	15,146	15,664
F Ending Stocks	17,160	13,523	12,727	14,144	12,727	12,739	14,139	15,980	16,433	17,455
Developing Market Economies										
W Production	62,449	67,541	79,903	74,619	79,710	84,504	89,423	92,174	95,718	103,076
F Production	103,765	113,710	116,389	109,797	114,304	116,999	119,806	124,697	129,114	130,513
W Net Imports	35,571	37,623	33,106	30,500	36,887	40,490	42,526	45,384	47,856	47,970
F Net Imports	6,249	4,934	6,906	9,100	12,628	14,632	16,339	17,620	19,637	21,887
W Ending Stocks	11,156	16,130	24,275	18,150	14,801	15,203	15,656	15,747	18,914	22,267
F Ending Stocks	7,671	10,482	12,975	9,649	10,517	10,578	10,706	11,498	11,930	11,387
China										
W Net Imports	5,695	2,200	3,100	8,600	9,000	7,500	8,000	8,000	8,000	8,000
F Net Imports	428	-115	-50	150	4,000	2,500	2,500	2,500	2,500	2,500

[a] W = Wheat; F = Feed Grains (Corn, Oats, Barley, Sorghum, and Rye); and GCAU = Grain Consuming Animal Units.
All Wheat and Feed Grain quantities are in thousand metric tons; prices are $/bushel.

Table 8C-2. Run 2—base assumptions, historical market shares, *w* price \$5.45, *F* price \$4.30 for all regions[a]

	1974/75	1975/76	1976/77	1977/78	1978/79	1979/80	1980/81	1981/82	1982/83	1983/84
United States										
W Price, Export	4.80	4.27	3.29	3.43	3.63	5.45	5.45	5.58	6.62	6.59
F Price, Export	3.55	3.10	2.80	2.54	2.50	4.30	4.30	4.30	4.30	4.30
W Production	48,879	58,078	58,432	55,139	48,962	57,500	57,788	60,089	63,082	66,007
F Production	150,469	184,926	193,083	201,914	212,070	224,700	217,579	219,559	220,005	220,607
W Consumption	19,068	20,112	21,037	22,800	23,600	22,015	22,502	22,884	20,615	21,564
F Consumption	121,788	133,700	132,385	136,900	153,200	141,002	124,956	124,443	131,311	136,433
W Net Exports	27,334	31,598	25,393	31,000	32,400	36,611	40,620	44,896	43,934	43,152
F Net Exports	35,091	49,279	49,959	51,800	56,000	56,863	52,604	55,864	63,494	71,039
W Ending Stocks	11,703	18,071	30,264	32,300	25,100	21,972	16,638	8,948	7,481	8,771
F Ending Stocks	15,414	17,361	30,022	41,200	45,600	70,313	110,307	149,336	174,262	187,115
GCAU	70	75	76	78	80	73	74	75	76	78
Canada										
W Production	13,295	17,078	23,523	19,651	21,145	17,300	20,338	20,438	20,733	22,498
F Production	17,436	19,987	21,198	22,362	20,016	18,100	23,296	24,148	24,745	23,416
W Consumption	4,607	4,827	4,875	4,800	4,800	5,051	4,997	4,982	4,953	5,032
F Consumption	15,923	16,800	16,953	16,300	17,000	13,791	12,937	12,344	11,902	11,320
W Net Exports	10,739	12,254	13,450	16,000	14,400	16,646	15,341	15,456	15,760	17,465
F Net Exports	2,102	4,333	3,727	3,370	5,172	5,411	5,317	5,985	6,959	7,760
W Ending Stocks	8,038	8,035	13,310	12,100	12,397	8,000	8,000	8,000	8,000	8,000
F Ending Stocks	5,626	4,483	5,188	7,579	6,474	5,371	10,413	16,231	22,114	26,449
GCAU	13,130	12,838	12,838	13,191	13,339	12,037	11,204	10,595	10,080	9,589
Australia										
W Production	11,357	12,024	11,800	9,200	18,300	16,000	11,761	11,548	11,420	11,874
F Production	4,453	5,611	5,334	3,983	7,100	5,900	5,834	6,060	6,199	5,696
W Consumption	3,025	2,764	2,925	2,600	2,800	3,087	2,978	2,868	2,663	2,557
F Consumption	1,717	1,753	2,222	2,351	2,393	1,812	1,620	1,357	1,056	672
W Net Exports	8,526	8,229	8,500	8,100	8,987	10,871	10,793	11,580	11,467	10,516
F Net Exports	2,865	3,628	2,812	1,819	3,974	4,197	3,924	4,178	4,658	5,085
W Ending Stocks	1,788	2,819	2,312	800	7,341	9,382	7,372	4,472	1,763	565
F Ending Stocks	501	731	787	791	790	681	970	1,496	1,981	1,920
GCAU	3,025	3,008	2,955	3,005	3,054	2,854	2,631	2,384	2,109	1,804

Argentina										
W Production	5,970	8,570	11,200	5,500	8,100	8,000	6,982	6,926	6,945	7,506
F Production	13,793	12,438	17,261	17,839	17,300	16,678	19,122	19,766	20,262	19,812
W Consumption	4,498	5,382	4,692	4,400	4,500	4,885	4,989	5,100	5,087	5,257
F Consumption	7,465	6,501	6,826	6,881	6,833	7,419	8,089	8,629	9,130	9,535
W Net Exports	1,784	3,160	6,000	1,800	2,582	3,115	1,993	1,826	1,857	2,249
F Net Exports	6,051	7,075	9,655	9,505	10,926	9,259	10,828	11,341	11,151	10,277
W Ending Stocks	714	742	1,400	500	269	269	269	269	269	269
F Ending Stocks	1,359	221	338	324	221	221	425	221	221	221
GCAU	3,928	3,749	3,631	3,948	3,841	3,811	3,978	4,154	4,340	4,537
Soviet Bloc										
W Production	117,869	94,650	131,519	126,603	155,300	111,600	132,914	134,970	136,969	138,912
F Production	156,945	125,439	173,829	146,252	162,300	143,300	170,350	175,268	180,241	185,269
W Net Imports	1,513	13,312	9,037	9,000	4,064	16,266	12,345	13,141	13,180	14,611
F Net Imports	6,857	19,291	10,865	17,805	18,997	22,138	19,377	19,963	21,411	22,697
W Ending Stocks	23,416	14,104	4,528	11,336	16,765	16,261	17,766	18,658	19,272	19,726
F Ending Stocks	4,768	6,487	6,223	4,340	6,858	6,445	9,457	8,009	8,013	8,016
Developed Market Economies										
W Production	58,213	51,205	54,139	50,510	53,739	56,299	54,003	54,783	55,766	58,325
F Production	93,161	87,889	82,189	98,400	101,300	100,722	106,566	109,107	111,432	112,086
W Net Imports	3,382	3,975	4,457	6,400	4,887	3,931	4,842	5,052	3,448	2,105
F Net Imports	32,421	33,799	44,717	35,955	33,500	37,321	33,329	35,265	40,224	43,801
W Ending Stocks	15,083	13,407	13,026	13,063	13,392	15,088	14,625	15,043	16,067	16,189
F Ending Stocks	17,160	13,523	12,727	14,145	12,727	17,763	18,401	18,072	18,050	17,884
Developing Market Economies										
W Production	62,449	67,541	79,903	74,619	79,710	84,504	85,808	89,987	94,732	102,736
F Production	103,765	113,710	116,389	109,797	114,304	117,000	122,938	126,578	129,955	130,800
W Net Imports	35,571	37,623	33,106	30,500	36,887	39,096	41,161	45,164	46,011	46,265
F Net Imports	6,249	4,934	6,906	9,100	12,628	12,234	13,960	16,061	18,529	21,563
W Ending Stocks	11,156	16,130	24,275	18,150	14,801	18,970	16,586	18,861	21,743	23,896
F Ending Stocks	7,671	10,482	12,975	9,650	10,515	10,817	12,001	12,132	12,142	11,390
China										
W Net Imports	5,695	2,200	3,100	8,600	9,000	7,500	8,000	8,000	8,000	8,000
F Net Imports	428	-115	-50	150	4,000	2,500	2,500	2,500	2,500	2,500

[a]W = Wheat; F = Feed Grains (Corn, Oats, Barley, Sorghum, and Rye); and GCAU = Grain Consuming Animal Units.
All Wheat and Feed Grain quantities are in thousand metric tons; prices are \$/bushel.

Table 8C-3. Run 3—base assumptions, historical market shares, w price ≥ \$6.80, F price ≥ \$5.37 for all regions[a]

	1974/75	1975/76	1976/77	1977/78	1978/79	1979/80	1980/81	1981/82	1982/83	1983/84
United States										
W Price, Export	4.80	4.27	3.29	3.43	3.63	6.80	6.80	6.80	6.80	8.09
F Price, Export	3.55	3.10	2.80	2.54	2.50	5.37	5.37	5.37	5.37	5.37
W Production	48,879	58,078	58,432	55,139	48,962	57,500	57,369	59,089	61,650	64,467
F Production	150,469	184,926	193,083	201,914	212,070	224,700	223,179	226,563	228,196	229,067
W Consumption	19,068	20,112	21,037	22,800	23,600	20,617	20,925	21,660	22,479	19,486
F Consumption	121,788	133,700	132,385	136,900	153,200	131,592	102,060	97,109	99,685	108,411
W Net Exports	27,334	31,598	25,393	31,000	32,400	37,910	38,888	43,840	46,535	47,594
F Net Exports	35,091	49,279	49,959	51,800	56,000	56,653	48,117	50,469	54,252	59,893
W Ending Stocks	11,703	18,071	30,264	32,300	25,100	24,069	21,628	15,215	7,849	5,236
F Ending Stocks	15,414	17,361	30,022	41,200	45,600	81,871	154,789	233,673	307,730	368,458
GCAU	70	75	76	78	80	69	69	70	71	73
Canada										
W Production	13,295	17,078	23,523	19,651	21,145	17,300	20,331	20,431	20,520	20,599
F Production	17,436	19,987	21,198	22,362	20,016	18,100	23,305	24,157	25,024	25,905
W Consumption	4,607	4,827	4,875	4,800	4,800	5,149	5,059	5,025	5,000	4,936
F Consumption	15,923	16,800	16,953	16,300	17,000	11,747	10,159	9,061	8,217	7,498
W Net Exports	10,739	12,254	13,450	16,000	14,400	16,548	15,272	15,407	15,521	15,663
F Net Exports	2,102	4,333	3,727	3,370	5,172	5,364	5,219	6,133	7,361	8,878
W Ending Stocks	8,038	8,035	13,310	12,100	12,397	8,000	8,000	8,000	8,000	8,000
F Ending Stocks	5,626	4,483	5,188	7,579	6,474	7,460	15,388	24,350	33,796	43,324
GCAU	13,130	12,838	12,838	13,191	13,339	11,232	9,907	8,963	8,187	7,466
Australia										
W Production	11,357	12,024	11,800	9,200	18,300	16,000	11,758	11,545	11,334	11,124
F Production	4,453	5,611	5,334	3,983	7,100	5,900	5,837	6,064	6,294	6,527
W Consumption	3,025	2,764	2,925	2,600	2,800	2,939	2,763	2,595	2,411	2,077
F Consumption	1,717	1,753	2,222	2,351	2,393	1,559	1,255	876	463	13
W Net Exports	8,526	8,229	8,500	8,100	8,987	10,754	10,496	11,406	11,894	11,200
F Net Exports	2,865	3,628	2,812	1,819	3,974	4,082	3,614	3,835	4,175	4,660
W Ending Stocks	1,788	2,819	2,312	800	7,341	9,647	8,146	5,689	2,718	565
F Ending Stocks	501	731	787	791	790	1,050	2,018	3,370	5,026	6,880
GCAU	3,025	3,008	2,955	3,005	3,054	2,719	2,360	1,975	1,560	1,111

Argentina										
W Production	5,970	8,570	11,200	5,500	8,100	8,000	6,979	6,923	6,865	6,806
F Production	13,793	12,438	17,261	17,839	17,300	16,678	19,127	19,771	20,424	21,086
W Consumption	4,498	5,382	4,692	4,400	4,500	4,695	4,797	4,924	5,057	5,007
F Consumption	7,465	6,501	6,826	6,881	6,833	7,189	7,862	8,519	9,136	9,683
W Net Exports	1,784	3,160	6,000	1,800	2,582	3,288	2,199	1,999	1,808	1,799
F Net Exports	6,051	7,075	9,655	9,505	10,926	9,489	9,971	10,582	11,519	12,857
W Ending Stocks	714	742	1,400	500	269	286	269	269	269	269
F Ending Stocks	1,359	221	338	324	221	221	1,515	2,186	1,955	502
GCAU	3,928	3,749	3,631	3,948	3,841	3,699	3,866	4,042	4,229	4,426
Soviet Bloc										
W Production	117,869	94,650	131,519	126,603	155,300	111,600	132,914	134,970	136,969	138,912
F Production	156,945	125,439	173,829	146,252	162,300	143,300	170,350	175,268	180,241	185,269
W Net Imports	1,513	13,312	9,037	9,000	4,064	16,918	13,002	13,948	15,169	15,114
F Net Imports	6,857	19,291	10,865	17,805	18,997	20,616	17,643	18,215	19,650	20,922
W Ending Stocks	23,416	14,104	4,528	11,336	16,765	16,261	17,766	18,662	19,272	19,726
F Ending Stocks	4,768	6,487	6,223	4,340	6,858	7,592	10,604	9,157	9,160	9,164
Developed Market Economies										
W Production	58,213	51,205	54,139	50,510	53,739	56,299	52,562	53,311	54,041	54,753
F Production	93,161	87,889	82,189	98,400	101,300	100,722	108,105	110,678	113,269	115,879
W Net Imports	3,382	3,975	4,457	6,400	4,887	3,788	4,723	5,205	5,163	3,657
F Net Imports	32,421	33,799	44,717	35,955	33,500	38,103	30,864	32,367	34,849	40,040
W Ending Stocks	15,083	13,407	13,026	13,063	13,392	16,395	15,795	16,222	16,221	17,464
F Ending Stocks	17,160	13,523	12,727	14,145	12,727	20,749	21,540	21,063	21,064	21,067
Developing Market Economies										
W Production	62,449	67,541	79,903	74,619	79,710	84,504	85,007	89,170	93,464	97,891
F Production	103,765	113,710	116,389	109,797	114,304	116,999	123,631	127,282	131,039	134,907
W Net Imports	35,571	37,623	33,106	30,500	36,887	37,895	38,731	43,098	45,025	47,084
F Net Imports	6,249	4,934	6,906	9,100	12,628	10,810	12,381	14,396	16,766	19,314
W Ending Stocks	11,156	16,130	24,275	18,150	14,801	22,217	19,288	21,786	21,876	25,061
F Ending Stocks	7,671	10,482	12,975	9,650	10,518	10,955	12,444	12,589	12,722	12,850
China										
W Net Imports	5,695	2,200	3,100	8,600	9,000	7,500	8,000	8,000	8,000	8,000
F Net Imports	428	-115	-50	150	4,000	2,500	2,500	2,500	2,500	2,500

[a]W = Wheat; F = Feed Grains (Corn, Oats, Barley, Sorghum, and Rye); and GCAU = Grain Consuming Animal Units.
All Wheat and Feed Grain quantities are in thousand metric tons; prices are $/bushel.

Table 8C-4. Run 4—base assumptions, cartel *w* price ≥ \$5.45, *F* price ≥ \$4.30 for all regions[a]

	1974/75	1975/76	1976/77	1977/78	1978/79	1979/80	1980/81	1981/82	1982/83	1983/84
United States										
W Price, Export	4.80	4.27	3.29	3.43	3.63	5.45	5.45	5.51	6.45	6.39
F Price, Export	3.55	3.10	2.80	2.54	2.50	4.30	4.30	4.30	4.30	4.30
W Production	48,879	58,078	58,432	55,139	48,962	57,500	57,927	59,963	62,662	65,566
F Production	150,469	184,926	193,083	201,914	212,070	224,700	217,271	219,240	220,949	221,605
W Consumption	19,068	20,112	21,037	22,800	23,600	22,015	22,508	23,089	21,089	22,129
F Consumption	121,788	133,700	132,385	136,900	153,200	141,002	124,956	124,233	130,819	135,850
W Net Exports	27,334	31,598	25,393	31,000	32,400	39,317	39,414	43,552	43,535	43,525
F Net Exports	35,091	49,279	49,959	51,800	56,000	59,018	49,943	51,564	57,847	65,573
W Ending Stocks	11,703	18,071	30,264	32,300	25,100	21,265	17,272	10,595	8,634	8,548
F Ending Stocks	15,414	17,361	30,022	41,200	45,600	70,082	112,095	155,708	187,465	207,110
GCAU	70	75	76	78	80	73	74	75	76	78
Canada										
W Production	13,295	17,078	23,523	19,651	21,145	17,300	20,338	20,438	20,622	22,232
F Production	17,436	19,987	21,198	22,362	20,016	18,100	23,296	24,148	24,891	23,765
W Consumption	4,607	4,827	4,875	4,800	4,800	5,104	5,087	5,024	4,953	5,025
F Consumption	15,923	16,800	16,953	16,300	17,000	13,739	12,848	12,302	11,908	11,340
W Net Exports	10,739	12,254	13,450	16,000	14,400	15,619	16,584	16,480	15,669	17,206
F Net Exports	2,102	4,333	3,727	3,370	5,396	4,971	7,780	10,148	11,973	12,492
W Ending Stocks	8,038	8,035	13,310	12,100	13,823	10,399	9,066	8,000	8,000	8,000
F Ending Stocks	5,626	4,483	5,188	7,579	6,250	5,639	8,307	10,005	11,014	10,947
GCAU	13,130	12,838	12,838	13,191	13,339	12,037	11,204	10,595	10,080	9,589
Australia										
W Production	11,357	12,024	11,800	9,200	18,300	16,000	11,761	11,548	11,375	11,769
F Production	4,453	5,611	5,334	3,983	7,100	5,900	5,834	6,060	6,249	5,812
W Consumption	3,025	2,764	2,925	2,600	2,800	3,087	2,978	2,874	2,676	2,572
F Consumption	1,717	1,753	2,222	2,351	2,393	1,812	1,620	1,357	1,060	681
W Net Exports	8,526	8,229	8,500	8,100	9,762	11,446	10,508	9,881	9,763	9,545
F Net Exports	2,865	3,628	2,812	1,819	3,727	4,518	4,321	4,566	4,955	5,065
W Ending Stocks	1,788	2,819	2,312	800	6,566	8,032	6,307	5,101	4,037	3,690
F Ending Stocks	501	731	787	791	1,038	609	501	638	871	936
GCAU	3,025	3,008	2,955	3,005	3,054	2,854	2,631	2,384	2,109	1,804

Argentina										
W Production	5,970	8,570	11,200	5,500	8,100	8,000	6,982	6,926	6,903	7,408
F Production	13,793	12,438	17,261	17,839	17,300	16,678	19,122	19,766	20,356	19,990
W Consumption	4,498	5,382	4,692	4,400	4,500	4,885	4,989	5,110	5,110	5,282
F Consumption	7,465	6,501	6,826	6,881	6,833	7,525	8,213	8,719	9,243	9,659
W Net Exports	1,784	3,160	6,000	1,800	2,218	2,861	2,239	1,936	1,834	2,043
F Net Exports	6,051	7,075	9,655	9,505	10,317	9,250	10,771	11,025	11,106	10,397
W Ending Stocks	714	742	1,400	500	634	888	642	522	482	565
F Ending Stocks	1,359	221	338	324	830	733	871	894	901	837
GCAU	3,928	3,749	3,631	3,948	3,841	3,811	3,978	4,154	4,340	4,537
Soviet Bloc										
W Production	117,869	94,650	131,519	126,603	155,300	111,600	132,914	134,970	136,969	138,912
F Production	156,945	125,439	173,829	146,252	162,300	143,300	170,350	175,268	180,241	185,269
W Net Imports	1,513	13,312	9,037	9,000	4,064	16,265	12,346	13,220	13,365	14,833
F Net Imports	6,857	19,291	10,865	17,805	18,997	22,138	19,377	19,963	21,411	22,697
W Ending Stocks	23,416	14,104	4,528	11,336	16,765	16,261	17,766	18,668	19,272	19,726
F Ending Stocks	4,768	6,487	6,223	4,340	6,858	6,445	9,457	8,009	8,013	8,016
Developed Market Economies										
W Production	58,213	51,205	54,139	50,510	53,739	56,299	54,003	54,783	55,646	58,038
F Production	93,161	87,889	82,189	98,400	101,300	100,722	106,561	109,103	111,555	112,385
W Net Imports	3,382	3,975	4,457	6,400	4,887	3,981	4,841	5,147	3,780	2,636
F Net Imports	32,421	33,799	44,717	35,955	33,500	37,325	33,354	35,125	39,778	43,145
W Ending Stocks	15,083	13,407	13,026	13,063	13,392	15,088	14,625	14,976	15,897	15,984
F Ending Stocks	17,160	13,523	12,727	14,144	12,727	17,763	18,398	18,070	18,060	17,899
Developing Market Economies										
W Production	62,449	67,541	79,903	74,619	79,710	84,504	85,808	89,987	94,496	102,174
F Production	103,765	113,710	116,389	109,797	114,304	116,999	122,933	126,573	130,150	131,270
W Net Imports	35,571	37,623	33,106	30,500	36,887	39,096	41,161	45,230	46,368	47005
F Net Imports	6,249	4,934	6,906	9,100	12,628	12,236	13,966	16,067	18,508	21,495
W Ending Stocks	11,156	16,130	24,275	18,150	14,801	18,970	16,586	18,692	21,187	23,203
F Ending Stocks	7,671	10,482	12,975	9,649	10,517	10,814	11,988	12,116	12,182	11,490
China										
W Net Imports	5,695	2,200	3,100	8,600	9,000	7,500	8,000	8,000	8,000	8,000
F Net Imports	428	-115	-50	150	4,000	2,500	2,500	2,500	2,500	2,500

[a]W = Wheat; F = Feed Grains (Corn, Oats, Barley, Sorghum, and Rye); and GCAU = Grain Consuming Animal Units.
All Wheat and Feed Grain quantities are in thousand metric tons; prices are $/bushel.

Table 8C-5. Run 5—base assumptions, cartel *w* price ⩾ \$6.80, *F* price ⩾ \$5.37 for all regions[a]

	1974/75	1975/76	1976/77	1977/78	1978/79	1979/80	1980/81	1981/82	1982/83	1983/84
United States										
W Price, Export	4.80	4.27	3.29	3.43	3.63	6.80	6.80	6.80	6.80	7.57
F Price, Export	3.55	3.10	2.80	2.54	2.50	5.37	5.37	5.37	5.37	5.37
W Production	48,879	58,078	58,432	55,139	48,962	57,500	57,459	58,889	61,091	63,635
F Production	150,469	184,926	193,083	201,914	212,070	224,700	219,007	227,795	234,570	240,119
W Consumption	19,068	20,112	21,037	22,800	23,600	20,618	20,929	21,652	22,456	20,993
F Consumption	121,788	133,700	132,385	136,900	153,200	131,593	102,060	97,109	99,685	106,870
W Net Exports	27,334	31,598	25,393	31,000	32,400	38,364	37,520	41,879	44,700	46,083
F Net Exports	35,091	49,279	49,959	51,800	56,000	55,262	41,787	41,889	45,236	50,422
W Ending Stocks	11,703	18,071	30,264	32,300	25,100	23,613	22,629	17,984	11,915	8,475
F Ending Stocks	15,414	17,361	30,022	41,200	45,600	83,194	161,961	249,611	333,676	406,876
GCAU	70	75	76	78	80	69	69	70	71	73
Canada										
W Production	13,295	17,078	23,523	19,651	21,145	17,300	20,331	20,431	20,520	20,599
F Production	17,436	19,987	21,198	22,362	20,016	18,100	23,305	24,157	25,024	25,905
W Consumption	4,607	4,827	4,875	4,800	4,800	5,203	5,160	5,093	5,006	4,952
F Consumption	15,923	16,800	16,953	16,300	17,000	11,694	10,658	8,992	8,217	7,482
W Net Exports	10,739	12,254	13,450	16,000	14,400	15,214	16,026	17,188	15,521	15,647
F Net Exports	2,102	4,333	3,727	3,370	5,396	6,005	9,669	12,799	15,192	17,206
W Ending Stocks	8,038	8,035	13,310	12,100	13,823	10,706	9,851	8,000	8,000	8,000
F Ending Stocks	5,626	4,483	5,188	7,579	6,250	6,647	10,224	12,589	14,203	15,420
GCAU	13,130	12,838	12,838	13,191	13,339	11,232	9,907	8,963	8.187	7,466
Australia										
W Production	11,357	12,024	11,800	9,200	18,300	16,000	11,758	11,545	11,334	11,124
F Production	4,453	5,611	5,334	3,983	7,100	5,900	5,837	6,064	6,294	6,527
W Consumption	3,025	2,764	2,925	2,600	2,800	2,939	2,763	2,595	2,411	2,130
F Consumption	1,717	1,753	2,222	2,351	2,393	1,559	1,255	876	463	13
W Net Exports	8,526	8,229	8,500	8,100	9,762	11,925	10,893	10,208	9,755	9,731
F Net Exports	2,865	3,628	2,812	1,819	3,727	4,878	4,582	5,188	5,607	6,174
W Ending Stocks	1,788	2,819	2,312	800	6,566	7,701	5,803	4,544	3,711	2,974
F Ending Stocks	501	731	787	791	1,038	501	501	501	724	1063
GCAU	3,025	3,008	2,955	3,005	3,054	2,719	2,360	1,975	1,560	1,111

Argentina										
W Production	5,970	8,570	11,200	5,500	8,100	8,000	6,979	6,923	6,865	6,806
F Production	13,793	12,438	17,261	17,839	17,300	16,678	19,127	19,771	20,424	21,086
W Consumption	4,498	5,382	4,692	4,400	4,500	4,695	4,797	4,924	5,057	5,083
F Consumption	7,465	6,501	6,826	6,881	6,833	7,295	7,991	8,499	9,033	9,597
W Net Exports	1,784	3,160	6,000	1,800	2,218	2,997	2,413	2,116	1,895	1,772
F Net Exports	6,051	7,075	9,655	9,505	10,317	9,460	10,996	11,249	11,380	11,480
W Ending Stocks	714	742	1,400	500	634	942	711	594	506	457
F Ending Stocks	1,359	221	338	324	830	752	891	914	926	935
GCAU	3,928	3,749	3,631	3,948	3,841	3,699	3,866	4,042	4,229	4,426
Soviet Bloc										
W Production	117,869	94,650	131,519	126,603	155,300	111,600	132,914	134,970	136,969	138,912
F Production	156,945	125,439	173,829	146,252	162,300	143,300	170,350	175,268	180,241	185,269
W Net Imports	1,513	13,312	9,037	9,000	4,064	16,916	13,002	13,948	15,169	15,703
F Net Imports	6,857	19,291	10,865	17,805	18,997	20,616	17,643	18,215	19,650	20,922
W Ending Stocks	23,416	14,104	4,528	11,336	16,765	17,766	18,658	19,272	19,726	
F Ending Stocks	4,768	6,487	6,223	4,340	6,858	7,592	10,604	9,157	9,160	9,164
Developed Market Economies										
W Production	58,213	51,205	54,139	50,510	53,739	56,299	52,562	53,311	54,041	54,753
F Production	93,161	87,889	82,189	98,400	101,300	100,721	108,100	110,674	113,265	115,872
W Net Imports	3,382	3,975	4,457	6,400	4,887	3,789	4,722	5,205	5,163	4,369
F Net Imports	32,421	33,799	44,717	35,955	33,500	38,106	36,885	32,388	34,870	38,879
W Ending Stocks	15,083	13,407	13,026	13,063	13,392	16,395	15,795	16,222	16,221	16,965
F Ending Stocks	17,160	13,523	12,727	14,144	12,727	20,749	21,537	21,061	21,462	21,063
Developing Market Economies										
W Production	62,449	67,541	79,903	74,619	79,710	84,504	85,007	89,170	93,463	97,891
F Production	103,765	113,710	116,389	109,797	114,304	116,998	123,626	127,278	131,035	134,899
W Net Imports	35,571	37,623	33,106	30,500	36,887	37,895	38,731	43,098	45,025	47,594
F Net Imports	6,249	4,934	6,906	9,100	12,628	10,811	12,386	14,401	16,773	19,325
W Ending Stocks	11,156	16,130	24,275	18,150	14,801	22,217	19,288	21,786	21,876	23,821
F Ending Stocks	7,671	10,482	12,975	9,649	10,517	10,953	12,433	12,574	12,703	12,822
China										
W Net Imports	5,695	2,200	3,100	8,600	9,000	7,500	8,000	8,000	8,000	8,000
F Net Imports	428	-115	-50	150	4,000	2,500	2,500	2,500	2,500	2,500

[a] W = Wheat; F = Feed Grains (Corn, Oats, Barley, Sorghum, and Rye); and GCAU = Grain Consuming Animal Units.
All Wheat and Feed Grain quantities are in thousand metric tons; prices are $/bushel.

Table 8C-6. Run 6—low income-high yields, current market conditions, no price policy[a]

	1974/75	1975/76	1976/77	1977/78	1978/79	1979/80	1980/81	1981/82	1982/83	1983/84
United States										
W Price, Export	4.80	4.27	3.29	3.43	3.66	3.81	3.52	3.43	3.41	3.42
F Price, Export	3.55	3.10	2.80	2.54	2.50	2.50	2.50	2.50	2.50	2.50
W Production	48,879	58,078	58,432	55,139	48,962	57,500	60,704	60,145	60,526	61,487
F Production	150,469	184,926	193,083	201,914	212,070	224,700	219,007	227,795	234,570	240,119
W Consumption	19,068	20,112	21,037	22,800	23,600	22,324	23,806	24,562	25,167	25,722
F Consumption	121,788	133,700	132,385	136,900	153,200	158,379	163,629	168,661	173,680	178,752
W Net Exports	27,334	31,598	25,393	31,000	32,400	35,025	30,655	31,809	33,572	35,226
F Net Exports	35,091	49,279	49,959	51,800	56,000	59,079	54,786	54,537	56,171	58,271
W Ending Stocks	11,703	18,071	30,264	32,300	25,100	25,250	31,491	35,264	37,050	37,587
F Ending Stocks	15,414	17,361	30,022	41,200	45,600	52,691	53,131	57,561	62,106	65,022
GCAU	70	75	76	78	80	81	82	83	83	84
Canada										
W Production	13,295	17,078	23,523	19,651	21,145	17,300	22,575	22,230	22,191	22,250
F Production	17,436	19,987	21,198	22,362	20,016	18,100	23,077	24,564	25,659	26,627
W Consumption	4,607	4,827	4,875	4,800	4,800	4,892	5,110	5,289	5,378	5,411
F Consumption	15,923	16,800	16,953	16,300	17,000	17,172	17,208	17,219	17,241	17,256
W Net Exports	10,739	12,254	13,450	16,000	14,400	14,337	13,371	15,540	16,950	17,677
F Net Exports	2,102	4,333	3,727	3,370	6,041	3,510	4,708	6,200	7,517	8,643
W Ending Stocks	8,038	8,035	13,310	12,100	12,647	10,718	14,812	16,213	16,076	15,237
F Ending Stocks	5,626	4,483	5,188	7,579	7,112	4,530	5,692	6,837	7,738	8,466
GCAU	13,130	12,838	12,838	13,191	13,339	13,354	13,289	13,170	13,009	12,812
Australia										
W Production	11,357	12,024	11,800	9,200	18,300	16,000	14,463	13,952	13,695	13,524
F Production	4,453	5,611	5,334	3,983	7,100	5,900	5,926	6,629	7,067	7,417
W Consumption	3,025	2,764	2,925	2,600	2,800	3,284	3,324	3,318	3,304	3,279
F Consumption	1,717	1,753	2,222	2,351	2,393	2,249	2,199	2,171	2,101	1,999
W Net Exports	8,526	8,229	8,500	8,100	8,106	9,780	10,167	10,303	10,326	10,300
F Net Exports	2,865	3,628	2,812	1,819	3,531	3,606	3,682	4,168	4,668	5,137
W Ending Stocks	1,788	2,819	2,312	800	3,501	6,438	7,409	7,740	7,804	7,749
F Ending Stocks	501	731	787	791	921	966	1,012	1,302	1,601	1,882
GCAU	3,025	3,008	2,955	3,005	3,054	3,079	3,079	3,056	3,007	2,933

Argentina										
W Production	5,970	8,570	11,200	5,500	8,100	8,000	8,084	7,730	7,584	7,509
F Production	13,793	12,438	17,261	17,839	17,300	16,678	18,143	19,260	20,044	20,717
W Consumption	4,498	5,382	4,692	4,400	4,500	5,096	5,249	5,359	5,472	5,588
F Consumption	7,465	6,501	6,826	6,881	6,833	7,789	8,297	8,800	9,245	9,688
W Net Exports	1,784	3,160	6,000	1,800	1,751	2,577	2,762	2,481	2,217	2,004
F Net Exports	6,051	7,075	9,655	9,505	9,030	8,901	9,768	10,403	10,766	11,007
W Ending Stocks	714	742	1,400	500	449	776	849	738	633	549
F Ending Stocks	1,359	221	338	324	713	701	780	837	870	892
GCAU	3,928	3,749	3,631	3,948	3,841	3,965	4,096	4,232	4,374	4,522
Soviet Bloc										
W Production	117,869	94,650	131,519	126,603	155,300	111,600	142,624	145,005	147,323	149,577
F Production	156,945	125,439	173,829	146,252	162,300	143,300	181,260	186,733	192,268	197,865
W Net Imports	1,513	13,312	9,037	9,000	6,543	13,609	6,824	7,066	7,599	8,316
F Net Imports	6,857	19,291	10,865	17,805	17,161	23,563	18,905	18,834	19,828	20,500
W Ending Stocks	23,416	14,104	4,528	12,236	16,191	15,982	18,428	19,815	20,681	21,288
F Ending Stocks	4,768	6,487	6,223	5,350	7,226	4,514	8,239	6,114	6,118	6,123
Developed Market Economies										
W Production	58,213	51,205	54,139	50,510	55,748	58,395	59,517	59,860	60,514	61,264
F Production	93,161	87,889	82,189	98,400	101,300	105,472	107,996	111,364	114,396	117,323
W Net Imports	3,382	3,975	4,457	6,400	2,915	745	529	700	467	60
F Net Imports	32,421	33,799	44,717	35,955	33,500	32,981	34,034	35,134	36,511	38,177
W Ending Stocks	15,083	13,407	13,026	12,882	13,606	13,511	13,086	12,924	12,931	12,947
F Ending Stocks	17,160	13,523	12,727	14,519	13,165	13,210	13,046	13,130	13,096	13,086
Developing Market Economies										
W Production	62,449	67,541	79,903	74,619	80,137	85,021	89,653	92,963	97,032	101,456
F Production	103,765	113,710	116,389	109,797	114,702	117,337	120,411	124,839	128,824	132,730
W Net Imports	35,571	37,623	33,106	30,500	34,967	37,464	39,200	41,969	44,599	46,431
F Net Imports	6,249	4,934	6,906	9,100	11,218	12,506	13,956	15,288	16,729	18,326
W Ending Stocks	11,156	16,130	24,275	18,150	15,149	15,093	14,226	13,105	13,569	13,825
F Ending Stocks	7,671	10,482	12,975	10,243	11,051	10,934	10,983	11,424	11,600	11,698
China										
W Net Imports	5,695	2,200	3,100	8,600	9,000	7,500	8,000	8,000	8,000	8,000
F Net Imports	428	-115	-50	150	4,000	2,500	2,500	2,500	2,500	2,500

[a] W = Wheat; F = Feed Grains (Corn, Oats, Barley, Sorghum, and Rye); and GCAU = Grain Consuming Animal Units.
All Wheat and Feed Grain quantities are in thousand metric tons; prices are $/bushel.

Table 8C-7. Run 7–low income-high yields, historical market shares, *w* price ⩾ \$5.45, *F* price ⩾ \$4.30 for all regions[a]

	1974/75	1975/76	1976/77	1977/78	1978/79	1979/80	1980/81	1981/82	1982/83	1983/84
United States										
W Price, Export	4.80	4.27	3.29	3.43	3.66	5.45	5.45	5.45	5.45	5.45
F Price, Export	3.55	3.10	2.80	2.54	2.50	4.30	4.30	4.30	4.30	4.30
W Production	48,879	58,078	58,432	55,139	48,962	57,500	58,829	58,949	59,541	60,258
F Production	150,469	184,926	193,083	201,914	212,070	224,700	231,468	238,934	245,429	251,726
W Consumption	19,068	20,112	21,037	22,800	23,600	21,872	22,141	22,637	23,181	23,745
F Consumption	121,788	133,700	132,385	136,900	153,200	140,651	124,080	122,568	125,660	130,152
W Net Exports	27,334	31,598	25,393	31,000	32,400	33,168	30,748	32,639	33,233	34,701
F Net Exports	35,091	49,279	49,959	51,800	56,000	51,912	44,029	45,314	47,708	49,562
W Ending Stocks	11,703	18,071	30,264	32,300	25,100	27,556	33,496	37,167	40,291	42,099
F Ending Stocks	15,414	17,361	30,022	41,200	45,600	77,553	140,784	211,651	283,484	355,264
GCAU	70	75	76	78	80	73	73	74	75	76
Canada										
W Production	13,295	17,078	23,523	19,651	21,145	17,300	21,532	21,646	21,748	21,839
F Production	17,436	19,987	21,198	22,362	20,016	18,100	24,424	25,320	26,232	27,160
W Consumption	4,607	4,827	4,875	4,800	4,800	5,095	5,101	5,148	5,169	5,184
F Consumption	15,923	16,800	16,953	16,300	17,000	13,695	12,697	11,935	11,331	10,757
W Net Exports	10,739	12,254	13,450	16,000	14,400	16,584	15,318	16,241	16,505	17,148
F Net Exports	2,102	4,333	3,727	3,370	4,778	4,994	4,790	5,525	6,542	7,731
W Ending Stocks	8,038	8,035	13,310	12,100	13,127	8,748	9,861	10,117	10,190	9,697
F Ending Stocks	5,626	4,483	5,188	7,579	8,375	7,784	14,720	22,580	30,939	39,612
GCAU	13,130	12,838	12,838	13,191	13,339	12,000	11,107	10,424	9,824	9,240
Australia										
W Production	11,357	12,024	11,800	9,200	18,300	16,000	13,629	13,490	13,349	13,207
F Production	4,453	5,611	5,334	3,983	7,100	5,900	6,822	7,131	7,447	7,768
W Consumption	3,025	2,764	2,925	2,600	2,800	3,078	2,955	2,843	2,715	2,569
F Consumption	1,717	1,753	2,222	2,351	2,393	1,823	1,648	1,397	1,116	803
W Net Exports	8,526	8,229	8,500	8,100	8,765	9,825	9,059	9,530	9,660	10,023
F Net Exports	2,865	3,628	2,812	1,819	3,591	3,782	3,308	3,445	3,676	3,882
W Ending Stocks	1,788	2,819	2,312	800	2,843	5,939	7,553	8,669	9,643	10,258
F Ending Stocks	501	731	787	791	861	1,156	3,022	5,312	7,967	11,051
GCAU	3,025	3,008	2,955	3,005	3,054	2,851	2,624	2,369	2,084	1,767

Argentina										
W Production	5,970	8,570	11,200	5,500	8,100	8,000	7,396	7,347	7,296	7,244
F Production	13,793	12,438	17,261	17,839	17,300	16,678	19,276	19,900	20,531	21,171
W Consumption	4,498	5,382	4,692	4,400	4,500	4,866	4,948	5,054	5,164	5,278
F Consumption	7,465	6,501	6,826	6,881	6,833	7,328	7,985	8,619	9,241	9,811
W Net Exports	1,784	3,160	6,000	1,800	1,930	3,004	2,577	2,293	2,133	1,967
F Net Exports	6,051	7,075	9,655	9,505	9,522	9,349	9,127	9,504	10,142	10,711
W Ending Stocks	714	742	1,400	500	269	399	269	269	269	269
F Ending Stocks	1,359	221	338	324	221	221	2,386	4,162	5,310	5,959
GCAU	3,928	3,749	3,631	3,948	3,841	3,778	3,908	4,044	4,186	4,335
Soviet Bloc										
W Production	117,869	94,650	131,519	126,603	155,300	111,600	142,624	145,005	147,323	149,577
F Production	156,945	125,439	173,829	146,252	162,300	143,300	181,260	186,733	192,268	197,865
W Net Imports	1,513	13,312	9,037	9,000	6,543	15,403	8,312	8,466	8,984	9,721
F Net Imports	6,857	19,291	10,865	17,805	17,161	21,004	15,987	15,894	16,866	17,515
W Ending Stocks	23,416	14,104	4,528	12,236	16,191	15,982	18,428	19,815	20,681	21,288
F Ending Stocks	4,768	6,487	6,223	5,350	7,226	6,445	10,170	8,045	8,049	8,053
Developed Market Economies										
W Production	58,213	51,205	54,139	50,510	55,748	58,395	55,933	56,698	57,446	58,175
F Production	93,161	87,889	82,189	98,400	101,300	105,472	111,879	114,788	117,718	120,669
W Net Imports	3,382	3,975	4,457	6,400	2,915	1,269	1,812	1,654	1,067	685
F Net Imports	32,421	33,799	44,717	35,955	33,500	32,865	28,168	29,537	31,362	32,978
W Ending Stocks	15,083	13,407	13,026	12,882	13,606	15,096	14,609	14,917	14,915	14,913
F Ending Stocks	17,160	13,523	12,727	14,520	13,165	18,234	18,456	18,108	18,110	18,112
Developing Market Economies										
W Production	62,449	67,541	79,903	74,619	80,137	85,021	86,248	90,440	94,763	99,220
F Production	103,765	113,710	116,389	109,797	114,702	117,337	123,353	127,001	130,755	134,618
W Net Imports	35,571	37,623	33,106	30,500	34,967	36,008	37,180	40,182	41,078	43,030
F Net Imports	6,249	4,934	6,906	9,100	11,217	10,109	11,046	12,276	13,738	15,287
W Ending Stocks	11,156	16,130	24,275	18,150	15,149	19,031	16,534	18,558	18,648	18,739
F Ending Stocks	7,671	10,482	12,975	10,248	11,054	11,171	12,269	12,321	12,388	12,467
China										
W Net Imports	5,695	2,200	3,100	8,600	9,000	7,500	8,000	8,000	8,000	8,000
F Net Imports	428	-115	-50	150	4,000	2,500	2,500	2,500	2,500	2,500

[a] W = Wheat; F = Feed Grains (Corn, Oats, Barley, Sorghum, and Rye); and GCAU = Grain Consuming Animal Units. All Wheat and Feed Grain quantities are in thousand metric tons; prices are $/bushel.

Table 8C-8. Run 8—low income-high yields, historical market shares, *w* price ⩾ \$6.80, *F* price ⩾ \$5.37 for all regions[a]

	1974/75	1975/76	1976/77	1977/78	1978/79	1979/80	1980/81	1981/82	1982/83	1983/84
United States										
W Price, Export	4.80	4.27	3.29	3.43	3.66	6.80	6.80	6.80	6.80	6.80
F Price, Export	3.55	3.10	2.80	2.54	2.50	5.37	5.37	5.37	5.37	5.37
W Production	48,879	58,078	58,432	55,139	48,962	57,500	58,458	58,081	58,219	58,575
F Production	150,469	184,926	193,083	201,914	212,070	224,700	237,212	245,910	253,552	260,801
W Consumption	19,068	20,112	21,037	22,800	23,600	20,475	20,567	21,033	21,559	22,110
F Consumption	121,788	133,700	132,385	136,900	153,200	131,242	101,184	95,621	97,527	101,685
W Net Exports	27,334	31,598	25,393	31,000	32,400	32,779	29,580	31,278	31,921	33,353
F Net Exports	35,091	49,279	49,959	51,800	56,000	49,687	39,432	40,131	41,848	42,526
W Ending Stocks	11,703	18,071	30,264	32,300	25,100	29,339	37,653	43,419	48,154	51,261
F Ending Stocks	15,414	17,361	30,022	41,200	45,600	89,141	185,579	295,465	409,305	525,468
GCAU	70	75	76	78	80	68	68	69	70	71
Canada										
W Production	13,295	17,078	23,523	19,651	21,145	17,300	21,525	21,638	21,740	21,831
F Production	17,436	19,987	21,198	22,362	20,016	18,100	24,434	25,330	26,242	27,170
W Consumption	4,607	4,827	4,875	4,800	4,800	5,193	5,167	5,207	5,222	5,234
F Consumption	15,923	16,800	16,953	16,300	17,000	11,651	9,915	8,636	7,629	6,699
W Net Exports	10,739	12,254	13,450	16,000	14,400	16,382	14,814	15,823	16,057	16,731
F Net Exports	2,102	4,333	3,727	3,370	4,778	4,955	4,747	5,916	7,654	10,000
W Ending Stocks	8,038	8,035	13,310	12,100	13,127	8,852	10,395	11,003	11,464	11,330
F Ending Stocks	5,626	4,483	5,188	7,579	8,375	9,865	19,636	30,412	41,371	51,842
GCAU	13,130	12,838	12,838	13,191	13,339	11,195	9,810	8,792	7,931	7,117
Australia										
W Production	11,357	12,024	11,800	9,200	18,300	16,000	13,625	13,486	13,345	13,204
F Production	4,453	5,611	5,334	3,983	7,100	5,900	6,826	7,135	7,451	7,773
W Consumption	3,025	2,764	2,925	2,600	2,800	2,930	2,741	2,560	2,360	2,140
F Consumption	1,717	1,753	2,222	2,351	2,393	1,570	1,283	916	516	77
W Net Exports	8,526	8,229	8,500	8,100	8,765	9,708	8,767	9,293	9,369	9,730
F Net Exports	2,865	3,628	2,812	1,819	3,591	3,666	2,993	3,120	3,354	3,559
W Ending Stocks	1,788	2,819	2,312	800	2,843	6,203	8,321	9,954	11,571	12,904
F Ending Stocks	501	731	787	791	861	1,524	4,074	7,173	10,754	14,891
GCAU	3,025	3,008	2,955	3,005	3,054	2,716	2,353	1,960	1,535	1,073

Argentina										
W Production	5,970	8,570	11,200	5,500	8,100	8,000	7,393	7,344	7,293	7,241
F Production	13,793	12,438	17,261	17,839	17,300	16,678	19,281	19,905	20,537	21,177
W Consumption	4,498	5,382	4,692	4,400	4,500	4,677	4,756	4,859	4,967	5,078
F Consumption	7,465	6,501	6,826	6,881	6,833	7,098	7,780	8,541	9,236	9,904
W Net Exports	1,784	3,160	6,000	1,800	1,930	2,968	2,680	2,796	2,327	2,163
F Net Exports	6,051	7,075	9,655	9,505	9,522	9,579	8,259	8,609	9,254	9,820
W Ending Stocks	714	742	1,400	500	269	624	580	269	269	269
F Ending Stocks	1,359	221	338	324	221	221	3,463	6,218	8,265	9,717
GCAU	3,928	3,749	3,631	3,948	3,841	3,666	3,796	3,932	4,075	4,223
Soviet Bloc										
W Production	117,869	94,650	131,519	126,603	155,300	111,600	142,624	145,005	147,323	149,577
F Production	156,945	125,439	173,829	146,252	162,300	143,300	181,260	186,733	192,268	197,865
W Net Imports	1,513	13,312	9,037	9,000	6,543	16,054	8,968	9,127	9,652	10,394
F Net Imports	6,857	19,291	10,865	17,805	17,161	19,482	14,252	14,146	15,105	15,740
W Ending Stocks	23,416	14,104	4,528	12,236	16,191	15,982	18,428	19,815	20,681	21,288
F Ending Stocks	4,768	6,487	6,223	5,350	7,226	7,592	11,318	9,193	9,197	9,201
Developed Market Economies										
W Production	58,213	51,205	54,139	50,510	55,748	58,395	54,441	55,174	55,890	56,587
F Production	93,161	87,889	82,189	98,400	101,300	105,471	113,494	116,437	119,401	122,385
W Net Imports	3,382	3,975	4,457	6,400	2,915	1,076	1,723	1,663	1,014	648
F Net Imports	32,421	33,799	44,717	35,955	33,500	33,645	25,647	26,890	28,812	30,421
W Ending Stocks	15,083	13,407	13,026	12,882	13,606	16,403	15,774	16,221	16,219	16,217
F Ending Stocks	17,160	13,523	12,727	14,520	13,165	21,220	21,603	21,097	21,098	21,099
Developing Market Economies										
W Production	62,449	67,541	79,903	74,619	80,137	85,021	85,444	89,618	93,924	98,364
F Production	103,765	113,710	116,389	109,797	114,702	117,336	124,048	127,703	131,465	135,336
W Net Imports	35,571	37,623	33,106	30,500	34,967	34,806	34,752	37,998	38,606	40,531
F Net Imports	6,249	4,934	6,906	9,100	11,217	8,685	9,466	10,614	12,035	13,542
W Ending Stocks	11,156	16,130	24,275	18,150	15,149	22,278	19,233	21,794	21,884	21,975
F Ending Stocks	7,671	10,482	12,975	10,248	11,054	11,310	12,713	12,770	12,839	12,915
China										
W Net Imports	5,695	2,200	3,100	8,600	9,000	7,500	8,000	8,000	8,000	8,000
F Net Imports	428	-115	-50	150	4,000	2,500	2,500	2,500	2,500	2,500

[a]W = Wheat; F = Feed Grains (Corn, Oats, Barley, Sorghum, and Rye); and GCAU = Grain Consuming Animal Units.
All Wheat and Feed Grain quantities are in thousand metric tons; prices are $/bushel.

Table 8C-9. Run 9—low income-high yields, cartel *w* price ≥ \$5.45, *F* price ≥ \$4.30 for all regions[a]

	1974/75	1975/76	1976/77	1977/78	1978/79	1979/80	1980/81	1981/82	1982/83	1983/84
United States										
W Price, Export	4.80	4.27	3.29	3.43	3.66	5.45	5.45	5.45	5.45	5.45
F Price, Export	3.55	3.10	2.80	2.54	2.50	4.30	4.30	4.30	4.30	4.30
W Production	48,879	58,078	58,432	55,139	48,962	57,500	59,225	59,368	59,824	60,377
F Production	150,469	184,926	193,083	201,914	212,070	224,700	230,583	237,994	244,785	251,453
W Consumption	19,068	20,112	21,037	22,800	23,600	21,872	22,157	22,654	23,193	23,750
F Consumption	121,788	133,700	132,385	136,900	153,200	140,652	124,080	122,568	125,669	130,152
W Net Exports	27,334	31,598	25,393	31,000	32,400	35,102	31,202	32,375	32,715	34,264
F Net Exports	35,091	49,279	49,959	51,800	56,000	51,155	36,919	35,733	37,019	38,226
W Ending Stocks	11,703	18,071	30,264	32,300	25,100	25,620	31,485	35,818	39,731	42,090
F Ending Stocks	15,414	17,361	30,022	41,200	45,600	78,245	147,515	226,899	308,689	391,441
GCAU	70	75	76	78	80	73	73	74	75	76
Canada										
W Production	13,295	17,078	23,523	19,651	21,145	17,300	21,532	21,646	21,748	21,839
F Production	17,436	19,987	21,198	22,362	20,016	18,100	24,424	25,320	26,232	27,160
W Consumption	4,607	4,827	4,875	4,800	4,800	5,077	5,167	5,279	5,326	5,352
F Consumption	15,923	16,800	16,953	16,300	17,000	13,713	12,632	11,804	11,174	10,590
W Net Exports	10,739	12,254	13,450	16,000	14,400	14,367	13,493	15,431	16,048	16,947
F Net Exports	2,102	4,333	3,727	3,370	6,041	5,209	8,472	11,302	13,482	15,280
W Ending Stocks	8,038	8,035	13,310	12,100	12,647	10,503	13,376	14,311	14,685	14,225
F Ending Stocks	5,626	4,483	5,188	7,579	7,112	6,288	9,607	11,821	13,397	14,687
GCAU	13,130	12,838	12,838	13,191	13,339	12,000	11,107	10,424	9,824	9,240
Australia										
W Production	11,357	12,024	11,800	9,200	18,300	16,000	13,629	13,490	13,349	13,207
F Production	4,453	5,611	5,334	3,983	7,100	5,900	6,822	7,131	7,447	7,768
W Consumption	3,025	2,764	2,925	2,600	2,800	3,078	2,955	2,843	2,715	2,569
F Consumption	1,717	1,753	2,222	2,351	2,393	1,823	1,648	1,397	1,116	803
W Net Exports	8,526	8,229	8,500	8,100	8,106	10,370	10,477	10,537	10,571	10,595
F Net Exports	2,865	3,628	2,812	1,819	3,531	4,437	4,898	5,421	5,990	6,601
W Ending Stocks	1,788	2,819	2,312	800	3,501	6,053	6,250	6,359	6,423	6,466
F Ending Stocks	501	731	787	791	921	561	837	1,149	1,490	1,855
GCAU	3,025	3,008	2,955	3,005	3,054	2,851	2,624	2,369	2,084	1,767

Argentina										
W Production	5,970	8,570	11,200	5,500	8,100	8,000	7,396	7,347	7,296	7,244
F Production	13,793	12,438	17,261	17,839	17,300	16,678	19,276	19,900	20,531	21,171
W Consumption	4,498	5,382	4,692	4,400	4,500	4,866	4,948	5,054	5,164	5,278
F Consumption	7,465	6,501	6,826	6,881	6,833	7,402	8,089	8,509	8,534	9,374
W Net Exports	1,784	3,160	6,000	1,800	1,751	2,742	2,531	2,361	2,197	2,032
F Net Exports	6,051	7,075	9,655	9,505	9,030	9,256	11,026	11,360	11,578	11,779
W Ending Stocks	714	742	1,400	500	449	841	758	690	626	560
F Ending Stocks	1,359	221	338	324	713	733	894	924	944	962
GCAU	3,928	3,749	3,631	3,948	3,841	3,778	3,908	4,044	4,186	4,335
Soviet Bloc										
W Production	117,869	94,650	131,519	126,603	155,300	111,600	142,624	145,005	147,323	149,577
F Production	156,945	125,439	173,829	146,252	162,300	143,300	181,260	186,733	192,268	197,865
W Net Imports	1,513	13,312	9,037	9,000	6,543	15,403	8,312	8,460	8,984	9,721
F Net Imports	6,857	19,291	10,865	17,805	17,161	21,004	15,987	15,894	16,866	17,515
W Ending Stocks	23,416	14,104	4,528	12,236	16,191	15,982	18,428	19,815	20,681	21,288
F Ending Stocks	4,768	6,487	6,223	5,350	7,226	6,445	10,170	8,045	8,049	8,053
Developed Market Economies										
W Production	58,213	51,205	54,139	50,510	55,748	58,395	55,933	56,698	57,446	58,175
F Production	93,161	87,889	82,189	98,400	101,300	105,471	111,877	114,787	117,718	120,669
W Net Imports	3,382	3,975	4,457	6,400	2,915	1,269	1,811	1,654	1,067	685
F Net Imports	32,421	33,799	44,717	35,955	33,500	32,868	28,179	29,543	31,362	32,978
W Ending Stocks	15,083	13,407	13,026	12,882	13,606	15,096	14,609	14,917	14,915	14,913
F Ending Stocks	17,160	13,523	12,727	14,519	13,165	18,233	18,454	18,108	18,110	18,112
Developing Market Economies										
W Production	62,449	67,541	79,903	74,619	80,137	85,021	86,248	90,440	94,763	99,220
F Production	103,765	113,710	116,389	109,797	114,702	117,336	123,351	127,000	130,755	134,618
W Net Imports	35,571	37,623	33,106	30,500	34,967	36,008	37,180	40,182	41,078	43,030
F Net Imports	6,249	4,934	6,906	9,100	11,218	10,110	11,049	12,278	13,739	15,287
W Ending Stocks	11,156	16,130	24,275	18,150	15,149	19,031	16,534	18,558	18,648	18,739
F Ending Stocks	7,671	10,482	12,975	10,243	11,051	11,167	12,261	12,314	12,383	12,464
China										
W Net Imports	5,695	2,200	3,100	8,600	9,000	7,500	8,000	8,000	8,000	8,000
F Net Imports	428	-115	-50	150	4,000	2,500	2,500	2,500	2,500	2,500

[a] W = Wheat; F = Feed Grains (Corn, Oats, Barley, Sorghum, and Rye); and GCAU = Grain Consuming Animal Units.
All Wheat and Feed Grain quantities are in thousand metric tons; prices are \$/bushel.

Table 8C-10. Run 10—low income–high yields, cartel *w* price ⩾ \$6.80, *F* price ⩾ \$5.37 for all regions[a]

	1974/75	1975/76	1976/77	1977/78	1978/79	1979/80	1980/81	1981/82	1982/83	1983/84
United States										
W Price, Export	4.80	4.27	3.29	3.43	3.66	6.80	6.80	6.80	6.80	6.80
F Price, Export	3.55	3.10	2.80	2.54	2.50	5.37	5.37	5.37	5.37	5.37
W Production	48,879	58,078	58,432	55,139	48,962	57,500	58,739	58,257	58,214	58,291
F Production	150,469	184,926	193,083	201,914	212,070	224,700	236,585	245,512	253,564	261,450
W Consumption	19,068	20,112	21,037	22,800	23,600	20,475	20,578	21,040	21,559	22,098
F Consumption	121,788	133,700	132,385	136,900	153,200	131,242	101,184	95,621	97,527	101,685
W Net Exports	27,334	31,598	25,393	31,000	32,400	34,148	29,330	30,572	30,610	32,075
F Net Exports	35,091	49,279	49,959	51,800	56,000	47,428	28,424	26,248	26,930	27,510
W Ending Stocks	11,703	18,071	30,264	32,300	25,100	27,969	36,802	43,444	49,486	53,599
F Ending Stocks	15,414	17,361	30,022	41,200	45,600	91,371	198,083	321,467	450,308	582,291
GCAU	70	75	76	78	80	68	68	69	70	71
Canada										
W Production	13,295	17,078	23,523	19,651	21,145	17,300	21,525	21,638	21,740	21,831
F Production	17,436	19,987	21,198	22,362	20,016	18,100	24,434	25,330	26,242	27,170
W Consumption	4,607	4,827	4,875	4,800	4,800	5,175	5,240	5,346	5,380	5,398
F Consumption	15,923	16,800	16,953	16,300	17,000	11,669	9,843	8,497	7,471	6,535
W Net Exports	10,739	12,254	13,450	16,000	14,400	13,963	12,945	15,186	15,753	16,702
F Net Exports	2,102	4,333	3,727	3,370	6,041	6,244	10,350	13,965	16,722	18,968
W Ending Stocks	8,038	8,035	13,310	12,100	12,647	10,809	14,149	15,254	15,862	15,592
F Ending Stocks	5,626	4,483	5,188	7,579	7,112	7,295	11,535	14,404	16,452	18,119
GCAU	13,130	12,838	12,838	13,191	13,339	11,195	9,810	8,792	7,931	7,117
Australia										
W Production	11,357	12,024	11,800	9,200	18,300	16,000	13,625	13,486	13,345	13,204
F Production	4,453	5,611	5,334	3,983	7,100	5,900	6,826	7,135	7,451	7,773
W Consumption	3,025	2,764	2,925	2,600	2,800	2,930	2,741	2,560	2,360	2,140
F Consumption	1,717	1,753	2,222	2,351	2,393	1,570	1,283	916	515	77
W Net Exports	8,526	8,229	8,500	8,100	8,106	9,780	10,167	10,303	10,326	10,300
F Net Exports	2,865	3,628	2,812	1,819	3,531	4,749	5,427	5,923	6,556	7,269
W Ending Stocks	1,788	2,819	2,312	800	3,501	5,722	5,745	5,787	5,852	5,945
F Ending Stocks	501	731	787	791	921	501	617	913	1,292	1,718
GCAU	3,025	3,008	2,955	3,005	3,054	2,716	2,353	1,960	1,535	1,073

Argentina										
W Production	5,970	8,570	11,200	5,500	8,100	8,000	7,393	7,344	7,293	7,241
F Production	13,793	12,438	17,261	17,839	17,300	16,678	19,281	19,905	20,537	21,177
W Consumption	4,498	5,382	4,692	4,400	4,500	4,677	4,756	4,859	4,967	5,078
F Consumption	7,465	6,501	6,826	6,881	6,833	7,172	7,868	8,290	8,715	9,155
W Net Exports	1,784	3,160	6,000	1,800	1,751	2,877	2,705	2,547	2,389	2,227
F Net Exports	6,051	7,075	9,655	9,505	9,030	9,466	11,252	11,585	11,802	12,003
W Ending Stocks	714	742	1,400	500	449	895	826	764	702	637
F Ending Stocks	1,359	221	338	324	713	752	915	945	965	983
GCAU	3,928	3,749	3,631	3,948	3,841	3,666	3,796	3,932	4,075	4,223
Soviet Bloc										
W Production	117,869	94,650	131,519	126,603	155,300	111,600	142,624	145,005	147,323	149,577
F Production	156,945	125,439	173,829	146,252	162,300	143,300	181,260	186,733	192,268	197,865
W Net Imports	1,513	13,312	9,037	9,000	6,543	16,054	8,968	9,127	9,652	10,394
F Net Imports	6,857	19,291	10,865	17,805	17,161	19,482	14,252	14,146	15,104	15,740
W Ending Stocks	23,416	14,104	4,528	12,236	16,191	15,982	18,428	19,815	20,681	21,288
F Ending Stocks	4,768	6,487	6,223	5,350	7,226	7,592	11,318	9,193	9,197	9,201
Developed Market Economies										
W Production	58,213	51,205	54,139	50,510	55,748	58,395	54,441	55,174	55,890	56,587
F Production	93,161	87,889	82,189	98,400	101,300	105,471	113,493	116,439	119,405	122,392
W Net Imports	3,382	3,975	4,457	6,400	2,915	1,076	1,722	1,663	1,014	648
F Net Imports	32,421	33,799	44,717	35,955	33,500	33,645	25,651	26,880	28,792	30,390
W Ending Stocks	15,083	13,407	13,026	12,882	13,606	16,403	15,774	16,221	16,219	16,217
F Ending Stocks	17,160	13,523	12,727	14,519	13,165	21,220	21,602	21,099	21,101	21,102
Developing Market Economies										
W Production	62,449	67,541	79,903	74,619	80,137	85,021	85,444	89,618	93,924	98,364
F Production	103,765	113,710	116,389	109,797	114,702	117,336	124,047	127,706	131,470	135,343
W Net Imports	35,571	37,623	33,106	30,500	34,967	34,806	34,752	37,998	38,606	40,531
F Net Imports	6,249	4,934	6,906	9,100	11,218	8,685	9,467	10,612	12,030	13,535
W Ending Stocks	11,156	16,130	24,275	18,150	15,149	22,278	19,233	21,794	21,884	21,976
F Ending Stocks	7,671	10,482	12,975	10,243	11,051	11,307	12,710	12,773	12,849	12,934
China										
W Net Imports	5,695	2,200	3,100	8,600	9,000	7,500	8,000	8,000	8,000	8,000
F Net Imports	428	-115	-50	150	4,000	2,500	2,500	2,500	2,500	2,500

[a] W = Wheat; F = Feed Grains (Corn, Oats, Barley, Sorghum, and Rye); and GCAU = Grain Consuming Animal Units. All Wheat and Feed Grain quantities are in thousand metric tons; prices are $/bushel.

Table 8C-11. Run 11—base assumptions, cartel w price $\geqslant$ \$5.45, F price $\geqslant$ \$4.30, soviet bloc, developed market and developing market economies only[a]

	1974/75	1975/76	1976/77	1977/78	1978/79	1979/80	1980/81	1981/82	1982/83	1983/84
United States										
W Price, Export	4.80	4.27	3.29	3.43	3.63	3.92	3.92	4.19	5.44	6.09
F Price, Export	3.55	3.10	2.80	2.54	2.50	2.50	2.53	3.37	3.30	4.34
W Production	48,879	58,078	58,432	55,139	48,962	57,500	59,643	60,772	61,076	65,771
F Production	150,469	184,926	193,083	201,914	212,070	224,700	205,613	210,161	220,300	216,500
W Consumption	19,068	20,112	21,037	22,800	23,600	22,141	23,058	25,068	21,733	23,303
F Consumption	121,788	133,700	132,385	136,900	153,200	159,055	165,235	160,978	160,673	153,132
W Net Exports	27,334	31,598	25,393	31,000	32,400	39,791	36,575	39,026	45,211	45,024
F Net Exports	35,091	49,279	49,959	51,800	56,000	62,053	59,408	61,553	61,198	69,628
W Ending Stocks	11,703	18,071	30,264	32,300	25,100	20,670	20,689	17,380	11,522	8,974
F Ending Stocks	15,414	17,361	30,022	41,200	45,600	49,053	29,992	17,592	15,983	9,691
GCAU	70	75	76	78	80	81	82	80	81	78
Canada										
W Production	13,295	17,078	23,523	19,651	21,145	17,300	21,490	21,543	20,382	22,643
F Production	17,436	19,987	21,198	22,362	20,016	18,100	21,793	22,704	25,205	23,225
W Consumption	4,607	4,827	4,875	4,800	4,800	4,916	5,018	5,179	5,015	5,134
F Consumption	15,923	16,800	16,953	16,300	17,000	17,201	17,353	15,727	15,599	12,726
W Net Exports	10,739	12,254	13,450	16,000	14,400	15,853	15,378	17,542	17,638	17,509
F Net Exports	2,102	4,333	3,727	3,370	5,396	2,651	4,045	5,801	7,974	9,713
W Ending Stocks	8,038	8,035	13,310	12,100	13,823	10,354	11,449	10,271	8,000	8,000
F Ending Stocks	5,626	4,483	5,188	7,579	6,250	4,500	4,914	6,116	7,782	8,598
GCAU	13,130	12,838	12,838	13,191	13,339	13,391	13,357	12,543	12,068	10,580
Australia										
W Production	11,357	12,024	11,800	9,200	18,300	16,000	12,603	12,326	11,263	12,177
F Production	4,453	5,611	5,334	3,983	7,100	5,900	4,938	5,222	6,371	5,361
W Consumption	3,025	2,764	2,925	2,600	2,800	3,285	3,320	3,252	3,044	2,875
F Consumption	1,717	1,753	2,222	2,351	2,393	2,237	2,151	1,842	1,739	1,059
W Net Exports	8,526	8,229	8,500	8,100	9,762	10,893	10,326	9,969	9,749	9,797
F Net Exports	2,865	3,628	2,812	1,819	3,727	3,687	3,136	3,548	4,211	4,596
W Ending Stocks	1,788	2,819	2,312	800	6,566	8,387	7,344	6,451	4,921	4,427
F Ending Stocks	501	731	787	791	1,038	1,015	667	501	926	635
GCAU	3,025	3,008	2,955	3,005	3,054	3,081	3,082	2,935	2,777	2,409

Argentina										
W Production	5,970	8,570	11,200	5,500	8,100	8,000	7,742	7,635	6,800	7,788
F Production	13,793	12,438	17,261	17,839	17,300	16,678	17,808	18,517	20,541	19,299
W Consumption	4,498	5,382	4,692	4,400	4,500	5,100	5,238	5,330	5,253	5,343
F Consumption	7,465	6,501	6,826	6,881	6,833	7,912	8,381	8,728	9,490	9,542
W Net Exports	1,784	3,160	6,000	1,800	2,218	2,707	2,561	2,378	1,781	2,257
F Net Exports	6,051	7,075	9,655	9,505	10,317	8,896	9,385	9,759	10,947	9,859
W Ending Stocks	714	742	1,400	500	634	827	770	697	461	649
F Ending Stocks	1,359	221	338	324	830	701	745	779	887	788
GCAU	3,928	3,749	3,631	3,948	3,841	3,999	4,162	4,250	4,445	4,533
Soviet Bloc										
W Production	117,869	94,650	131,519	126,603	155,300	111,600	132,914	134,970	136,969	138,912
F Production	156,945	125,439	173,829	146,252	162,300	143,300	170,350	175,268	180,241	185,269
W Net Imports	1,513	13,312	9,037	9,000	4,064	16,266	12,346	13,286	14,501	15,270
F Net Imports	6,857	19,291	10,865	17,805	18,997	22,138	19,377	19,963	21,411	22,634
W Ending Stocks	23,416	14,104	4,528	11,336	16,765	16,261	17,766	18,668	19,272	19,726
F Ending Stocks	4,768	6,487	6,223	4,340	6,858	6,445	9,457	8,009	8,013	8,062
Developed Market Economies										
W Production	58,213	51,205	54,139	50,510	53,739	56,299	57,641	58,381	56,683	59,908
F Production	93,161	87,889	82,189	98,400	101,300	100,722	102,676	105,273	110,458	110,407
W Net Imports	3,382	3,975	4,457	6,400	4,887	3,981	2,759	2,970	4,597	2,750
F Net Imports	32,421	33,799	44,717	35,955	33,500	37,323	36,132	38,000	38,225	43,544
W Ending Stocks	15,083	13,407	13,026	13,063	13,392	15,088	14,972	14,914	14,682	15,768
F Ending Stocks	17,160	13,523	12,727	14,144	12,727	17,763	18,014	18,078	18,334	17,932
Developing Market Economies										
W Production	62,449	67,541	79,903	74,619	79,710	84,504	89,546	93,633	94,099	103,823
F Production	103,765	113,710	116,389	109,797	114,304	116,999	119,700	123,446	129,984	129,880
W Net Imports	35,571	37,623	33,106	30,500	36,887	39,096	39,333	42,256	47,334	48,828
F Net Imports	6,249	4,934	6,906	9,100	12,628	12,235	14,418	16,639	18,615	21,559
W Ending Stocks	11,156	16,130	24,275	18,150	14,801	18,970	19,139	18,487	16,424	23,457
F Ending Stocks	7,671	10,482	12,975	9,649	10,517	10,815	11,025	11,484	12,640	11,460
China										
W Net Imports	5,695	2,200	3,100	8,600	9,000	7,500	8,000	8,000	8,000	8,000
F Net Imports	428	-115	-50	150	4,000	2,500	2,500	2,500	2,500	2,500

[a]W = Wheat; F = Feed Grains (Corn, Oats, Barley, Sorghum, and Rye); and GCAU = Grain Consuming Animal Units.
All Wheat and Feed Grain quantities are in thousand metric tons; prices are \$/bushel.

Table 8C-12. Run 12—base assumptions, cartel *w* price ⩾ \$6.80, *F* price ⩾ \$5.37, soviet bloc, developed market and developing market economies only[a]

	1974/75	1975/76	1976/77	1977/78	1978/79	1979/80	1980/81	1981/82	1982/83	1983/84
United States										
W Price, Export	4.80	4.27	3.29	3.43	3.63	3.90	3.81	3.91	4.46	5.84
F Price, Export	3.55	3.10	2.80	2.54	2.50	2.50	2.50	2.85	3.25	3.62
W Production	48,879	58,078	58,432	55,139	48,962	57,500	59,504	60,217	61,913	63,266
F Production	150,469	184,926	193,083	201,914	212,070	224,700	205,919	211,244	218,281	221,946
W Consumption	19,068	20,112	21,037	22,800	23,600	22,219	23,318	24,585	24,621	22,155
F Consumption	121,788	133,700	132,385	136,900	153,200	158,978	165,333	167,155	165,093	164,069
W Net Exports	27,334	31,598	25,393	31,000	32,400	39,291	34,476	36,790	41,491	46,131
F Net Exports	35,091	49,279	49,959	51,800	56,000	59,955	64,935	67,633	59,279	62,059
W Ending Stocks	11,703	18,071	30,264	32,300	25,100	21,090	22,806	21,660	16,477	11,465
F Ending Stocks	15,414	17,361	30,022	41,200	45,600	51,224	36,765	23,193	17,062	12,839
GCAU	70	75	76	78	80	81	82	82	81	81
Canada										
W Production	13,295	17,078	23,523	19,651	21,145	17,300	21,450	21,429	20,997	21,151
F Production	17,436	19,987	21,198	22,362	20,016	18,100	21,845	22,852	24,399	25,182
W Consumption	4,607	4,827	4,875	4,800	4,800	4,916	5,024	5,158	5,145	5,015
F Consumption	15,923	16,800	16,953	16,300	17,000	17,200	17,419	16,848	15,938	14,828
W Net Exports	10,739	12,254	13,450	16,000	14,400	15,620	14,514	17,022	19,183	16,554
F Net Exports	2,102	4,333	3,727	3,370	5,396	2,651	3,882	5,194	7,130	9,079
W Ending Stocks	8,038	8,035	13,310	12,100	13,823	10,586	12,498	11,747	8,417	8,000
F Ending Stocks	5,626	4,483	5,188	7,579	6,250	4,500	5,057	5,890	7,257	8,568
GCAU	13,130	12,838	12,838	13,191	13,339	13,391	13,386	13,027	12,367	11,505
Australia										
W Production	11,357	12,024	11,800	9,200	18,300	16,000	12,754	12,256	11,625	11,413
F Production	4,453	5,611	5,334	3,983	7,100	5,900	4,969	5,297	5,975	6,207
W Consumption	3,025	2,764	2,925	2,600	2,800	3,287	3,330	3,306	3,187	2,951
F Consumption	1,717	1,753	2,222	2,351	2,393	2,237	2,163	2,002	1,776	1,433
W Net Exports	8,526	8,229	8,500	8,100	9,762	10,885	10,278	9,844	9,523	9,587
F Net Exports	2,865	3,628	2,812	1,819	3,727	3,687	3,137	3,347	4,009	4,604
W Ending Stocks	1,788	2,819	2,312	800	6,566	8,394	7,361	6,468	5,385	4,261
F Ending Stocks	501	731	787	791	1,036	1,015	685	635	829	1,003
GCAU	3,025	3,008	2,955	3,005	3,054	3,081	3,087	3,018	2,861	2,615

Argentina										
W Production	5,970	8,570	11,200	5,500	8,100	8,000	7,715	7,572	7,134	7,075
F Production	13,793	12,438	17,261	17,839	17,300	16,678	17,853	18,629	19,943	20,596
W Consumption	4,498	5,382	4,692	4,400	4,500	5,173	5,254	5,367	5,410	5,350
F Consumption	7,465	6,501	6,826	6,881	6,833	7,912	8,395	8,857	9,407	9,890
W Net Exports	1,784	3,160	6,000	1,800	2,218	2,704	2,531	2,297	1,886	1,770
F Net Exports	6,051	7,075	9,655	9,505	10,317	8,895	9,413	9,746	10,474	10,690
W Ending Stocks	714	742	1,400	500	634	826	757	665	502	457
F Ending Stocks	1,359	221	338	324	830	701	748	778	844	864
GCAU	3,928	3,749	3,631	3,948	3,841	3,999	4,165	4,305	4,450	4,609
Soviet Bloc										
W Production	117,869	94,650	131,519	126,603	155,300	111,600	132,914	134,970	136,969	138,912
F Production	156,945	125,439	173,829	146,252	162,300	143,300	170,350	175,268	180,241	185,269
W Net Imports	1,513	13,312	9,037	9,000	4,064	16,916	13,002	13,948	15,169	16,583
F Net Imports	6,857	19,291	10,865	17,805	18,997	20,616	17,643	18,215	19,650	20,922
W Ending Stocks	23,416	14,104	4,528	11,336	16,765	16,261	17,766	18,668	19,272	19,726
F Ending Stocks	4,768	6,487	6,223	4,340	6,858	7,592	10,604	9,157	9,160	9,164
Developed Market Economies										
W Production	58,213	51,205	54,139	50,510	53,739	56,299	57,599	58,307	58,076	58,371
F Production	93,161	87,889	82,189	98,400	101,300	100,722	102,721	105,352	108,977	112,038
W Net Imports	3,382	3,975	4,457	6,400	4,887	3,788	1,841	2,070	2,856	3,416
F Net Imports	32,421	33,799	44,717	35,955	33,500	38,100	34,739	36,582	37,937	39,752
W Ending Stocks	15,083	13,407	13,026	13,063	13,392	16,395	16,275	16,219	16,129	16,179
F Ending Stocks	17,160	13,523	12,727	14,144	12,727	20,750	21,005	21,068	21,166	21,110
Developing Market Economies										
W Production	62,449	67,541	79,903	74,619	79,710	84,504	89,462	93,420	96,397	100,710
F Production	103,765	113,710	116,389	109,797	114,304	116,999	119,773	123,629	128,536	132,517
W Net Imports	35,571	37,623	33,106	30,500	36,887	37,895	36,553	39,533	43,659	47,418
F Net Imports	6,249	4,934	6,906	9,100	12,628	12,810	12,926	15,074	17,226	19,680
W Ending Stocks	11,156	16,130	24,275	18,150	14,800	22,218	22,329	21,647	20,977	21,889
F Ending Stocks	7,671	10,482	12,975	9,649	10,517	10,955	11,284	11,839	12,539	12,751
China										
W Net Imports	5,695	2,200	3,100	8,600	9,000	7,500	8,000	8,000	8,000	8,000
F Net Imports	428	-115	-50	150	4,000	2,500	2,500	2,500	2,500	2,500

[a]W = Wheat; F = Feed Grains (Corn, Oats, Barley, Sorghum, and Rye); and GCAU = Grain Consuming Animal Units.
All Wheat and Feed Grain quantities are in thousand metric tons; prices are $/bushel.

Table 8C-13. Run 13—base assumptions, cartel *w* price ⩾ \$5.45, *F* price ⩾ \$4.30, soviet bloc and developed market economies only[a]

	1974/75	1975/76	1976/77	1977/78	1978/79	1979/80	1980/81	1981/82	1982/83	1983/84
United States										
W Price, Export	4.80	4.27	3.29	3.43	3.63	3.97	4.08	4.57	5.85	6.02
F Price, Export	3.55	3.10	2.80	2.54	2.50	2.50	2.72	3.49	3.52	4.25
W Production	48,879	58,078	58,432	55,139	48,962	57,500	59,891	61,225	62,157	66,175
F Production	150,469	184,926	193,083	201,914	212,070	224,700	205,064	210,416	218,412	216,591
W Consumption	19,068	20,112	21,037	22,800	23,600	21,995	23,041	24,188	21,053	23,274
F Consumption	121,788	133,700	132,385	136,900	153,200	159,199	163,414	158,316	156,999	150,622
W Net Exports	27,334	31,598	25,393	31,000	32,400	40,675	38,583	41,228	44,978	44,156
F Net Exports	35,091	49,279	49,959	51,800	56,000	64,855	61,453	61,854	63,456	70,160
W Ending Stocks	11,703	18,071	30,264	32,300	25,100	19,933	18,209	13,831	9,964	8,731
F Ending Stocks	15,414	17,361	30,022	41,200	45,600	46,096	26,267	16,476	14,390	10,181
GCAU	70	75	76	78	80	81	81	79	80	76
Canada										
W Production	13,295	17,078	23,523	19,651	21,145	17,300	21,565	21,431	20,756	22,867
F Production	17,436	19,987	21,198	22,362	20,016	18,100	21,695	22,850	24,715	22,932
W Consumption	4,607	4,827	4,875	4,800	4,800	4,914	5,025	5,130	4,977	5,127
F Consumption	15,923	16,800	16,953	16,300	17,000	17,202	16,989	15,414	14,997	12,674
W Net Exports	10,739	12,254	13,450	16,000	14,400	16,264	16,112	18,040	16,414	17,741
F Net Exports	2,102	4,333	3,727	3,370	5,415	2,633	4,266	6,101	8,236	9,635
W Ending Stocks	8,038	8,035	13,310	12,100	13,822	9,945	10,372	8,634	8,000	8,000
F Ending Stocks	5,626	4,483	5,188	7,579	6,232	4,500	4,960	6,325	7,846	8,506
GCAU	13,130	12,838	12,838	13,191	13,339	13,391	13,206	12,358	11,760	10,514
Australia										
W Production	11,357	12,024	11,800	9,200	18,300	16,000	12,657	12,200	11,452	12,220
F Production	4,453	5,611	5,334	3,983	7,100	5,900	4,880	5,358	6,165	5,313
W Consumption	3,025	2,764	2,925	2,600	2,800	3,282	3,300	3,196	2,984	2,863
F Consumption	1,717	1,753	2,222	2,351	2,393	2,237	2,099	1,803	1,628	1,039
W Net Exports	8,526	8,229	8,500	8,100	9,762	10,910	10,399	10,062	9,906	9,765
F Net Exports	2,865	3,628	2,812	1,819	3,727	3,687	3,190	3,664	4,220	4,487
W Ending Stocks	1,788	2,819	2,312	800	6,565	8,374	7,333	6,276	4,839	4,432
F Ending Stocks	501	731	787	791	1,038	1,015	608	502	823	614
GCAU	3,025	3,008	2,955	3,005	3,054	3,081	3,057	2,894	2,704	2,358

Argentina										
W Production	5,970	8,570	11,200	5,500	8,100	8,000	7,791	7,521	6,974	7,829
F Production	13,793	12,438	17,261	17,839	17,300	16,678	17,723	18,719	20,229	19,225
W Consumption	4,498	5,382	4,692	4,400	4,500	5,093	5,217	5,270	5,200	5,355
F Consumption	7,465	6,501	6,826	6,881	6,833	7,912	8,329	8,734	9,398	9,555
W Net Exports	1,784	3,160	6,000	1,800	2,218	2,712	2,613	2,353	1,938	2,322
F Net Exports	6,051	7,075	9,655	9,505	10,317	8,896	9,356	9,936	10,762	9,766
W Ending Stocks	714	742	1,400	500	634	829	790	687	523	675
F Ending Stocks	1,359	220	338	324	830	701	742	795	870	780
GCAU	3,928	3,749	3,631	3,948	3,841	3,999	4,143	4,238	4,422	4,542
Soviet Bloc										
W Production	117,869	94,650	131,519	126,603	155,300	111,600	132,914	134,970	136,969	138,912
F Production	156,945	125,439	173,829	146,252	162,300	143,300	170,350	175,268	180,241	185,269
W Net Imports	1,513	13,312	9,037	9,000	4,064	16,265	12,346	13,286	14,045	15,262
F Net Imports	6,857	19,291	10,865	17,805	18,997	22,138	19,377	19,963	21,411	22,696
W Ending Stocks	23,416	14,104	4,528	11,336	16,765	16,261	17,766	18,668	19,272	19,726
F Ending Stocks	4,768	6,487	6,223	4,340	6,858	6,445	9,457	8,009	8,013	8,017
Developed Market Economies										
W Production	58,213	51,205	54,139	50,510	53,739	56,299	57,721	58,010	56,919	59,640
F Production	93,161	87,889	82,189	98,400	101,300	100,722	102,591	105,667	110,207	110,479
W Net Imports	3,382	3,975	4,457	6,400	4,887	3,981	2,713	3,178	3,935	2,563
F Net Imports	32,421	33,799	44,717	35,955	33,500	37,326	36,193	37,725	39,304	43,468
W Ending Stocks	15,083	13,407	13,026	13,063	13,392	15,088	14,979	14,871	15,130	15,671
F Ending Stocks	17,160	13,523	12,727	14,144	12,727	17,763	18,006	18,125	18,270	17,848
Developing Market Economies										
W Production	62,449	67,541	79,903	74,619	79,710	84,504	89,702	93,260	95,398	104,127
F Production	103,765	113,710	116,389	109,797	114,702	116,999	119,565	123,765	129,387	129,623
W Net Imports	35,571	37,623	33,106	30,500	36,887	40,413	42,245	44,816	47,811	47,916
F Net Imports	6,249	4,934	6,906	9,100	13,197	15,111	16,648	17,795	19,872	21,811
W Ending Stocks	11,156	16,130	24,275	18,150	14,801	15,411	15,957	16,017	18,126	23,021
F Ending Stocks	7,671	10,482	12,975	9,612	10,434	10,474	10,538	11,173	12,044	11,134
China										
W Net Imports	5,695	2,200	3,100	8,600	9,000	7,500	8,000	8,000	8,000	8,000
F Net Imports	428	-115	-50	150	4,000	2,500	2,500	2,500	2,500	2,500

[a] W = Wheat; F = Feed Grains (Corn, Oats, Barley, Sorghum, and Rye); and GCAU = Grain Consuming Animal Units.
All Wheat and Feed Grain quantities are in thousand metric tons; prices are $/bushel.

Table 8C-14. Run 14—base assumptions, cartel *w* price ⩾ \$6.80, *F* price ⩾ \$5.37, soviet bloc and developed market economies only[a]

	1974/75	1975/76	1976/77	1977/78	1978/79	1979/80	1980/81	1981/82	1982/83	1983/84
United States										
W Price, Export	4.80	4.27	3.29	3.43	3.63	3.99	4.07	4.46	5.75	6.06
F Price, Export	3.55	3.10	2.80	2.54	2.50	2.50	2.62	3.40	3.39	4.18
W Production	48,879	58,078	58,432	55,139	48,962	57,500	59,975	61,251	62,005	66,296
F Production	150,469	184,926	193,083	201,914	212,070	224,700	204,877	209,470	218,335	215,709
W Consumption	19,068	20,112	21,037	22,800	23,600	21,944	22,844	24,327	21,850	22,995
F Consumption	121,788	133,700	132,385	136,900	153,200	159,250	164,612	160,388	159,868	153,779
W Net Exports	27,334	31,598	25,393	31,000	32,400	40,971	38,384	40,737	45,341	44,925
F Net Exports	35,091	49,279	49,959	51,800	56,000	64,148	58,846	59,873	60,288	66,717
W Ending Stocks	11,703	18,071	30,264	32,300	25,100	19,687	18,442	14,641	10,263	8,646
F Ending Stocks	15,414	17,361	30,022	41,200	45,600	46,749	28,140	17,319	15,460	10,700
GCAU	70	75	76	78	80	81	82	80	81	79
Canada										
W Production	13,295	17,078	23,523	19,651	21,145	17,300	21,591	21,604	20,762	22,969
F Production	17,436	19,987	21,198	22,362	20,016	18,100	21,661	22,624	24,708	22,797
W Consumption	4,607	4,827	4,875	4,800	4,800	4,913	5,009	5,136	4,985	5,130
F Consumption	15,923	16,800	16,953	16,300	17,000	17,203	17,195	15,656	15,376	12,994
W Net Exports	10,739	12,254	13,450	16,000	14,400	16,402	15,967	17,865	16,803	17,840
F Net Exports	2,102	4,333	3,727	3,370	5,415	2,632	4,041	5,757	7,825	9,173
W Ending Stocks	8,038	8,035	13,310	12,100	13,822	9,807	10,422	9,026	8,000	8,000
F Ending Stocks	5,626	4,483	5,188	7,579	6,232	4,500	4,945	6,182	7,723	8,364
GCAU	13,130	12,838	12,838	13,191	13,339	13,391	13,288	12,483	11,953	10,689
Australia										
W Production	11,357	12,024	11,800	9,200	18,300	16,000	12,676	12,342	11,458	12,314
F Production	4,453	5,611	5,334	3,983	7,100	5,900	4,860	5,204	6,158	5,210
W Consumption	3,025	2,764	2,925	2,600	2,800	3,281	3,308	3,224	3,013	2,886
F Consumption	1,717	1,753	2,222	2,351	2,393	2,237	2,123	1,826	1,686	1,085
W Net Exports	8,526	8,229	8,500	8,100	9,762	10,916	10,396	10,070	9,906	9,837
F Net Exports	2,865	3,628	2,812	1,819	3,727	3,687	3,131	3,503	4,138	4,380
W Ending Stocks	1,788	2,819	2,312	800	6,566	8,369	7,342	6,391	4,931	4,522
F Ending Stocks	501	731	787	791	1,038	1,015	622	501	839	585
GCAU	3,025	3,008	2,955	3,005	3,054	3,081	3,070	2,920	2,749	2,412

Argentina										
W Production	5,970	8,570	11,200	5,500	8,100	8,000	7,808	7,650	6,979	7,916
F Production	13,793	12,438	17,261	17,839	17,300	16,676	17,693	18,491	20,220	19,066
W Consumption	4,498	5,382	4,692	4,400	4,500	5,090	5,220	5,291	5,215	5,351
F Consumption	7,465	6,501	6,826	6,881	6,833	7,912	8,345	8,720	9,426	9,547
W Net Exports	1,784	3,160	6,000	1,800	2,216	2,713	2,623	2,434	1,953	2,391
F Net Exports	6,051	7,075	9,655	9,505	10,317	8,896	9,313	9,736	10,710	9,619
W Ending Stocks	714	742	1,400	500	634	830	794	719	529	702
F Ending Stocks	1,359	221	338	324	830	701	739	777	865	766
GCAU	3,928	3,749	3,631	3,948	3,841	3,999	4,153	4,248	4,436	4,550
Soviet Bloc										
W Production	117,869	94,650	131,519	126,603	155,300	111,600	132,914	134,970	136,969	138,912
F Production	156,945	125,439	173,829	146,252	162,300	143,300	170,350	175,268	180,241	185,269
W Net Imports	1,513	13,312	9,037	9,000	4,064	16,916	13,002	13,948	15,169	16,583
F Net Imports	6,857	19,291	10,865	17,805	18,997	20,816	17,643	18,215	19,650	20,922
W Ending Stocks	23,416	14,104	4,528	11,336	16,765	16,261	17,766	18,668	19,272	19,726
F Ending Stocks	4,768	6,487	6,223	4,340	6,858	7,592	10,604	9,157	9,160	9,164
Developed Market Economies										
W Production	58,213	51,205	54,139	50,510	53,739	56,299	57,749	58,331	57,053	60,137
F Production	93,161	87,889	82,189	98,400	101,300	100,722	102,561	105,326	110,065	110,167
W Net Imports	3,382	3,975	4,457	6,400	4,887	3,788	1,755	2,049	3,448	2,463
F Net Imports	32,421	33,799	44,717	35,955	33,500	38,103	34,852	36,613	37,146	41,005
W Ending Stocks	15,083	13,407	13,026	13,063	13,392	16,395	16,289	16,206	16,029	16,445
F Ending Stocks	17,160	13,523	12,727	14,144	12,727	20,750	20,990	21,081	21,277	20,819
Developing Market Economies										
W Production	62,449	67,541	79,903	74,619	79,710	84,504	89,757	93,698	95,479	104,445
F Production	103,765	113,710	116,389	109,797	114,304	116,999	119,517	123,390	129,318	129,356
W Net Imports	35,571	37,623	33,106	30,500	36,887	40,398	42,212	44,707	47,875	47,952
F Net Imports	6,249	4,934	6,906	9,100	13,197	15,124	16,790	17,981	20,087	21,951
W Ending Stocks	11,156	16,130	24,275	18,150	14,801	15,452	15,959	16,006	17,638	23,297
F Ending Stocks	7,671	10,482	12,975	9,612	10,434	10,472	10,510	11,045	12,031	11,062
China										
W Net Imports	5,695	2,200	3,100	8,600	9,000	7,500	8,000	8,000	8,000	8,000
F Net Imports	428	-115	-50	150	4,000	2,500	2,500	2,500	2,500	2,500

[a]W = Wheat; F = Feed Grains (Corn, Oats, Barley, Sorghum, and Rye); and GCAU = Grain Consuming Animal Units.
All Wheat and Feed Grain quantities are in thousand metric tons; prices are $/bushel.

Table 8C-15. Run 15—low income-high yields, cartel *w* price ⩾ \$5.45, *F* price ⩾ \$4.30, soviet bloc, developed and developing market economies only[a]

	1974/75	1975/76	1976/77	1977/78	1978/79	1979/80	1980/81	1981/82	1982/83	1983/84
United States										
W Price, Export	4.80	4.27	3.29	3.43	3.66	3.84	3.48	3.36	3.32	3.31
F Price, Export	3.55	3.10	2.80	2.54	2.50	2.50	2.50	2.50	2.50	2.50
W Production	48,879	58,078	58,432	55,139	48,962	57,500	60,865	59,736	59,593	60,097
F Production	150,469	184,926	193,083	201,914	212,070	224,700	218,647	228,716	236,686	243,292
W Consumption	19,068	20,112	21,037	22,800	23,600	22,244	23,941	24,758	25,404	25,999
F Consumption	121,788	133,700	132,385	136,900	153,200	158,461	163,504	168,450	173,406	178,420
W Net Exports	27,334	31,598	25,393	31,000	32,400	35,606	28,655	29,035	30,526	32,038
F Net Exports	35,091	49,279	49,959	51,800	56,000	54,186	46,637	46,071	47,389	49,180
W Ending Stocks	11,703	18,071	30,264	32,300	25,100	24,749	33,012	38,954	42,613	44,670
F Ending Stocks	15,414	17,361	30,022	41,200	45,600	57,464	65,764	79,711	95,294	110,669
GCAU	70	75	76	78	80	81	82	83	83	84
Canada										
W Production	13,295	17,078	23,523	19,651	21,145	17,300	22,619	22,160	22,071	22,092
F Production	17,436	19,987	21,198	22,362	20,016	18,100	23,020	24,655	25,814	26,831
W Consumption	4,607	4,827	4,875	4,800	4,800	4,891	5,104	5,318	5,435	5,483
F Consumption	15,923	16,800	16,953	16,300	17,000	17,173	17,213	17,193	17,189	17,190
W Net Exports	10,739	12,254	13,450	16,000	14,400	14,606	12,328	14,655	16,318	17,201
F Net Exports	2,102	4,333	3,727	3,370	6,041	3,344	4,490	6,162	7,608	8,825
W Ending Stocks	8,038	8,035	13,310	12,100	12,647	10,450	15,637	17,823	18,141	17,549
F Ending Stocks	5,626	4,483	5,188	7,579	7,112	4,695	6,012	7,312	8,329	9,145
GCAU	13,130	12,838	12,838	13,191	13,339	13,354	13,289	13,170	13,009	12,812
Australia										
W Production	11,357	12,024	11,800	9,200	18,300	16,000	14,498	13,896	13,602	13,404
F Production	4,453	5,611	5,334	3,983	7,100	5,900	5,889	6,689	7,169	7,550
W Consumption	3,025	2,764	2,925	2,600	2,800	3,282	3,329	3,321	3,309	3,266
F Consumption	1,717	1,753	2,222	2,351	2,393	2,249	2,196	2,175	2,108	2,008
W Net Exports	8,526	8,229	8,500	8,100	8,106	9,789	10,162	10,270	10,264	10,209
F Net Exports	2,865	3,628	2,812	1,819	3,531	3,606	3,660	4,195	4,737	5,240
W Ending Stocks	1,788	2,819	2,312	800	3,501	6,430	7,437	7,742	7,771	7,681
F Ending Stocks	501	731	787	791	921	966	999	1,318	1,643	1,944
GCAU	3,025	3,008	2,955	3,005	3,054	3,079	3,079	3,056	3,007	2,933

Argentina										
W Production	5,970	8,570	11,200	5,500	8,100	8,000	8,112	7,684	7,507	7,409
F Production	13,793	12,438	17,261	17,839	17,300	16,678	18,096	19,337	20,175	20,889
W Consumption	4,498	5,382	4,692	4,400	4,500	5,093	5,256	5,368	5,483	5,601
F Consumption	7,465	6,501	6,826	6,881	6,833	7,789	8,290	8,812	9,264	9,711
W Net Exports	1,784	3,160	6,000	1,800	1,751	2,579	2,778	2,447	2,144	1,903
F Net Exports	6,051	7,075	9,655	9,505	9,030	8,901	9,730	10,459	10,873	11,152
W Ending Stocks	714	742	1,400	500	449	777	855	724	605	509
F Ending Stocks	1,359	221	338	324	713	701	776	843	880	906
GCAU	3,928	3,749	3,631	3,948	3,841	3,965	4,096	4,232	4,374	4,522
Soviet Bloc										
W Production	117,869	94,650	131,519	126,603	155,300	111,600	142,624	145,005	147,323	149,577
F Production	156,945	125,439	173,829	146,252	162,300	143,300	181,260	186,733	192,268	197,865
W Net Imports	1,513	13,312	9,037	9,000	6,543	15,403	8,312	8,466	8,984	9,721
F Net Imports	6,857	19,291	10,865	17,805	17,161	21,004	15,987	15,894	16,866	17,515
W Ending Stocks	23,416	14,104	4,528	12,236	16,191	15,982	18,428	19,815	20,681	21,288
F Ending Stocks	4,768	6,487	6,223	5,350	7,226	6,445	10,170	8,045	8,049	8,053
Developed Market Economies										
W Production	58,213	51,205	54,139	50,510	55,748	58,395	59,562	59,786	60,388	61,099
F Production	93,161	87,889	82,189	98,400	101,300	105,472	107,947	111,443	114,529	117,499
W Net Imports	3,382	3,975	4,457	6,400	2,915	1,269	-265	-311	-587	-980
F Net Imports	32,421	33,799	44,717	35,955	33,500	32,865	30,996	32,222	33,611	35,245
W Ending Stocks	15,083	13,407	13,026	12,882	13,606	15,096	14,955	14,865	14,901	14,912
F Ending Stocks	17,160	13,523	12,727	14,519	13,165	18,234	18,066	18,166	18,125	18,113
Developing Market Economies										
W Production	62,449	67,541	79,903	74,619	80,137	85,021	89,740	92,822	96,793	101,141
F Production	103,765	113,710	116,389	109,797	114,702	117,337	120,335	124,958	129,026	132,994
W Net Imports	35,571	37,623	33,106	30,500	34,967	36,008	35,473	37,852	40,456	42,208
F Net Imports	6,249	4,934	6,906	9,100	11,218	10,110	11,472	12,692	14,030	15,536
W Ending Stocks	11,156	16,130	24,275	18,150	15,149	19,031	18,918	17,800	18,408	18,665
F Ending Stocks	7,671	10,482	12,975	10,243	11,051	11,168	11,360	11,979	12,243	12,398
China										
W Net Imports	5,695	2,200	3,100	8,600	9,000	7,500	8,000	8,000	8,000	8,000
F Net Imports	428	-115	-50	150	4,000	2,500	2,500	2,500	2,500	2,500

[a] W = Wheat; F = Feed Grains (Corn, Oats, Barley, Sorghum, and Rye); and GCAU = Grain Consuming Animal Units. All Wheat and Feed Grain quantities are in thousand metric tons; prices are $/bushel.

Table 8C-16. Run 16—low income-high yields, cartel *w* price ≥ \$6.80, *F* price ≥ \$5.37, soviet bloc, developed and developing market economies only[a]

	1974/75	1975/76	1976/77	1977/78	1978/79	1979/80	1980/81	1981/82	1982/83	1983/84
United States										
W Price, Export	4.80	4.27	3.29	3.43	3.66	3.82	3.43	3.30	3.26	3.23
F Price, Export	3.55	3.10	2.80	2.54	2.50	2.50	2.50	2.50	2.50	2.50
W Production	48,879	58,078	58,432	55,139	48,962	57,500	60,726	59,150	58,654	58,844
F Production	150,469	184,926	193,083	201,914	212,070	224,700	218,958	230,036	238,516	246,154
W Consumption	19,068	20,112	21,037	22,800	23,600	22,314	24,092	24,908	25,558	26,162
F Consumption	121,788	133,700	132,385	136,900	153,200	158,391	163,347	168,276	173,215	178,208
W Net Exports	27,334	31,598	25,393	31,000	32,400	35,104	26,527	26,714	28,090	29,494
F Net Exports	35,091	49,279	49,959	51,800	56,000	52,087	42,050	41,194	42,343	44,001
W Ending Stocks	11,703	18,071	30,264	32,300	25,100	25,181	35,281	42,809	47,823	51,007
F Ending Stocks	15,414	17,361	30,022	41,200	45,600	59,632	72,988	93,253	116,141	139,705
GCAU	70	75	76	78	80	81	82	83	83	84
Canada										
W Production	13,295	17,078	23,523	19,651	21,145	17,300	22,581	22,073	21,973	21,982
F Production	17,436	19,987	21,198	22,362	20,016	18,100	23,069	24,768	25,941	26,974
W Consumption	4,607	4,827	4,875	4,800	4,800	4,892	5,112	5,355	5,487	5,545
F Consumption	15,923	16,800	16,953	16,300	17,000	17,173	17,206	17,160	17,141	17,133
W Net Exports	10,739	12,254	13,450	16,000	14,400	14,374	11,456	14,098	15,912	16,874
F Net Exports	2,102	4,333	3,727	3,370	6,041	3,273	4,407	6,199	7,718	8,981
W Ending Stocks	8,038	8,035	13,310	12,100	12,647	10,681	16,693	19,312	19,886	19,449
F Ending Stocks	5,626	4,483	5,188	7,579	7,112	4,766	6,222	7,631	8,713	9,572
GCAU	13,130	12,838	12,838	13,191	13,339	13,354	13,289	13,170	13,009	12,812
Australia										
W Production	11,357	12,024	11,800	9,200	18,300	16,000	14,467	13,628	13,527	13,320
F Production	4,453	5,611	5,334	3,983	7,100	5,900	6,921	6,763	7,252	7,643
W Consumption	3,025	2,764	2,925	2,600	2,800	3,284	3,332	3,324	3,312	3,290
F Consumption	1,717	1,753	2,222	2,351	2,393	2,249	2,199	2,180	2,113	2,015
W Net Exports	8,526	8,229	8,500	8,100	8,106	9,781	10,136	10,226	10,206	10,139
F Net Exports	2,865	3,628	2,812	1,819	3,531	3,606	3,679	4,245	4,804	5,320
W Ending Stocks	1,788	2,819	2,312	800	3,501	6,437	7,437	7,715	7,723	7,616
F Ending Stocks	501	731	787	791	921	966	1,010	1,348	1,683	1,991
GCAU	3,025	3,008	2,955	3,005	3,054	3,079	3,079	3,056	3,007	2,933

Argentina										
W Production	5,970	8,570	11,200	5,500	8,100	8,000	8,088	7,627	7,440	7,339
F Production	13,793	12,438	17,261	17,839	17,300	16,678	18,137	19,431	20,281	21,009
W Consumption	4,498	5,382	4,692	4,400	4,500	5,096	5,263	5,374	5,490	5,609
F Consumption	7,465	6,501	6,826	6,881	6,833	7,789	8,296	8,825	9,278	9,726
W Net Exports	1,784	3,160	6,000	1,800	1,751	2,577	2,755	2,396	2,079	1,829
F Net Exports	6,051	7,075	9,655	9,505	9,030	8,901	9,762	10,536	10,965	11,256
W Ending Stocks	714	742	1,400	500	449	776	846	704	579	480
F Ending Stocks	1,359	221	338	324	713	701	779	850	889	915
GCAU	3,928	3,749	3,631	3,948	3,841	3,965	4,096	4,232	4,374	4,522
Soviet Bloc										
W Production	117,869	94,650	131,519	126,603	155,300	111,600	142,624	145,005	147,323	149,577
F Production	156,945	125,439	173,829	146,252	162,300	143,300	181,260	186,733	192,268	197,865
W Net Imports	1,513	13,312	9,037	9,000	6,543	16,054	8,968	9,127	9,652	10,394
F Net Imports	6,857	19,291	10,865	17,805	17,161	19,482	14,252	14,146	15,104	15,740
W Ending Stocks	23,416	14,104	4,528	12,236	16,191	15,982	18,428	19,815	20,681	21,288
F Ending Stocks	4,768	6,487	6,223	5,350	7,226	7,592	11,318	9,193	9,197	9,201
Developed Market Economies										
W Production	58,213	51,205	54,139	50,510	55,748	58,395	59,523	59,695	60,285	60,984
F Production	93,161	87,889	82,189	98,400	101,300	105,472	107,989	111,540	114,639	117,623
W Net Imports	3,382	3,975	4,457	6,400	2,915	1,076	-1,186	-1,202	-1,472	-1,861
F Net Imports	32,421	33,799	44,717	35,955	33,500	33,642	29,603	30,796	32,184	33,818
W Ending Stocks	15,083	13,407	13,026	12,882	13,606	16,403	16,258	16,167	16,207	16,218
F Ending Stocks	17,160	13,523	12,727	14,519	13,165	21,221	21,857	21,158	21,113	21,101
Developing Market Economies										
W Production	62,449	67,541	79,903	74,619	80,137	85,021	89,665	92,648	96,597	100,921
F Production	103,765	113,710	116,389	109,797	114,702	117,337	120,400	125,106	129,191	133,178
W Net Imports	35,571	37,623	33,106	30,500	34,967	34,806	32,688	35,108	37,690	39,400
F Net Imports	6,249	4,934	6,906	9,100	11,218	8,685	9,980	11,133	12,417	13,673
W Ending Stocks	11,156	16,130	24,275	18,150	15,149	22,279	22,115	20,981	21,640	21,696
F Ending Stocks	7,671	10,482	12,975	10,243	11,051	11,309	11,618	12,323	12,626	12,809
China										
W Net Imports	5,695	2,200	3,100	8,600	9,000	7,500	8,000	8,000	8,000	8,000
F Net Imports	428	-115	-50	150	4,000	2,500	2,500	2,500	2,500	2,500

[a]W = Wheat; F = Feed Grains (Corn, Oats, Barley, Sorghum, and Rye); and GCAU = Grain Consuming Animal Units.
All Wheat and Feed Grain quantities are in thousand metric tons; prices are $/bushel.

Table 8C-17. Run 17–low income–high yields, cartel *w* price ⩾ \$5.45, *F* price ⩾ \$4.30, soviet bloc and developed market economies only[a]

	1974/75	1975/76	1976/77	1977/78	1978/79	1979/80	1980/81	1981/82	1982/83	1983/84
United States										
W Price, Export	4.80	4.27	3.29	3.43	3.66	3.89	3.56	3.45	3.43	3.43
F Price, Export	3.55	3.10	2.80	2.54	2.50	2.50	2.50	2.50	2.50	2.50
W Production	48,879	58,078	58,432	55,139	48,962	57,500	61,128	60,472	60,791	61,724
F Production	150,469	184,926	193,083	201,914	212,070	224,700	218,058	227,056	233,970	239,577
W Consumption	19,068	20,112	21,037	22,800	23,600	22,107	23,728	24,518	25,132	25,690
F Consumption	121,788	133,700	132,385	136,900	153,200	158,597	163,727	168,719	173,726	178,793
W Net Exports	27,334	31,598	25,393	31,000	32,400	36,543	31,698	31,996	33,766	35,400
F Net Exports	35,091	49,279	49,959	51,800	56,000	57,095	49,995	49,856	51,475	53,575
W Ending Stocks	11,703	18,071	30,264	32,300	25,100	23,949	30,247	34,205	36,096	36,727
F Ending Stocks	15,414	17,361	30,022	41,200	45,600	54,459	56,636	66,916	75,478	82,428
GCAU	70	75	76	78	80	81	82	83	83	84
Canada										
W Production	13,295	17,078	23,523	19,651	21,145	17,300	22,693	22,283	22,223	22,276
F Production	17,436	19,987	21,198	22,362	20,016	18,100	22,924	24,496	25,617	26,593
W Consumption	4,607	4,827	4,875	4,800	4,800	4,889	5,089	5,274	5,370	5,405
F Consumption	15,923	16,800	16,953	16,300	17,000	17,175	17,224	17,231	17,247	17,260
W Net Exports	10,739	12,254	13,450	16,000	14,400	15,041	13,253	15,404	16,911	17,668
F Net Exports	2,102	4,333	3,727	3,370	6,060	3,431	4,482	6,060	7,429	8,584
W Ending Stocks	8,038	8,035	13,310	12,100	12,647	10,017	14,368	15,972	15,914	15,116
F Ending Stocks	5,626	4,483	5,188	7,579	7,093	4,587	5,806	7,010	7,951	8,701
GCAU	13,130	12,838	12,838	13,191	13,339	13,354	13,289	13,170	13,009	12,812
Australia										
W Production	11,357	12,024	11,800	9,200	18,300	16,000	14,557	13,993	13,720	13,544
F Production	4,453	5,611	5,334	3,983	7,100	5,900	5,825	6,584	7,040	7,395
W Consumption	3,025	2,764	2,925	2,600	2,800	3,279	3,326	3,318	3,304	3,279
F Consumption	1,717	1,753	2,222	2,351	2,393	2,249	2,192	2,168	2,099	1,998
W Net Exports	8,526	8,229	8,500	8,100	8,106	9,805	10,203	10,337	10,356	10,325
F Net Exports	2,865	3,628	2,812	1,819	3,531	3,606	3,623	4,120	4,634	5,111
W Ending Stocks	1,788	2,819	2,312	800	3,501	6,416	7,446	7,785	7,844	7,784
F Ending Stocks	501	731	787	791	921	966	976	1,273	1,581	1,866
GCAU	3,025	3,008	2,955	3,005	3,054	3,079	3,079	3,056	3,007	2,933

Argentina										
W Production	5,970	8,570	11,200	5,500	8,100	8,000	8,161	7,764	7,605	7,525
F Production	13,793	12,438	17,261	17,839	17,300	16,678	18,015	19,203	20,009	20,688
W Consumption	4,498	5,382	4,692	4,400	4,500	5,086	5,248	5,358	5,471	5,587
F Consumption	7,465	6,501	6,826	6,881	6,833	7,789	8,279	8,793	9,242	9,685
W Net Exports	1,784	3,160	6,000	1,800	1,751	2,584	2,820	2,524	2,244	2,025
F Net Exports	6,051	7,075	9,655	9,505	9,030	8,901	9,667	10,348	10,733	10,981
W Ending Stocks	714	742	1,400	500	449	779	872	755	644	557
F Ending Stocks	1,359	221	338	324	713	701	771	833	867	890
GCAU	3,928	3,749	3,631	3,948	3,841	3,965	4,096	4,232	4,374	4,522
Soviet Bloc										
W Production	117,869	94,650	131,519	126,603	155,300	111,600	142,624	145,005	147,323	149,577
F Production	156,945	125,439	173,829	146,252	162,300	143,300	181,260	186,733	192,268	197,865
W Net Imports	1,513	13,312	9,037	9,000	6,543	15,403	8,312	8,466	6,964	9,721
F Net Imports	6,857	19,291	10,865	17,805	17,161	21,804	15,987	15,894	16,866	17,515
W Ending Stocks	23,416	14,104	4,528	12,236	16,191	15,982	18,428	19,815	20,681	21,288
F Ending Stocks	4,768	6,487	6,223	5,350	7,226	6,445	10,170	8,045	8,049	8,053
Developed Market Economies										
W Production	58,213	51,205	54,139	50,510	55,748	58,395	59,640	59,915	60,547	61,291
F Production	93,161	87,889	82,189	98,400	101,300	105,472	107,863	111,304	114,359	117,291
W Net Imports	3,382	3,975	4,457	6,400	2,915	1,269	-310	-369	-681	-1,092
F Net Imports	32,421	33,799	44,717	35,955	33,500	32,862	31,054	32,325	33,730	35,392
W Ending Stocks	15,083	13,407	13,026	12,882	13,606	15,096	14,962	14,870	14,904	14,915
F Ending Stocks	17,160	13,523	12,727	14,519	13,165	18,234	18,058	18,161	18,123	18,110
Developing Market Economies										
W Production	62,449	67,541	79,903	74,619	80,137	85,021	89,888	93,068	97,096	101,508
F Production	103,765	113,710	116,389	109,797	114,702	117,337	120,208	124,747	128,769	132,685
W Net Imports	35,571	37,623	33,106	30,500	34,967	37,400	38,970	41,783	44,574	46,388
F Net Imports	6,249	4,934	6,906	9,100	11,801	13,122	14,679	16,103	17,610	19,263
W Ending Stocks	11,156	16,130	24,275	18,150	15,149	15,268	14,463	13,062	13,577	13,849
F Ending Stocks	7,671	10,482	12,975	10,181	10,950	10,804	10,767	11,234	11,399	11,478
China										
W Net Imports	5,695	2,200	3,100	8,600	9,000	7,500	8,000	8,000	8,000	8,000
F Net Imports	428	-115	-50	150	4,000	2,500	2,500	2,500	2,500	2,500

[a]W = Wheat; F = Feed Grains (Corn, Oats, Barley, Sorghum, and Rye); and GCAU = Grain Consuming Animal Units.
All Wheat and Feed Grain quantities are in thousand metric tons; prices are $/bushel.

Table 8C-18. Run 18—low income-high yields, cartel *w* price ⩾ \$6.80, *F* price ⩾ \$5.37, soviet bloc and developed market economies only[a]

	1974/75	1975/76	1976/77	1977/78	1978/79	1979/80	1980/81	1981/82	1982/83	1983/84
United States										
W Price, Export	4.80	4.27	3.29	3.43	3.66	3.90	3.55	3.45	3.42	3.42
F Price, Export	3.55	3.10	2.80	2.54	2.50	2.50	2.50	2.50	2.50	2.50
W Production	48,879	58,078	58,432	55,139	48,962	57,500	61,213	60,464	60,735	61,639
F Production	150,469	184,926	193,083	201,914	212,070	224,700	217,868	227,074	234,097	239,771
W Consumption	19,068	20,112	21,037	22,800	23,600	22,961	23,737	24,534	25,150	25,712
F Consumption	121,788	133,700	132,385	136,900	153,200	158,643	163,722	168,703	178,765	178,768
W Net Exports	27,334	31,598	25,393	31,000	32,400	36,842	30,897	31,785	33,575	35,202
F Net Exports	35,091	49,279	49,959	51,800	56,000	56,397	47,107	46,240	48,412	50,487
W Ending Stocks	11,703	18,071	30,264	32,300	25,100	23,965	30,270	34,410	36,424	37,146
F Ending Stocks	15,414	17,361	30,022	41,200	45,600	55,079	61,920	73,250	84,978	95,180
GCAU	70	75	76	78	80	81	82	83	83	84
Canada										
W Production	13,295	17,078	23,523	19,651	21,145	17,300	22,718	22,280	22,214	22,264
F Production	17,436	19,987	21,198	22,362	20,016	18,100	22,892	24,499	25,629	26,608
W Consumption	4,607	4,827	4,875	4,800	4,800	4,889	5,085	5,270	5,374	5,418
F Consumption	15,923	16,800	16,953	16,300	17,000	17,175	17,226	17,230	17,245	17,255
W Net Exports	10,739	12,254	13,450	16,000	14,400	15,179	13,098	15,325	16,878	17,643
F Net Exports	2,102	4,333	3,727	3,370	6,460	3,407	4,378	6,014	7,416	8,588
W Ending Stocks	8,038	8,035	13,310	12,100	12,647	9,879	14,414	16,893	16,254	15,265
F Ending Stocks	5,626	4,483	5,188	7,579	7,093	4,611	5,899	7,154	8,123	8,888
GCAU	13,130	12,838	12,838	13,191	13,339	13,354	13,289	13,170	13,009	12,812
Australia										
W Production	11,357	12,024	11,800	9,200	18,300	16,000	14,577	13,991	13,713	13,535
F Production	4,453	5,611	5,334	3,983	7,100	5,900	5,804	6,587	7,447	7,485
W Consumption	3,025	2,764	2,925	2,600	2,800	3,278	3,327	3,318	3,304	3,279
F Consumption	1,717	1,753	2,222	2,351	2,393	2,249	2,190	2,168	2,099	1,999
W Net Exports	8,526	8,229	8,500	8,100	8,106	9,810	10,208	10,339	10,363	10,320
F Net Exports	2,865	3,628	2,812	1,819	3,531	3,606	3,611	4,110	4,637	5,118
W Ending Stocks	1,788	2,819	2,312	800	3,501	6,414	7,456	7,791	7,846	7,782
F Ending Stocks	501	731	787	791	921	966	969	1,271	1,583	1,871
GCAU	3,025	3,008	2,955	3,005	3,054	3,079	3,079	3,056	3,007	2,933

Argentina										
W Production	5,970	8,570	11,200	5,500	8,100	8,000	8,178	7,762	7,599	7,518
F Production	13,793	12,438	17,261	17,839	17,300	16,678	17,989	19,206	20,009	20,781
W Consumption	4,498	5,382	4,692	4,400	4,500	5,084	5,248	5,359	5,472	5,588
F Consumption	7,465	6,501	6,826	6,881	6,833	7,789	8,275	8,794	9,243	9,687
W Net Exports	1,784	3,160	6,000	1,800	1,751	2,586	2,832	2,520	2,240	2,018
F Net Exports	6,051	7,075	9,655	9,505	9,030	8,901	9,646	10,348	10,740	10,992
W Ending Stocks	714	742	1,400	500	449	779	877	755	642	555
F Ending Stocks	1,359	221	338	324	713	701	769	833	868	891
GCAU	3,928	3,749	3,631	3,948	3,841	3,965	4,096	4,232	4,374	4,522
Soviet Bloc										
W Production	117,869	94,650	131,519	126,603	155,300	111,600	142,624	145,005	147,323	149,577
F Production	156,945	125,439	173,829	146,252	162,300	143,300	181,260	186,766	192,268	197,865
W Net Imports	1,513	13,312	9,037	9,000	6,543	16,054	8,968	9,127	9,652	10,394
F Net Imports	6,857	19,291	10,865	17,805	17,161	19,482	14,252	14,146	15,164	15,740
W Ending Stocks	23,416	14,104	4,528	12,236	16,191	15,982	18,428	19,810	20,681	21,288
F Ending Stocks	4,768	6,487	6,223	5,350	7,226	7,592	11,318	9,193	9,197	9,201
Developed Market Economies										
W Production	58,213	51,205	54,139	50,510	55,748	58,395	59,666	59,912	60,538	61,279
F Production	93,161	87,889	82,189	98,400	101,300	105,472	107,835	111,307	114,366	117,304
W Net Imports	3,382	3,975	4,457	6,400	2,915	1,076	-1,267	-1,334	-1,620	-2,032
F Net Imports	32,421	33,799	44,717	35,955	33,500	33,642	29,714	30,968	32,375	34,044
W Ending Stocks	15,083	13,407	13,026	12,882	13,606	16,403	16,272	16,174	16,211	16,222
F Ending Stocks	17,160	13,523	12,727	14,519	13,165	21,221	21,041	21,150	21,110	21,097
Developing Market Economies										
W Production	62,449	67,541	79,903	74,619	80,137	85,021	89,937	93,062	97,578	101,485
F Production	103,765	113,710	116,389	109,797	114,702	117,337	120,165	124,752	128,784	132,703
W Net Imports	35,571	37,623	33,106	30,500	34,967	37,386	38,930	41,777	44,614	46,425
F Net Imports	6,249	4,934	6,906	9,100	11,801	13,138	14,715	16,142	17,046	19,300
W Ending Stocks	11,156	16,130	24,275	18,150	15,149	15,305	14,493	13,012	13,652	13,820
F Ending Stocks	7,671	10,482	12,975	10,181	10,950	10,802	10,749	11,232	11,396	11,472
China										
W Net Imports	5,695	2,200	3,100	8,600	9,000	7,500	8,000	8,000	8,000	8,000
F Net Imports	428	-115	-50	150	4,000	2,500	2,500	2,500	2,500	2,500

[a] W = Wheat; F = Feed Grains (Corn, Oats, Barley, Sorghum, and Rye); and GCAU = Grain Consuming Animal Units.
All Wheat and Feed Grain quantities are in thousand metric tons; prices are $/bushel.

9 SUMMARY AND POLICY IMPLICATIONS

The first eight chapters have focused on the analysis of the potential impacts of the imposition of a grain export cartel in the narrow context of the world grain trade. In the first part of this concluding chapter we provide a brief summary of the key issues surrounding the introduction of a cartel. In the remainder of the chapter we broaden the focus to recognize that a cartel would have to be imposed on an existing set of policies related to food and agriculture. These discussions focus first on how for political reasons nations intervene in domestic agriculture. The discussion is then broadened to recognize international relations dimensions. The chapter concludes with a brief discussion of three possible world supply-demand situations which might exist in the 1980s. Conditions in nations around the world as well as in world markets clearly will influence the potential success of any cartel.

BRIEF SUMMARY

Factual and Conceptual Issues

The quantitative characteristics of international trade in grains around which the cartel issue was discussed are:

1. The volume of trade in 1979–80 was 195 million metric tons of grain or 7.4 billion bushels, the equivalent of one U.S. corn crop or three and one-half U.S. wheat crops.
2. Its value (at export points) in 1979–80 was in excess of $35 billion.
3. Grain exports are increasingly concentrated in the hands of a few exporters, five or six in number, with the importance of the U.S. increasing.
4. The LDCs have emerged as the dominant importers of wheat, while the DCs have declined in importance.
5. The CPEs entered the wheat and feed grain markets as major importers during the 1970s.
6. The USSR has switched from being an exporter to being a net importer, but its forays into the market are erratic with significantly destabilizing results.
7. The EEC has become a net exporter of wheat but remains a steady importer of coarse grains.
8. The most rapid and sustained *increases* in the demand for wheat and feed grains in the world market are coming from OPEC countries and middle-income LDCs with foreign exchange, such as South Korea and Taiwan. OPEC countries, however, are still relatively small importers of food and feed grains.
9. The overall volume in trade is increasing, with the rate of increase in coarse grains being much more rapid than that of wheat.
10. The proportion of world wheat production traded has remained constant between 15 and 20 percent of production, while the proportion of coarse grain production traded has doubled from 6 percent to over 13 percent in the last twenty years.

In addition to the above, there are several interesting structural characteristics of the world grain trade:

1. Some 95 percent of international wheat transactions involve state traders on at least one side of the transaction—as exporters or as importers. About one-third of the trade in wheat involves state-trader to state-trader transactions. State trading can be done either through direct government purchase and sale or through some government agency having internal monopoly power such as, for example, the Canadian Wheat Board.

2. Over 40 percent of world feed grain trade involves state traders on at least one side of the transaction.
3. It is generally accepted that a few multinational grain firms account for a large proportion of U.S. grain exports; and they handle well over three-quarters of the world grain trade. Two privately held firms may account for 50 percent of U.S. and world trade.
4. These same five firms are involved in virtually all state-trading activities, in that the firms handle the logistical functions of the trade after price-quantity bargains are reached by state-trading agencies.
5. Five countries (the U.S., Canada, Australia, Argentina, and France) account for over 85 percent of world wheat exports. Canada, the U.S., and Australia alone account for 70 percent; the U.S. by itself, 40 percent.
6. One country, the U.S., exports more than 50 percent of world coarse grain exports. Only six countries account for 80 percent of coarse grain exports.
7. Most countries involved in the grain trade support domestic agriculture through price supports and the accompanying necessary trade restrictions; in fact, most countries isolate (completely or partially) domestic prices from world prices.
8. It follows (from item 7) that grain policy is a political variable of significant magnitude in the domestic policy concerns of virtually all market participants which involves, among other things, attempts to export domestic price and production instability. Most countries try to prevent events in the international market from disrupting domestic policy objectives, and consider grain-trading relations as diplomatic or international relations variables as well as commercial trade variables.

In the above context we have suggested the hypothesis that frequently the world grain market is a buyer's rather than a seller's market. This occurs in part because of the use of trade barriers such as tariffs by importers. The latter (as shown in this book) if properly managed can result in net economic gains to importers as long as world prices are below internal support prices. If this is true, how is it that importers have been able to exert monopsony (buying) power in trade and export instability to major grain exporters? The structural characteristics listed above do not necessarily prove that the world grain market is not competitive and freely working. But they do suggest that the influence of government policy and the potential market power of private traders cannot be ignored. It is demonstrated that a cartel which attempts to increase the bargaining power of exporters, for example, is opposed by the private grain trade.

An important distinction was made between a producer cartel where grain producers in exporting countries receive the benefits and a government cartel where grain producers, livestock producers, and consumers generally share the benefits. The distinction between these two types of cartels is necessary because of the large domestic demand for grains in exporting countries, especially feed grains. The domestic meat sector is a large user of feed grains. It was stressed that a grain cartel has to be discussed in the context of both grains and livestock. In addition, different types of cartels were discussed. For example, a cartel may well want to charge low-income countries a lower price than high-income countries.

Different types of cartel instruments and institutions were presented and discussed. At a minimum, exporters would have to agree on an export price below which importers could not buy regardless of who was doing the day-to-day trading. More severe instruments could be used, but if exporters do not cooperate, an export cartel will fail regardless of its initial design.

There is the important question of how importers would respond to a cartel. The work to date on supply and demand response in major importing regions is limited (our empirical results are based on the best estimates available). One hypothesis is that the threat of an export cartel would result in a policy response of freer trade. This would be a marked departure from the current structure of the grain market. In addition we discussed the implications of state trading by importers in terms of their direct response to a cartel. The question raised is what do conventional estimates of supply and demand responses mean when viewed from the eyes of an importer that is a state trader?

Quantitative Impacts

Several key theoretical points are crucial when interpreting the empirical results from the introduction of a cartel. First is the distinction between a producer cartel and a government cartel discussed above. Results were presented for both types of cartels. Second, the grain trade is not now a "free trade" market. One of our models starts from the position that importers, especially Japan and the EEC, use barriers to trade to improve their position vis-a-vis exporters; and through these trade instruments, they are able to obtain economic benefits from exporters by the use of optimal tariffs. Results were presented for an export cartel which would have the effect of offsetting trade barriers. In addition, results were presented for an ideal export cartel wherein exports are restricted below free trade but exporters collect the export tax revenue rather than importers collecting the tariff revenue as is currently the case.

Our results show that the gains from an effective export cartel could be quite large. The analysis assumes that importers would not impose even higher barriers to trade in response to a cartel than currently exist. A government cartel in both wheat and feed grains could easily yield exporting nations over $15 billion in benefits. A government feed grain export cartel could also benefit livestock producers in exporting countries by keeping feed grain prices relatively low for the domestic market. In absolute terms, the U.S. has the most to gain from an export cartel in wheat and feed grains since it is the largest exporter of both commodities. Relatively, however, it has more to gain in feed grains since it has roughly 60 percent of the export market and 40 percent of the wheat market. It follows that Canada and Australia have relatively more to gain from a wheat export cartel. Also, because a wheat cartel requires more cooperation among exporters than does a feed grain cartel, perhaps the latter would be more attractive but we must keep in mind that because of the substitution effect, an export cartel would probably entail *both* wheat and feed grains.

The important conflict between a producer cartel and a government cartel is shown empirically. Wheat and feed grain producers in exporting countries could, in fact, lose from a government export cartel unless they were compensated in some manner. On the other hand, grain producers would gain substantially from a producer cartel. In the government cartel case, unlike the producer case, prices increase for importers but decrease for domestic users. The largest gain, therefore, from a government cartel could go to consumers in exporting countries—that is, to the consumers of products made from grain directly (for example, bread) and products made from grain indirectly, (for example, meat). This conflict may not only be internal to each country. It could be a stumbling block for a cartel since one country, for political reasons, might want a producer cartel while the others may prefer a government cartel.

THE BROADER POLICY ENVIRONMENT

The establishment of a grain export cartel would not occur in a policy vacuum. World trade in grain is already influenced by government action. In this section we briefly discuss the broader food and agriculture policy environment which could influence a cartel. Here we recognize that governmental intervention may be politically rational even if it is not in terms of economists' notions of economic efficiency and rationality. Our discussion has two parts. The first deals with policy intervention for domestic political reasons. The second discusses some international relations aspects which relate to the grain trade.[a]

Domestic Politics

Domestic government policy influencing the grain trade is of three types: (1) direct market intervention to support farm prices and farmer income; (2) policies to maintain low food prices; and (3) general economic policies which use the management of trade relationships to accomplish national economic and political objectives.

Farm Price and Farmer Income Support. Most DCs have for a long time attempted policy measures to reduce the instability of farm prices and to increase farm income by managing agricultural supplies to enhance domestic prices. For this purpose, nations have had to enact trade policies which prevent external (world market) fluctuations from disrupting domestic objectives. Thus, domestic agricultural policy is inherently protectionist. For importing countries, the task is quite simple. For over a century, the European countries have used trade policies (primarily tariffs) as the basic instrument of

[a]Much of the discussion draws on an earlier paper by McCalla (1980).

domestic farm policy. Such barriers to trade enhance income of producers in importing nations.

The task for exporters is more complicated. If domestic prices are to be enhanced by domestic supports, then supply management, export dumping, or a combination of these is necessary at least during periods of excess production. The schemes used by countries are many and varied. At various times, the United States has used overseas surplus disposal in the form of Public Law 480, export subsidies, two-price systems, direct payments to farmers, and management of the land input. Canada and Australia—and sometimes other exporters such as Argentina and Brazil—have used state-trading agencies, along with supply quota allocations to producers, multiple exchange rates, and bilateral pricing agreements to achieve separation between domestic and international prices.

These increasingly complicated regimes of domestic farm income support with accompanying trade restrictions or attempts at trade liberalization (by exporters) are implemented because governments perceive that farmers are important politically and deserve economic support. As the international market becomes more important relative to the domestic market, these kinds of programs become more expensive as well as more complicated. Still, the international market is treated as a residual, at least in the sense that international ramifications are considered after domestic parameters are set. Thus, at least for short-run analysis of an export cartel, the political-economic reality of domestic support programs seems to be a required dimension of any world trade analyses.

Domestic Food Costs. Farm products are consumed as food by consumers, many of whom are urban dwellers. Consumer interests in general are the opposite of farmer interests—consumers want low prices. For obvious survival reasons, governments, too, attempt to take consumer interests into account. For analysis one must divide countries into three camps: exporters, high-income importers, and the rest of the world (including the CPEs and LDCs). Each approaches the problem differently. DC exporters of grain have typically attempted to support farm income by modest domestic supply management, mainly via income transfers to farmers while keeping domestic prices reasonably low. Via tariffs and other trade restrictions, high-income importers have maintained farm and food prices at relatively higher levels than have exporters but, as suggested in this book, this is partly because tariff revenues collected from grain imports are given consumers in forms other than low food prices. As long as the rate of personal income growth in both exporters and high-income importers exceeds the rate of inflation in general and food prices in particular, consumer groups do not become a disruptive political force. However, economic stagnation plus high rates of inflation during the 1970s, coupled with the rapid run-up in commodity prices in 1972–73, threw this delicate balance between food and farm prices into disarray and catipulted protective farm policies into the national political-economic arena.

The rest of the world (CPEs and LDCs) has dealt with the food-farm price dilemma in a remarkably similar way. In general, the lower the level of per capita income, the higher the proportion of that income spent on food. Thus, food prices are crucial to production costs because they are the major wage goods, they are crucial to real-income growth or decline, and they are ultimately crucial to governmental political survival. Therefore, retail food prices must be kept low and basically constant. As long as cheap or subsidized imports (Public Law 480) are available, both the LDCs and the CPEs could use the international market as an increasingly important alternative to domestic production. Thus, domestic production incentives via increased farm prices could be deferred at substantial savings to the national budgets. The rapid escalation of international commodity prices during the 1970s severely damaged these strategies principally because of foreign exchange shortages. Most countries responded by trying to expand domestic production through an increase in farm prices while of necessity keeping food prices basically constant. The result, of course, is obvious—staggering increases in governmental budgetary costs for food subsidies. It appears, for example, that both Poland and Egypt spend more on food subsidies than on national defense. It goes without saying that these policies require management of the trade interface, most frequently by direct government purchases or imports via state-trading agencies. As these countries now completely dominate the world wheat market, national policy intervention greatly influences import demand, as we have clearly shown earlier in the book.

National Economic and Political Objectives. As long as prices are reasonably stable, real income growth is positive, and the difference between desired internal prices and world prices is small, agricultural policy can be viewed as benign by national macro-policymakers. If one of the above is not realized, agricultural policy becomes an element of national policy rather than sectoral policy for special interests. During most of the 1970s, at least two and sometimes all three of the above key elements were absent. Rapid increases in international grain prices are translated indirectly into bread and meat prices because countries cannot in the long run completely offset the basic tendencies of supply and demand. Thus, inflation is exacerbated which increases the costs of food subsidies. Slow rates of income growth, coupled with high food prices, reduce real income—a politically distasteful outcome for most politicians. Increased disparities between world and internal prices cost more, given the requirement that domestic prices remain nearly constant.

Interposed on these internal developments of the 1970s was OPEC which exerted substantial and continuous pressure on the balance-of-payments situation of all oil importers (most of the world). Importers sought to economize on foreign exchange for imports of grain to pay for oil but ran into extreme political protest when they attempted to raise food prices. The result was either a growing budget deficit or a foreign exchange deficit, neither of which contributed to domestic, economic, or political stability.

The above picture is not painted to argue that the grain trade is a central causative agent in these broader national economic issues. If grain exports and imports are in part residuals of domestic food and agricultural policy, and these policies, during periods of inflation and international price instability, are escalated into national policy issues, then the pure economics of grain commodity trade pales in the face of powerful domestic objectives which attempt internal stabilization by exporting instability into the international grain market.

If one now adds national diplomatic efforts—such as U.S. attempts to barter grain for oil (1975), the USSR grain embargo (1980), increasing numbers of bilateral agreements made for political as well as economic reasons, and food shipments made for defense and alliance objectives (for example, to Egypt and Israel)—one begins to understand the character of the policies influencing the grain trade as a result of domestic political intervention. It is into this complicated set of policy issues that a grain export cartel would come into existence. Clearly policy responses of importers as well as exporters are crucial to actual outcomes.

International Politics

For purposes of this limited discussion, international politics is defined as interactions among nations whose own sovereign interests are enhanced by cooperation or conflict with one or more other nations. We deal only with some limited examples where the grain trade appears to have intersected with diplomatic issues. These are diplomatic retaliation (USSR grain embargo) reenforcement of political alliances (Public Law 480), economic retaliation (grain OPEC), the recapturing of economic gains or profits (grain cartel), and the lessening of potential economic and political instability (world food security and the UNCTAD proposals).

Diplomatic Retaliation. It becomes more attractive to use grain embargoes to retaliate for diplomatic reasons, the greater the dependence of the target country (or countries) upon external grain supplies. The USSR became increasingly dependent on the world grain market during the 1970s for several reasons: rising incomes, which increased the demand for meat and, therefore, feed grains; the apparent policy decision to maintain consumption levels in the face of production shortfalls; and production instability. Thus, an embargo by the United States in retaliation for Russian aggression in Afghanistan seemed plausible. Such an action against a diplomatic enemy would not be subject to the usual criticism of food as a diplomatic weapon—namely, that it causes the poor and hungry to suffer rather than the political regime. This measure failed as can be inferred from the preceeding chapters largely for two reasons: (1) other exporters were less diligent in cooperating and (2) the complexity of the international grain trade made enforcement virtually impossible.

Reenforcing Political Alliances. Patterns in Public Law 480 shipments can partially be explained by whom the U.S. perceives as friends. Food aid can have many desirable characteristics. It has a humanitarian element and in some cases—for example, India in 1965–66—may have prevented mass starvation. It also has the potential for developing markets—for example, Japan. It can be one arrow in the diplomatic quiver to reward those who find the donor nation's favor—for example, our turnaround with respect to Egypt. It is clear that these objectives in most instances have been conditioned by domestic concerns for surplus disposal. Therefore, it is hard to unravel the precise impacts of this element of global politics on the grain trade, but it clearly had some impact, at least during the 1960s.

Economic Retaliation. The cry, "A bushel for a barrel," is clearly couched in terms of economic retaliation, in this instance against OPEC. Yet, as this book stresses, even if a grain exporter cartel could be enforced against OPEC, its impact would be limited because most OPEC countries are sparsely settled and thus import relatively little grain; therefore, the monopoly revenue to be gained would be limited. Beyond this, foreign exchange wealth is not in short supply in OPEC countries. Thus a partial cartel is likely to have less chance for success than a global approach.

Lessening Potential Economic and Political Instability. Increasing disparities between rich and poor nations are potentially destabilizing to the world order. An element of this disparity is hunger and starvation existing simultaneously with food surpluses and overeating. Thus, there is continuing dialogue on a world food security program and proposals to transfer income from DCs to LDCs via commodity agreements as proposed by UNCTAD. Although these are laudable objectives, little progress has been made to date on either front—perhaps because economic development assistance is difficult and, if too successful, runs counter to the interests of donor countries.

These issues do nothing more than introduce the notion that a grain cartel could contribute to or detract from broader international political issues. A political economic analysis, therefore, seems desirable in addition to the economic analysis presented in this book.

CONCLUDING COMMENTS

The dominance of the United States in both the world wheat and feed grain markets means that U.S. grain policy, as well as general economic and diplomatic policy, greatly influences world markets. For example, the loan rate in the U.S. sets an absolute floor under world grain prices. Also, the call price in the farmer-held reserve sets a ceiling on prices as long as reserves exist. Further decisions with respect to target prices and acreage restrictions have direct impacts on world markets. But as previously stressed, the United States along with Canada and Australia do not exercise their tremendous potential market power. Instead the exercise of power is by importers. Most developed country importers such as Japan and the EEC use variable levies and quotas and in the process collect substantial import taxes. Why shouldn't exporters capture these benefits by collectively raising world prices? Our book argues that the gains from doing so are substantial.

It is interesting to analyze major grain exporter domestic and trade policies such as price supports, farmer-held reserves, and the like in conjunction with policies used by importers. Are exporter policies a response to importer policies or vice versa? Or are the policies of both exporters and importers set together in order to maximize the welfare of all nations jointly? We contend that exporter policies are set in response to importer policies and that high-income importers may be getting the upper hand. An export cartel, at one extreme (which would likely be an unstable equilibrium), has the importers responding to the policies of exporters. Thus, for a stable equilibrium, both importers and exporters would have to design policies wherein the welfare of all countries jointly is considered.

Very recently, suggestions have been made (because of the rapid rise in grain prices in 1980) that the U.S. consider a policy which creates internal stability and that the export market be used to handle the residual quantity not needed for internal stability (for example, the government export cartel discussed in this book). This type of policy is interesting since it implies that both exporters and importers could try to export instability, but to whom? Also, exporters would not respond passively to the policies of importers. Our text on cartels stresses two points related to the above. A cartel implies that perhaps many of the past policies used in the United States—such as price supports, acreage controls, farmer-held reserves, and the like—would no longer be necessary to support farm income. The income needed for these policies would not come from the treasury as in the past but rather would come from importers who, in essence, extract this revenue via their domestic and international trade policies. This is assuming that a cartel would result in freer trade. Second, a government export cartel would in essence create price stability internally by charging different prices abroad than in the home market.

It is clear that historically the true comparative advantage of at least the grain sectors of the large food-exporting nations has never been fully reflected. Trade barriers and overvalued exchange rates have been two inhibiting factors. An expansion of trade for the grain sector through a cartel, or whatever, results in an increase in price of land and other factors used to produce grains. Real income to grain farmers would increase. However, in view of the importance of livestock, internal grain prices would likely have to be kept relatively low in order to keep this sector viable. At least in the United States because of the increased political power of consumer groups, managing exports only for the benefit of grain producers is politically unfeasible. Thus the nature of a government cartel has more appeal then a grain producer cartel. As stressed in this book, a government grain export cartel takes into account grain producers, livestock producers, and consumers generally.

In closing, the empirical results in Chapters 7 and 8 should be interpreted with caution partly because it is difficult to predict abnormal changes in weather and also, as Chapter 6 stresses, very little is known about importers' response to abrupt changes in agricultural policy among exporters (for instance, a grain export cartel). Thus it is useful to consider the implications of three quite different future courses of events (any of which, in our opinion, could happen with equal probability). First, suppose the world will experience a continued substantial growth in demand relative to supply. In essence, food imports will expand with accompanying price increases. In this case, likely many of the trade barriers used by importers would be less effective and there would be fewer benefits to be gained by exporters in implementing a cartel. Short-term instability due to weather could be handled by stock policies. Second, suppose the long-term trend is that supplies increase faster then demand in a world interwoven with all sorts of domestic price supports. This picture seemed to depict the realities of most of the 1950s and 1960s. It is during such a period when, as we argue in the text, the grain market is a buyer's market and import policies exploit the agricultural sector of exporting countries. In this environment cartels could play a role by at least using export policy to deal equitably with importers. The latter should have to carry some of the world grain stocks and partially accommodate the oversupply situation (oversupply is in part due to price supports among importers). Lastly, consider the world where for four or five years there is a deficit, then a surplus, then again a deficit, and so on. The 1970s seemed to be such a period, as evidenced from the prices in Table 1–1. Also, as our empirical results show, tariff policies respond differently to these different situations. In tight market periods the barriers to trade are minimal, which in essence is why price instability is transmitted from importers to exporters. If this is the world of the future, our cartel analysis also makes economic sense. Long-term agreements, export taxes, and the like can greatly improve the exporters' bargaining position during such an unstable grain market.

We cannot predict the fundamental market characteristics of the 1980s. However, whether the outcome is a seller's, buyer's, or unstable market has significant implications for the potential benefits from a export cartel. These fundamental conditions of world food balances, coupled with the policies influencing agricultural trade discussed in this chapter, suggest that our analysis of the potential outcomes of a grain export cartel should be carefully interpreted within this broader environment.

REFERENCE

McCalla, A.F. 1980. "Political Economy of the World Grain Trade." In *International Affairs and U.S. Agriculture.* Report of Seminar sponsored by M.G. and Johnnye D. Perry Foundation and the University of Missouri. Special Report 259, Agricultural Experiment Station, University of Missouri—Columbia.

INDEX